WOMEN'S MAGAZINES 1693-1968

Cynthia L. White, Ph.D.

MICHAEL JOSEPH   LONDON

First published in Great Britain by
MICHAEL JOSEPH LTD
52 Bedford Square
London, W.C.1
1970

7181 0687 3

Set and printed in Great Britain by
Unwin Brothers Limited at the Gresham Press, Woking,
in Imprint type, ten-point leaded, and bound by
James Burn at Esher

WOMEN'S MAGAZINES 1693-1968

MICHAEL JOSEPH BOOKS ON
LIVE ISSUES

Series Editors: H. L. Beales O. R. McGregor

Dedication

This book is gratefully and affectionately dedicated

To my friends

and to all those whose concern is focussed upon the fundamental issues of our time and whose work is involved with them.

'. . . of those to whom much is given, much is required. And when at some future date the high court of history sits in judgment on each of us, recording whether in our brief span of service we fulfilled our responsibilities . . . our success . . . will be measured by the answers to four questions:

First, were we truly men of courage . . . ?
Second, were we truly men of judgment . . . ?
Third, were we truly men of integrity . . . ?
Finally, were we truly men of dedication . . . ?'

JOHN F. KENNEDY
January, 1961.

The major part of this work has been approved by the University of London for the award of the Degree of Doctor of Philosophy.

Acknowledgements

ARCHIVES

I should like to thank the following institutions and their staffs for their assistance with source material:

The Audit Bureau of Circulations, 19 Dunraven St., W.1: I much appreciate the co-operation I have received from the Secretary, Mr G. Brand, C.A., and his staff in compiling the tabulations of circulation figures included in the Appendices, and for his permission to reproduce them.

Bedford College Library: I am most grateful to Mrs Brewster and her assistants for all their help.

British Museum Copyright Office: I am particularly indebted to the Superintendent, Mr Damery, to Mr Jackson, Mr Bexley and other staff for their unstinting efforts to locate early records and unaccessioned material, and for their kind hospitality over many weeks of research.

British Museum Newspaper Library, Colindale: my very sincere thanks go to Mr Holland and Mr Wilson (Superintendents), and all the Library staff who worked tirelessly over a period of twelve months to trace, and keep me supplied with, obscure and often war-damaged periodicals. I should like to pay special tribute to their excellent service.

British Museum Reading Room: I greatly appreciate the assistance of the Superintendent and his staff during many years' research, and equally, their courtesy and kindness.

The Fawcett Library, 27, Wilfred Street, S.W.1: my special thanks are due to the former Librarian, Miss Vera Douie, O.B.E., whose encyclopedic knowledge of literature relating to women has been of the utmost value, and also to the present Librarian, Miss Mildred Surry, A.L.A., for her continued help.

(i) Great Britain

INTERVIEWS

I am greatly in the debt of the many representatives of the British women's publishing industry who have given up so much of their time to assist me with a survey of women's magazines in the 1960s, granting interviews, arranging further introductions, organising visits of observation, and supplying unpublished research and other data. I should like to record here my deep appreciation of their co-operation, and add my warmest thanks for the friendliness and hospitality with which I have everywhere been received and entertained.

My outstanding debt is to Mr Gordon Brunton, Managing Director of the Thomson Organisation. His most generous assistance in arranging interviews with his publishing colleagues on both sides of the Atlantic has provided the foundation for my research into current trends in women's publishing, and his sustained interest has been a continuing source of encouragement. I thank him most sincerely for the important contribution he has made.

Mr Alex McKay (Director, IPC Group Management Ltd.) has likewise given me every possible help with interviews inside the IPC, and I am particularly grateful for the time he has personally spent in giving me the benefit of his long and varied experience in publishing, which has been invaluable. Mr Marcus Morris (Managing Director, National Magazine Co.) has also given freely of his time. I much appreciate his readiness to make unpublished material available to me, and his many other kindnesses. Mr W. D. McClelland (Research Director, IPC) has on several occasions generously contributed supplementary data from his own files, and I gratefully acknowledge his help. To Mr Walter Brown (Production Services, Sun Printers, Watford) I owe a thorough insight into magazine printing by gravure and letterpress and my thanks are due to him, and to all those listed here:*

INTERNATIONAL PUBLISHING CORPORATION (IPC)
International Printers Ltd.
Mr Gordon Allen, Director.

I.P.C. Group Management Ltd.
Mr I. Page, (Personal Assistant to Mr McKay).

Fleetway Publications Ltd.
Miss Ailsa Garland, Editor, *Woman's Home Journal.*
Miss Jean Twiddy, Editor, *My Home, Woman and Home, Woman's Weekly.*
Miss Sheila Weston, Cookery Editor, *Woman's Home Journal.*

* *N.B.* Positions mentioned are those held when the representative was first interviewed; many have since changed.

Mr William J. Jackson, Advertising Manager, and other staff of the Advertising Department.

George Newnes Ltd.
Lady Georgina Coleridge, Director.
Mrs Emma Powell, Editor, *Flair*.
Mr Denis Hackett, Editor and Director.
Mr John Mendes, Editor, *Homes and Gardens*.
Mr George Rogers, Editor, *Woman's Own*.

Odhams Press Ltd.
Mr Archie Kay, Editorial Director.
Miss Josie Argy, Editor, *Woman's Realm*.
Miss Barbara Buss, Editor, *Woman*.
Miss Graeme Hall, Editor, *Everywoman*.
Mrs Veronica Snobel, Editor, *Mother*.
Miss Constance Walsh, Editor, *Housewife*.
Mr Alan Morgan, Art Director, *Ideal Home*.
Also:
Miss Mary Grieve, ex-Editor, *Woman*.
Mr Harris Kamlish, ex-Advertisement Director.

C. Arthur Pearson Ltd.
Miss Patricia Lamburn, Director, *Hers, Mirabelle, '19', Rave, True*.

THE LADY LTD.
Miss Margaret Whitford, Editor, *The Lady*.

THE NATIONAL MAGAZINE CO. LTD.
Mrs Pamela Carmichael, Editor, *She*.
Miss Hazel Meyrick-Evans, Editor, *Vanity Fair*.
Miss Laurie Purden, Editor, *Good Housekeeping*.
Mr Michael Griffith, Art Editor, *She*
Mr Michael Bird, and other staff of the Research Department.

THE THOMSON ORGANISATION
Standbrook Publications Ltd.
Mr Geoffrey Perry, Managing Director, *Family Circle*.
Mr Roy McConnell, Vice-Chairman.
Miss Joyce Ward (ex-Editor, *Woman's Realm*), Editorial Consultant to *Family Circle*.
Mr Peter Finch, Marketing Supervisor.

ACKNOWLEDGEMENTS

Illustrated Newspapers Group.
Mr Victor Hawkins, Circulation Manager.

BOWATERS U.K. PULP AND PAPER MILLS LTD.
Mr Grahame Martin-Turner, Director.
Mr Barclay.

BRITISH PRINTING CORPORATION

Hazell Sun.
Mr Russell Pearce, Sales Director.

Hazells Offset Ltd., Slough.
Mr D. Emerson, Sales Executive.

Taylowe Ltd., Maidenhead.
Mr O. P. Hassell, Director.

Sun Printers Ltd., Watford.
Mr W. Ford, F.O.C. (Gravure Machine Room), N.G.A.
Mr J. Neighbour (Compositor for *Woman's Own*).
Mr J. Swan, F.O.C. (Div. I) S.O.G.A.T.

(*ii*) *United States of America*

During my research in America, I received every possible assistance
from representatives of the women's publishing industry, who gave
generously of their time and made a large amount of material available
to me. Their contributions form an important part of Chapter 8, 'The
Women's Press in America'. In particular, I am very grateful to Mr
Gardner Cowles, Chairman of Cowles Communications Inc., for kindly
arranging for me to meet a number of his colleagues. To all those
mentioned below I should like to extend my sincere thanks:

CONDÉ NAST.
Mr Ruston, Executive Vice-President.
Mr Alexander Liberman, Editorial Director.
Mrs Kate Lloyd, Features Editor, *Vogue*.
Mrs. Betsy Talbot Blackwell, Editor-in-Chief, *Mademoiselle*.

COWLES COMMUNICATIONS INC.
Mr Arthur Hettich, Editor, *Family Circle*.

CURTIS PUBLISHING CO.
Mr John Mack Carter, Editor, *Ladies' Home Journal.*

DELL PUBLISHING CO.
Mr George Delacorte, Chairman.
Mrs Silvy Reice, Editor, *Ingenue.*

FAWCETT PUBLICATIONS.
Mrs Geraldine Rhoads, Editor, *Woman's Day.*

HEARST CORPORATION.
Mrs Helen Gurley Brown, Editor, *Cosmopolitan.*
Mr Wade Nichols, Editor, *Good Housekeeping.*

McCALL CORPORATION.
Mr Robert Stein, Executive Assistant to the President (Former Editor, *McCall's*).
Mr Sey Chassler, Editor, *Redbook.*
Mr Walter, Research Department.

MACFADDEN-BARTELL CORPORATION.
Mr Frederick Klein, President.

MADISON AVENUE MAGAZINE.
Mr Carl Rogers, Publisher and Editor.

MARTIN GOODMAN PUBLICATIONS.
Mr Noah Sarlat, Editor, and other representatives.

MAGAZINE PUBLISHERS' ASSOCIATION.
Mr Robert Kenyon, Executive Vice-President.

TRIANGLE PUBLICATIONS.
Mrs McMurtry, Fashion Editor, *Seventeen.*

I should like to add here a special word of thanks to Miss Dee Knapp (*IPC Magazines* Representative, U.S.A.) Her generosity and kindness, extended in so many (practical!) ways, leaves me greatly in her debt.

RESEARCH ASSISTANCE
Part of this research was carried out in the United States of America at the University of Michigan. I owe a special debt of gratitude to the Horace H. Rackham School of Graduate Studies through which I was invited to study at the University as a Visiting Scholar and where I was accorded full guest privileges. The hospitality shown me by Professor

Leon Mayhew (Associate Chairman, Department of Sociology), Professor R. O. Blood and other members of the Faculty, together with their assistance and advice, is deeply appreciated.

FINANCIAL ASSISTANCE
In addition to the award of a State Studentship, I am indebted to the following bodies for grants and travel bursaries:

The Council, Moira House School, Eastbourne, Sussex
(Charles B. Ingham Scholarship).
The Council, College Hall, University of London
(Pfeiffer Research Fellowship).
The Sir Richard Stapley Educational Trust.
The Reid Trust, Bedford College.
The Central Research Fund Committee (University of London).
The Lady Robinson Travel Scholarship Committee (College Hall).

I should like to acknowledge with sincere thanks all the help, professional and otherwise, which I have received from members of the *Department of Sociology, Bedford College* (University of London), mentioning particularly Professor Lady Williams, Professor A. R. Ilersic, and the Secretary to the Department, Miss Madge Simonis.

Special thanks for their encouragement and support go also to friends from *College Hall* (University of London), *London House* and *William Goodenough House,* particularly Miss Patricia Ede, B.Sc., the Reverend Philip S. Jones, and Miss Joanna Dannatt, M.A.; also to Mr Roydon Sacks for his valued criticism of the technological sections of the *ms.*

It is impossible to acknowledge all the personal contributions from which this study has benefited, but no list would do justice to them which failed to include the following; only I know how much I owe them: Professor James Barnes (Wabash College, Indiana, U.S.A.) and Mrs Patience Barnes, Miss Evelyn Born, Ph.D., Miss Marilyn Davis, M.A. (University of Saskatchewan, Canada), Dr and Mrs Arthur Day, Professor Martha England (Queens University, New York City, U.S.A.), Dr and Mrs Fulvio Ferrari, Mrs Tresna Fletcher B.A., Dr F. H. Gillett, M.R.C.S., L.R.C.P., Mr Robert Gray, Mr Graeme Johnson, F.R.C.S., Miss Diane Kirkpatrick, M.F.A., M.A., Ph.D., Miss Elizabeth Lewis, F.R.C.S., Mr Stephen Muller, F.R.C.S.I., Dr and Mrs Barnett Malbin, Mr Ronald Prather, Miss Philippa Randall, B.A., Mr Victor H. Riddell, F.R.C.S., Dr and Mrs John Royle, Miss Thalia Shuttleworth, F.R.C.S., Mr James Shuttleworth, Miss Mona Swann, Dr and Mrs Frank Taylor, Miss Mary Taylor, M.A. (University of Toronto, Canada), Dr and Mrs C. W. Timbrell, and Mr Charles W. Timbrell, M.M.

Finally, I should like to add my warm thanks to my former teacher and supervisor, Professor O. R. McGregor, Head of the Department of Sociology, Bedford College. This study owes a very great deal to his interest, guidance and criticism, and I acknowledge his invaluable (though invisible) contribution to it with sincere appreciation.

CYNTHIA L. WHITE

May, 1969.

Contents

Introduction

Following the huge expansion in publishing for women since the war, women's magazines have become important mass communication media reaching the majority of British women. As such, they have attracted a large and increasing volume of advertising, the revenue from which has made them lucrative and desirable properties. In 1961, a succession of mergers, begun four years earlier, culminated in 'the most significant and far-reaching heavyweight take-over contest ever experienced in the publishing industry'.[1] It ended with the International Publishing Corporation winning control of Odhams Press, then the largest magazine publishing firm in the world, at a cost of £38 million; with this development, women's magazines, for the first time in their history, became subject to monopolistic control.

In view of their potentially considerable social and economic influence, women's magazines have for too long escaped the attention of sociologists. The need for systematic study of their character and functioning is all the more pressing now that the bulk of them are owned by a single publishing combine. Of prime significance are the factors which together determine magazine content, and the changing balance between them. It is no less important to ascertain what is actually being communicated to women, week by week, both as an initial step in estimating the nature and extent of the influence of the women's press, and to provide a basis for an evaluation of the medium in sociological terms. The case for such evaluations by sociologists, in contravention of the 'First Commandment' of modern positivist Sociology, 'Thou shalt not commit a value judgement',[2] has been powerfully argued by Lord Simey who advocates their reintroduction into sociological analysis on the ground that, 'no attempt can or should be made to separate the study of a society from the values embodied in it',[3] and that it is part of the responsibility of a sociologist to interpret, judge and prescribe according to those values.

Correct interpretation, and a complete understanding in the two areas of magazine production mentioned above, depends upon the ability of the researcher to supply an historical perspective in the field of publishing for women. Apart from one short literary study of women's periodicals in the period 1700–1760, no history of the women's press exists, and the state of the magazine industry in contemporary Britain has been similarly neglected. The aims of this survey, therefore, are to analyse the modern women's periodicals against their historical background, relating the development of the industry to social, economic and technological change, and showing how these three sets of factors have affected its structure and evolution, and influenced the scope and character of magazine content.

The survey is based on an analysis of a representative sample of women's magazines appearing between 1800 and 1968. For the purposes of the study, a 'women's magazine' is defined as any periodical intended primarily for female consumption, excluding only those journals which are the organs of women's societies, and those which are highly specialised in their content, such as publications dealing with maternity and child care, knitting and needlework. The term 'periodical' includes all publications appearing regularly, from weeklies to annuals, where the latter are produced as a continuing series and not as isolated issues.

To provide a sampling frame, a list of all traceable women's periodicals was compiled for the period under review. Every available title was examined and a brief description of its contents and characteristics recorded. Each was then classified according to type of content, and the class and age-grouping of its readership. From this classified list, a sample was drawn in such a way as to give, as far as possible, representative, chronological coverage of all women's magazines published between 1800 and 1968, 42 titles being selected for detailed analysis. Those chosen were mainly the leading journals of each successive period, as indicated by their length of run and by other evidences of their popularity such as descriptions in the trade press and comments from other literary sources, circulations for the early period being either unobtainable or unreliable. However, some short-run magazines were also included in the sample in order to show, if possible, the reasons why they failed, thereby indicating the criteria of success operating in publishing for women at different times.

The sample magazines were analysed at intervals of 25 years in the nineteenth century (1800, 1825, 1850, 1875 and 1900), 10 years between 1900 and the Second World War (1910, 1920, 1930 and 1938), and 5 years in the post-war period (1946, 1951, 1956, 1961 and 1966), the intervals being progressively compressed to allow for the accelerating pace of social change. The periods were slightly adjusted so as to exclude the two world wars, on the assumption that the content of women's magazines during the war years would be unrepresentative of normal coverage during peace-time.

At each point of time a year's issues of each selected periodical were analysed. The analysis was two-fold. First, a comprehensive check-list of basic content categories was compiled and the cumulative composition of each year's issues of a publication compared with it. All magazine content was thus recorded in terms of all content categories, thereby revealing significant omissions and variations between one magazine and another, and between different periods. The system of recording was also designed to give a broad indication of the proportional representation of the various classes of content within a single magazine.

Second, both editorial and advertising matter was analysed to yield information in six areas: (1) the effects of social and economic change, (2) readership, (3) advertising ratios and techniques, (4) modes of presentation, including editorial approach, (5) function (as seen by the magazines themselves) and (6) editorial attitudes and values, paying particular attention to those bearing upon the social role and position of women.

In order to relate this analysis of the developing character and functions of the women's press more accurately to the social background of its readers, an independent survey was made of the changing social position of women over the past two centuries, together with a special statistical study of the demographic trends affecting their life and labour. Similarly, a technological survey was undertaken, covering advances in paper manufacture and printing over the same period, to provide the historical background to the achievement of mass production in periodical publishing.

These surveys, and the actual sampling of magazine content, have been supplemented by visits of observation to printing works and magazine offices, together with approximately sixty interviews with representatives from all branches of the publishing trade. From the latter much valuable information has been gained concerning the modern approach to the production of women's magazines, and in addition, access to a considerable amount of unpublished promotion and research material has been obtained, which has helped to provide a more complete picture of the women's press in the 1960s. Circulation and readership figures have also been made available by the publishing houses and by the Audit Bureau of Circulations. Statistics, and other material relevant to advertising, have been supplied by the Institute of Practitioners in Advertising.

In order to provide a basis for comparison with women's publishing in another industrialised society, a short survey of contemporary American women's magazines was undertaken during July–October, 1967, comprising research in the Sociology Department and the periodical archives of the University of Michigan, and a series of interviews with magazine publishers and editors in New York. A summary of the find-ings is contained in Chapter 8.

The study falls into two parts. Part One describes the pre-war history of the women's press, which has been consistently neglected in all contemporary assessments of women's magazines. Early experi-ments in the eighteenth century are shown to be the origins of our modern women's periodicals, and their development into more 'orthodox' publications is traced, culminating in the birth of a clearly recognisable industry in the last quarter of the nineteenth century under the guiding hand of Alfred Harmsworth (Lord Northcliffe). Part One concludes with an account of how these late-Victorian foundations were built upon in the first forty years of the twentieth century, dealing in particular with the crystallisation of a clearly definable editorial for-mula, and the widening of the social base of magazine readership.

Part Two is concerned with the vast expansion of the women's press in post-war Britain, and its metamorphosis into a huge business enter-prise, dominated by, and dependent upon, advertising. The effects of the socio-economic revolution are considered, together with the recent decline in sales throughout the industry which has led publishers into a thorough reappraisal of the traditional approach to publishing for women and experiments with new techniques and new formulae.

As this survey shows, women's magazines are entering a crucial phase in their history. Much attention is currently being focussed upon them and there is widespread speculation as to their future. The 'rescue operations' now being mounted throughout the women's press are in danger of being rendered ineffectual through the almost total lack of information bearing upon the needs, interests and attitudes of British women in the 'sixties. Policy-making tends to be arbitrary, often causing conflict between management and editorial staff and dissatisfaction amongst readers. Moreover, the industry seems to be no nearer solving its problems than it was five years ago. It is hoped that this study, by contributing for the first time a sociological insight into more than one hundred and fifty years of publishing for women, will provide lessons from the past which are applicable to the present, and indicate the lines along which research in the future may most profitably be directed.

NOTES
1   Hugh Cudlipp, *At Your Peril*, p. 98.
2   Alvin Gouldner in his Presidential Address to the American Society for the Study of Social Problems, 1961.
3   T. S. Simey, *Social Science and Social Purpose*, Constable, 1969. See also: T. S. Simey, 'What is Truth in Sociology?' in *New Society*, July 23rd, 1964.

Part One

Laying the foundations
1693-1939

I

The Origins of the
Women's Press: 1693-1865

(i) *First Experiments in Publishing for Women*

Isolated periodicals for women began to appear at the end of the
seventeenth century, but it was almost two hundred years before they
were published in sufficient numbers to justify their classification as an
industry. Nevertheless, the curious and diverse collection of feminine
literature which grew up in the eighteenth century, long before a
women's press as such was thought of, provides an interesting and
informative introduction to the history of women's magazines.*

The publications characteristic of this early period were entirely
individual in their approach. Intended primarily 'to amuse and instruct'
the female reading public, their contents were determined more by the
caprice of the author than by any objective estimate of the requirements of the woman reader. It would therefore be unjustified to base any
sociological generalisations upon them. However, they throw some useful light upon the climate of thought and social attitudes prevailing in
the eighteenth century, as well as giving some interesting glimpses of
everyday life in Georgian England.

The publication which may fairly be called the very first periodical
for women was *The Ladies' Mercury*, published by John Dunton, a
London bookseller, and intended as a sister paper to *The Athenian
Mercury*. Dunton had, in 1691 and 1692, given over monthly, fort-

---

* No sociological study of these early periodicals has ever been made. There
is, however, a literary study[1] encompassing women's publications of the period
1700-1760, which, with the exception of *The Ladies' Mercury* (1693), are the
earliest on record. In the absence of any sociological data, and in view of the
difficulty of gaining access to some of these early titles, the writer has been
grateful to draw extensively upon this survey to supplement collected material
relating to the second half of the eighteenth century.

nightly, and then weekly issues of that paper to 'the Fair Sex', and out of this experiment grew the idea for a regular publication entirely for women. Dunton assured his new readers, 'We shall be ready to answer all questions you shall vouchsafe to send us'[2] and he was as good as his word. The paper teemed with answers to 'all the most nice and curious questions concerning love, marriage behaviour, dress and humour of the female sex, whether virgins, wives or widows'[2] and the most intimate problems were aired in its pages with a forthrightness typical of an age which was bawdy, lusty and uninhibited:

> 'I am a man of Honour, and not a twelvemonth since I married a young woman, to whom I was the most faithful and fondest of Husbands; but . . . I had not been married half a year before I took her in the very act of Adultery. Now . . . being neither obliged as a Gentleman or a Christian to take Infamy and Pollution into my Embraces, and, to lay open my Constitution, not able to live without a woman, I at present keep a Mistress, a Companion so dear to me that with all my very soul I could marry her; but as the highest Favour the straitlaced Drs Common will give me is a Divorce only *a mensa et thoro* from my first-hand bargain, that performance is above my power. Now my Question to you Gentlemen is this. How far am I sinful in this last conversation, and whether Adultery or not, together with your opinion of our present Law, that in cases of Adultery will no farther unty the Marriage-Knot than a separation only from Bed and Board?'

The Editor's reply was candid but sympathetic:

> 'Truly, Sir, we think your case one of the hardest in the world . . . but a man must neither Whore nor Marry while she lives for the Pulpit Law pronounces it both ways Whoredom, so that if he be not gifted with a Saint like Countenance . . . is somewhat hard upon him, for they that have drunk, the Proverb says, are apt to be dry . . .'[3]

The growth of women's periodicals continued during the early years of the eighteenth century, since there was 'a feminine audience . . . ready and waiting . . . to patronise enterprises directed to women'.[4] There seems to have been a definite growth in the female reading public dating from the turn of the century, due mainly to the increased leisure forced upon upper and middle-class women by economic changes which reduced their domestic tasks to a minimum. This expanding readership was made up of new recruits from the commercial classes as well as a substantial number of domestic servants whose conditions of work gave them both facilities for reading and access to reading matter. But, excluding this last group, reading spread no further down the social scale, and, moreover, remained confined to the Capital and its environs.

Neither potential circulation, nor printing capacity was large enough at this time to support a sizeable periodical press. One estimate gives the weekly circulation of newspapers and periodicals in 1704 as 43,000, a figure which implies 'less than one newspaper buyer per hundred persons per week'.[5] By 1753, however, newspaper sales had tripled to reach a daily total of 23,673,[6] facilitated by an increase in printing capacity. A contemporary printer quoted the number of printing presses in London in 1724 as 70,[7] a figure which had risen to between 150 and 200 by 1757,[8] contributing to an estimated four-fold increase in printed literature of all kinds by the close of the century.[9]

The pioneer publications for women were of two kinds. The first group cannot truly be classed as 'women's magazines' but were rather the forerunners of the pocket diaries of modern times. They appeared annually, described variously as 'pocket-books', 'almanacks' and 'chronologers', and contained, in addition to a calendar, a wealth of extraneous information on a variety of topics, together with conundrums, poetry and other entertainments. A typical example is *The Ladies' Diary* which came out in 1704 and continued to appear annually until 1841 when it merged with *The Gentleman's Diary*. The first issue, 'dearer by one half' than any other almanack of the time, sold out quickly and maintained its popularity under the Editorship of John Tipper of Coventry until he died in 1713.

Tipper's intention was to provide something for all conditions of women. For Ladies, there would be 'information concerning essences, perfumes and unguents', for Waiting-women and Servants, 'excellent directions in cooking, pastry and confectionary'; for Mothers, 'instructions for the advancement of their families', and for Virgins, 'directions for love and marriage'. Above all, Tipper was determined that the contents of his *Diary* should reflect 'what all women ought to be—innocent, modest, instructive and agreeable', a normative approach quite different from that found in modern women's magazines.

The actual content of the annual fell into two parts: a Calendar, consisting of 'a great variety of Particulars all at length because few women make reflections or are able to deduce consequences from premises', and a miscellaneous collection of items including sketches of famous women, 'excellent receipts of divers kinds', stories, articles on health and education, enigmas and mathematical questions. In 1706,

Tipper advertised for contributions from readers in the form of 'verses, enigmas, and pleasant stories', and apparently got them from all over the kingdom. In 1707, he decided to revise his formula, and claiming to be 'convinced by a multitude of letters that enigmas and mathematical questions give the greatest satisfaction and delight to the obliging Fair', proposed to substitute these for the cooking recipes, an amendment which he later stated had proved highly acceptable to the ladies.

Side by side with these entertaining and informative annuals there was a growing collection of more orthodox literary works, for instance those published by Richard Steele, which can more justifiably rank as the ancestors of modern women's magazines. Long before he brought out a paper exclusively for their amusement, Steele confessed that his publications were largely intended for women readers. *The Tatler* in its opening number (April, 1709) promised instruction to the general public and entertainment to the fair sex, and during the twenty-one months of its existence continued to supply stories and anecdotes dealing with feminine interests. Steele admitted being preoccupied with 'the improvement of ladies'. As 'Nestor Ironside', he aired his views in *The Guardian* upon the education and reading of young ladies and upon the use and abuse of leisure, regretting particularly the onset of the age of gallantry which threatened to substitute the Lady for the Woman. According to a contemporary observer, his sorties into female territory proved so acceptable that, 'you should scarce find a lady dressing or drinking tea in the morning with her friend, but Mr St—le's paper made up the first part of the entertainment'.

The betterment of women was a theme which also commended itself to Ambrose Phillips who brought out another women's journal, *The Free-Thinker*. He made clear his intention to give the minds of his readers 'as beautiful a turn as nature has bestowed upon their persons', and a second women's periodical, *The Visiter*, copied this approach, devoting itself to those subjects 'which tend to the improvement of the Mind and Manners as they are relative to a Domestic Life'. This framework did not, apparently, allow the inclusion of current events and social problems, which the Editor earnestly undertook never to introduce. Instead, he appealed for edifying contributions from his readers, which he saw as the best way of stimulating their minds and convincing them that 'knowing how to make a pudding and pleat their husbands' neckcloths [was] not the only knowledge necessary to them'.

The Editor never slackened his efforts to inculcate a love of learning among women, and his recognition of the need for comprehensive female education showed that, in company with many other eighteenth century thinkers, he had a high regard for the female intellect. The following quotation sums up the viewpoint which his magazine was designed to propagate and at the same time catches out a female Editor, who had previously masqueraded as a man:

'If one woman among a hundred is fired with the laudable ambition of mounting higher in the rational world than the rest of her neighbours, she is immediately shunned by her own sex and ridiculed by the other. Barbarous injustice! If it is owned that we are endu'd with rational Faculties, why are we denied the due Improvement of them? Why are we kept in total ignorance of everything but Domestic affairs? Drudging in a family, or perhaps taught to set off our persons—in order to arrive at the Summum Bonum of every woman—a husband?'[10]

The only other publications of note appearing at this time were *The Female Tatler*, *The Ladies' Journal* (which came out in Dublin), and *The Parrot*. The first of these, published under the fictitious editorship of 'Mrs Crackenthorpe' in 1709, circulated abuse and scandal to such an extent that after only a few months it occasioned an indictment as a 'Nuisance' from a Grand Jury. This effectively curbed its licentiousness and it afterwards became 'as insipid as anything in print'. *The Ladies' Journal*, which appeared three years after *The Visiter*, imitated that magazine's liberal championship of women's education, while *The Parrot* (1728) was yet another example of a well-intentioned attempt on the part of an Editor (in this case 'Mrs Penelope Prattle'), to 'put things right in the world' by focussing attention on current vices and preaching virtue.

From the foregoing examples it is evident how much the personal views of Editors were allowed to dictate the content of these early periodicals. In all of them, there was a sustained campaign to impose a personal set of standards and values on the woman reader. Indeed, many writers regarded this as their *raison d'être*, and intended their periodicals to be a medium through which they could criticise women and reclaim them by moral teaching. Thus the professed 'amusement' function of these early works was frequently subordinated to that of instruction.

Such periodicals dominated the literary scene until 1731. In that year, the 'magazine proper' entered the field, under the guiding hand of Edward Cave. Cave was a printer, who coined the word 'magazine' to describe his new periodical for gentlemen, which was an entirely new type of journal containing material drawn from many literary sources, carrying the motto '*e pluribus unum*'. This was evidently a successful formula for the plagiarists were soon at work and among its imitators was *The Lady's Magazine*, published at one shilling, which faithfully reproduced Cave's design, omitting only the accounts of parliamentary debates. The new formula was a popular departure from the old-style journals, heavy with moral and philosophical treatises, and from 1731 onwards, the old and the new vied with each other for public approval.

Mrs Eliza Haywood continued in the old traditions with her *Female Spectator* (1744–47) in which she sought to uplift her female contemporaries. Each small volume, completely lacking in illustrations, contained in its seventy pages a diverting commentary on the life of the times. Anonymously, and very entertainingly, a group of ladies ran what might be called a 'social intelligence bureau', with the object of holding up to public condemnation the customs and morality of the age. Real life examples of immoral conduct were used, though no names were ever divulged, and using these instances as a platform, Mrs Haywood preached and exhorted, advised and reprimanded, urging her young readers to 'renounce cards and masquerades' in favour of books and needles. Her strictures on the irresponsible pursuit of pleasure would have won the approval of the most austere of Victorians. She was equally concerned to 'bring learning into fashion', which, as she defined it, included Philosophy, Geography, History and Mathematics and involved fairly rigorous mental exercise. Her 'syllabus' bore the first signs of the onset of the intellectual revival, during which the cultivation of the intellect became fashionable for women.

A second periodical of the new type, *The Lady's Weekly Magazine*, appeared in 1747. Only one issue has survived, but its design is interesting. The Editor, 'Mrs Penelope Pry', once again promised to feed the female mind with essays 'treating upon the most useful subjects' in which the principles of virtue and morality were inevitably to be taught, but she also accepted the need to 'alleviate and refresh the imagination and excite innocent mirth'. However, this enlightened approach produced nothing more imaginative than 'a poetical enigma, a dialogue on the present Political History of the world', several dull items from Scotland, four columns of equally dull comment on affairs in London, and a list of births, deaths, promotions, casualties and bankrupts'.[11] The Editor continued to regale her public in this placid manner for about three years, and those with an appetite for more dramatic entertainment must have relished the arrival of a more spirited successor in 1749, namely, *The Ladies' Magazine*, published by Jasper Goodwill and sold for twopence at the corner of Elliott's Court, Little Old Bailey.

The Ladies' Magazine was the brightest and most gripping women's publication that had yet been produced. Averaging seventeen pages and coming out fortnightly, the magazine was designed to make 'one handsome complete volume at the end of the year', and could be obtained 'from any of the persons who serve newspapers or subscription books'. In the opening number, Goodwill told his readers what they might expect:

> 'How common soever the method is grown of entertaining the public with a collection under the title of a magazine, yet I apprehend it is not therefore the less agreeable . . . It will be a most agreeable amusement either in the parlour, the shop or the Compting house, in retirement, as it will contain an agreeable variety of subjects in the circle of wit, gallantry, love, history, trades, science and news. And it will be a most innocent, elevating and profitable entertainment for young masters and misses by giving them an early view of the polite and busy world. It certainly is, and shall be the cheapest thing of its kind and price ever published.'

The proprietor appealed to his readers to recommend his magazine to their neighbours in order to publicise it, for the reason that several of the London papers had 'refused to advertise it, the reason of which may be easily seen into'. The 'reason' can only have been the magazine's *pièce de résistance* which was a detailed and grisly record of contemporary crimes and punishments, many of the descriptions being supplied by eye-witnesses. This core of sensation was supplemented with verse, riddles and puzzles, a diary of events at home and abroad, play reviews, and short discourses on topics of general interest, particularly the vulnerability of the female sex to the depravity of the age. As part of the attempt to educate readers, a course of History by question and answer ran for a considerable time, together with advice columns dealing with readers' queries. The success of the magazine enabled Goodwill to enlarge it and to aspire to clearer and smaller type, which he hailed as a great achievement. In response to popular demand, a romance was started, but no other new or original contributions were forthcoming, and the periodical's continued success no doubt rested in large measure upon its crime section. It was finally brought to an end by Goodwill's death in 1753.

The contents of *The Ladies' Magazine* indicate the important function which many periodicals of this time discharged in circulating domestic and foreign news, and in publishing lists of births, marriages, deaths and other announcements. These features were common to most magazines in the eighteenth and early nineteenth centuries, and it is the topical interest of such publications as Goodwill's which makes them unique in the history of publishing for women. With the growth of the daily press, and the development of an efficient system of communications which rendered topical material a highly perishable commodity, this news-giving service was gradually superseded.

The middle of the century brought the last of the 'essay-periodicals'.* There were four of them: *The Lady's Curiosity or Weekly Apollo* (1752) edited by Nestor Druid and printed by C. Sympson at the Bible in Chancery Lane, *The Old Maid* (1755) by Mary Singleton, Spinster, *The Young Lady* by 'Euphrosine', and *The Lady's Museum* by Charlotte Lennox. *The Lady's Curiosity* emphasised love and marriage and gave advice and instruction to all those contemplating matrimony, either by answers to correspondents or by means of stories and anecdotes. Mary Singleton, who produced *The Old Maid*, typifies the eighteenth-century Editor in her capricious approach to the formulation of content. She wrote on whatever topic happened to take her fancy, ranging over 'the fashions, plays, masquerades and the follies and vices of the sex', with no attempt at planning or continuity. The fact that this journal lasted only six months suggests that the reading public was growing more discerning and demanding more from their periodicals than the re-presentation of the views and interests of a single author. *The Young Lady* fared even worse, for 'Euphrosine's' desire to 'improve and entertain her public' was thwarted after a mere seven weeks. It would seem that her audience recoiled from the sober life she advocated as determinedly as she embraced it.

Charlotte Lennox offered the eighteenth-century reader the last of the 'essay-periodicals', which, unlike some others, reached a high standard due to her considerable literary talent. She contributed essays, novels, poetry and translations from the French, together with short narratives, philosophical pieces and songs. It was her mission, too, 'artfully to cajole fair readers into seriousness', but she warned against indiscriminate study which might 'blunt the finer edge of their wit, and change the delicacy in which they excel into pedantic coarseness'.

With the passing of *The Lady's Museum*, the pioneer phase in publishing for women came to an end. These fleeting works, often colourful and outspoken, seldom bland, and never sickly, were remarkable for their individuality and enterprise and for the high degree of reader-participation they managed to achieve proportionate to their small circulations. While they reflected the spirit of the age which gave them birth, they nevertheless made use of their opportunities for influencing

* The description is Miss Stearns'.

women and assumed responsibility for guiding their tastes and beha-viour. In this respect they were trend-setters rather than trend-follow-ers, trying to stamp out vice and promote virtue through learning. This paternalistic approach does not seem to have been resented. Rather, judging by their ready response to requests for contributions and their partiality for debating moral and other questions through correspondence, women readers regarded it as a stimulus and a challenge.

After 1760, as the 'magazine' format became more widely adopted, women's periodicals began to take on a new look. Their numbers multiplied and more than a score of publications of the new type appeared before the end of the century. There were 'Museums', 'Magazines' and 'Miscellanies', their titles denoting the diversity of their contents and the characteristic 'collecting together' of a variety of features. This expansion in the range of content together with a greater professionalism in its manner of treatment, differentiates these maga-zines from the idiosyncratic journals which preceded them.

The year 1770 brought what may perhaps be regarded as the first objective and professional effort to create a magazine acceptable to women. This was *The Lady's Magazine* which ran for seventy-seven years and became a firmly entrenched favourite with women of the leisured classes. In its opening number the Editor expressed surprise that, although reading had become more popular with women than in former times, no periodical existed expressly designed for their amuse-ment and improvement. The magazine aimed to fill this gap and blend entertainment and instruction in such a manner that it would suit 'the housewife as well as the peeress'.

Whilst it closely adhered to the principles of cultivating the mind and upholding virtue, *The Lady's Magazine* did not underestimate the im-portance to women of 'the external appearance', assigning a special department to fashion, illustrated with engravings, and promising 'an earliness of intelligence which shall preclude anticipation'. This was a completely new departure, and, together with the embroidery patterns given away in each number and inset sheet music, made the sixpenny monthly a particularly attractive bargain, which the proprietors were careful to emphasise. Besides these innovations, the magazine carried a variety of literary contributions from readers (including poetry) which made up the bulk of its content, supplemented with foreign and home news, notices of births, marriages, deaths, promotions and bankruptcies, fiction and correspondence. Men were frequent contributors and made free use of the magazine to air their views (or their grievances) concern-ing the female sex. The ladies were quick to retaliate in kind:

31

'I am the eldest daughter of a tradesman who had acquired a
considerable fortune by his indefatigable industry, and brought
me up a gentlewoman. [He] would not suffer me to give myself
the least trouble about his family affairs so that I am entirely ignorant of everything belonging to that vulgar character, a good housewife. But tho' I was brought up a gentlewoman, I chose a husband
for myself who was much my inferior in point of fortune—he is,
however, according to the language of the world, a frugal, indus-
trious man . . . [and] extremely fond of me; but then he is so
provokingly absurd as to expect me to look after his household
matters, tho' he knows I have always lived without having my mind
disturbed by any domestic cares. Now, Sir, I appeal to the Public,
whether I can, consistently with my character as a gentlewoman,
pay the slightest attention to my family.'[12]

From the first, *The Lady's Magazine* offered readers a varied and
stimulating diet and an editorial approach which was sturdy and
realistic. It was enthusiastically received, and soon a plagiarised version
appeared, the work of 'a desperate Adventurer' cited as 'Mr Wheble'.
The publishers, Robinson and Roberts, applied to the King's Bench,
and on July 8th, 1771, the defendant was pronounced guilty of fraud,
both in publishing a periodical 'under a false Signature, and endeavouring to impose it on the Public as a Continuation of the genuine Work',
and also, 'in pretending that the real Magazine, purchased by the
Plaintiffs, was surreptitious and an Imposition upon the Public'.[13]

Twenty years later in 1790, the authors were commenting on 'the
prevailing taste for improvement in female education' which had enabled them to extend the scope of the magazine beyond their original
intention. No longer were 'learning and genius, taste and study' considered 'incompatible with the duties of female life, superior to their
understanding and pernicious to the morals of the sex', a revolution
which the writers took credit for having anticipated in the initial design
of the work.

The Lady's Monthly Museum, written to a similar formula, appeared
in 1798 and also enjoyed a long run. It was written by 'a society of
ladies . . . of established reputation in literary circles', and was intended
to be 'an assemblage of whatever can tend to please the fancy, interest
the mind, or exalt the character of the British Fair', an antidote to 'the
indolent habit of loitering away time in an unprofitable manner'.
The magazine clearly set forth its attitudes concerning the responsibilities of the women it addressed, giving household duties first priority
but stressing also the importance of improving the mind. The Editors

considered that 'the acquisition of languages, simple mathematics, astronomy, natural and experimental philosophy, with history and criticism may be cultivated by the sex with propriety and advantage', while for lighter amusement they recommended the study of music, poetry and painting, together with geography, chemistry, electricity, botany, animals and gardening.

The magazine was carefully compiled to remain consistent with this view of female improvement, but the informative features were supplemented with fiction which had by this time become an indispensable ingredient in periodical literature. Every six months a Cabinet of Fashion was also included, illustrated by coloured engravings, the first to appear in a women's periodical. There was no attempt to predict coming styles. The 'Cabinet' served merely as 'a record' of what Society women all over the country were already wearing. This small but bulky magazine, (it measured 7 inches by 5 inches and contained around eighty-five pages) claimed for itself both 'a flattering reception' and 'an extensive circulation', though no figures were ever quoted.

Unlike the majority of women's publications which preceded them, these late-eighteenth century magazines were intended to be lasting leisure companions and were destined for the bookshelf. For this reason they were made available in annual volumes, the monthly parts having been bound together and a supplement or index added. They were basically literary productions, and their growth was consequent upon a widespread revival of interest in literature. The art of conversation was also being recultivated at this time, in imitation of the French Salons, and these journals no doubt played an important part in providing stimulating ideas for the adroit hostess to deploy at her supper table. The subjects treated were not 'feminine' in the modern sense in that they rarely ventured outside the neutral territory of the intellect. Many contributions came from, and were enjoyed by men, and it is often impossible to discover for which sex a periodical was primarily intended without reference to the title, and even the title was frequently misleading.

The 'intellectual' approach could be maintained as long as men and women were considered to be mental equals, and as long as the concept of the ideal social role for women included their participation in affairs outside the home. The eighteenth century began with an intellectual revival in which women participated, but it ended with Mary Wollstonecraft's impassioned denunciation of sexual discrimination showing that the intervening years had witnessed a marked change in social attitudes. The extent of this change can best be illustrated by a comparison of two works, Thomas Brown's *Legacy for the Ladies*, written at the turn of the century, and Thomas Gisborne's *An Enquiry into the Duties of The Female Sex* which appeared in 1797.

The striking fact about Brown's essay is its complete lack of deference to women. Unlike the Victorians, who worshipped at the shrine of Womanhood, Brown wrote with vision unclouded by the 'Feminine Illusion' and laid bare the vices of the sex as he saw them. He mounted a vitriolic attack upon the female character, and upon 'the softe and easy life' he claimed women led. The ferocity of this attack itself implies equal status between the sexes, since the converse holds that an age of chivalry denotes an age of female subjugation. Indeed, throughout his argument, Brown made it quite clear that he regarded men and women as human beings with equal endowments, but felt that women were weakened by self-centredness and 'the perpetual need to make themselves agreeable'. He strongly rejected any notion of their inferiority and blamed female education for feminine idleness and dissipation.

Gisborne's treatment was, by contrast, moderate and restrained. He ranged over many of the same aspects of the character and duties of women, but drew very different conclusions. Almost as if he were replying to Brown's critique across the decades, he set out to reverse the earlier writer's analysis. He claimed that, 'The Creator has with consummate wisdom conferred differential mental abilities upon the sexes', but to compensate for those respects in which they were inferior, had also invested them with certain desirable qualities. This was the opposite of Brown's view which went so far as to postulate the mental superiority of women, obscured by pride and weakness.

Both authors were severely critical of female education, but while Brown advocated improvement on the grounds that it led to useless lives and wasted talents, Gisborne wanted to re-cast the system so that it might provide the cloistered female with an effective opiate to 'supply [her] hours of leisure with innocent and amusing occupations'. Gisborne quoted extensively from, and approved, the Pauline doctrine on the duties of women, which clearly lay at the root of his views. He favoured a purely domestic role for women and believed that their sole and entire duty was to be sober and prudent wives:

> 'To guide the home and superintend the various branches of domestic management is the indispensable duty of the married woman. No mental endowments furnish an exemption from it; no plea of improving pursuits can excuse the neglect of it.'[14]

A comparison of these two works leaves no doubt that social attitudes to women changed considerably as the century progressed and that by its end the belief in the inherent mental inferiority of women had gained ground. As late as 1770, the Editor of *The Lady's Magazine* could still assert that 'The minds of the sex when properly cultivated are not inferior to those whose honour it is to be protectors and instructors of the fair', and the women's periodicals of the time continued to include material which presupposed a fairly high intellectual level. But as the doctrine of the mental, physical and moral inferiority of women became more firmly entrenched, and as their horizons contracted commensurately, these thought-provoking, informative, literary magazines were superseded by periodicals of an entirely different character, insipid, limited in scope and lacking all mental stimulus, being designed for a new breed of woman whose interests and activities were confined wholly to the domestic sphere.

None of these trends had become apparent in 1806 when a new magazine, *La Belle Assemblée*, entered the field. It endorsed the current approach to publishing for women, promising to provide the same fare as its rivals, only more comprehensively, elegantly, and with greater variety. The Proprietors were quick to realise the popularity of contributions from readers, particularly letters, and they announced their intention that the magazine should be made 'the channel of those Public Communications, Correspondence, Queries, Answers and Co. which such as honour it with their Patronage may choose to engage in or put to each other'. They readily admitted that this was no more than their rivals were doing, but claimed that 'in providing a classification and order for whatever correspondence suitable to the nature of the work, our Readers may honour us with, we flatter ourselves that we have introduced a material improvement so far as method, arrangement and elegance of display may be considered as enticements to readers in periodical publications'. This was in fact one of the first publications to introduce a table of contents, and the greater attention beginning to be paid to techniques of presentation indicated a growing professionalism in publishing for women, associated with the passing of the age of the single, amateur Proprietor-Editor.

La Belle Assemblée offered a service of a particularly novel kind. Georgian women were seemingly burdened with erring and irritating relatives and friends to whom they felt unable to speak their minds. The practice therefore grew up of writing to women's periodicals for the purpose of 'conveying, under the assumed fiction of a story of exactly resembling circumstances, some precept or admonition which could not have been communicated or would not have been attended to in any direct manner'. The Editors recommended the use of their correspondence columns to any readers wishing to avail themselves of this 'delicate, suitable and not least effectual method'. Another innovation was a series of articles on the 'culinary system', in which general hints were given on keeping accounts, ordering and preserving foodstuffs and avoiding waste, particularly of bread, which at the time was 'a heavy article of expence'. These articles apparently proved unpopular, for they were soon discontinued, an indication, perhaps, of a disinclination amongst women of the time to mix business with pleasure.

In most other respects, the new magazine duplicated the policies of its rivals and reflected their views on women. It, too, committed itself to the improvement of the female mind justifying this on the grounds that women were 'beings endowed with reason and consequently capable of the highest degree of intellectual improvement'. Any apparent inferiority in the female sex it ascribed to 'an improper mode of education and study, or an inexcusable indulgence of parents'. It deplored the fact that:

'More attention is paid to the graces, accomplishments and decorations of the person and the fashion of the times, than to the virtues of the heart, the correctness of judgement, or the energies of the mind . . . the principles which insure . . . domestic happiness, social harmony and universal respect.'[15]

The sum of these attitudes indicates the faint beginnings of a reaction against the licentiousness of eighteenth-century life, but not as yet a narrowing of the accomplishments considered desirable for women to acquire, nor any sign of a belief in their moral, physical or mental inferiority. Instead, there seems to have been a general desire to educate women to an even higher level so that they might be more stimulating companions for their menfolk and occupy their time more fruitfully. Gentlewomen were expected to take an interest in, and to understand, social and political matters, and to read widely and intelligently. Consequently, their magazines fed them with stimulating, topical literature. They led full social lives, and in recognition of this fact, notes on music, the arts and the theatre were included, as well as book reviews. For lighter amusement there was poetry, serial and complete fiction, plays, biographical sketches, conundrums and diagrams for handwork, together with miscellaneous short essays on topics ranging from 'Sensibility' to 'Beards'—anything which might interest or amuse. Fashion articles often contained clothes for men, and men joined with women in contributing letters and compositions.

Only the *Monthly Museum* made any provision for readers' personal difficulties. It carried an advice feature conducted by 'The Old Woman' which was intended primarily for the young. For the most part it consisted of 'think-pieces' on subjects raised in readers' letters, but occasionally a letter would be printed in full, giving an insight into the preoccupations and perplexities of the young women of the time. From Cheltenham, 23-year-old 'Biddy Willing' wrote:

'... my papa and mama have been trying for the last three years to match me, and have for that purpose carried me from our country seat to London, from London to Brighton, from Brighton to Bath, and from Bath to Cheltenham, where I now am, backwards and forwards, till the family carriage is almost worn out, one of the horses is become blind and another lame, without my having more than a nibble, for I have never yet been able to hook my fish. I begin to be afraid that there is something wrong in their manner of baiting for a husband, or of mine of laying in the line to catch him ... though I have ... never acted the prude but at every proper advance have looked as much as to say, Come on, if you dare. I know not how it is, no one has ever offered me anything beyond a fashionable compliment.'[16]

She begged for an opinion on her lack of success in the matrimonial stakes, and no doubt triumphantly conveyed to her parents the Old Woman's reply:

'... eagerness always defeats its own end, and sometimes is attended with the most fatal consequences to the unhappy woman who is the object of such indelicate and mischievous conduct ... I think the parents of my lively correspondent are much more to blame for their impotency, than she is for her ill success. I allow it is a natural and laudable wish to see a daughter matched to a man of probity and sense, who possesses an independent fortune, or who has abilities and diligence enough to acquire a decent competence at least, but this should not be too plainly expressed ... nor should she be dragged from one scene of gaiety to another, till every fop knows her face, and the weakest understanding can penetrate the design. Jewels are not worn every day, nor should beauty be too much exposed to the vulgar eye ... men will ever be more enamoured of the flower which they have found in the shade.'[16]

In other publications advice came in the form of moral discourses and editorial exhortations, for the Editors of the day clearly took their responsibilities seriously, conscientiously and consistently directing

37

their efforts towards the improvement of their readers. Their approaches naturally differed: *The Lady's Magazine* tended to be heavily philosophical, while *The Lady's Monthly Museum*, written for younger women, imparted its teaching with lively good humour.

The aims underlying these enterprises were evidently endorsed and appreciated by the general public. The Editors of both magazines claimed, respectively, to have received 'the most satisfactory and pleasing proofs' and 'most flattering remarks' of approbation. Unfortunately, no evidence is available regarding the actual size of this enthusiastic readership. There is only the statement made by the *Monthly Museum* that its circulation had been raised to 'a number beyond our most sanguine hopes'.

Thus, during the first decade of the nineteenth century, women's magazines continued to be frank, vigorous and mentally stimulating, representing a cross-section of feminine (and often masculine) opinion, and reflecting a broad spectrum of interests and activities. Editors saw as their prime function the cultivation of women's minds, whilst rigidly practising 'purity of selection'. In consequence, space devoted to beautifying the female person was kept to a minimum, an interesting reversal of the priorities which obtain in women's periodicals today. As late as 1813, *The Female Preceptor* entered the field, dedicated to Hannah More and intent on providing the 'rationally devout' with 'a repast suitable to their tastes'. The anonymous Lady Editor explained that she had deliberately chosen this medium because 'It is generally acknowledged that Periodical Works have a direct tendency to effect the grand object of all laudable exertions, viz. the *expansion* and *illumination* of the mind',[17] and having been assured by several ladies of eminence that there was a 'paucity of publications *expressly* designed for Females', undertook to provide a literary work that would meet the requirements of the 'vast portion of Females ambitious to obtain other information than of that destructive kind which is generally communicated through the medium of a great majority of novels and romances'.[17]

Her monthly magazine carried a high proportion of essays 'Chiefly on the Duties of the Female Sex', poetry, news from the provinces, fashion, notes on astronomy, school prospectuses, and notices of births, marriages, public lectures and prices in the London markets. The magazine also published its list of subscribers, 325 in all, which was headed by H.R.H. Princess Charlotte of Wales and included a number of members of the aristocracy.

By 1825, however, significant changes in the content and tone of women's magazines had occurred consistent with a much narrower view of the role and status proper to women, and indeed there was abundant evidence to show that attitudes to women had undergone considerable modification since 1800. The Editor of *The Lady's Magazine* regretfully commented:

'The times are changed . . . women have completely abandoned all attempts to shine in the political horizon, and now seek only to exercise their virtues in domestic retirement. The wise (who happily form the majority) perceiving the bad taste manifested in striving for mastery with man, are contented with truly feminine occupations, but in discarding their follies, and in endeavouring to become the rational companions instead of the toys and tyrants of men have fallen from their high estate and dwindled into comparative insignificance . . . the proud lords used to acknowledge the equality of the sexes—but now if a lady should dare to aspire to literary distinction, she meets with little encouragement. Magazines, journals and reviews abound with sarcastic comments upon the blue-stockings and their productions. Intellectual acquirement, when applied to a woman is used as a term of reproach. Writers . . . proclaim the mental as well as the bodily inferiority of the weaker sex.'[18]

This passage chronicled an important era in the history of upper-class women: the sudden reversal of the trend which promised their wider participation in social affairs, and their gradual withdrawal into the home. This development was of crucial importance in the evolution of the women's press. Women's magazines were no longer required to contribute to the intellectual improvement and advancement of women, merely to provide innocent and amusing reading matter as an alternative to the daily newspapers which were now considered to be too tainted for female perusal. The broad-based formula and intellectual approach evolved during the eighteenth century became obsolete and was gradually replaced by one more suited to the restricted lives and interests of early Victorian women.

The onset of these changes was visible in the magazines of 1825. There was a significant reduction in the coverage of domestic and foreign news, politics, and public affairs generally, all such items having disappeared completely from *La Belle Assemblée*, and *The Lady's Magazine*. Gone, too, were the boisterous debates on topical questions in which both sexes had once enthusiastically engaged, together with all other signs of reader-involvement apparent in the magazines of 1800. In all respects there was a definite sobering of magazine content and signs of growing introversion. The reaction against the excesses of the

39

Regency period gave rise to a new emphasis on propriety and the purging of every indiscretion and lapse of taste. The *Monthly Museum* had taken on a prim, correct character, a marked contrast to its former liveliness and candour, and *The Lady's Magazine* had similarly become entirely humourless, remarking:

'Conversation . . . is the means by which wisdom may obtain an influence over weakness and folly and piety over irreligion and immorality . . . Women . . . to whom devolves the charge of rising generations . . . should be cautious not to utter any sentiment, or to indulge in any conversation inconsistent with virtue and piety.'

Contraction in one area was balanced by expansion in another. Female dress at this period was becoming increasingly elaborate and the women's press paid more and more attention to it. Several new publications devoted almost entirely to the fashions appeared during the early years of the nineteenth century, and fashion coverage was also increased in some existing periodicals. The need for women to be informed about matters of dress was undoubtedly intensifying at this time. With the increase in wealth and productive capacity resulting from the spread of industrialisation, both the demand for and supply of consumer goods was rising. More important still, a new class of consumers was beginning to emerge, a class of wealthy industrialists who rose to social eminence via horse-power rather than horseflesh, and who had money to spend but little inbred taste to guide them. As they breached the ranks of the landed aristocracy, either by marriage or land purchase, it was incumbent upon them to assume the modes and manners of the leisured classes, and for their womenfolk particularly to observe the socially accepted rules of dress and decorum. Here was wide scope for the women's magazines, and many of them took to supplying detailed descriptions, with sketches, of what fashionable Society women were wearing, an important new service at a time when communications were still unreliable, and fashion intelligence difficult to come by.

The older journals tended to resist the new cult of appearances, adamantly refusing to indulge female vanity. *The Lady's Magazine* in particular deplored the lengths to which women were willing to go to follow prevailing fashions or enhance their personal beauty:

'How could one ever for an instant acknowledge as beautiful, a female waist so artificially contracted . . . ? There is no standard of beauty other than that which nature herself has set up. Vile advertisements hint that a row of ivory teeth may be *supplied* . . . the charming brilliancy of complexion for which the British Fair are so noted, is to be attributed as much to the use of the incomparable Kalydor as to the partiality of nature.'[19]

The Editor roundly condemned all such 'quack nostrums . . . at exhorbitant prices',[20] claiming that they could never do anything but injury.

Such Editors, steeped in a different tradition which gave women social and intellectual freedom in addition to their domestic obligations, found it hard to accept the narrowing of their frame of reference and the substitution of a new scale of priorities. *The Lady's Magazine*, in response to the new social requirements, introduced a regular feature giving 'instructions to young married ladies on the management of their households and the regulation of their conduct in the various relations and duties of conjugal life', one of the first magazines to do so. But it added a characteristic rider that it should be possible for a lady to be 'a good manager of her household and still find time to attend to the cultivation of her mind'. It was a losing battle, and the old-style journals with their roots in the eighteenth century lost ground to a new type of 'feminine' literature exemplified by such periodicals as *The Ladies' Pocket Magazine* (1825) which were designed solely to entertain, being composed of fiction, fashion and miscellaneous light reading of a superficial kind.

In the years between 1825 and 1850 there took place the first recorded merger in the field of publishing for women. The three leading women's magazines, *The Lady's Magazine*, *The Lady's Monthly Museum* and *La Belle Assemblée* joined forces. From 1832 until they ceased publication in 1847, their content was identical, though they appear to have been printed at separate establishments. The disappearance from the Victorian publishing scene of these vintage periodicals marked the passing of an era. With their going, the last vestiges of Georgian influence were erased and the field left wide open to Victorian Editors to evolve a formula expressly to meet the needs of the new industrial age.

(ii) Magazines in Transition

The Victorian age gave birth above all to 'the Feminine Illusion' by which is meant the glorification of Womanhood and the worship of female purity as the antithesis of, and antidote for, the corruption of Man:

B*

'[Woman was] given to man as his better angel, to dissuade him
from vice, to stimulate him to virtue, to make home delightful and
life joyous . . . in the exercise of these gentle and holy charities, she
fulfils her high vocation. But great as is the influence of the maiden
and wife, it seems to fade away when placed by that of the mother.
It is the mother who is to make the citizens for earth . . . and happy
are they who thus fulfil the sacred and dignified vocation allotted
to them by Providence.'[21]

Such was the new ideal of Womanhood: a holy vocation demanding
lifelong sacrifice and submission, exemplified not by a Virgin Queen, but
by a dutiful and virtuous young wife and mother. All women were
encouraged to model their lives on hers, so that from her pedestal
Victoria mutely dictated the rules of female conduct as effectively as if
they had been written into the legal code. She had, moreover, set a new
example by marrying for love, and magazine fiction was full of the unhappiness brought upon themselves by those who married solely for
money.

The new vision of Womanhood, compounded of piety and domesticity, had a profound effect upon the character of women's magazines,
narrowing their scope and eliminating all mental stimulus. Those who
still believed that the female intellect was worth cultivating steadily lost
ground to those who desired to foster in women an all-sufficing
pride in home and family. The new generation of Victorian Editors
upheld the latter view, and set out both to propagate it and to prepare
women for their calling by moral exhortation. One Editor was ecstatic
about the new female role:

'Let man take his claimed supremacy . . . let him be supreme in
the cabinet . . . the camp . . . the study . . . to woman will still
remain a goodly heritage of which neither force nor competition
can deprive her. The heart is her domain, and there she is an empress
. . . to watch over the few dear objects of regard with an eye that
never sleeps, and a care that cannot change: to think, to act, to suffer,
to sacrifice, to live, to die for them, their happiness, their assured
safety—these constitute Woman's true triumph . . . her love
sustained by highest Genius.'[22]

Assisted by such seductive language as this, the Victorian ideal of
exalted, self-effacing womanhood swept over society and into the
women's press. *The New Monthly Belle Assemblée*, launched in 1847,
provides a measure of the changes which had taken place since the

mid-'twenties. The magazine, which enjoyed the patronage of the Duchess of Kent, was dignified, correct, and morally vigilant. Designed purely for entertainment, it carried a large proportion of fiction, all of which was intended as a vehicle for moral teaching. Every story carried its lesson, usually the triumph of the good over the bad, the pious and virtuous over the vain and heartless, or the folly of idleness and extravagance contrasted with the rectitude of diligence and charity. Frequently, the writer would pause in the narrative to deliver a warning or an exhortation. In addition to fiction, there were reviews of plays and books, a series on English Churches, some poetry, a fashion section, and occasional articles on social questions such as 'late-closing' and 'sweating', a collection which accurately reflected the interests and activities of ladies of rank and breeding. *The Ladies' Cabinet* settled for a similar formula and an equally high moral tone, and in all such upper-class periodicals the trend away from topical and intellectual contributions was confirmed, together with the reduction in correspondence and other items from readers.

Only *The Lady's Newspaper and Pictorial Times* (1847) condemned the fact that:

'... in works professedly published for feminine perusal, no attempt has been made to consult also the intellectual capacity of women, or to advance in any way the cultivation of her mind. A series of frivolous articles, alike destitute of genius in their conception, or of talent in their execution were expected to meet with a grateful reception from the taste and discernment of those to whom they were offered.'[23]

Its editor was determined to reverse the trend and to 'raise the female mind to its true level'. The definition of this 'true level' was significant, being: 'whatever tends to enlarge the range of observation, awake the reason, and to lead the imagination into agreeable and innocent trains of thought, . . . and adds the captivating charms of mental culture to those of female loveliness'. Clearly, this was a debasement of the vision of the mental improvement of women held by writers at the turn of the century. Learning was then seen as a vital attribute in promoting harmonious relationships between the sexes. According to this Editor, it was no more than a pretty accomplishment, and the syllabus he recommended bore no comparison to the tough, educational programmes prescribed for women in 1800. Nevertheless, this was the only attempt made during the early years of Victoria's reign to bridge the gap left by the demise of the more serious-minded journals.

Until the middle of the century, the women's press remained an upper-class institution. But in 1852, an important new development occurred in the introduction of the first 'cheap' magazine to be produced for women of the middle classes. This was *The Englishwoman's Domestic Magazine*, brought out by Samuel Beeton and issued monthly at twopence. The customary price for a monthly had previously been one shilling, which placed them beyond the reach of those with moderate incomes. Beeton, aged twenty-one, was one of the first to recognise the untapped potential of the middle-class market, and his experiment opened the eyes of other publishers to the rich profits to be reaped by catering to women of all classes, paving the way for the vast expansion in publishing for women which took place at the end of the century. The decision to launch a low-priced monthly for a new class of reader altogether was a courageous enterprise. Some time later, the Editor revealed the thinking that lay behind his venture:

'We took the field in the belief that there was room for a cheap serial combining practical utility, instruction and amusement, and the flattering encouragement we have received during the progress of our work has confirmed us in this opinion. The experiment was a bold one, as apart from the nature and quality of the information supplied, and the number of engravings given for so small a charge, the Golden Prizes (given at the end of each volume), added materially to the risk.'[24]

Despite this uncertainty, the magazine could hardly have failed. There was no other publication for middle-class women at this time, nor did any of the 'quality' journals attempt to cater for their special needs. The proprietors saw their role as 'public instructors' whose first duty was to educate. However, they wished to dissociate themselves completely from 'that kind of education which prevails almost universally among the higher circles', for 'showy accomplishments may win a husband, but can do little toward making him a happy one'. That this approach was influenced as much by the Protestant Ethic as by traditional attitudes to the role of women, is evident from Beeton's own 'Receipt for succeeding in the world', which was 'to work much and spend little', and to practise 'wholesome thrift as will disinduce us to spend our time or money without an adequate return either in gain or enjoyment'. The contents of the magazine were geared to these objectives, and were intended to provide 'a fund of practical information and advice tending to promote habits of industry and usefulness, without which no home can be rendered virtuous or happy'.

Dedicated to 'the improvement of the intellect, the cultivation of the morals and the cherishing of domestic virtues', the magazine was mainly concerned with domestic management. Isabella Beeton, whose own *Book of Household Management* was to become a domestic classic, contributed weekly Notes on cookery and on fashion, travelling to Paris twice a year to cover the Spring and Autumn Collections. To help women put these Notes to practical use, Beeton conceived the idea of a 'Practical Dress Instructor', the forerunner of the paper dress-making pattern, one of the most heavily patronised services offered by the modern women's press. Another of his innovations were the 'Prize Compositions' which he introduced to encourage young women to improve their minds and which won an enthusiastic response from them, attracting upwards of a hundred competitors for each essay subject.

In addition to these novelties the magazine carried serial fiction, literary criticism, and articles on gardening and household pets, as well as poetry and miscellanea. Its advice on hygiene and the care of the sick foreshadowed the coming sanitary revolution and embarked the women's periodicals on another important service, but most significant, in terms of future publishing trends, was a new feature entitled 'Cupid's Letter Bag'. In this Beeton undertook to dispense advice to correspondents on the subject of courtship, and the problems confided to him might well have been taken from the postbag of a modern magazine counsellor:

From '*Drooping Snowdrop*' (Greenwich):
'Having been several times to a theatre in London, I have there become enamoured of a certain performer whose name I dare not mention; but I would give the world could I but gain an introduction to him . . . Do pray advise me . . .'

In this instance Beeton urged his fair correspondent 'by all means to gain an introduction to the party . . . as (without disparagement to the profession generally) a hero *on* the stage is anything but a hero *off* it'.[25]

From '*Jessie A.*' (Brompton):
'I am about to be married, but am sorely afraid of being compelled to give up going to balls and routs, of which I am excessively fond. My intended husband is of a very quiet turn of mind while I have a great taste for pleasure . . . Under these circumstances could I be happy?'

To this Beeton replied with some astringency:

'We are quite sure that if Jessie could be happy, her husband would not . . . Let Jessie remain single until she can learn the disregard of *self*.'[26]

The *Englishwoman's Domestic Magazine*, the first women's periodical to deal systematically with the subject of domestic management, achieved a greater popularity than even Beeton himself had anticipated. Within two years of publication it had reached a sale of 25,000 copies a month, rising to 37,000 by 1856, and when the first series ended in 1860 its circulation stood at 50,000. In that year Beeton launched a new and enlarged series,* printed (in anticipation of the repeal of the newspaper duty) on better quality paper, and introducing coloured fashion engravings which were imported from Paris. Following the signing of the Commercial Treaty with France which considerably reduced tariffs between the two countries, Mrs Beeton had visited Paris and there arranged with Adolphe Goubaud for the *E.D.M.* to use the fashion plates commissioned for his fashion monthly *Le Moniteur de la Mode*. These added greatly to the attractiveness of the new sixpenny edition which *The Standard* described as 'a wonderful production in size, matter and above all in price', adding: 'We have the authority of "Materfamilias" for saying that the house would go to sixes and sevens if the magazine failed to put in its monthly appearance.'

Meanwhile, social and economic changes which in the space of fifty years were to transform the position of women, their education and their employment, and profoundly influence the development of the women's press, were already becoming apparent. Magazine fiction in the 1840s was full of the plight of families who had fallen victim to the economic uncertainties of the times. Harrowing tales of misery and want were unfolded as first one family and then another was caught and ruined by the fever of speculation attendant upon the accelerating pace of industrialisation. Movement up or down the social scale was a striking feature, and dozens of romantic dramas were woven around doomed love-matches between penniless couples which were saved by a sudden reversal of fortune. By 1850, the distress of thousands of cultured but untrained gentlewomen thrown summarily onto an overcrowded labour market, was gaining prominence. Articles on the subject appeared in the women's magazines, together with discussions on the evils of

---

* Certain volumes of this series are on restricted loan at the British Museum, being classed as 'pornography'. One subject, the corporal punishment of children, evoked a year-long correspondence, in the course of which the corrective measures employed were fully described, throwing a new and sadistic light on the concept of the 'pious' Victorian mother.

the late-hour system, emigration schemes, the relief of poverty, female prostitution, and the Deceased Wife's Sister's Marriage Bill.

This was also the period during which the movement for the extension of women's rights put down its roots and thrust itself into the public eye. It was heralded by the appearance in 1846 of *The Female's Friend*, a magazine which dedicated itself to 'elevating the character and condition of women'. It pointed out that women were currently exposed to 'serious evils', which had to be extensively published if they were to be remedied. Already, institutions were being formed to secure the improvement and enforcement of the laws protecting women, and the magazine reported regularly on their progress during the few months it remained in print. Over the next twenty years, these protest groups multiplied and their demands grew more insistent. An organised campaign began to develop, impinging more and more upon public notice and using as mouthpieces some of the most eminent Victorian political, literary and Society figures. The Woman Question was fast becoming the most widely aired topic of the day.

Yet the leading periodicals for women were careful to avoid the whole subject of women's rights. Only the most casual references to feminist activities were made, and these were infrequent and invariably derogatory. From 1850 onwards a number of new magazines entered the field, but it is significant that no periodical which espoused the women's cause survived for more than a year or two. On the other hand, several publications which proffered the usual mixture of fiction, fashion, and needlework, were immediately successful and embarked upon long runs of between twenty-five and thirty years.

The Ladies' Treasury (1858) was one such magazine, expressly intended to 'illustrate and uphold "each dear domestic virtue, child of home" '. It offered a bland collection, including lessons in French and German, practical direction for flower and landscape painting, instructions for fancy work of all kinds and for the making of wax and paper flowers, all of which were intended to provide innocent and amusing occupations to fill the interminable leisure hours of young Victorian women. The Editor rigorously excluded everything which might tend to 'enervate or bewilder' the pure female mind. Hence the poetry was compounded of 'pure thought and high feeling', and the fiction never failed to display the triumph of 'Principle over Passion'.

The success of this magazine, which ran until 1895, provides some measure of popular tastes and the daily routine of young women in the leisured ranks of society. The values it projected indicate the strengthening hold of Victorian morality which demanded from women the utmost in purity and piety. One of the first magazines to challenge this limited conception of women's needs and interests was *The Lady's Review*. Coming out in 1860, it proposed to devote itself to 'what may truly be called the best and entire, rather than the fragmentary interests of women' and to represent 'the intelligence and sentiments of the Ladies of England, as well as their wants and services . . . their individual claims and proper social position'. This was the first known attempt to incorporate any discussion of the social changes affecting women into a women's magazine, and the Editor justified this new departure on the grounds of 'the advance of society . . . the increasing complication of the concerns of women and their progressing importance in the community', drawing the conclusion that such an organ was 'a want of the day'.

The public verdict on *The Lady's Review* was unfavourable, and it ceased publication within the year. Six years later, another attempt was made to launch a magazine in tune with the growing movement to improve the status and rights of women. This was *Woman's World*, a severely practical magazine which refused to indulge women's sartorial tastes, giving prominence instead to politics. A contemporary critic, whilst praising its talented and well-written articles, high-quality fiction and unobtrusive refinement and beauty, condemned the political features as being neither wise nor useful, advocating as they did disestablishment and women's suffrage. In 1869 the magazine changed its name to *The Kettledrum*, subtitled *The Woman's Signal for Action*, emphasising its feminist leanings. Elaborating the magazine's policy, the Editor agreed that there existed 'a line beyond which feminine minds and feminine pens must not venture' but argued that the line was elastic and included a wide variety of subjects, all of which would certainly be discussed in its pages. *The Kettledrum* thus set out to combine art and literature with social improvement, but it was forced to beat a predictable retreat in less than a year.

Even the mildest advocates of the advancement of women trespassed too far to be acceptable. *The Ladies*, a sixpenny monthly published in 1872, was in every respect, save one, a model publication. It was 'A journal of the Court, Fashion and Society', and true to the traditions of polite literature for the upper classes, set out to 'aid woman to be beautiful in her person, elegant in her dress and artistic in her tastes'. In case this might be thought too frivolous a programme, the Editor assured readers that the magazine would by no means neglect a woman's 'less conspicuous but more needful duties which fit her to take a proper place in the home as a wife and mother'. In all these respects, the periodical faithfully adhered to the formula which had brought success to its competitors, but it nevertheless survived for only one year. The reason for this may well have been the Editor's admission that:

'We are heartily and earnestly at one with those who claim for women many rightful, political, and social privileges from which they are now unfairly excluded.'[28]

Sympathising with the Women's Movement was sufficient to drive otherwise orthodox magazines out of print. The majority of women, lacking the incentives which drove the hard-pressed minority to fight for the rights which would make them self-supporting, recoiled in horror from the 'unfeminine' behaviour of the advocates of women's emancipation and followed the lead of their Sovereign in condemning them. Ordinary women everywhere clung to the belief that Providence had assigned them a limited and submissive role and accepted it uncomplainingly and (for the most part) contentedly. Thus, whilst one section of the female population campaigned to widen their sphere of work and their share in the business of life, the remainder were either actively hostile to their efforts or passively withheld their support, unconvinced that women's destiny and true happiness lay along this road to freedom.

That the well-to-do middle classes tended towards greater conservatism than the upper classes in this respect is apparent from the reactions of two correspondents to the passing of the Women's Disabilities Bill and the Married Women's Property Bill. Commenting on the passage of the first, a contributor to *The Englishwoman's Domestic Magazine* wrote:

'That women as a body desire a vote in Parliament I do not think. The women who do have such a wish form but a very small proportion of those whose opinions they say they represent. I think most sensible women will say that they prefer their own sphere to that offered them in the terms and inferences of the Bill.'[29]

Again, referring to the Property Bill, a reader commented:

'It is absurd to think that because these rights are granted to married women marriage is thence to be regarded as a sort of partnership ... Nothing could be more unfounded than the idea that men should cease to be masters of their own households'[30]

a view which betrayed a fundamental desire, shared by the majority of women, to uphold the traditional relationship in marriage.

The campaign to extend women's rights consistently failed to win prominence in the women's press. The women's magazines continued to reinforce the *status quo*, and adhered to a restricted formula. The emergence of *The Queen* in 1861, a publication which was to span a century, strengthened this approach. In declaring its policy, *The Queen* with royal contempt brushed aside any revolutionary ideas concerning the proper nature and scope of a women's magazine. It said:

> 'When we write for women we write for the home. We shall offend very few when we say that women have neither heart nor head for abstract political speculation, while as for our own liberties, or our political principles, they may be safely left to men . . . therefore our survey of foreign affairs and of politics generally will be recorded in a few notes.'[31]

The Queen was Samuel Beeton's attempt to follow his successful monthly, *The Englishwoman's Domestic Magazine*, with a high-class newspaper for women which would provide 'a weekly Record and Journal which ladies can read and profit by; one in which their understandings and judgements will not be insulted by a collection of mere trivialities, but which will be to them a help in their daily lives . . .' Edited by his friend Frederick Greenwood (and later by himself), the magazine's sixteen folio pages were filled, in addition to events of the day, with needlework designs, fashion articles (written by Isabella Beeton), engravings of fine art subjects, literary topics, gossip, Society intelligence and details of public entertainments. As a newspaper it provided women with more topical and factual information than the orthodox magazines, and soon achieved the status of being the foremost periodical for ladies of rank and breeding.

1869 brought a light-hearted protest against 'Defeminisation' in the shape of a sixpenny monthly, *The Girl of the Period Miscellany*, which sided with those young women who preferred balls and beaux to campaigning for women's rights. Written by the fictitious 'Miss Echo' and a bevy of voluble female assistants, it accepted the evidence of the Census that 'it is possible to have too much of a good thing', but warned against the dangers of dealing with the problem of the Surplus Woman in ways that might ultimately lead (through lack of use) to the withering away of her feminine character and functions.

Challenging John Stuart Mill's implied criticism* that for a woman to prefer to gain her livelihood by being a wife and mother was evidence of 'a poor, mean spirit', the magazine set out to show that the 'Girl of the Period' was 'not such a mere weed as she has been made out to be', but was rather 'the natural outgrowth of the Circumstances . . . an

---

* *Political Economy*, J. S. Mill, Book IV, Ch. VII, Section 3.

involuntary Protest . . . the Irony of the Situation'. Fully illustrated with black and white engravings which included a number of cartoons satirising the follies and vanities of the age, the magazine was an entertaining blend of irreverent fiction and social comment reminiscent of *Punch*, a sharp and revealing contrast to the orthodox journals for gentlewomen.

Finding that none of the regular women's journals would espouse their cause, those working for the advancement of women were obliged to provide their own publications. One of these was the *Woman's Gazette* (1875), a functional magazine designed to put needy women in touch with employment opportunities. Conscious of the ever-increasing number of women's periodicals coming on to the market, the proprietors felt bound to justify the addition:

'We think there is urgent need of a special organ to represent the many branches of women's work, to print correspondence, to supply the latest information, and be a medium for advertisements.'

In the absence of labour exchanges and a co-ordinated system for advertising vacancies, there was certainly a place for such a publication, as the ranks of unemployed and penniless women swelled. It promised to provide an invaluable service to the thousands of unmarriageable women thrown on to the labour market without the knowledge or resources to find work for themselves. Yet despite this pressing need, the *Woman's Gazette* was poorly supported, and reported in 1879 that it had been forced to change its title and widen its scope in order to become self-supporting. As *Work and Leisure*, it continued to supply information about professional bodies and give advice concerning employment, but broadened its base to include entertainment, adding correspondence, fiction, holiday features, pastimes, anecdotes and prize competitions. This was evidently a change for the better, and the magazine continued in print until 1893.

Meanwhile, magazines generally were preoccupied with catering on the one hand to the rising middle classes who kept their women in idleness and luxury, and on the other to the growing number of gentlewomen with no hope of marriage who had been reduced to penury. The magazines of the 'seventies reflected the extremes of wealth and poverty, the mixed harvest of the first phase of the industrial revolution. The third quarter of the century was characterised by 'a degree of opulence, luxury and refinement unheard of in the palmiest days of the Roman commonwealth',[32] which showed itself in 'the immense amount of money which seems to be at liberty to be spent in the purchase of art treasures . . .', in luxury furniture, 'which is more useful, convenient and costly every year', and in the extravagance of female dress.

The amassing of industrial property was beginning to have its effect upon the class structure, permitting an unprecedented degree of social mobility. In consequence, women born to a lowly station were now required, by virtue of their husbands' success in business, to take their place alongside ladies of rank and breeding. The latter did not welcome these *parvenues*. Their attitude was put by a correspondent to *The Englishwoman's Domestic Magazine*:

> 'The terrible persons one now comes in contact with are a positive calamity to the nation. What can you hope for when you meet in first class railway carriages, ladies who talk and tell their fellow-travellers all about their 'usbands 'aveing 'orses who 'unt with the 'ounds three times a week? . . . They are not unfrequently good-looking, almost always clean and usually arrayed in purple and fine linen. But well-dressed! . . . to bedizen oneself with rings and earrings, brooches and chains and clothe oneself in sealskin and furs and velvets for half-an-hour's railway journey, or a walk to a shop—oh it is miserable work and altogether monstrous. We can frown down I hope . . . and cold-shoulder out of Society, if ever by chance they enter therein, these miserable persons . . . with their 'ouses, their 'omes, their 'arness and their 'air.'[33]

For such women, ignorant of Society's modes and manners, the women's magazines proved an indispensable guide. More and more publications began to include features on etiquette, undertaking to answer readers' queries on all matters of dress and taste. Fashion notes occupied an increasing amount of space as styles grew ever more elaborate and succeeded each other with increasing rapidity. Advertisements now began to figure largely in several magazines, testifying to the big expansion in mass-produced consumer goods and rising incomes. The economy was booming, and industrial property-owners contributed to the growth of the retail trade by channelling their newly acquired wealth into display expenditure to buttress their social position.

While this orgy of spending benefited the newly rich, it placed a severe strain upon the financial resources of established Society, for whom landed property was a far less fruitful source of income than industry and commerce. Commenting on the high pressure of life, *The Queen* apportioned some of the blame to women:

> 'We cannot say we think women entirely guiltless in the matter of urging on the race for wealth.'[34]

In an earlier issue it had advocated 'strict economy in the management of every middle-class household'[35] in the face of 'social pressures' stemming from 'the luxury, not to say ostentation that characterises our period'.

There was a corresponding broadening in the range of leisure pursuits. With the later years of the nineteenth century came a relaxation of some of the restraints inhibiting social intercourse for women, who were able to participate in many new outdoor activities. The *E.D.M.* commented:

'We are no longer afraid of croquet . . . [or] long walks. The archery ground delights many . . . [also] the swimming bath.'

The girl of the period had 'more freedom of action . . . healthy development . . . confidence . . . a go-ahead spirit',[36] which gave the women's magazines considerable new scope. The undercurrent of change was expressed in a lighter, gayer atmosphere and the introduction of new pastimes. By 1875, the oppressive moral gloom of the earlier period was giving place to new freedom of expression, literally reflected in the faces of the fashion models which were becoming pert and alive, in marked contrast to those of the 'fifties and 'sixties which had been prim and lifeless, bespeaking silent purity.

The magazines were now meeting a heightened demand for romantic fiction, advice about dress and 'the toilette', and for fancy work, since these were still the chief interests and occupations of well-bred young ladies. One of the main functions of periodicals at this time was to keep readers *au fait* with the latest fad or novelty. It was an age of 'crazes', in needlework and in dress. It was fashionable, for instance, to ape masculine dress, to do 'Berlin work', to live for the ballroom, and finally to surrender to a *mariage de convenance*.

But for married women life had far less variety and excitement to offer. With her children given into the care of nursemaids, and the housekeeping devolving upon an increasing army of servants, the young wife had little to occupy her time. One lady, driven to seek help with this problem, received the following reply:

'Your case is that of thousands of women and arises from the present state of society. In old times when one servant did the rough work, and the mistress worked with her, time did not hang heavily upon the wife's hands, and her labour saved her husband's pocket very materially. Employment at home is difficult for women to get, and remuneration is very little. We advise you taking a few children to teach, or giving music lessons: or if your husband's position prevents this being done, economise his income and spend your time in working at your own clothing and his, and in assisting in the housekeeping.'[37]

Many thousands of women found their chief difficulties arising from the growing shortage of domestic servants, and few issues of the magazines of the time lacked some reference to 'the servant problem'. The reasons for the shortage were attributed to the diverting of female labour into other forms of work (chiefly clerical posts and the retail distributive trade) created by the spread of industrialism. Correspondents were keen to offer solutions through the columns of the women's press including, if all else failed, means for self-help. The *E.D.M.*, writing for households where few servants were employed, published information about the latest labour-saving appliances which were flooding onto the market. These included machines for knife-cleaning, boot and shoe cleaning, carpet-sweeping, bread-making, washing, wringing, goffering and crimping as well as those for the garden and stable, a list which gives some idea of the many operations requiring manual labour carried out in Victorian homes. Two important inventions coming into use at this time were the electric bell and the American refrigerator.

The servant problem grew year by year, disrupting the hitherto unruffled calm of the wealthier Victorian households. Families lower down in the social hierarchy were not so seriously affected since their womenfolk had long been accustomed to taking on themselves a large share of the housekeeping. As paid help grew scarcer and more expensive, women had to assume even more of these responsibilities. A writer in the *E.D.M.* sympathised with 'those overworked mothers who find all pleasantness crowded out of their lives by the ever-accumulating piles of work to be got through by one pair of hands', and advocated the purchase of one of the new sewing machines on 'the gradual payment system'. None of these women could be accused of dissipating their lives in idleness, but considerable concern was voiced in the women's press over the numerous young women, educated at fashionable boarding schools to shine in the pretty accomplishments suited to the drawing-room, who were totally unfitted to assume the management of a household should circumstances require it.

The servant shortage having exposed this serious deficiency in female education, the women's magazines began to try and fill the gap. A few introduced items on home management ranging from 'handy hints' to detailed recipes and advice on superintending servants, as well as dealing with readers' domestic queries. But nowhere was there a systematic attempt to instruct women in the domestic arts. Moreover, the advice given was too general to be of much help to the uninitiated, either assuming a good deal of prior knowledge or intended to be passed on by a mistress to her servants. At this time it was not considered a prime function of women's magazines to provide such a service. They were still primarily a medium of entertainment and as such were mainly composed of fiction, fashion, fancy-work and social gossip.

However, as the problem of domestic help intensified, hints and recipes began to be regularly included and readers sent in their queries to be answered in print, a service which was to expand greatly in future years. Also, as the century progressed and more became known about the distressed condition of various groups in the population, the women's magazines began to develop a social conscience, devoting considerable space to these problems and enlisting readers' help in their relief. Foremost amongst them was the plight of the thousands of unmarriageable women forced onto a hopelessly overcrowded labour market in an attempt to be self-supporting. The problem evinced the greatest concern amongst contributors to *The Queen* and the *E.D.M.* many of whom must have had personal knowledge of the sufferings of impoverished, unskilled, and unemployable gentlewomen in their own families or amongst their friends. There was evidence of in-group sympathy, deeply felt, which came across in letters, articles and editorials. The Editor of *The Queen* called it 'One of the greatest social problems of our day', and, 'one of the burning questions of modern political economy'.[38]

Also reflected, was the growing involvement of women in charitable enterprises. For the first time both magazines began to carry articles on the 'ragged schools', servants' homes and night refuges for the homeless poor, and contributions in the form of money and clothing were solicited. Thus, at a time when the doctrine of *laissez-faire* and sheer ignorance were hampering social reformers in their efforts to win support from the public at large, at least two leading women's publications helped to publicise the appalling condition of the poor and sought to mobilise funds and other help for their relief.

In 1875 the women's press was still comparatively small. In that year, however, among a group of new journals intended for middle-class consumption, there appeared two important magazines, *Myra's Journal of Dress and Fashion* and *Weldon's Ladies' Journal. Myra's Journal* was run by Mrs Matilda Browne who had formerly edited *The Young Englishwoman* under the pen-name 'Myra' and was a close friend of Samuel Beeton. In her new venture she received a good deal of help from Beeton who advised her on many technical and financial matters and even arranged for Weldon's to publish the magazine. He stressed the importance of appealing to a wide audience and the *Journal* was offered to the public in several different editions priced between 2d. and 6d. to suit all pockets. The novelties of coloured fashion plates and paper dress-making patterns, which Beeton had earlier experimented with so successfully, assured the magazine of an enthusiastic reception, and indeed the response was so overwhelming that its size had to be increased to cope with the flood of correspondence.

Weldon's was also well patronised, and this threepenny weekly, perhaps more than any other periodical, supplied the blue-print for the 'home weeklies' which crowded onto the market during the closing years of the century. It lasted until 1963, proof that it had assessed correctly the needs of the mass female reading public, and during its life the proprietors brought out many auxiliary publications specialising in dress-making and needlework, subjects which could not be given full coverage in the parent magazine.

With the coming of *Weldon's* the field of publishing for women began to assume the characteristics of an industry. Publishing firms were waking up to the fact that there was a vast potential demand for useful and entertaining periodical literature among women of all classes, but particularly in the middle and lower-middle ranks. The proportion of advertising was steadily increasing, indicating that manufacturers and retailers too were becoming aware of the potential of the women's press —as a selling medium.

The transitional years in the history of women's magazines were coming to an end. They were on the verge of an era of explosive growth, which gave birth at the turn of the century to an important communications industry, capable, once a mass readership had built up, of far-reaching social and economic influence over the women of Britain. This development was founded upon social, economic and technological changes, all of which must now be examined in some detail.

NOTES

1 'Early English Periodicals for Ladies', Bertha Monica Stearns.
2 *The Ladies' Mercury*, 1693, p. 1.
3 *Op. cit.*
4 B. M. Stearns, *op. cit.*, p. 38.
5 Ian Watt, *The Rise of the Novel*, Ch. 2, p. 35.
6 A. S. Collins, *Authorship in the Days of Johnson*, p. 255.
7 *Ibid.*, p. 236.
8 Austen Leigh, 'William Strahan and His Ledgers', p. 272.
9 Marjorie Plant, *The English Book Trade*, p. 445.
10 *The Visiter*, December, 1723.

11 B. M. Stearns, *op. cit.*, pp. 55-6.
12 *The Lady's Magazine*, May, 1771, Vol. 1, p. 462.
13 *Ibid.* (Postscript to Index), Vol. 1, 1771.
14 Thomas Gisborne, *An Enquiry into the Duties of the Female Sex*, p. 271.
15 *La Belle Assemblée*, 1806, p. 73.
16 *The Lady's Monthly Museum*, October, 1798, Vol. 1, p. 289.
17 *Op. cit.* (Preface to launch issue.)
18 *Op. cit.*, 1825, p. 64.
19 *Ibid.*, p. 528.
20 *Ibid.*, p. 631.
21 *The Ladies' Cabinet*, 1847, p. 156.
22 *Ibid.*, p. 138.
23 *Op. cit.*, 1850, Vol. 1. (Editorial Preface.)
24 *Op. cit.*, Vol. 1, 1852. (Preface.)
25 *Englishwoman's Domestic Magazine*, February, 1853, Vol. 1, p. 318.
26 *Ibid.*, July, 1852, Vol. 1, p. 96.
27 *Op. cit.*, January 25th, 1863.
28 *The Ladies*, 1872. (Preface to launch issue.)
29 *Op. cit.*, Vol. 8, 1870, p. 124.
30 *Ibid.*, Vol. 9, p. 188.
31 *Op. cit.*, 1861. (Preface to launch issue.)
32 *Ibid.*, 1875, p. 253.
33 *Op. cit.*, Vol. 8, 1870, p. 377.
34 *Op. cit.*, 1875, p. 121.
35 *Ibid.*, p. 86.
36 *Op. cit.*, Vol. 9, 1870. p. 254.
37 *E.D.M.*, 1870, p. 298.
38 *Op. cit.*, 1875, p. 72.

2

An Industry is Born: 1875-1910

(i) Exploring the Market

The last two decades of Victoria's reign were years of unparalleled expansion in publishing for women. Excluding family journals and all-fiction periodicals, both of which had a feminine bias, not less than forty-eight new titles entered the field between 1880 and 1900. The 'explosion' was frequently commented upon, and new publications felt they had to justify adding to the number. As early as 1887, before the phase of concentrated expansion had begun, *Mother's Companion* was concerned about overloading the market:

> 'At first it might appear that there are magazines enough in this field and that there is certainly no room for one addressed to a particular class in the community. But those to whom the *Mother's Companion* will appeal, constitute a very numerous, and very important section of society.'[1]

This accelerated rate of growth continued through the first ten years of the twentieth century, but by this time the seller's market of the 1890s was beginning to give place to a buyer's market, in which it was becoming increasingly difficult to achieve lasting success. While magazines were few, the novelty value of any newcomer was usually sufficient to sustain it and to compensate for low standards of content and presentation. But with heightened competition, readers began to demand reliability and value for money, and the early years of the new century brought a rapid turnover in titles as substandard journals perished.

In their haste to capitalise in a booming industry, publishers too readily assumed that where women were concerned it was only necessary to throw together a mixture of traditionally 'feminine' ingredients to produce a magazine they would flock to buy. Thomas Gibson Bowles, a journalist of long experience who started *Vanity Fair** and who was also Founder-Editor of *The Lady*, exploded this fallacy in a letter to his Manager in which he criticised an early issue of the latter magazine and demanded improvements. He wrote:

'We are bound to get rid, once for all, of the old idea that "anything will do for women". It is not true... for women, though less good perhaps at creating, are better than men at criticising, and will damn us at once if we are not up to a fairly high standard. Give them quality *now* at any rate—the quantity will come.'[2]

The sudden spurt of growth was not confined to the women's press. The publishing industry as a whole was entering a phase of rapid expansion consequent upon social, economic and technological change. The main social development responsible for the publishing boom was the spread of state education which created a vast new potential market for cheap literature. The Education Act of 1870 had made provision for the setting up of elementary schools by local boards. A further Act (1876) made education compulsory to the age of thirteen, and with the passing of new legislation in 1891, it became free to all.

The results were far-reaching. In 1892, *The Young Woman* commented:

'The progress of education has touched all classes. There is no more startling phenomenon in the life of today than the enormous increase of journals and newspapers. We have now reached the point where the full effect of national education is being felt. Everyone can read. Books have become cheaper and cheaper. The entire intellectual life of the nation has received an enormous quickening. Hence journals play a part in national life wholly undreamed of in the days when the realm of letters was governed by *The Edinburgh Review and Quarterly*.'[3]

The publishing empires of such men as Alfred Harmsworth, Arthur Pearson and George Newnes were founded upon the new generation of readers issuing from the Board schools. Cheaper railway travel, too, helped to swell the demand for 'half-hour literature'. *The Ladies' Gazette* (1895) which kept its dimensions small, was, according to one correspondent, 'the ideal size for reading in the train as so many of us like to do'. Another contributory factor was the gradual change in the pattern

---

* Not to be confused with a modern fashion magazine of the same name.

of life of the female population. In the 'seventies, the pendulum started to swing back towards greater social freedom for women. They began to participate more fully in leisure activities outside the home, mixing more freely and intimately with men. Publishers were quick to see in these developments new scope for periodicals which would both reflect the widening social ambit and interests of the female sex, and assist those married women who were forced to be maids-of-all-work in understaffed households.

Social changes supplied the great impetus to expansion; technological advances facilitated it. The growth of cheap literature for the masses was founded upon developments in paper manufacture and printing, and upon the rise of organised retail distribution, which was itself dependent upon improved communications over the country as a whole. The production of cheap paper in large quantities, the mechanisation of type-casting and setting, and the introduction of fast, rotary presses were crucial, and these advances were made during the last quarter of the nineteenth century.

In paper-making, as a result of mechanisation, the period 1800–60 brought a seven-fold increase in output and a marked improvement in finish, strength and regularity, particularly in the cheaper grades of paper. The invention of the Fourdrinier machine lowered production costs, and made possible the manufacture of larger sheets. Costs were further reduced by the introduction of bleaching powder and cheaper kaolin, soda and salt. But the fundamental problem preventing further expansion was the shortage of raw materials. Rags were still the main source of supply but these were scarce and expensive, and totally inadequate to meet the growing demand for paper of all kinds. The search for a substitute intensified. Cotton and flax waste were important new discoveries, but the real breakthrough came from Sweden where sulphite was successfully produced from wood-pulp. This invention, introduced into Britain in the 1880s, revolutionised the industry and made possible a huge increase in productive capacity, especially for the cheaper grades of paper needed by the periodical press.

Equally important was the development of printing processes capable of turning out newspapers and periodicals by the million at high speed. Attempts to accelerate the time-consuming type-casting and composing processes had been in progress since the beginning of the century. Mechanised type-casting was developed by Bruce under an American patent much earlier, but it was not used in this country until the 1840s owing to strong prejudice against mechanical methods. This gave way before the efficiency of the Bruce caster and all subsequent models were based on it until, in 1881, Frederick Wicks produced a new rotary machine which pushed up the casting rate to 6,000 characters an hour, allowing printers to save time by discarding used type and re-casting it as needed.

Efforts were also being made to speed up the type-composing process, which was still carried out manually. The 'piano-type', introduced early in the nineteenth century, was the first effective advance. It was followed by the Hattersley in 1857 and various other models, including one driven by electricity brought out in the 1870s. But, just as wood-pulp provided the break-through for the paper industry, all previous type-casting and setting inventions were eclipsed by the Linotype, introduced in 1889, which cast whole lines of type mechanically. At first it was operated by one man using hundreds of matrices struck by hand punches. Soon, a punch cutting machine made the process simpler, cheaper and faster, and a new era in the production of cheap, printed literature began.

Another abvance came with the perfecting of illustrative techniques. Fully illustrated copy is a feature of modern publications, but picture papers only began to appear at the close of the nineteenth century, the pioneer being the *Daily Graphic*, published in 1890. One of the earliest methods of illustration was wood-engraving, and in the 1830s electrotyping was developed from it. The next advance was the photographic reproduction of line drawings, which were etched in relief on zinc. This was the first of the photo-process engraving techniques which revolutionised methods of illustration in the last quarter of the century.

The first photograph had been obtained in 1822 and the first negative followed thirteen years later. However, the first photo-mechanical blocks were not made until the 1880s, and even then no tones could be reproduced until Meisenbach invented the 'half-tone' process in 1882. This method translated the original into a regular 'dot' texture, and was so successful that, by 1900, it had almost completely replaced woodengravings.

Half-tone reproduction required greater accuracy, and finer quality, quick-drying inks, which were subsequently developed, together with a wider range of pigments. The American gas-blacks, which combined strong colour with excellent printing properties, were one notable improvement. These new inks were not suitable for colour printing, which relied upon synthetic organic colours invented by Perkins in 1858. But in colour-work, too, progress was being made. In 1900, chromo-lithography was being challenged by an entirely new method, photogravure, consequent upon the discovery of scientific colour analysis in 1861, but it was not as yet widely used.

Concurrent with these developments in preparation processes, progress was also being made in increasing the speed and capacity of printing presses. In the eighteenth century, the only means of printing was by hand-operated wooden presses of the platen type. The first major improvement came with the introduction of iron presses, first devised by Earl Stanhope, perfected in America and brought to England in 1817. A lighter and simpler version, the 'Albion', came into use in 1820. Meanwhile, power-operated presses were being experimented with in Germany, where Koënig constructed a steam-driven, flat-bed cylinder machine in 1811. *The Times*, which pioneered many printing advances in the nineteenth century, brought it to England, speeded it up, and later installed an improved version initially capable of printing both sides of the paper simultaneously, and latterly four sheets at once on one side.

These innovations pushed the efficiency of the flat-bed press to its limit, and it was obvious that only a rotary model could cope with the faster production rates necessary to keep pace with modern requirements. The first successful horizontal rotary press, the Hoe, was built in America in 1846, and installed by *The Times* in 1857. In conjunction with the improved presses, other advances were being made in stereotyping, culminating in the production of curved papiermâché plates, which allowed several duplicates to be made from one type-setting, as well as rotary printing on both sides of the paper.

Paper was still being fed into the machines in single sheets, and the next step was the introduction of reeled paper (which allowed continuous feeding) and a folding attachment, first used in Liverpool in 1885. The Hoe underwent successive modifications, until in 1895, a model was developed which could deal with three rolls of paper simultaneously. By 1908 Hoe and Goss presses were printing 32-page copies of *The Times* at the rate of 25,000 copies an hour.

Thus, to help them meet the needs of a newly educated and literate population hungry for cheap reading matter, printers had the advantages of mechanical type-casting and setting, the two new illustrative techniques of photogravure and the half-tone process, stereotyping, fast rotary presses and large quantities of cheap, good quality newsprint. In addition, the coming of the railways provided a fast, direct method of distribution over all parts of the country and created a more satisfactory link between publishers and the reading public in the provinces, building up a National, in place of a Metropolitan press.

Economic conditions, too, favoured expansion. Business was booming in the 1890s and businessmen were seeking new areas of investment. The high costs of publishing, due mainly to excise duties on imported paper and rags and the stamp duty on newspapers, had long been disincentives to prospective publishers. But, following the 14th Report of the Commissioners of Excise, these surcharges were gradually reduced and finally abolished. The advertisement and stamp duties were repealed in 1853 and 1855, and those on paper and rags were lifted in 1860 and 1861. These 'taxes on knowledge' had latterly pressed hardly on the cheaper publications using low grade paper, and their removal gave a new stimulus to this section of the trade particularly. With the market opening up and taxes falling, publishing now offered good prospects to investors, and an increasing number of firms, attracted by the growing potential of the women's section of the market, began specialising in the production of women's magazines. Among the leading multiple publishers of women's journals at this time were Beeton's, Harrison's, Newnes, Pearson's, the Periodical Publishing Company, Schild's, Simpkin, Marshall and Co. and Weldon's.

But, while there were unlimited prospects for expansion in the women's press, production costs rose with higher output. Publishers were forced to turn to advertisers to finance their new ventures, though they were reluctant to admit the extent to which they were dependent upon an advertising subsidy. One of the first public admissions appeared in an Editorial in the launch issue of *The Gentlewoman*, a 'quality' weekly brought out in 1898. It said:

'Advertisements are indispensable because every copy costs the proprietors nearly double the price for which it is sold.'

The Editor further expressed the hope that the advertisement columns (just under half the total content) would provide 'a useful directory for ladies'.

This acceptance of advertising as fundamental to the financing of the women's press marked an important stage in the growth of the magazine industry. In 1800, the amount of advertising carried by the women's journals was extremely small. No advertisements appeared in the annual volumes of either the *Lady's Magazine* or the *Lady's Monthly Museum*, though there is evidence to suggest that some may have appeared on the covers of the original monthly issues. *La Belle Assemblée* in 1806 was a pioneer in adding to its annual volume an eight-page compendium of advertisements for a variety of products ranging from books and remedies, to dress, furnishings and entertainments. By 1825, there were signs of a change of policy. The *Lady's Magazine* had begun featuring advertisements both on its back pages and on its covers 'to respectfully inform the Nobility and Gentry', though it was careful to warn its patrons against numerous inferior and inefficacious preparations'. Advertisements for artificial teeth, oriental dentifrice and 'antibilious family pills' vied for the reader's attention with 'patent, ever-pointed pencils', fruit lozenges, composition wax candles and an assortment of dresses, bonnets, shawls and 'chintz furnitures'.

La Belle Assemblée was now making a definite bid for advertising custom. In 1823 it issued the following announcement:

'To Advertisers: The proprietors of this magazine offer its pages to commercial men and others as a cheap and advantageous method of claiming public attention. The admission of this miscellany into the families of the Nobility and Gentry of the first distinction, must render it a most respectable medium for advertisements.

'The Editors, finding the sale of *La Belle Assemblée* progressively increasing, have in consequence been induced to extend the limits hitherto appropriated for the insertion of public announcements, as much to prevent the disappointment of applicants, as to afford a better notion of typographical beauty to the favours they shall in future receive.

'Those persons, therefore, who may feel inclined to give the preference to this magazine, may be assured of having their advertisements exhibited to the best effect, and in a conspicuous style, upon more reasonable terms than any other periodical publication of equal circulation in the metropolis.'

The sudden need to attract advertising was evidently due to higher production costs occasioned by the increase in the size of the magazine. It prided itself on formal elegance and the beauty of its engravings, which must have added considerably to these, and in 1829 it reported 'new achievements in illustrative techniques' claiming 'an unsurpassed standard of excellence both in the tinted fashion plates and in the Society portraits'. *The Lady's Magazine* was encountering similar difficulties in meeting rising costs and it, too, claimed better standards of presentation as the justification for an increase in its cover price:

'... it has been deemed expedient to increase its [the magazine's] claims to public encouragement by the elegance and beauty of imitative art. This is the consideration which impels us to propose an advance of sixpence for each of our future numbers. Our expenses are great and have been lately increasing.'

The increase brought the price of the annual volume up to £1 6s. 6d.,

making it a costly item, though the reading public got value for its
money in the engravings alone, which were highly prized, and made
available separately by the publishers for framing.

A bar to advertising in the early nineteenth century was the punitive
advertisement tax of three and sixpence, levied in 1803. In 1833, this
was lowered to one and sixpence, and there was an immediate expansion
in advertising. Meanwhile, its focus was changing. As mass production
increased, and a new range of cheaper consumer goods became available,
manufacturers grew more interested in reaching potential purchasers
among the lower-income groups. They received an added stimulus in
this direction by the removal of the newspaper stamp duties which
increased the volume of 'penny literature' and created an ideal selling
medium.

But as late as the 1860s, the women's press was still only mildly interested in attracting advertising. The proprietors of *The World of Fashion*
were among the few publishers who patronised the trade press in an
effort to get custom. *Willing's Press Guide* for 1862 carried the following
announcement inserted by them:

'The immense circulation which this magazine enjoys amongst
the best classes of society renders it a most valuable medium for
advertisers. The sale is much larger than any other magazine of the
kind in Europe. A few advertisements are printed on the wrapper.'

Advertising in women's periodicals remained limited until the third
quarter of the century. Even in 1876, high-class journals such as *Le
Follet* and *World of Fashion* were only willing to accept a small amount
of advertising matter. The former announced to advertisers through the
Newspaper Press Directory that: 'A limited number of Approved advertisements may be specially arranged for'[5] while the latter maintained
its policy of confining them to its covers.

But among the newer publishing firms there were signs of a change
of attitude. They began to see in advertising the answer to their financial
difficulties, and set out to increase it. Whereas in the past the women's
magazines had resolutely slammed the door against commercial interests,
some of them began to woo advertisers in earnest, and by 1900 were
clamouring for all the advertising custom they could get. The *Newspaper
Press Directory* for 1901 provides evidence of this change of front. In it,
magazines vied with each other to convince advertisers of their superior
advantages as selling media. *Home Notes*, claiming to be 'A pioneer of
its class', cited 'crowded advertisement columns' as evidence of its
pulling power. *Myra's Journal* described itself as 'a valuable advertising

medium' with 'a large circulation'. Newnes advertised their periodicals as a group emphasising their wide market coverage, while *The Lady's Pictorial* stressed its special merits as a 'First Class medium for all advertisements appealing to Ladies'.

The Gentlewoman, claiming a circulation of 250,000 amongst the upper classes, summed up the appeal of the women's press to the trade:

> 'Astute advertisers will observe *The Gentlewoman* is bought by women, read by women, and as women spend nine-tenths of what men earn, the moral is obvious.'

Its advertising rate was quoted as: 'One inch—10s.; one page—£30; half-page—£15; one col.—£7 10s. Position pages, £35'.[6] These rates make an interesting comparison with those of the present day,* as does the deadline for advertising copy, which was quoted as the 'Friday in week preceding date of issue'. The only other periodical to publish its advertisement rate was *The Young Ladies' Journal* which quoted: 'Whole page £40 and pro rata. £30 in monthly parts. Positions by arrangement.' On this last point it assured advertisers:

> 'Advertisements are so placed that subscribers can read them. All go in the weekly parts and the monthly numbers. Our old advertisers say it pays to advertise in the *Y.L.J.*'[7]

The expansion of the women's periodical press was in fact being underwritten by advertisers from the 1880s onwards, and this dependency greatly enhanced the status of the advertising industry and modified editorial attitudes to advertising copy. The older generation of publishers had consistently frowned on advertising as an obnoxious nuisance and treated it with suspicion and contempt. The expansion in advertising following the repeal of the advertisement tax drew the following warning from *The Athenæum*:

> 'It is the duty of an independent journal to protect as far as possible, the credulous, confiding and unwary from the wily arts of the insidious advertiser.'[8]

Most Editors shared this opinion of the advertiser, looking on him as 'a pariah to be frustrated and disciplined as much as possible. He

---

* The 1968 rate for a 'facing matter', four-colour page in *Woman* was £4,450; for black-and-white, £3,060.

must be made to pay in advance and he must bring his copy, cap in hand, to be edited'.[9]

The growing importance of advertising revenue dramatically changed this situation. As indicated in the various publishers' announcements, advertisements which had once been relegated to the back pages and covers of magazines now enjoyed more advantageous positions, interspersed throughout the content or given special placings by arrangement. They suffered none of the restrictions upon size and style of earlier years, and Editors even began to be enthusiastic about them:

'Advertisements nowadays are so attractive, it may even be said . . . interesting. . . . It is impossible to glance through the advertisement pages of a paper like *The Ladies' Field* without being struck by the differences in the methods by which different men of fine business capacity and long experience set to work to bring about the same, or similar results.'[10]

There could be no more convincing evidence that advertising had now become socially accepted than the fact that many of the leading women's journals allowed their names to be used to lend prestige to advertising copy. Among the periodicals which permitted their reputations to be used in this way were: *The Ladies' Field*, *Hearth and Home*, *The Lady*, *The Lady's Realm*, *The Lady's Pictorial*, *Madame*, *Myra's Journal*, *The Queen*, *The Ladies' Gazette* and *The Gentlewoman*, all of them 'quality' magazines.

As larger firms began to patronise the women's press more heavily, a new professional approach became evident in the content and presentation of advertising copy. Some advertisers made capital out of current events, such as the full-page soap advertisement in colour which ran, 'I don't mind Mumma getting Women's Rights as long as I have Baby's Wright's'.[11] Manufacturers were also directing their attention increasingly to the middle classes, 'the sort of people', to quote one shopkeeper, 'who will lay out a sovereign more freely than the richer classes would spend five shillings'.[12] In their efforts to stimulate consumption, firms switched to new techniques. The respectful, dignified and understated copy of the Victorian period gave place to more coercive and insistent methods, some of which led to ethical controversies and resulted in the passing of the 'Truth in Advertising' resolution at a meeting of the Associated Advertising Clubs of the World in 1911.

As the pressure from commercial interests increased, Editors found themselves in a difficult position, since their magazines were being turned into glittering shop-windows at a time when increasing numbers of people needed to cut back on expenditure to stay within their incomes. *The Queen* commented:

'Housekeepers want to know what is commonly purchased by those who can afford it, as well as what it is wise to refrain from purchasing when money is short. Nor is it concerning the plainest of everyday cookery that each post brings questions to the Editor of a woman's paper.'[13]

The more responsible Editors tried to stress the folly of overspending on a limited income for the sake of keeping up appearances, but other magazines, particularly the new 'glossies' of the Edwardian era, were full of fresh ideas for spending time and money, which *The Queen* for one deplored:

'Some printed matter has without doubt tended to extravagance. Grave assertions that "every woman who respects herself nowadays must have at least three silk petticoats" are amusing only so long as one is able to believe that there are no girls silly enough to be influenced by them.'

Thus, advertisers were getting a considerable amount of support from a formerly hostile women's press. It came indirectly, with every feature encouraging women to spend more on beautifying themselves or their homes, or suggesting new leisure time activities or publicising new entertainments, and increasingly it came directly, through editorial mentions and recommendations, and the incorporation of advertising matter indistinguishable from editorial content. In return, advertising revenue helped to keep cover prices down and permitted the galloping growth of the infant magazine industry.

The expansion of the women's press between 1885 and 1910 was thus based upon social changes, facilitated by technological progress and financed by advertising. The extent of the industry's growth in terms of total circulation is difficult to estimate, since all but a very few journals concealed their actual sales.* The most successful periodicals claimed 'large circulations', but the description is relative and the figures quoted are likely to have been considerably inflated. The lack of certified figures was in fact a serious obstacle to advertisers, who, having pressed in vain

---

* *The Lady* quotes a weekly sale of 1,683 in 1885, 17,687 in 1895 and 27,949 in 1905. Figures available at the offices of The Lady Publishing Co.

for public audit, eventually formed the Advertisers' Protection Society in 1900 in an attempt to redress the balance. However, some idea of the industry's expansion can be gained from the increase in the number of titles, which more than doubled between 1875 and 1900.

A large number of these periodicals were launched hastily and without any attempt to study the market, for example, *The Lady's Own Magazine* (1898) which admitted it had no particular *raison d'être*:

> 'A great deal is learned from reading, and the demand for periodicals will increase rather than decrease. This being so, the *Lady's Own* is sent forth today, if not to 'fill a long-felt want', to find favour with the fair ones and to secure a corner in every household.'

However, the more discerning publishers began to notice the existence of sub-groups within the female population and to cater specifically for these, instead of trying to appeal, as in the past, to 'The Sex' as a whole. The spur to diversification and specialisation within the industry came as competition from a host of 'carbon copy' opportunist literature intensified. New areas of the female market were explored and opened up, and the women's press ceased to be an institution functioning almost exclusively for the benefit of the upper classes.

The new firms by no means eschewed the higher ranks in their concern to win new readers. At least ten new 'Society' journals were launched during the period, seven of which enjoyed long runs ranging from fourteen to eighty years. The two most noteworthy of these were *The Gentlewoman* (1890) and *The Lady* (1885), which is still in print, and the only remaining privately published newspaper for women. *The Gentlewoman* proved to be a typical 'quality' journal and quickly became an established favourite. *The Lady*, however, was 'a journalistic novelty', inspired by Thomas Gibson Bowles who 'conceived the idea that a woman's paper of greater practical usefulness and having a rather lighter literary touch than that of its predecessors might be welcome'.[14] It was designed especially to appeal to 'women of education' and to provide 'information without dullness and entertainment without vulgarity', undertaking 'whether . . . in the more serious business of women's life, or on those matters apparently more trivial, yet scarcely less important, which relate to its adornment and beautification . . . to furnish them with all such useful and worthy aid as can possibly be given in the pages of a weekly journal'.[15]

Despite a varied table of contents, which included general news concerning women and women's interests, the Church, a Teacher's column, social events, fashion and shopping news, reviews, articles on housekeeping, hygiene and child care, a children's corner, competitions, exchange and sale advertisements and a parliamentary report—a list which included some interesting innovations—*The Lady* did poorly at first, selling 'under 2,500 copies a week'. But in 1894, when Miss Rita Shell became Editor, it forged ahead, having been completely re-cast 'according to her own ideas'. Two new features were added, the 'where-to-live' columns, and a section of 'small-ads', both of which proved extremely popular. This is an early example of the importance of editorial 'flair' in publishing for women: the intuitive knowledge of what women appreciate, and the ability to present it in the way that evokes a response.

Notwithstanding these additions to the 'quality' journals, the advent of a new group of publications, stretching further down the social scale than any of their predecessors, showed that publishers were beginning to look beyond the servant-keeping classes for new readers. Typical of this new type of periodical was *Woman's World*, which came out in 1903 and lasted well into the 1950s. It was intended to appeal to 'the housewife . . . to ladies in shops or offices, as a cheerful and amusing companion during journeys and tea-breaks . . . to busy factory workers [as] an interesting, pleasant, and useful friend'. It incorporated the usual features, with particular emphasis on 'solid, sensible articles on household economy', but had a bias towards sensational fiction.

As the horizons of women's employment expanded, so did the scope for magazines which would meet the special needs, and mirror the interests of, the unmarried working woman. At the lower end of the scale, lurid, all-fiction weeklies appeared, destined for the mill-girl, the shop-assistant and the lady's maid—popularly known as 'the penny dreadfuls'. They frequently bore titles of spurious gentility, 'spurious' because, as the Editor of *Ladyland* observed:

'It needs but a superficial glance at most of the so-called "ladies' papers" to convince anyone that they were not written for the boudoir or the parlour, and their travesties of English homes show that their authors have no more intimate knowledge of the domestic life of the upper and middle classes than might be gleaned from a surreptitious conversation with Sarah Jane at the back-garden gate. The trashy novelette, and the serial "shocker" which form the staple of the penny periodicals dedicated to woman kind, are doubtless largely read by the classes for whom they are written, but notwithstanding their high-sounding titles, they never reach the realms of "ladyland".'[16]

Such was the judgement of the established press on upstart journals such as *My Lady's Novelette, The Lady's Own Novelette* and others. But the spread of literacy had opened up a valuable new market for any publisher ready to meet the demand for romantic melodrama growing up amongst women of the working classes. Good literature in any form was extremely scarce amongst the lower ranks, and it was in recognition of this fact that, as far back as 1877, one publisher brought out *The Homely Friend for Young Women and Girls* to help cultivate their minds by giving them 'good and pleasant things to think of'. The Editor, in her introduction, said:

'We know that most of you have not much time for reading, or many opportunities of getting books (except bad ones), so we want in this little paper, which everyone can have for her very own, and which will not take long to read, to collect for you everything that will interest or help you.'

This was an early example of a magazine designed to fill a particular gap, and its success, measured by a run of almost fifty years, suggests that the proprietors had detected (and satisfied) a real need.

Not all periodicals were 'cheap and nasty'. As the industry expanded, many all-purpose magazines were introduced intended for the housewife with limited means. These publications straddled the artisan and lower-middle classes. In essence, they followed the pattern of the more expensive journals, but they tended to emphasise economy, and ran articles on employment together with hints on dressing suitably and cheaply for the business world, a fact which suggests they were also read by single women. These magazines met the requirements of women workers in higher-grade occupations, such as clerks, shop-assistants and teachers, many of whom came from good homes though their circumstances forced them to be self-supporting.

Significant developments were taking place in other sections of the market, mainly in the form of new publications catering to specific groups. For the first time publishers were turning their attention to younger readers. They were beginning to realise that there was room for magazines catering to girls, as distinct from young women. As far back as 1864, Samuel Beeton had recognised this and brought out a penny weekly, *The Young Englishwoman*, especially for them. It was full of 'Fiction and Entertaining Literature', as well as fashion, poetry and needlework, a journal that could be 'placed without the slightest fear in the hands of girls of tender age'. Beeton, who had consulted his wife as to the formulation of the magazine, edited it himself until 1866, when the failure of the renowned banking house of Overend, Gurney and Co. caused his financial ruin and his publications were taken over by Ward, Lock and Tyler.

It was some years, however, before other magazines for girls appeared. One of the first and most successful was the *Girls' Own Paper*. It came out in 1880, promising 'to foster and develop that which is highest and noblest in the girlhood and womanhood of England'. It started life as a weekly and subsequently became a monthly in response to readers' requests for a larger magazine with more illustrations. At first, fashion was conspicuous by its absence, but it was introduced later for the benefit of older women who apparently enjoyed the magazine as much as their daughters did, and asked for special features to be included for them.

A crop of similar journals appeared during the 1880s and 1890s, all aimed at the adolescent market (though 'adolescence' had yet to be discovered), and it would seem that some, at least, of these enterprises were encouraged by an increase in the spending-power of this age-group, for the Editor of the *Girls' Own* remarked:

'Girls didn't used to have so much pocket-money. Now they can afford sixpence.'

This magazine was one of many which enjoyed long runs, remaining in print until 1950.

Another interesting venture was an attempt to cut right across the limits imposed by social stratification and to cater instead to an 'attitude group', composed of like-minded women wherever they were to be found, 'in churches, business houses, the mills, public and high schools, and in the innumerable employments', women 'who read, who think, and who have a real interest in social effort, religious truth, and for whom the fashion plate and the novelette have little charm'. This was the editorial aim of *The Young Woman*, a magazine brought out in 1892. Related to it, was the provision of reading matter expressly for 'the educated woman'. At this time the criticism was frequently made that 'the average educated woman . . . is not adequately represented in that branch of the press that professes to speak for her'.[17] This was usually countered by the argument that a woman 'may turn for her general reading to the great daily, weekly and monthly organs of contemporary literature and thought'. However, a new generation of publishers thought otherwise, and the Editor of *Hearth and Home* (1891), one of several publications launched to fill the gap, commented:

'Good as our journals of everyday reading are, it is hardly to be

expected that they should deal with the masses of matter they have
to consider from a point of view women should take when discussing
it among themselves.'

Implicit in this statement was the belief that however general the
topic, it had to be written up differently, according to the sex of the
reader, a view which has profoundly influenced the development of the
women's press, encouraging romanticism rather than realism, and
driving out fact in favour of fiction. Of all the experiments to provide
for the educated woman, the magazines which did best were those such
as *Woman* (1890),* which took the middle road, offering 'something more
than the "Lady's", or "Society" paper or cookery book, and something
less than the ponderous daily leader and parliamentary reports, or the
academic weekly or monthly review'.

Two other publications which entered the field at this time showing
the readiness of publishers to exploit any potential market, were *The
Matron* (1906) and *Woman's Health and Beauty* (1902). The former
claimed to be 'the first [magazine] . . . published wholly and solely in the
interests of the Matron'. Evidently the proprietors felt that the older
woman had been neglected in the rush to bring out magazines for
young women, and they produced a special paper for her, mainly devoted
to fashions, which carefully omitted features on child-rearing and all
'personal' queries connected with early married life. Its success
(deduced from a ten-year run) suggests that there was definite scope for
publications catering to middle-aged women despite the assertion in a
Queen editorial that this age-group had ceased to exist:

> 'Many mothers nowadays to all intents and purposes are as young
> as their daughters. In fact, the disappearance of the middle-aged
> woman is a marked sign of the period. Our London world is
> divided into girls, young married women, and old ladies in the
> 70s and 80s. Everyone has bright eyes, a flower face and a slender
> figure, and everyone is dressed to perfection. The "fair, fat and
> forty" has ceased to exist. Women of fifty and sixty hunt, shoot,
> dance, play golf and hockey, and drive their own motors . . . are
> forever on the go over to Paris to fit a frock or make trips on their
> own to New York, India, etc. Eternal youth has come to stay.'[19]

No doubt many of these sprightly women owed more of their
youthfulness to their magazines than they would have cared to

---

* Not to be confused with the current magazine of the same name.

admit, particularly those which helped them make the best of their features and figures. One new periodical specialising in this area was *Woman's Health and Beauty*. Its main function was to instruct women in health, beauty and physical culture, and even its fiction was used to reinforce the desire to achieve physical perfection. The magazine ran for eighteen years under a male Editor and claimed in 1902 to have amassed a total of '375,000 paid up subscribers in Great Britain and abroad'.

The most important development during this period, as regards the future evolution of the women's press, was the new concern on the part of publishers to service the housewife. In 1875 the *Saturday Review* had carried a shattering analysis of life in the average Victorian household, rudely dispelling the 'halo of sham sanctity' which customarily surrounded it. According to this *exposé*, the modern woman:

'rises late and has made no provision for breakfast; her husband starts for his work hungry and savage; her toilet is hurried, her temper and her hair are ruffled; she blunders in giving orders to the cook, declines the morning walk to market, by her own slovenliness and carelessness sets the servants a wretched example, and affords them endless opportunities for speculation.'

This critique provoked widespread discussion, jolting society out of its complacency, and making it clear that, far from presiding over domestic Avalons, the vast majority of women were incapable of the most rudimentary domestic management. The servant shortage was growing more acute and hired help of any kind was becoming a luxury. Aggravating the situation, prices in general were soaring, forcing women to economise in every department of housekeeping. Numbers of them, particularly the newly married, proved wholly unequal to the task, which often imposed intolerable strains upon their marriages. At the same time, social standards in respect of nutrition, hygiene, health and child-care were also rising, demanding even more of women than formerly.

Here was wide scope for the women's press, and a rash of new publications were brought out devoted to home topics. The last twenty years of the nineteenth century witnessed the arrival of, among others, the *Housewife** (1886), *The Mother's Companion* (1887), *The Ladies' Home Journal†* (1890), *Woman at Home* (1893), *Home Notes* (1894),

---

* Not to be confused with a modern publication of the same name.
† This magazine had no connection with its American namesake.

Home Chat (1895), and the *Home Companion* (1897). These were mostly aimed at the middle and lower-middle classes where the need for domestic guidance was greatest. Magazines like *Housewife* and the *Woman at Home* dealt only superficially with household subjects. It was left to other publications to perceive, and respond to, the need for more thoroughgoing domestic manuals. One of the first to do so was the *Mother's Companion* which voiced the opinion that 'the many and varied subjects that affect mothers in the duties they have to fulfil to their children, their homes and to society, have not yet been so dealt with in a popular way as their increasing importance demands'.

Three years later, it was followed by the *Ladies' Home Journal* which deplored the fact that, despite the appearance of 'numerous so-called home journals . . . there is not a single publication which may be confidently relied upon as a reference and guide in the conduct and management of the home'.[20] It condemned their treatment of domestic art, science, health and other important subjects as 'superficial . . . unpractical and indifferent' and set out to remedy these deficiencies in a publication which was intended to combine 'practical information with useful recreation', devoting space to health, law, fashion, housekeeping, 'popular science', cookery, fancy-work, home furnishing, toilet hints, patterns and competitions. It also invited correspondence upon any subject.

These early attempts to provide regular and comprehensive coverage of home management met with immediate success, and they were followed throughout the 'nineties by a crop of journals written to a similar formula. Never slow to recognise the potential of a new market, Alfred Harmsworth was in the vanguard of this expansion. In 1891, with £500 capital, he formed the Periodical Publishing Company, the parent of the Amalgamated Press, for the sole purpose of publishing women's magazines. His first publication, *Forget-Me-Not*, was edited by Miss Winifred Ruth ('Biddy') Johnson, the renowned architect of a number of modern mass-selling women's periodicals. Sub-titled 'A Pictorial Journal for Ladies', the magazine was intended as a cheap but superior weekly for the middle classes, offering better value for a penny than any of its rivals. Upholding the highest editorial standards ('It will be as bright and pure as the flower from which it gets its name'), and arousing the reader's interest with such items as 'The Diary of a Professional Beauty' and 'Confessions of a Wall-Flower', *Forget-Me-Not*, after a slow start, gradually won favour with thousands of women. By July, 1894, its circulation had risen to 141,000, and Harmsworth later claimed for it 'a circulation larger than all the ladies' journals that have been established for twenty years'.

Harmsworth's next venture was to bring out a rival to *Home Notes*, a successful home monthly launched by Pearson's in 1894 and reputedly making an annual profit of £12,000. His extraordinary flair for publishing guaranteed full support from the trade for any periodical he promoted. Thus, when *Home Chat* appeared in 1895, 'with the aim of providing a weekly woman's journal for a penny which should be equal in the quality of its contributions both editorial and pictorial to any of the sixpenny journals',

'. . . insistent, clamorous crowds beseiged the publishing offices, every individual anxious to make certain of supplies. The usual publishing staff, unable to deal with the crush enlisted the services of their colleagues on the business and editorial sides. Shirt-sleeved men, perspiring, but never pausing, flung the papers to the waiting crowds, which never seemed to lessen. From morning to night the work continued, and ever the paper selling, selling, selling, and the great machines roaring as they flung out the stream of copies.'[21]

Although *Home Chat* was designed as a cheap weekly, it was characteristic of Harmsworth that he would countenance no compromise over editorial or artistic quality. He respected the reading public, believing that it appreciated 'clear sanity' in its literature; thus the magazine was to be both daintily attractive and thorough, and in this it 'established a new note in journalism like nothing that had preceded it'. *Home Chat* proved to be lively, entertaining and above all practical, covering as far as possible all the interests and occupations of the home-loving woman and setting new standards of service. With *Home Notes*, it helped to lay the foundations upon which the mass circulation weeklies of the twentieth century were built, for the two magazines became the indispensable companions of middle-class women, in fact the *Woman* and *Woman's Own* of late-Victorian England. And not only of these women. *Home Chat* was enthusiastically received by a wide readership:

'Women in West End Squares and in middle-class houses were equally interested. It became a favourite in the suburban villa and in the country cottage. Everywhere, women of every age and class were to be seen immersed in its pages.'[22]

Despite this encouraging start, *Home Chat* soon ran into difficulties. Competition from Pearson's, faulty advertising arrangements and printing troubles combined to undermine its sales and Harmsworth was soon expressing anxiety at the large numbers of returns from newsagents. Even so, the magazine was selling just under 186,000 copies in June, 1895, and once its early problems had been overcome, proved to be yet another publishing triumph for Harmsworth, remaining in print until 1958.

(ii) Finding a Formula

The years between 1885 and 1910 produced many new experiments in publishing for women. Not only was there greater provision for women in the lower divisions of the social hierarchy, but there were also attempts to cater to special groups, in particular the young, the educated, middle-aged women, housewives and working girls. At the same time, a change occurred in the character of the women's press as a whole. It became a medium of communication not only between editorial staff and their readers, but between women all over the country, a reflection of an undercurrent of social change which was gradually creating the conditions for free and easy contact. Schemes were started to promote 'both the easier intercommunication of woman with woman and also the development of her individuality and of her intellectual powers',[23] some of which ultimately led to the establishment of women's clubs. These clubs catered for 'all sections of society and all grades of opinion' and gave women new opportunities for exchanging ideas and seeking mutual help and advice. At this period, many of the women's magazines were filling a similar role, acting as a forum where subjects of interest to women could be discussed. *The Lady*, commenting on this trend, said:

'They [women] read more, they think more, they do more, and this shows in their conversation. Subjects are discussed which would not have been whispered about a generation or two ago.'[24]

The widening social participation of women was everywhere reflected in the women's press. The magazines followed them as they engaged in sports of all kinds, rode bicycles, went motoring, took an interest in breeding and showing animals, did gardening as well as needlework, joined sketching and camera clubs, wrote, painted and travelled abroad.

Through these new interests and activities, social contacts for women increased. Moreover, society itself was opening up. A new 'public' was emerging—a public composed of people of all stations of life, who jostled each other on railway platforms, ate 'together' (geographically at least) in restaurants, used the same polling booths, and shopped at that most egalitarian of institutions, the department store. The gulf between classes was as great as ever, perhaps even magnified, with the aristocracy strenuously resisting dilution from below, and the aspirant middle classes obdurately turning their backs on their humble origins. But in the absence of nearness of approach, there was now nearness of view, and the lorgnette of wider society was held up to scrutinise the upper classes in a way that had been impossible when their life went on behind closed doors. This had the effect of drawing society together and stimulating interest in life in the Capital, even in lower-class magazines, which increasingly carried 'gossip' columns, and 'Society chat'.

By 1910, the various experiments with magazine content had crystallised into a clearly definable, and almost entirely predictable formula for each class of publication. Magazines for the upper classes were chiefly chronicles of Society at play, with extensive reporting of Court and Society functions throughout the United Kingdom and abroad, coverage of the arts, music and the theatre (with reviews) and commentaries on sport. The 'Society' columns were an important feature, functioning as an in-group news service for the 'Upper Ten Thousand', to whom it was essential to know Who went Where, When. These surveys were wide-ranging, covering Scotland and Ireland and taking in attendances at the latest 'Drawing Rooms', the hunting field, 'Hymen's Realms', and even the Birmingham Fatstock Show, where, it was solemnly reported on one occasion, 'Her Majesty the Queen met with unique success carrying off all the Champion cups for fat cattle'. Such columns were in themselves a compulsive spectator-sport for those on the fringes of Society.

The Queen had, by 1900, begun to feature *débutante* portraits, and the extensive reporting of Court Presentations and other functions indicated an enormous upsurge in social activity, together with heightened public interest. *The Queen* commented:

'This is an inquisitive age: all daily papers from the august *Times* downwards have now their daily column of personal news, and few are the magazines which do not publish monthly some report of an interview with this or that celebrity. So keen is the general thirst for information touching the private life of every individual. The telegraph wire and the penny post, the periodical press and the special reporter have, during the last half-century provided the curious with new and extraordinary means of gratifying their relish for personal detail.'[25]

Another standard ingredient in all upper-class periodicals was advice on Etiquette. Social life in Edwardian, as in Victorian England was closely circumscribed by ritual and by formal rules of behaviour which operated as a powerful screening device to preclude the entry of 'undesirables' into the 'best circles'. The mysteries of this intricate social code were assumed to have been revealed to the nobility and gentry at the same time that blue blood was injected into their veins. But the queries which appeared regularly in the 'quality' journals suggested that many Society women found themselves perplexed and defeated by their own system. Card-leaving occasioned the greatest number of enquiries. Besides being the most complicated of all procedures, it was also the most important since it was the accepted way of indicating whom one wished to number among one's friends, and whom one 'preferred not to know', and the strictest attention was paid to it.

If these rules of conduct occasionally gave established Society women pause for thought, they posed almost insuperable problems for the uninitiated. This was the one area in which money could not buy success, as every wealthy social aspirant eventually discovered. A writer in the *Lady's Companion* observed:

'Amongst the ignorant classes the notion prevails that money and money alone is the passport to society . . . but there was never a greater mistake made. A man may be a multi-millionaire, but if his wife bears the unmistakable hall-mark "plebeian", no amount of diamonds will ever light her into the charmed circle of our aristocracy. Society men will fraternise with the millionaire and ignore his misplaced "h's" and the absence of good breeding while they drink his wine, but the wives and daughters of those men will not visit his wives and daughters, nor receive them in their own houses if they lack refinement and culture. The penniless daughter of an underpaid curate would (provided she were a gentlewoman) have the entrée into houses that would resolutely close their doors on the pretensions of the millionaire's family.'[26]

It was therefore vital to such women to become socially adept if they were to discharge the social duties necessary to the advancement of their husbands' careers. But, as the same magazine pointed out:

'There is a certain indefinable pride that prevents a woman even admitting to her nearest and dearest that she does not know the ordinary usages of polite society. . . . A woman prefers it to be taken for granted that she has always moved in what is known as good society and that she is perfectly *au fait* with all the intricacies of modern etiquette.'[27]

Thus more and more women turned for guidance to the 'quality' magazines through which their queries could be dealt with under the assurance of complete anonymity.

Grooming women in matters of good taste in dress was equally necessary, and fashion coverage in the 'sixpenny' journals continued to increase. The art of being well-dressed was becoming a profession:

'. . . there is a passion for dress and ornament nowadays which has probably never been surpassed. Monsieur Worth has recently stated that in the middle of the century women of high fashion went through the Season with two silk dresses and a cashmere shawl. To dress well today partakes of the nature of a fine art, and demands as much time, study and capital from its devotees as the steady pursuit of an artistic career. These dresses of course must be shown and hence the modern feminine craze for living, as it were, in public.'

The importance of the 'quality' magazines as sources of information on the latest fashion trends grew with the rapid expansion of the fashion trade on both sides of the Channel. This development was marked by the issue of an English edition of France's reigning fashion journal, *Le Moniteur de la Mode*, an expensive, glossy magazine which had already run for thirty-two years. One of the British fashion journals, *The Ladies' Gazette of Fashion*, was at the same time undergoing changes which underlined the growing demand for fashion intelligence. In 1895, it published the following statement:

'The times have changed since this periodical was first issued . . . and popular requirements have changed with them. The changes in fashion are so rapid and so many, the variety of costumes and other articles of apparel so great, that ladies took to a weekly rather than a monthly supply of information on these important subjects. Recognising this fact, it has been decided to publish the *Ladies' Gazette* every week at one penny.'

Beauty culture, too, began to have a recognised place, indicating that values had changed sufficiently to permit the pursuit of personal beauty for its own sake. While some journals still held tenaciously to the principle that only 'hussies' wore make-up, the more broad-minded among them began to accept the fact that Nature sometimes needed assistance. The new trend was evident in occasional editorial comments such as the following:

'We must make the best of ourselves till the end. Of course it is easy to overstep the mark in this direction, and those who are too eager in their efforts to beautify themselves generally defeat themselves in becoming too studied and artificial. Looks, manners, dress, deportment are all worth our best consideration.'[29]

This was not merely a piece of enlightened advice born of the liberalising influences of female emancipation, but one of the 'laws of subsistence' for any girl who was staking everything on finding a husband to support her. It applied equally to women obliged to support themselves. As a writer in *Woman* pointed out:

'Many business women are forced to make-up because nobody wants elderly-looking people about them in these modern times. They simply dare not grow old if they wish to retain their situations.'[30]

The problem of surplus women was no nearer solution. Far from improving, the marriage rate fell to fifteen per thousand in 1910, twelve below the average for the previous decade. Fewer persons under twenty-one were married than ever before, and the average age of spinsters over the country as a whole was twenty-five years. Re-marriage among the widowed was also decreasing, while the number of divorces had risen by 50 per cent. An article in *The Queen* showed that the upper and middle classes were still encumbered with a host of helpless women. The author, Mary Spencer, who was conducting an enquiry into the functions of the new Employment Bureaux, drew attention to 'the comparative youth of many unemployable women'. Her survey over five years showed that 42 per cent of those for whom no work could be found were under 30 years of age, and she added:

'It is quite a mistake to suppose that the "poor lady" has faded away and been replaced by the well-educated, well-trained professional or industrial worker. . . . All over the kingdom there are troops of girls . . . who will find themselves in a most helpless state if . . . they should need to obtain anything by their own exertions. . . . The education of girls is still too much directed towards the matrimonial market and the facilities for trade training outside London leave much to desire.'[31]

Thus the numbers of women forced to support themselves continued to multiply, and it was chiefly for their benefit that *The Queen* and

The Lady ran their 'Women's Employment' and 'How to Live' columns, which brought new ways of earning money to the notice of readers. Single women were not the only ones to take advantage of these. Many married women, unable to seek gainful employment outside the home, turned to these features for help in supplementing inadequate incomes. The Editor of *The Lady* wrote:

'My sympathies are very much with those of my readers who, owing to home ties, are debarred from many professions which hold out prospects for future gain to their more fortunate friends. Letters constantly reach me asking for some fresh hints as to how a few extra shillings can be made.'[32]

The upper-class journals were the only ones which catered to the more socially conscious and serious-minded women. *The Lady* and *The Queen*, who numbered amongst their readers a substantial core of those whose aristocratic upbringing had instilled into them a sense of involvement with wider social concerns, reported on parliamentary proceedings and the public activities of women, and also ran appeals for various charities. They were, however, reaching a progressively smaller section of the women's market as the numbers of middle and lower-class journals increased, and it was the latter whose pattern of development had the greatest influence in shaping the future content of the women's press.

The middle-class magazines, in contrast to the 'quality' periodicals, concentrated much more on home topics. They were written to a formula which now included child-care articles, dress-making and needlework, personal problem pages and advice on all kinds of household queries. They did not entirely neglect the social round, but their commentaries were couched in very general terms, suited to a class more accustomed to observing these activities from a respectful distance than participating in them. As a general rule, the lower the class of readership, the more home-centred a magazine's contents tended to be, so that the lower-middle class publications restricted themselves entirely to a domestic formula.

At this stage, there was still no attempt to provide a comprehensive household service, only to give general guidance. The approach of the cookery columnist in the *Lady's Companion* was typical:

'In order to help my young friends who are not very experienced in housekeeping, I give a plain dinner from time to time with very precise instructions.'[33]

Shorter and simpler menus were in fact coming into vogue, chiefly owing to the lack of domestic help, and likewise professional hairdressing. Too often, however, magazine consultants told their readers what to do, but omitted to show them how to do it; for example, 'In flats or small houses where space is scarce . . . it is often advisable to use combined furniture'[34]—a suggestion made without any advice as to what form these 'combinations' should take. Ten years later, advice on household management was still largely theoretical, though readers could obtain help with specific problems through the correspondence columns, which covered most areas of housekeeping. Taken as a whole, the coverage of household topics throughout the women's press was grossly inadequate by modern standards, but relative to the standards of the past, it represented a considerable advance.

The middle-class magazines were used increasingly to discuss ways and means and to assist women with budgeting. That some members of the wealthier classes were also beginning to suffer from an insufficiency of means was suggested by requests in magazines like the *Ladies' Field* for less costly menus suited to the budgets of, for example, officers' wives, and those who had to adapt their housekeeping 'to incomes as low as £600 a year'. It was, however, the middle-class family which was most severely hit by inflated prices and the continually mounting cost of keeping pace with society's expectations, and it was the middle-class periodicals which devoted most space to managing on modest incomes.

Not all families started out in financial difficulties. Many were thrown into reduced circumstances as a result of business failures. This was 'an age of bogus companies, of fraudulent prospectuses adorned by the names of peers, soldiers and publicists, names . . . intended to hoodwink the investor, and to induce the widow and the clergyman, the half-pay officer and the struggling professional man to pour their meagre savings into a financial sieve with handsome offices in Cheapside'.[35] Fluctuations in the trade cycle brought bankruptcy and unemployment, and while fortunes were being made at the century's close, they were also being lost. For those reasons, Economy was the order of the day in many thousands of homes.

As far as they were able, and drawing upon readers' experiences as well as their own, the household columnists tried to give advice on household economy. One woman, writing for advice on how to manage an income of £168, who admitted to being £50 a year overspent, was sharply told to stop giving parties while in debt. *The Ladies' Treasury* frequently dealt with correspondents who had to exist on even less, on £150, or perhaps £100 per annum. At one time it carried a serialised account of the difficulties facing a fictitious married couple who were obliged to exist on the former amount. The wife was well-bred and well-educated by Society standards, but totally incapable of managing a house on a limited income, and her step-by-step instruction by a 'neighbour' in simple cookery, routine household duties and budgeting, provided the model for all readers in similar circumstances.

The strain on the family income often meant that a wife was hard put to it to clothe herself in the manner her station of life required. Here again, the magazines came to her aid, suggesting the best ways of deploying limited resources and showing her stratagems by which she could stretch them still further. Writers encouraged both optimism and resourcefulness:

> 'Can a woman be well-dressed on an allowance of from £30 to £50 a year? Well I think she can if only she will be prudent and sensible. No woman who makes a figure in society can dress on twice these sums; but there are thousands of girls and women gently born who do not spend their days in a whirl of balls and bazaars and house-party diversions.'[36]

The magnitude of the problem of keeping up appearances in an age when so much importance was attached to being well-dressed was underlined by the setting up of 'West End Toilette Exchanges' which apparently did a brisk trade. One magazine claimed that, 'Many women with daughters to clothe depend almost entirely on these exchanges as a means of dressing themselves and their children fashionably and well'.[37] Other women had recourse to home dressmaking, and the magazines at this period were full of diagrams and instructions including (for the first time) clothes for children.

Running a home efficiently involved more than budgeting wisely, and it is interesting to note how standards were rising at this time. The publicity given by social reformers to the need for improving the sanitary condition of the population and also its diet was evidently having some effect, for in 1900, the Editor of *The Young Woman* pronounced it the duty of women to acquaint themselves before marriage with 'physics, hygiene, the chemistry of food, architecture, room arrangement and the kitchen', adding that 'no person ought to be a mother who has not given especial thought to the study of children'.[38]

There was evidence both of a growing concern for child welfare, and a fundamental change in the whole approach to the upbringing of children. The affectionless discipline of the whip had been superseded, a writer in *Woman's Life* stating categorically that:

'Corporal punishment for children is growing both obsolete and unnecessary. With patient and sympathetic treatment, the most unruly of children can be handled and made to do the reasonable will of an older person.'[39]

Middle-class mothers were now spending more time with their children, and were encouraged to do so by magazine counsellors who suggested, for instance, that they should devise 'play-lessons' to help their children to count. In addition, features written especially for children began to occupy a corner in most magazines. As time went on, the decline in births aroused serious concern, and magazine editors tried wherever possible to counteract the trend by stressing the joys of motherhood, castigating those women who preferred to absorb their energies in the social round.

One of the most important services that the middle-class magazines were rendering at this time was probably less in the field of domestic management than in the area of personal relationships. The old, rigid patterns of behaviour which governed the associations of men and women in mid-Victorian England were breaking up. Relationships within the family, too, were changing, and a new ideal of family life was gradually being evolved. Not only were women gaining wider social experience before marriage, they were being called upon to assume greater personal responsibilities after it, and the 'New Woman' as she was called, by throwing off her chrysalis of parental protection and dominance, was cutting herself off to some extent from their solace and help, creating a need for new counsellors and new friends.

The magazines were aware of this need. The *Lady's Companion* was sympathetic:

'For the working wife there is no relief and no release, and where there is a large family and a small income, there is no limit to her anxieties nor her sphere of duty. She is Chancellor of the Exchequer, Officer of Health, food and clothes provider, charwoman and nurse, queen and slave, and expected to be the infallible guardian of the family fortune and honour and happiness. The organisation of such duties is a feat in itself, but when the executive also falls on the same individual, little wonder that heart and mind and nerves . . . seek relief in the temporary handing over of a few perplexities . . .'[40]

In response, a new department emerged in the women's press, the 'problem page', though these features were never included in the

'Society' journals. Previously, many periodicals had included correspondence from readers, in which queries on dress, travel, health and
housekeeping were dealt with, but personal problems had been
conspicuously absent. Called variously, 'Between Ourselves', 'The
Spiritual Side of Everyday Difficulties', 'Chats with Young Wives' or
simply 'Advice to Girls', they invited readers 'to consult our expert . . .
on any matter relating to yourself', if they were in need of reliable
advice. The 'difficulties' mainly concerned courtship and marriage, but
these columns were sometimes used to bring back truanting daughters,
or to advise mothers how to manage their independent-spirited
offspring.

There was evidence in all such correspondence of a growing tension
between the two generations, and of a general restiveness among young
women. For some, the chief problem was boredom:

> 'There are evidently dozens of young folks whose lives seem to
> them flat, stale and unprofitable—"we are so dull!" is the mournful
> chorus of these young maidens—"we live in the country. Will you
> get us some nice occupation, please, dear Estelle?" '41

If parents had been unaware of this pent-up frustration, it was
sharply brought to their notice as many girls fled their homes, bent on
carving out independent careers in London. While the magazines were
full of grim, cautionary tales of the dangers and disillusionment that
awaited them—descriptions of sleeping cubicles in boarding-houses,
skimpy meals, severe competition and low pay—they were nevertheless
prepared to encourage young women to strike out on their own, even
in the face of parental opposition. These counsellors, in befriending and
advising lonely, dispirited women, and consoling and enlightening
bewildered parents, performed an important service in the absence of
professional help.

Their value to young married women was equally great, as is shown
by the following testimonial from a reader:

> '. . . I am so very lonely, having no friend at all to talk to about
> household matters, and I do not care to worry my husband with
> them when he comes home tired from his day's work. Your columns
> form my only "chum" for such matters, and I have a large scrap-
> book in which . . . I put both the article and the correspondents' page
> and treasure them up.'42

In response to this need for friendship, or simply contact with other
women similarly placed, the women's magazines made a special effort

to foster communication between subscribers by setting up 'social clubs', inviting correspondence and encouraging the exchange of ideas and experiences.

By 1910, fiction was a staple ingredient in almost all women's magazines. As a general rule, the amount of fiction included varied in inverse proportion to the class of readership. Upper-class journals carried very little, and inclined towards a more sophisticated approach, with plots frequently built around events of the day. One romance, set against a background of political intrigue, described, in torrid and sensual vein, the development of an adulterous relationship, showing how far Victorian morality had been left behind. Middle-class fiction tended to be more sentimental but was equally sensational in its own way. As *The Lady* pointed out, many of the plots provided excellent 'openings for conversation, not to speak of subjects for discussion', and as such were no doubt welcomed by hostesses.

This form of entertainment had definite therapeutic value for women of all classes, a fact of which magazine writers were well aware. A writer in *The Lady* observed: 'No-body is any the worse for being lifted for a short time out of the worries of everyday life into a world of imagination', and the demand for such literature steadily increased. There was at this time 'a limitless field for short stories of about 2,000 to 2,500 words', the greatest demand coming from the penny periodicals such as Harmsworth's *Forget-me-not*. To succeed, they had only to conform to a few simple rules:

> 'They must be complete, have two or three characters and a mild love interest, a little bit of mystery, and deal with everyday or "romantic" affairs in a way that most people can understand.'[43]

The blue-print for the mass weeklies of the future was evolved from a blend of these lower-middle class journals and the new periodicals for the working-class housewife. *Home Notes* and *Home Chat* led the way, but the all-important concept of 'reader-identification' the cornerstone of modern publishing for women, did not crystallise until some years later. Evidence of its growth was provided by an important new periodical, *My Weekly*, brought out by D. C. Thomson in 1910, intended for working-class women. Its Editor prefaced the launch issue with the following remarks:

> 'My editorial experience has left me impressed with one thing in particular and that is the need for what is called the "personal note" in journalism . . . I will try to appeal to readers through their

human nature and their understanding of everyday joys and sorrows. For I know well that, in order to get into active and intimate relationship with the great public, one must prove oneself fully acquainted with its affections, sentiments and work. . . . I understand, too, how that human nature is strangely and pathetically eager for friendship. I mean willingly to become the confidant of readers, young and old, rich and poor, who can safely trust me with their ideas and difficulties.'[44]

The magazine was written to a simple, but now classic formula comprising romantic fiction, household hints, cookery and dress-making, a children's feature, and advice on personal problems, interspersed with interesting tit-bits of news and gossip and introduced with a 'plain talk' from the Editor. In itself, this formula was unexceptional, but it appealed to the lowest common denominator of the mass female market, and so provided the best basis for future expansion. *My Weekly* enjoyed considerable success and is still in print. Its editorial policy of getting into 'active and intimate relationship' with readers has since been copied by all the successful mass weeklies, and its adherence to a simple, home-centred recipe in its content indicated the direction which an increasing number of women's periodicals were to take in the years between the wars.

The success achieved by magazines such as *My Weekly* showed that the interests and activities of the majority of women were still centred upon the home, and that their attitudes concerning their social role had been largely unaffected by the campaign to extend women's rights. Editors and readers alike supported the view, voiced by Lord Curzon, that 'Political activity will tend to take away woman from her proper sphere and highest duty which is maternity, and the vote is not desired, so far as can be ascertained by the large majority of women'.

Women's magazines confined themselves almost entirely to servicing women in their domestic role, and they paid little attention to the possibilities of widening their sphere of influence. Any reference to improving the status of women was in the context of a new humanitarian recognition of the rights of the individual, rather than positive support for equality between the sexes. Taking an active part in life outside the home was never presented as being a desirable extension of a woman's sphere. Nor was the practicability of combining the roles of wife and worker ever properly investigated. The majority of editors inclined towards the view that 'the most adequate contribution to the welfare of the state must, speaking roughly, always be rendered by women, no matter what their social rank, in their own homes',[45] a belief which has greatly influenced the formula for women's journalism in the twentieth century.

As a result of the conflict between their traditional beliefs and the propaganda of the Women's Rights Movement, many women found themselves confused and uncertain, 'neither able to sit at ease in the old confines, nor dash ahead with [their] pioneering sisters'.[46] A correspondent to *The Queen* described the situation of the 'intermediate' woman:

> 'Higher education and the *Zeitgeist* have conspired to place me intellectually on a platform to which all my instincts, my inherited sympathies are opposed. I hold the most enlightened views about my sex, and do my utmost to help on its movements, except in the one small matter of privately acting upon my own principles. . . . My feelings, impulses, likes and dislikes stand right in the way of my convictions . . . it is the outcome of heredity from a long line of oppressed female ancestors.
>
> 'That woman's sphere should be widened, that she should have more to do with shaping the larger issues of life, that she should have independence of thought and action and assert her ideals, instead of being passively dragged along . . . of all this I am thoroughly convinced.'

Yet, in common with the majority of women of all classes and educational levels, this writer admitted that her overwhelming desire was to be 'a quite unillustrious, more or less hampered and dependent wife and mother'. As she went on to explain:

> 'I detest responsibility . . . I require sympathy and encouragement in all that I do. I am bored with things in general, I love things in particular. The near and the personal appear to me primarily interesting and important . . . the small jobs, the varied details of private and domestic life possess extraordinary charm.'[47]

These sentiments were deep-rooted in the female population, and in the absence of an ideology suggesting alternative or additional long-term goals, the impetus towards advancement provided by the campaign for women's emancipation remained too narrowly channelled to influence more than a relatively small number of women. The women's press, though it gave greater coverage to the Women's Movement than in former years, remained non-commital about its aims. Editorially, the women's magazines reflected and reinforced the traditional views held by the average reader, and tailored their content to suit the needs and interests these implied. Unlike the pioneer journals of the eighteenth and early-nineteenth centuries, the periodicals of late-Victorian and Edwardian England were content to be trend-followers rather than trend-setters. In view of the failure of the few publications which did try to take an independent line they had little choice. *Woman Citizen*, for example, founded on the assumption that an opening existed 'for a weekly paper appealing primarily to the increasing class of educated women who have intellectual, industrial or public interests', endeavoured 'to fill in the gaps left, on the one hand by the so-called "women's papers", and on the other by the daily newspapers', but it met the fate of all such experiments.

In the years leading up to the First World War, several more magazines were brought out, including a number for home-loving women of the working classes, but only a few came through the war-time upheavals in the publishing trade. One which did survive was *Woman's Weekly*, launched in November 1911. Edited for the woman 'who lives in the villa or the cottage, in a large house or a small house', but definitely not for 'the women of Mayfair', it set out to help 'the woman who rules the destinies of the home . . . in her life, her work, and her recreation'. From the start, its contents were carefully compiled to be both practical and useful, remembering readers' modest circumstances. Its recipes were simple—'how to make rice-pudding, jam roll, and how to cook a joint of roast beef'—and its fashions, ignoring the extremes of taste, consisted of 'the ordinary garments which will be worn by the average woman', supplemented by a complete wardrobe of patterns for home dressmaking which readers could collect over several months. In addition, there were a number of short advice features, on child health, 'girls' affairs' (e.g. 'The Business Girl as a Wife') and housekeeping, the range of which gradually expanded. There were also prizes to be won, either for competitions, or for letters giving tested hints and recipes, and accounts of readers' 'real love stories'. The fiction, also intended to be 'useful' without touching upon 'the sordid side of life', was an important feature, and for one penny a week the magazine gave full value in considerable variety. It got off to a shaky start, however, and was later remodelled by Miss 'Biddy' Johnson, under whose guiding hand it survived to become one of Britain's most popular women's magazines, reaching a half-million sale by the 1930s.

Many existing magazines came to a premature end as a result of the war, and there were few new titles to replace them between 1914 and 1918. One important newcomer was *Vogue*, which crossed the Atlantic in 1916 and added new colour and vitality to the publishing scene. For one shilling' it offered one hundred and twenty glossy pages fortnightly, plus a colour supplement, and it covered a wide range of subjects besides fashion, including Society news, entertainments, cultural and discussion features, which were of a high literary standard.

The Editor justified this policy of intellectual challenge by reference to the philosophy underlying women's publishing in America:

'America believes in the higher education of women as does no other country on earth. She knows perfectly well that marriage and motherhood, paramount as they are, are not to be the whole of this girl's life. First, there are the years between college and marriage, often a very considerable period, since the modern girls insist on waiting till they get what they want. Next, a woman of this class doesn't spend the whole twenty-four hours of her day rocking her baby and making a good man happy. Finally, after the baby period is over this girl is going to have fifteen or twenty years of unimpaired vitality when her children don't need, and certainly don't want her individual attention. She has been given an abundance of surplus time and energy. . . . Do we realise it in England?'[48]

England did not realise it. She was too busy fighting a global war, and those who had so zealously campaigned for the advancement of women prior to 1914, by common consent shelved their demands and turned their energies to helping the war effort.

NOTES

1   *Op. cit.*, 1887. (Preface to launch issue.)
2   Leonard E. Naylor, *The Irrepressible Victorian*, p. 110.
3   *Op. cit.*, 1892. (Preface to launch issue.)
4   *Op. cit.*, 1862, p. 173.
5   *Op. cit.*, 1876, p. 210.
6   *Op. cit.*, 1901, p. 380.
7   *Ibid.*, p. 342.
8   *Op. cit.*, July 17th, 1830.
9   E. S. Turner, *The Shocking History of Advertising*, p. 79.
10 *Op. cit.*, 1910, p. 129.
11 *Ladies' Field*, March 19th, 1910.
12 *Woman's Life*, 1910, p. 748.
13 *Op. cit.*, 1910, p. 129.
14 *The Lady*, 50th Birthday number, 1935.
15 *Ibid.*, 1885. (Launch issue.)
16 *Op. cit.*, 1898. (Preface to launch issue.)
17 *Hearth and Home*, 1891. (Preface to launch issue.)
18 *Op. cit.*, 1890. (Preface to launch issue.)

19 *Op. cit.*, February, 1910, p. 26.
20 *Op. cit.* (Preface to launch issue.)
21 George Dilnot, *The Romance of the Amalgamated Press*, p. 23.
22 *Ibid.*
23 *Ladies' Field*, 1900, p. 252.
24 *Op. cit.*, January, 1910, p. 126.
25 *Op. cit.*, 1900, p. 372.
26 *Op. cit.*, March 10th, 1900.
27 *Ibid.*, March 3rd.
28 *Ladies' Field*, 1900, p. 452.
29 *The Lady*, March 17th, 1910, p. 457.
30 *Op. cit.*, November 28th, 1900.
31 *Op. cit.*, 1910, p. 23.
32 *Op. cit.*, 1910, p. 28.
33 *Op. cit.*, 1900, p. 145.
34 *Woman*, 1900, p. 24.
35 *Ladies' Field*, 1900, p. 452.
36 *Woman*, October 10th, 1900.
37 *Ibid.*, January, 1900.
38 *Op. cit.*, p. 64.
39 *Op. cit.*, 1900, p. 524.
40 *Op. cit.*, 1910, p. 305.
41 *The Lady*, 1900, p. 306.
42 *Cartwright's Lady's Companion*, 1900, p. 239.
43 *Ibid.*, December 10th, 1910.
44 *Op. cit.*, 1910. (Preface to launch issue.)
45 *The Queen*, 1900, p. 3.
46 *Ibid.*, p. 58.
47 *Ibid.*
48 *Vogue*, 1916. (Preface to launch issue.)

3
Growth between the Wars: 1920-1938

The social and economic changes produced by the First World War profoundly affected the women's press. Between 1920 and 1939, the structure of the industry changed considerably. The 'Society' journals which had formerly dominated the publishing scene steadily lost ground to a rising group of magazines catering to the middle and lower-middle classes. This change was precipitated by the post-war re-distribution of wealth which created two broad categories, the 'New Rich' and the 'New Poor', a classification which was frequently used in the magazines of the time.

The 'New Rich' were those who had made money out of the war-time boom in the economy, both the entrepreneurial classes (the industrial property-owners) and the workers, who had benefited from regular employment and higher wages. Many of the latter were women, who had been employed in the munitions factories and elsewhere. The 'New Poor' were to be found amongst

'those classes of education and refinement who have to meet the enormous increases in the cost of barest necessities with steadily decreasing incomes, often enough on incomes reduced to vanishing point by the loss of husband and father, or heavily encumbered, having the erstwhile breadwinner ill or disabled by wounds.'[1]

A clear sign of this new poverty was the proliferation of money-lenders whose circulars were 'very cunningly worded . . . to appeal especially to teachers, officials and other classes who have fixed incomes, the purchasing power of which has seriously dwindled'.[2]

The changed fortunes of various groups in the population reacted upon the character and content of the women's magazines according to their readerships. Some of the 'quality' publications, which before the war had epitomised carefree prosperity, underwent a complete transformation which reflected the straitened circumstances of the classes to which they catered. Those most severely hit were the magazines serving the gentry and the aristocracy, particularly *The Lady* and *The Queen*.

Conversely, there were those magazines whose readers were largely untouched by economic adversity, and which, moreover, were attracting additional custom from the ranks of the newly rich. *Vogue* was one of these. Having departed somewhat from its original aims, it now confined itself to parading a garish and esoteric assortment of fashions designed to appeal to those with extravagant tastes and ample resources. The eighteenth-century crinoline, 'after Velasquez', and the Victorian bustle, competed side by side with exotic creations from the Orient, Czechoslovakia and Egypt. The fashion pages were flanked by sumptuous advertisements featuring a glittering array of luxury merchandise, and employing skilful selling devices to tempt the unwary. Altogether the magazine transformed the simple desire to be well-dressed into an exorbitantly expensive and time-consuming profession, beyond the reach of all but the most affluent.

Eve, a new publication brought out in 1920, was aimed at the daughters of the New Rich, 'young souls whose subconscious minds are not burdened by any remembrance, and who just enjoy the good things of this world'.[3] Using an entirely unconventional approach, it abandoned the usual content categories and wove a lively mixture of fiction, fashion, social notes, beauty, home-furnishing, recipes, sport and gossip into an extravagantly worded, sparkling narrative interspersed with exaggerated and fanciful illustrations. In its exuberance and its determination to break with the past, *Eve* embodied the spirit of the 'roaring twenties'. Symbolising the revolt against the *ancien régime*, it embraced the new social freedoms of the post-war years:

'For good or ill we are coarse today. ... Tired of shams, we have torn down the musty hangings which the Victorians erected. We talk of everything, we consider everything; we do not rule out one single emotion or experience as being impossible or improper to any person or set of persons. We are determined to let in the air—to ventilate every corner of our mansion. ...'[4]

The Editor of *The Lady*, as spokeswoman for a considerable number of the 'dispossessed', took a practical and optimistic view of the new order:

'In these days of increasing expenditure and diminishing income, it behoves us—the New Poor—to adapt ourselves to altered circumstances, and to learn how comparatively simple it is to do many things for ourselves that formerly necessitated sending for a workman. . . . Having shed the last remnants of our false pride, our terror of "what the neighbours will think", we can arrange our domestic life on the principle that "when no-one's anybody, then everyone is somebody", a much more comforting state of affairs . . . also of far more use to the country at large and ourselves in particular.'[5]

The magazine went on to apply itself to the task of helping its readers make the best of their circumstances, supplying both advice and information, particularly with regard to employment.

But advertising support was crucial to the economic health of most magazines, and the reduced circumstances of this class of readership did not encourage commercial patronage. Some firms, particularly those dealing in 'bread and butter' lines, continued to advertise in a range of periodicals, a few of them adapting their copy to suit the financial status of different readerships. In 1920, *The Lady* carried the following advertisement for medium-priced footwear:[6]

'Lotus and Delta shoes are not for the "new rich" at all, either in quality or price. They are not flashy, obtrusive, catch-the-eye shoes, nor are they by any means "the dearest that can be bought for the money". The qualities of Lotus and Delta appeal far more to the "new poor": quiet, good style, comfort, durability and wonderfully reasonable prices.'*

The bulk of advertising, however, was re-directed into the new magazines created for the affluent middle classes, and many of the older 'quality' journals, starved of their life-blood, shrank in size and finally disappeared.

They were replaced by a group of publications, most of them intended for middle and lower-middle class consumption, whose titles were to become household words in the 'forties and 'fifties. The list included, in chronological order, *Good Housekeeping* (1922), *Modern Woman* (1925), *Woman and Home* (1926), *My Home* and *Modern Home* (1928), *Wife and Home* (1929), *Woman and Beauty* (1930), *Everywoman's* (1934) and *Mother* (1936), together with three titles for a slightly higher class of readership, *Woman's Journal* (1927), *Harper's Bazaar* (English

---

* An advertisement by the same firm for the same article appeared simultaneously in the *Ladies' Field* (a magazine for the wealthier classes), using an entirely different approach.

Ed. 1929) and a glossy 'pocket' magazine, *Housewife* (1939), which later became full-size. All these were monthly periodicals. Among the new middle-class weeklies were three magazines destined to become the first of the mass circulation periodicals, *Woman's Own* (1932), *Woman's Illustrated* (1936) and *Woman* (1937).

The prime function of these magazines was to render the woman reader 'intimate personal service', with a secondary emphasis on entertainment. This order of priorities is characteristic of the women's press in contemporary Britain, but at the time it marked a turning point in women's publishing, being a reversal of the functions of women's magazines before the First World War. The trend was associated with the reorientation of women's journalism away from the servant-keeping leisured classes, and towards the middle ranks.

Woman and Home (a monthly sister-paper to the resoundingly successful *Woman's Weekly*), *My Home* and *Modern Home* were all published as home advisers for middle-class women who had little outside help. *Modern Home*, in common with other magazines of its type, subscribed to the view that to run a house efficiently required both knowledge and planning. Accordingly, it provided 'technical pages for those who are building or furnishing . . . entertainment features and a craft section to help the hostess', and, in recognition of the fact that a house must also be a home, it undertook to help with personal as well as practical difficulties, including 'more intimate articles [to] discuss the more subtle side of home-making'.

The new weeklies, catering to the lower-middle classes, were similarly based on service, and written to a formula which is clearly recognisable as the standard recipe for mass-selling periodicals in the 1960s. The concept of 'reader-identification' had strengthened and the editorial approach was friendly and reassuring. *Woman's Own* came out as 'The new big-value weekly for the up-to-date wife and wife-to-be', and was introduced with free gifts and 'a pictorial supplement produced by the new photo-tone process', heralding the growth of fully-illustrated periodicals for women printed by colour-gravure. Intended primarily for women in charge of small homes, it offered:

'special domestic articles, cooking features, personal pages of sensible beauty advice, fashion-to-make, baby care, knitting and needlework, tense, human and true-to-life stories, and help with personal problems and worries.'[7]

It was followed in 1936 by *Woman's Illustrated*, put out by the Amalgamated Press, which was very similar in layout and approach.

Both magazines enjoyed considerable success, being as attractive and interesting as they were helpful. In the same year, Odhams replied with *Mother*, carefully planned to be 'the greatest occasion of the century in magazine journalism for women'.

But the greatest event in publishing for women was not after all to be *Mother*, but the magazine which Odhams launched (almost by accident) the following year to utilise their new photogravure plant at Watford which was standing idle pending the transfer of *John Bull*. This magazine was *Woman*, 'The National Home Weekly', one of the first periodicals to try and reach a cross-section of women all over the country. It described itself as a magazine of two parts, stating a clear duality of function:

'In the first we seek to entertain you with vivid, vital stories and articles touching every side of life and human interest. In the second we give you practical help and inspiration concerning your home.'

Though its content did not, at this stage, bear the editorial hall-mark of Mary Grieve, and did not differ significantly from its closest rivals, it had one vital ingredient to offer which its competitors had not, namely colour. *Woman* was the first women's magazine to be printed by colour-gravure, and in the drab environment of the mid-'thirties it was a glamorous novelty. Initially, it failed to reach its guaranteed net sale, but, due to the editorial flair of Mary Grieve, the magazine had topped three-quarters of a million by the time war broke out and soared to a sale of more than three and a half million copies in the late 'fifties. In 1968, it was still maintaining its position as 'Britain's greatest direct sales force to women'.

The big inter-war expansion in publishing for women confirmed and strengthened the trend towards the growth of a middle-class women's press. At the same time, new additions were being made to the working-class sector of the market. Two of these, *Woman's Friend* (1924), and *Woman's Companion* (1927) were 'service' magazines for housewives, which proved extremely popular, remaining in print, respectively, until 1950 and 1961. But the majority were in the 'pulp fiction' category and intended purely for entertainment.

Peg's Paper was the fore-runner of this new group of fiction weeklies. It came out in 1919, with the following Editorial introduction:

'It is going to be your weekly pal girls. My name is Peg, and my one aim in life is to give you a really cheery paper like nothing you've ever read before. Not so very long ago, I was a mill-girl too.

D
97

Because I've been a worker like you, I know what girls like, and I'm going to give you a paper you'll enjoy. . . . Look on me as a real friend and helper. I will try to advise you on any problems.'

Here, too, there was a determined effort to achieve close identification with readers, which evidently paid dividends, since the paper continued until the Second World War. It was joined by a succession of similar periodicals throughout the 'twenties and 'thirties, including *Red Star* (1929), *Secrets* (1932), *Oracle* (1933), *Lucky Star* and *Miracle* (1935) and *Glamour* (1938), to name but a few. Their staple content was fiction—'really grand stories that will make you eager to draw up your chair to the fire and have a real good read . . . the true-to-life stories that every woman enjoys'—was how the Editor of *Miracle* described them. Their chief ingredients were romance, glamour, sensation, mystery and revenge, showing the deep need of hard-worked, poorly-paid girls and women to escape from their drab surroundings into a colourful, action-packed dream-world, where love and riches were for once within reach. Despite the lurid illustrations and inferior writing, the values projected were always moral, if sometimes naïve in their assumption that in this life the good always triumphs over the bad.

The kind of need such fiction was meeting is illustrated in this editorial précis prefacing a story in *My Weekly*:

'Once upon a time there was a milliner, young, beautiful and attractive and her name was Peggy. She sold wonderful model hats to old, plain dowagers and pretty young girls; but none of her wealthy customers could boast of the beauty and charm which Peggy possessed, though she had not a penny to her name. Then one sunny morning, Romance stepped right across Peggy's path with such allurement and witchery that it well-nigh turned Peggy's head. For it led her right away from the hat-shop and the drabness which had made up her life, and introduced her to an absolutely new world, where wealth made life easy and love paved the way to happiness. . . .'[8]

This fictional escapism was supplemented and reinforced by the numerous horoscope, fortune-telling and face-reading features which formed a regular and popular part of all such cheap literature.

The growth of the cinema generated more romance and glamour which the pulp weeklies were quick to exploit. *Peg's Own*, for example, carried a problem page undersigned by Ramon Novarro. By the mid-'thirties, the film-craze had become so intense that a special magazine,

Woman's Filmfair (1935) was launched to capitalise on the allure of filmland. Trying to appear respectably utilitarian, it proposed to combine 'glamour with practicality', looking at films 'from a really practical woman's point of view', an approach which encompassed such 'vital' matters as 'How do film-stars keep their figures?' and 'How will the fashions be influenced by the stars?', and including a collection of 'the smartest discoveries gleaned from the world of the screen'. It ran for only six years before it became a casualty of the war.

The growing middle-class orientation of the women's press and the new emphasis on home service were accompanied by an intensification of the pressures encouraging a domestic role for women, associated with the psychological aftermath of the war. In the immediate post-war period there were signs of a new social consciousness among women and a reluctance to return to the old domestic confines. As part of their contribution to the war effort, many thousands of women had for the first time engaged in public work, both paid and voluntary, which had vastly increased their social experience and broadened their horizons. With the return to peace, large numbers of them were ready to consolidate these gains, but when the men came back from the war they expected their womenfolk to reassume their 'rightful' position in society and to devote themselves to bringing to life the 'dream of home' which had sustained them in the trenches.

Women's involvement in activities outside the home gradually lessened and the new climate of thought produced 'the return of the feminine type', heralded by *Woman's Life* in 1920:

'The tide of progress which leaves woman with the vote in her hand and scarcely any clothes upon her back is ebbing, and the sex is returning to the deep, very deep sea of femininity from which her newly-acquired power can be more effectively wielded.'[9]

Most magazines applauded the trend and encouraged it. In one, the Editor implored her readers not to emulate 'the woman who tries to be a man . . . those stiff-collared, short-haired, tailor-suited imitation males with which our clubs and streets are now abounding'.[10] She urged them never to exchange their charm or their womanhood 'for the masculinity which men hate so much', finishing up with the dictum, 'Miss Fluffy Femininity carries off the prizes'. This piece of advice was strongly reminiscent of a Victorian anecdote used to demonstrate the same truth:

'Heroic girl: "Where's the young man who applauded so loudly when I rescued that little boy from drowning?" Reply: "He's over there, proposing to the girl who screamed and fainted".'

The women's press reinforced the trend back to 'dear housewifeliness'. Almost without exception, the new periodicals dedicated themselves to upholding the traditional sphere of feminine interests and were united in recommending a purely domestic role for women. *Housewife*, which appeared just before the outbreak of the Second World War, provides a good illustration of the typical editorial approach in the introduction to its launch issue which was undersigned by the celebrated Christopher Stone:

'. . . happy and lucky is the man whose wife is houseproud, a woman who revels in the fact that she has a home of her own to make, and who is determined to make it attractive for him and for herself, a woman who likes to do things well, to make him proud of her and of their children, and yet who endeavours to do all this cheerfully on a limited income.'

Existing publications were also adapting to the new trend. *The Lady* drastically cut its employment features (though the problem of surplus women was still serious), and substituted several new home-making articles, including a guide to dressmaking, with patterns, and columns on the 'nursery and school-room'. *The Queen* introduced 'Cooking made easy', a home management bureau to which readers were encouraged to send recipes and hints for five-shilling prizes, a children's supplement, and two special items, 'Your domestic problems solved' and a forum where topics of interest to women at home could be aired.

For these two journals, the new emphasis on domestic subjects was undoubtedly partly due to the servant shortage, aggravated by the need to economise with the onset of the Depression. But for a new 'quality' magazine like *Woman's Journal*, catering to more affluent readers, the trend was clearly unrelated to expediency since the magazine devoted itself to the decorative, rather than the practical side of home-making. The image of home life it projected was cosy and sentimental, while its powerful romantic fiction, illustrated by ethereal pastel drawings, portrayed throughout the new ideal of femininity.

The *Lady's Companion* echoed this approach, but in so doing allowed itself to degenerate into the kind of cloying, patronising journalism which has brought the women's press its indifferent reputation. The tone of the Editorial content is well illustrated in its table of contents which offered: fashion-to-make (for the 'busy little housewife'), a beauty column, ('hubby likes you to keep that girlish prettiness you know') and a page for 'Every little mother and mother-to-be [who] has moments of worry and doubt when she wonders whether she is doing the very best she can for the tiny life entrusted to her'. Wives and husbands who did not wish for a brood of 'wee darlings' were castigated for their selfishness and assured that 'the richest home in the world is a poor place without the treasure of a child to call you "mummy"'.

Throughout the fiction, the chat, and the answers to correspondents in this and other magazines, there was a sustained effort to curb restlessness on the part of wives and to popularise the career of housewife and mother. *Home Chat* in particular rejoiced in the fact that 'we are feminine again', and cautioned the growing brigade of modern women who were refusing to join the ranks of 'married drudges', that 'men's attitudes to Home Comfort are still B.C.'. Underlining this truth, a male reader wrote:

> 'I married . . . because she was an admirable example of the "hearth-cat". I knew she would see to it that every detail was perfect in my home, from taking care that there was always a sheaf of fresh shaving-papers in the bath-room, to having exactly the right sort of dinner for the evenings I'd been kept late at the office.'[11]

Home Chat, too, fell into the habit of using coy phrases, such as 'the little bride' and 'the little mother'. The pulp weeklies, sharing the same ideals, copied this technique, and focused their fiction and editorials on the cosy security of home and the love of husband and children. It was an attractive picture compared to the hard struggle facing most working girls, and mirrored the day-dreams of most readers, of whom this fictional character was typical:

> 'Why, every time I think of the little home Will and I are getting together, I know that I'll never want to type another word when I get scrubbing and cleaning and cooking in it.'[12]

Another issue contained the story of a girl who pretended not to like housework because she felt obliged to discourage an admirer. But so passionately did she yearn for the joys of cleaning and polishing that she took to donning her overall in private—a predictably 'feminine', if impractical, creation in pink with white smocking. She was one day caught in the act, and wedding bells pealed joyously through the final paragraph.

The editorial platform was everywhere founded on the unshakable conviction that for the modern woman, marriage was 'The Best Job of All'. But whether or not this was true for all women, it was definitely becoming as demanding an occupation as any, both in the standard of housekeeping expected from women, and in the more difficult territory of marital relationships, the character of which was changing as a result of the new social freedoms. Social standards in respect of family care continued to rise in response both to new scientific discoveries (which advanced knowledge in such areas as nutrition, maternity, child-care, therapeutics, public health and mental welfare), and the fixing of minimum statutory standards.

The spread of medical and other knowledge was widely documented. As far down the scale as *Woman's Weekly*, reference was now being made to the importance of ante-natal care, and at the request of the Great Northern Central Hospital, this magazine publicised a new ante-natal clinic opened for the benefit of those unable to afford the services of a family doctor. This was one of the first instances of a magazine being officially asked to further public welfare. The *Lady's Companion* gave details of a voluntary-service nursery for under-fives, available to mothers at a cost of 1s. 2d. per week, and *The Queen* publicised the Basil Blackwood Day Nursery for the 'new poor', as well as hostels for mothers and babies. The new prominence given to nursery education, which culminated in special statutory provisions, was a direct result of the work of Margaret McMillan who contributed articles on the subject to the women's magazines.

By the early 'twenties, household management had come to be regarded as a demanding and responsible profession, requiring systematic instruction if competence were to be achieved in all its many branches. Accordingly, the women's press began to treat household topics in greater depth. Magazines began to employ professional experts as advisers, and gradually a departmental service was evolved, the various sections being presided over by special writers who were responsible to the Editor, but who had increasing autonomy in their own spheres. Thus the way was being paved for the Section Editors of contemporary women's journalism, who work with their own staffs as separate teams under a co-ordinating Editor.

However, a professional and comprehensive household service was still lacking, and it took an American magazine to point the way. In 1922, the English edition of the American home monthly *Good House-keeping* was brought out. It set out to give an all-round home-making service, demonstrating techniques in detail, laying down guiding principles, and giving up-to-date information on available goods and services. Justifying this thorough-going approach, its Editor wrote:

'Any keen observer of the times cannot have failed to notice that we are on the threshold of a great feminine awakening. Apathy and levity are alike giving place to a wholesome and intelligent interest in the affairs of life, and above all, in the home. We believe that the time is ripe for a great new magazine which shall worthily meet the needs of the housekeeping woman of today.'[13]

At first, *Good Housekeeping* did not confine itself to home topics. It also included a variety of serious articles likely to interest the intelligent reader, in which topical questions were vigorously debated. There was also a small amount of superior fiction. But it was primarily a manual of housecraft and it aimed at dealing with each subject as thoroughly as possible, claiming a factual foundation for everything found in its pages. Later, all goods and services mentioned were subjected to rigorous testing, on the basis of which manufacturers were awarded (or denied) the Good Housekeeping Seal of Guarantee, which soon became synonymous with quality and reliability in the minds of women consumers. Lavishly illustrated, professionally run according to the best American standards, and backed by a consumer service, the magazine offered incomparable value at a cover price of one shilling, and had no rival. Because it brought impressive new standards of expertise to bear on a wide range of home subjects it quickly established itself as leader in the field.

The arrival of *Good Housekeeping* proclaimed the accession to the domestic throne of the professional 'Queen of the House'. But, while the professionalisation of housewifery was beneficial in raising standards, it was disadvantageous to women in two important respects. On the one hand, it increased their domestic burden by making higher demands upon them in terms of achievement and efficiency at a time when auxiliary help was almost impossible to obtain; on the other, it encouraged women to spend more time than ever in the discharge of their household duties, to the exclusion of external interests and activities, thereby narrowing their outlook and contributing to the revival of an insular feminine role.

An important change was the higher status housewifery was now acquiring. *Good Housekeeping* proudly christened housewives 'The craft-workers of today', and in advocating the application of craftsmanship to home management praised it as 'a form of service which is appreciated by everyone', bringing 'instant material and spiritual rewards'. It even urged women to take up a scientific training so that they could use scientific principles to help them solve their domestic difficulties.

The existence of a platform for the exchange of ideas helped, in the case of *Good Housekeeping*, to offset to some extent its concentration on housecraft. Outwardly, it adhered to the principle that married women should look further than the kitchen and the nursery, but it nevertheless betrayed an underlying acceptance of traditional attitudes. The Editor confessed to finding it 'surprising and distinctly gratifying to our sense of womanliness' that more than half the respondents to its questionnaire admitted to making, rather than buying, their own underwear. As long as these views remained paramount, there was little prospect of a reduction in the domestic commitments of women.

In other magazines there was no counterbalancing influence whatsoever to the cult of 'Home, sweet home'. Editors expatiated in unison on the sacrificial joys of being a wife and mother. They elevated housewifery into a craft, gave it the status of a profession, and sold it to readers on the most attractive of terms, thereby nullifying all that had been achieved by the Women's Rights Movement in securing greater social freedom for women, and letting slip the opportunities opening up for them as a result of the war. In addition they created the perfect buying climate for every kind of household commodity which advertisers soon began to exploit. As early as 1920, the effects were beginning to make themselves felt. In that year *Woman's Weekly* carried this advertisement for baby food:

'Do you realise, Mother of a Baby—that you can be one of the greatest creative artists in the world?—Just like every other artist a mother must study her Art—the greatest Art of all—the great art of creating strong, straight, noble men and women.'[14]

The onset of the Depression imposed a new set of responsibilities on the women's press, chiefly those of helping women of all classes to manage on dwindling incomes, and encouraging thrift and economy. The servant shortage had never been more acute, ten out of every eleven families being servantless. *The Lady* later prophesied:

'It looks as though a good deal of suburban elegance will have to be abandoned, and simple household ways adopted. The luxury of an attendant almost constantly on duty will have to go the way of candlelight, open fires and other amenities now only possible to the rich.'[15]

But even the rich were finding life difficult. *The Queen* commented:

'Without going into high finance, there is the outstanding fact

that taxation in this country has over-reached its peak point . . . and
so many people have still the same liabilities as they were shoulder-
ing before the war . . . what are they to do when increased taxation
and depreciation in market values make a hitherto adequate income
utterly inadequate?'[16]

The alternatives were to continue living beyond their means, or to
cut back on expenditure, and *The Queen* indicated how these classes
were reacting:

'Life on the whole is less extravagant; people of the leisured
classes are foregoing many of their former luxuries in the laudable
attempt to live within their incomes. Of course, exceptions to this
are to be met with, and undoubtedly capital is in new hands today.
There are more workers amongst those of the leisured classes, fewer
of the *jeunesse dorée* to be found. . . . Parents in their endeavour to
live within their incomes are bringing up their children to be more
practical and self-reliant to enable them if necessary to earn their
living.'[17]

Magazines from *The Queen* downwards came to the aid of hard-
pressed housekeepers, showing them how to stretch the weekly budget,
and in some cases giving estimates of costs for use as a guide in appor-
tioning incomes.* They offered ideas for economising in dress, catering,
and furnishing. Even *Vogue* ran a series of 'budget' articles called
'Mathematics for the Million without a Million—or How to Make
Ingenuity Take the Place of Hard Cash'. One periodical, the *Home Mail
and Women's Guide* (1933) made an unusual attempt to tackle the problem of deflation at its source, on the basis of the economic principle

---

* Some examples of living costs were given in *The Queen*, February 15, 1930,
p. 32:

A. For luxury living in a large household where menservants are kept:
    40s. to 60s. per head per week, in the dining room
    25s. per head per week, in the school-room/nursery
    25s. per head per week, for upper staff
    18s. per head per week, for under staff.
B. For nice living in a large household which is not run on luxury lines, 20s.
    per head per week all round. In cases where there is a large family of
    children and the living is quite simple, 17s. or 18s. per head.
C. For luxury living in a small, childless household where four or five very
    experienced women servants are kept, 40s. per head in the dining-room and
    20s. per head for the staff.
D. For nice living in a two or three servant-keeping house, 20s. per head.
E. For plain, sufficient living, 16s. per head.
F. For very plain living, 14s. per head.

that 'Prosperity depends on Expenditure'. Having accepted that 'the purchasing power of every housewife is the basis of industrial activity', the proprietor reasoned that 'to induce her to buy more she must be given more to spend'. He therefore proposed to offer, for a twice-yearly subscription of five shillings, 'a first-class magazine catering exclusively for women and all home-lovers', through which a rebate of one shilling in the pound would be made on all goods bought through its advertising columns. In addition, there were the attractions of a free insurance scheme, and free 'small-ad' facilities monthly for all subscribers. The experiment was short-lived, but it is an interesting example of a purposive magazine, and one which, in common with other publishers and advertisers, recognised the growing importance of the housewife as a consumer.

The new responsibilities of the women's press were not confined to to giving budgetary advice. Economic stagnation was accompanied by signs of new stresses within the family, and by widespread spiritual depression. Commentators spoke of an apparent listlessness, a lack of vigour and a predominating attitude of fatalism. In 1930, an article in *Good Housekeeping* described the change that had come over the youthful population:

'Today's youth . . . and men and women in their early thirties seem to expect nothing, to look forward to nothing, to believe in nothing . . . it has a real danger of sterility, and sterility is the beginning of the end of family, national and spiritual life. . . . The want of real merriment is startlingly, terribly evident; people enjoy themselves in a very half-hearted way, just as they work.'[18]

Accompanying this spiritual sterility, and perhaps partly issuing from it, was a new and serious decline in fertility. During the post-war period the birth-rate took a sudden steep plunge which, together with a heavy net annual migration loss, gave rise to grave concern about the possibility of future depopulation. Contemporary observers agreed that the downward trend in births was due to deliberate family limitation:

'How general this is may be gathered from a comparison of our families with those of just one generation ahead of us. Then the common number of children was from four to eight, and now young couples feel they have done their duty if they have simply reproduced themselves. Many do not feel any obligations to shoulder even so much responsibility, so that the one-child family and the childless home are widespread.'[19]

The decline in fertility was one manifestation of the economic strains being imposed upon the family. Equally serious were the stresses arising out of the new era of equality between the sexes. The tensions associated with changing relationships both outside and within marriage issued in illegitimacy, adultery, divorce and child-neglect, and above all, in a new and all-pervasive preoccupation with sex. The *Lady's Companion* drew attention to it as early as 1920:

'Literature dealing with sex problems was pushed into the background during the war, but a leading journalist prophesied that with the return of peace, it would be revived with renewed force. That prophecy is already being fulfilled, and quite recently, another leading journalist has suggested that "the change in the sex relation may well prove to be the gravest of the enduring results of the war in western society". The question therefore arises, how are the girls of the period prepared for a state of society wherein sex relations are in this transition stage and difficult to define? Have we arrived at a stage of evolution when it is not merely desirable but imperative that our young people should be definitely informed as to the facts of life and thus placed upon their guard against the dangers and pitfalls of a world in solution?'[20]

Significantly, the question was not *when* sex instruction should be given, but whether it should be given *at all*, a clear indication of the level of ignorance in this area. Another magazine asserted that 'Eve's bite of the fruit of the Tree of Knowledge of Good and Evil' did not take place until 1914, and felt she was 'in for a lot of trouble over her dessert'. It was proved right. Throughout the 'twenties there was growing evidence of marital failure, but not until the 1930s was the root cause brought into the open.

The major factor responsible for breaking through the 'conspiracy of silence' was the spread of psychological theories about sex, in particular those of Sigmund Freud. In attributing sexuality to women, and even to children, he shocked public opinion into a radical reassessment of the customary sexual roles of men and women, and though, initially, his assault upon the tenderest area of their sensibilities was met with complete disgust and rejection, eventually it came to be accepted that women were far from being sexually passive. A writer in *Good Housekeeping* indicated the ramifications of Freud's work:

'Freud, whether right or wrong, did succeed in convincing [women] that they had sex desires and that these desires were not wicked; that to repress them was as difficult and dangerous to women as to men, and that they need no longer pretend that all they wanted was at most motherhood, when it was quite as natural for them to want lover-hood. This has been an astounding change . . . even to know what marriage meant was formerly regarded as unsuitable in women, and to want to know indecent. . . . The result of such a violent fracture has been bad as well as good. Instead of the terrifying repression of the old maid, we have the complete repudiation of any kind of self-control as a danger to her sanity, or at least to the normal and free development of her age. It was perhaps an inevitable reaction from the false belief that the physical side of marriage meant nothing to a woman, to the obsession with sex which has prevailed now for some years.'[21]

The discovery that women were sexual creatures sent the ideal of pure and innocent womanhood finally crashing to the ground and with it went the strongest justification for the double standard of morality carried over from the Victorian era. Women now had the right to 'accept for themselves the standard always accepted by men', and the assumption of this right was, according to Dr Maude Royden writing in *Good Housekeeping*, the explanation for the change in moral standards between the wars. It doubtless also contributed to the changed moral climate in magazine fiction, in which moral lapses were treated ever more tolerantly.

However, it is doubtful whether the Freudian theories concerning female sexuality contributed much to the enlightenment of the majority of women. The women's magazines of the period were full of evidence to the contrary. The Editor of *Woman's Own* could confidently claim that, judging by her post-bag, 'ignorance of the obligations, privileges and marvels of married life is as widespread today as it was in the darkest ages of the history of women'.[22] *The Lady's Companion* admitted that the blame lay with the consistent refusal to treat the subject openly:

'Until recent years, sex was something which we did not discuss; it was hidden away, suffered in silence, and what might have been a thing of exquisite beauty was distorted and treated as though it did not matter. Generations paid for this treatment of the most vital angle of life, and today hundreds of men and women are unhappy.'[23]

The problems of the declining birth-rate, the high incidence of marital failure and sexual ignorance presented the women's press with new challenges. To combat the first, they intensified their advocacy of marriage and motherhood, though they were forced to make allowances for the strictures imposed by the recession. *The Lady's Companion* recognised the difficulties facing newly married couples:

> ' "Just at first we cannot see our way clear to having babies"— this is a constant cry. Today many women have to help towards supporting the house, as well as men. They have to go to business and come back at night and they cannot do this and have babies as well.'[24]

As a remedy the Editor recommended sensible planning, but added a reminder that marriage was ordained primarily for the bearing of children and that Nature worked to that end. *The Lady* pointed out what it regarded as the folly of sacrificing children in order to maintain a certain standard of living:

> 'The pity is that young people bringing up one or two babies on an income insufficient for their standards of gentility and pleasure (both of which are often false) do not realise how short a time a small family lasts.'[25]

Some magazine counsellors used the new theories to exert psychological pressure on their readers in an attempt to persuade them into marriage. *Woman's Fair* printed an analysis of the various 'types' of single women with comments on the 'psychological' reasons which prevented them marrying. The discussion closed with the flat statement that:

> 'Any girl who declares she prefers to stay single is only fooling herself. No matter how full of life she may be, it isn't complete without marriage. Nothing else can satisfy this fundamental need. If you are clinging to single blessedness, the chances are that there is something wrong with your emotional make-up or your attributes, or that you are the victim of false ideas. Knowledge and guidance may help.'[26]

Thus, at a time when it was becoming increasingly common for women to have careers of their own, psychological theory was one more factor adding its weight to the consensus of influence being brought to bear upon women to look no further than the domestic sphere, with magazine writers using it to quell the independent-spirited, and to encourage women to play down their intelligence if they wished to avoid spinsterhood and make a successful marriage. *Woman*, for example, urged the newly-married woman to 'Be the Junior Partner Madam!', cautioning all those capable and efficient women coming to marriage from full lives in the outside world to guard against becoming dictatorial wives or competing with their husbands. The persistence of Victorian attitudes regarding the proper role for a wife made this warning necessary. The husband who wrote to *Woman's Own* to put his views about married women working, summed up the attitude of the majority of men:

> 'I'm afraid I'm old-fashioned enough to want a whole-time wife, whose main interest in life will be her home, her children and me ... I want a wife to listen to my troubles, to be ready and willing to soothe and comfort me. I don't want to come back [from work] tired, and find myself having to comfort her. In fact, I want a wife whose first and only interest is me—and then, our home. . . . Later on, there ought to be children. A wife who earns will not be at all keen to have them. . . . So let me do the earning. Let her stick to the whole-time job of being my wife.'[27]

The women's magazines in general endorsed this view, but they realised the difficulties arising out of the clash between the old order and the new. They began to treat personal problems in greater depth, and opened their columns to a discussion of particular areas of difficulty. Throughout, they upheld the *status quo* and remained non-commital about women's advancement. One reader who wrote to the *Lady's World* in 1920 asking for support for, and information about, the campaign for women's rights, was stiffly told that, 'It would be outside the purpose of these columns to show the partizanship you desire'. As late as 1938, ten years after the granting of universal female suffrage, *The Queen* took the same position, stating that it was beyond its scope to discuss the merits or demerits of this achievement.

Instead, the magazines set about the task of helping women to be better wives and mothers, and in the years leading up to the Second World War, this increasingly included instruction in matters of sex. For the first time they offered booklets on family planning and related subjects, and dealt with marital problems in special articles. Meanwhile, the spread of psychological theories of sex were producing a different attitude to marriage on the part of some magazine counsellors. Whereas they had once stressed only the joys of maternity and family life, they now began to recommend it in very different terms:

'Nobody envies the old bachelor and the poor old maid. Marriage is the one *métier* of life and most of us aim at it. Not with the idea of having a home of our own, or of having a companion, but simply for the one truth for which marriage stands.'[28]

But in general the customary taboos surrounding sexual topics remained sufficiently strong to prevent the magazines dealing with these problems in all but the vaguest terms. Correspondents writing for advice usually failed to receive specific guidance, and often got no help at all, such as the *Home Chat* reader who was told by 'Mrs Jim':

'I am sorry I cannot answer so intimate a question through these columns, and I am rather amazed at your ignorance about the facts of life. Ask an older friend to tell you.'[29]

The majority of the women's periodicals confined themselves to giving practical help in more straightforward areas, showing women how to make themselves more physically attractive, their homes more comfortable, and their families more content. They encouraged them to look no further.

By the time war broke out for the second time, the majority of women's magazines had become 'homely friends', cosy and introverted, offering women a retreat from the world and a respite from the grim struggles of everyday living. Over-sweet commiseration was beginning to replace the astringent counselling of an earlier period. *Woman's Weekly* had recruited every woman's ideal male companion in 'The Man-Who-Sees' to dispense a weekly dose of soothing wisdom: 'a man who has woven for himself a warm cloak of Philosophy, Courage, Kindliness and a sense of Humour, which he is prepared to throw over others as well as himself'. Features of this type testified to the deep need most women felt for some sort of opiate to sustain them through their days of quiet, desperate struggle, and the amateur philosophers and friendly counsellors filled a role that was once the prerogative of the parish priest. Religious columns also began to appear, and together they offered women comfort, guidance and inspiration, reinforcing as they did so the enduring tenets of faith, hope and charity, and the traditional female virtues of endurance, tolerance and self-sacrifice.

The best of these women's periodicals managed to convey warmth, friendliness, sincerity, and a deep concern with the fundamental values of life as they were understood by the large mass of the population. Even the lowest-grade publications, the pulp-fiction weeklies, conformed to these basic standards. Of these papers Professor Hoggart has said:

'They are in some ways crude, but often more than that. They still have a felt sense of the texture of the life of the group they cater for. . . . Most of the material is conventional, that is, it mirrors the attitudes of its readers. But those attitudes are not as ridiculous as one might at first be tempted to think. In comparison with these papers, some of those more recently in the front are as a smart young son . . . beside his sentimental, superstitious, and old-fashioned mother. . . . The world these stories present is a limited and simple one, based on a few accepted and long-held values. It is often a childish and garish world and the springs of the emotions work in great gushings. But they do work; it is not a corrupt or a pretentious world. It uses boldly words like "sin", "shame", "guilt", "evil", with every appearance of meaningfulness which serious writers for more sophisticated audiences understandably find difficulty in using today. . . . It accepts completely . . . the notion that marriage and a home founded on love, fidelity and cheerfulness are the right purpose of a woman's life.'[30]

These were the principles which guided most magazine writers. Of the popular journals, *Woman* was alone in its progressive view that women's journalism should, in addition to reinforcing home values, have a social conscience. For a while the magazine experimented with articles dealing with social problems, but was forced to abandon them when they produced a chastening 30 per cent drop in sales. This demonstration of the failure of a popular women's weekly to arouse interest in subjects of importance outside domestic concerns underlined the extent to which the progress of women had been retarded in the inter-war years. In the magazine's first issue, the Editorial drew attention to the fact that, 'In the last ten years there has been a movement, a tendency which the suffrage generation calls backward, "retrogressive". . . . ' The Editor felt that this charge of retrogression was 'neither exactly true or entirely fair', going on to explain:

'We are trying to do something difficult, to blend our old world with our new. [Women are] trying to be citizens and women at the same time. Wage-earners and sweethearts. But while they work, filling a tremendous place in professional and industrial life, they are still greedy for the pleasures and responsibilities which the sweet stay-at-home, that domestic tyrant, had so well in hand.'

This in essence was the dilemma facing women in the years between the wars. Opportunities such as they had never previously known were opening up on all sides, but the choice was still between these and marriage. Few of them could have both; few of them wanted both, because traditional attitudes concerning a woman's true sphere were still strong, in society and in themselves. Their magazines were powerful advocates of the *'Kinder, Küche, Kleider'* role, for most Editors welcomed and encouraged both the return to 'femininity', and the new appreciation of home life which manifested themselves during these two decades.

These trends, together with the re-distribution of income, heightened the attraction of the women's press to advertisers. Astute businessmen, particularly in the fashion and cosmetic trades, soon realised the benefits to be gained from co-operating with magazine publishers. The fashion industry which was enjoying a post-war boom, allied itself still more closely to the women's journals and increased its consumption of advertising space. This development was precipitated by the increasing popularity (and availability) of good, ready-to-wear clothes, which were steadily ousting the expensive, couturier-designed models, thereby bringing the fashion departments of the large stores into prominence and into the market for advertising space. The *Lady's Companion* observed:

'. . . the ultra-smart set are at present amusing themselves in experimenting in economy. Refusing to pay the exorbitant sums asked by the exclusive West-End dressmakers, it has become the fashion amongst a great many smart débutantes to wear those wonderful ready-to-wear frocks that are sold for three, four and five guineas in the big stores.'[31]

Eve added: 'Fashion was never less tyrannical, or more elastic', which was certainly true of the 1920s, when the freedom to follow personal inclinations in dress was but one more indication of the uprooting of the old codes and conventions all over society. For the fashion 'glossies' this change resulted in a new approach. They became trend-setters, rather than trend-followers and soon occupied a position from which they could exert great influence over patterns of expenditure and the formation of tastes. Coupled with the increased spending-power of many groups within the female population, this singled them out as a prime target for firms keen to expand their markets, and a close association began to develop between them.

By 1938, there was clear evidence of the growing co-operation between advertisers and the women's magazines in all areas of consumption. A new type of advertisement feature had been introduced which was presented as part of editorial content. *Woman's Weekly*, for example, carried 'Shopping Lists', which consisted of a selection of proprietary items recommended by the magazine. *Woman's Journal*, too, ran a 'Shopping Service' in which branded goods were given editorial support. All the items advertised in *Woman* and *Good Housekeeping* were covered by a cash refund guarantee, while *Miracle* ran a series of 'beauty offers' by arrangement with cosmetic firms. *Home Chat* did likewise, prefacing one of its 'Special Offers' with the following appeal to the ingenuous:

'I was so tremendously enthusiastic about this wonderful new lemon hand jelly, that I have prevailed upon the nice manufacturer to allow me to send you a really generous "gift-tube".'

There were signs, too, of a new concern to collect readership data for commercial purposes. *Good Housekeeping* was one of the first magazines to recognise the importance of market research, and as part of a survey designed to investigate readers' buying habits, a personal questionnaire was sent out to ascertain how much women were spending, where, and on what. It revealed that, in 1930, the 'typical, moderately well-off woman' had an average dress allowance of £65 a year; that only 20 per cent, 7 per cent and 5 per cent of women respectively, used lipstick, rouge and scent, and that $7\frac{1}{2}$ per cent used no make-up of any kind, figures which no doubt gave a stimulus to cosmetic manufacturers.

This type of research vastly expanded after the war when the growth of advertising custom encouraged publishers to investigate the potential buying-power of their readers more fully, both as a service to existing advertisers and as a means by which to attract more custom. Another related pre-war development was *Vogue*'s decision to bring out a supplementary *Beauty Book*, after first canvassing readers to assess the nature and extent of their interest in beauty topics. Significantly, these commercially-biased experiments were pioneered by American-owned companies.

By contrast, English firms were still more concerned with pleasing the reader than the advertiser. In 1938, *Home Chat* carried out a small survey, not to discover the consumption potential of its readers, but to find out how far it was meeting their requirements editorially, in what it recognised was a period of sweeping social change. The Editor explained the purpose of the survey:

'For nearly forty-five years *Home Chat* has been guide, philosopher and friend to you and your mother before you. But fashions change, folk change, and I wonder sometimes if I am giving you in your little paper just what you want and in the way you want it.'[32]

To encourage readers to comply with her request to complete and return the questionnaire printed in the magazine,* the Editor offered a free gift to all respondents.

The more commercial interests encroached into editorial territory, the less scope there was for Editors to mould their magazines strictly according to their own views. In 1920 there was no question about editorial freedom to control pernicious advertising practices. Nor did Editors hesitate to discourage women from purchasing certain commodities if they considered it necessary. Disregarding the cosmetic advertising carried by the magazine, *Home Chat*'s Editor pointed out, 'Paint and powder may be pretty, but it won't wash!'. *Harrison's Journal* went so far as to prepare a guide to the traps in advertising waiting to ensnare the gullible. Later, as magazines became even more heavily dependent upon advertising revenue, and advertisers themselves became more demanding, Editors were forced into a position first of neutrality, then of concurrence, and finally of collusion.

This process took place faster in the daily press, where, even before the Second World War, editorial autonomy was being seriously eroded. In 1933, the Brewers' Society, launching a big publicity campaign, made it clear to the national press that the continuation of their patronage depended upon editorial support being given to their advertisements. It was quickly slapped down but it was a warning of things to come. The P.E.P. Report on the Press in 1938 found disturbing evidence that newspapers had begun both to suppress minor items likely to be disadvantageous to advertisers and to discourage the airing of issues which might cause publicity unfavourable to them. Also, greater efforts were being made by publishers to ensure the most advantageous placing of advertising matter. These practices were not necessarily a result of direct negotiations with advertisers. Often they were automatically carried out at the sub-editing stage in accordance with general newspaper policy to safeguard advertising revenue.

In the 'thirties, the women's press was still unaffected by severe pressures of this kind, but 'concessions' to advertisers were growing. Special positions were arranged, and some advertising copy was so skilfully written that only its recurrence in other journals revealed that it was not editorial matter. As the need to secure more advertising revenue became acute, publishers were ready to co-operate still further.

* See Appendix II.

Advertisements in the trade press showed that magazine proprietors were stepping up their campaigns to sell advertising space and doing all they could to convince firms of the superiority of the women's press as an advertising medium. But advertisers were hard to convince that women's publications, with their circulations of (at best) a few hundred thousand, were as profitable a proposition as the daily papers with a multi-million sale.

To attract the advertising revenue they needed, publishers had to increase their sales. But with every increase in circulation, production costs soared. Since the beginning of the century, printing methods had become progressively more efficient. Gradually, electricity supplanted gas and steam-engines in supplying motive power and by 1920 almost all printing machines were operated by it. Automatic ink-pumping was another important innovation, patented in 1915. In response to the increasing demands of the rapidly expanding newspaper industry, the deck system for web-rotary presses was abandoned and floor-level installations substituted, which later facilitated multiple-unit printing. A 'flying paster', patented in 1924, saved time formerly lost in stopping the presses to feed in a new reel, and other refinements at various stages of the preparation and printing processes increased their speed and versatility. By the 1930s, Hoe and Goss presses had been perfected which were capable of turning out printed, cut and folded copies, counted and wrapped if necessary, in a continuous operation. In paper manufacture, too, continuous processing had been achieved, by which raw wood was converted into reeled paper within a single plant. Quality was being improved at the same time. New techniques in finishing produced better printing surfaces on cheaper grade papers, allowing finer reproduction, which benefited the cheapest publications. Machine coating, which was developed in America and introduced into Britain in 1934, brought coated paper within reach of a much wider range of periodicals giving them the advantage of a superior printed result at a comparatively low price.

Despite these developments, the cost of printing periodicals by letterpress was high, and it increased with output. Publishers began to look around for an alternative method which could print by the million cheaply and efficiently and also give better quality reproduction. Preferably it should be one capable of being adapted to take colour. Lord Southwood, impressed by American achievements with photogravure, decided to install an experimental plant at Watford to print *John Bull*. But Odhams were not the first to try out this process. It was, as already noted, in limited use at the turn of the century, but for a long time it was thought that rotary machines printing in four colours were technically impossible. Through the persistence of David Greenhill, the Sun Engraving Co. eventually succeeded in getting such a press built to their specifications, and installed it at their Watford printing works in the 1920s. The early trials more than justified their efforts and soon the Company was printing sections of magazines by this method.

The perfecting of rotary colour-gravure provided the breakthrough so badly needed by periodical publishers. The method, despite heavy preparation costs, reaped huge economies of scale and gave the industry the capacity to accommodate a mass-circulation periodical press, turning out good quality, colour-illustrated magazines at newspaper speeds and newspaper prices. As has already been mentioned, the first women's magazine to be wholly produced by it was *Woman* in 1937, but it was soon joined by *Everywoman* and *Woman's Own*. The new method vastly improved the appearance of all three in comparison with other journals. The spur of this competition, together with a typographical revolution, drove rival publications to modernise their presentation, and in the years leading up to the Second World War there was a noticeable improvement in format and illustration throughout the women's press. Particularly noticeable was the standardisation of dimensions in accordance with technical requirements, so that women's magazines, superficially at least, tended towards uniformity.

On the production side, the magazine industry was getting into gear ready for the accelerated growth of the 'forties and 'fifties. Circulations were still a closely guarded secret with the majority of publishers, but for some a new era of frankness had begun with the founding of the Audit Bureau of Circulations in 1931. Women's magazines were slow to register, however, and advertisers looked increasingly to market research to supply the data they needed. One of the first of these surveys was carried out in 1927 by the London Research and Information Bureau, its aim being to provide a more accurate guide to the circulations of newspapers, magazines and periodicals by class and area. The design of the survey, its sampling methods, and the conduct of the interviews were inadequate by modern standards, but it gave a general indication of the distribution, by class, of the readerships of leading women's magazines.

From a sample of more than 20,000 respondents divided between middle-class, lower-middle class and working class readers* in the ratio of 5,020, 6,290, and 8,830 respectively, it emerged that *Home Chat*

* Class definitions were as follows: *Middle class*—'well-to-do and comfortably off'; *Lower-Middle class*—'buying capacity limited, but same buying habits and social outlook as the middle class'; *Working class*—'steadier types of workers' (slums and poor areas excluded).

and *Home Notes* had universal appeal, their readers being spread fairly evenly over all three classes, but with the highest concentration in the lower-middle class. *Woman's Weekly* was another magazine with wide popularity, drawing its readers chiefly from the lower-middle and working classes. It was followed closely by *Woman and Home*, whose readers came from the same two groups but in the reverse order. Amongst the middle classes, the *Lady's Home World* was also popular, together with *Vogue* and *Eve*, while *Peg's Paper* had one of the largest followings with working-class women. However, no magazine could claim more than 867 readers, or 4·3 per cent of the total sample.

Ten years later, more figures were available, though few of them were publicly audited, and by this time considerable expansion was evident, *Woman* having leapt ahead of its rivals *Woman's Weekly*, *Woman's Own* and *Woman and Home* to reach a sale of around three-quarters of a million. The success of this colour-gravure magazine, designed for mass circulation, signified that the old era in publishing for women was drawing to a close. The rise of the large publishing firms and the growth in the consumption potential of women meant that it was only a matter of time before the women's press would be lifted out of its quiet backwater and into the fore-front of big business. The process would transform it from a miscellaneous collection of amateurish productions catering to minority readerships into a highly competitive and professional medium of communication reaching five out of six women in Britain.

The Second World War acted as the catalyst for this change, producing yet another social revolution which fused the fragmented readerships of the pre-war years into a unified and homogeneous reading public of millions, and so gave women's magazines new prominence and significance as specialised media capable of influencing the buying decisions of the bulk of British women. As such, they became a magnet for advertisers, and as their patronage increased, the women's press became progressively more vulnerable to commercial influence. The effects of that influence, both upon the structure of the industry and upon magazine content, is the most crucial aspect of their post-war history.

NOTES

1 *The Queen*, January, 1920, p. 190.
2 *Home Chat*, 1920, p. 119.
3 *Ladies' Field*, January, 1910.
4 *Op. cit.*, April 8th, 1920.
5 *Op. cit.*, June 24th, 1920, p. 744.

6 *Ibid.*, February 12th, 1920, p. ix.
7 *Op. cit.*, 1932. (Launch issue.)
8 *Op. cit.*, January 17th, 1920, p. 44.
9 *Op. cit.*, February, 1920, p. 120.
10 *Ibid.*, January 10th, p. 13.
11 *Op. cit.*, February 22nd, 1930, p. 418.
12 *My Weekly*, May 3rd, 1930, p. 531.
13 *Op. cit.*, 1922. (Launch issue.)
14 *Op. cit.*, 1920. (Advertisement for Glaxo.)
15 *Op. cit.*, January 27th, 1938, p. 97.
16 *Op. cit.*, June 25th, 1930, p. 15.
17 *Ibid.*
18 *Op. cit.*, May, 1930, p. 14.
19 *Ibid.*, May, 1930, p. 208.
20 *Op. cit.*, 1920, p. 240.
21 *Op. cit.*, 1938, p. 22.
22 *Op. cit.*, February 5th, 1938, p. 11.
23 *Op. cit.*, April 2nd, 1938, p. 18.
24 *Ibid.*, April 23rd, 1938, p. 8.
25 *Op. cit.*, January 13th, 1938, p. 38.
26 *Op. cit.*, February, 1938, p. 19.
27 *Op. cit.*, April 30th, 1938, p. 7.
28 *Lady's Companion*, April 23rd, 1938, p. 8.
29 *Op. cit.*, March 15th, 1930, p. 644.
30 Richard Hoggart, *Uses of Literacy*, pp. 121–9.
31 *Op. cit.*, 1920, p. 217.
32 *Op. cit.*, October 8th, 1938.

Part Two

From Rationing to Rationalisation

The Women's Press: 1946–1968

4
Utility Journals: 1946-1956

(i) 'Make Do and Mend': 1946–1951

The Second World War profoundly affected the magazine industry. It struck at its capacity to print by rationing paper and the number of copies that could be produced, cut back its profits from advertising, and pruned the contents of every magazine down to an essential core of guidance in coping with conditions of scarcity. Many titles ceased publication early on and never reappeared; others amalgamated. The remainder soldiered on, thin and colourless by pre-war standards, but fiery in spirit, their contents wholly directed towards helping the war effort on the home front. The Government, realizing the importance of the women's magazines as channels of communication through which instructions and announcements could be broadcast to women all over the country, maintained a close liaison with their editorial staffs. The Ministry of Food and the Ministry of Fuel and Power were two Government Departments which used this medium extensively, urging upon women the need to economise and suggesting ways to stretch rations and save fuel.

Because of the restrictions on printing, magazines inevitably became a scarce commodity for which there was an insatiable demand. Every available copy enjoyed multiple readership, and the editorial teams who worked long hours with skeleton staffs under extremely difficult conditions to maintain an unbroken record of issues, sowed the seeds which were to bear fruit by the million in peace-time. The content of these war-time publications was remarkable for the practical ingenuity shown in all departments of home service. Women were told how to make 'fruit' flans with carrots and brassières out of lace curtains (good for upholding morale if nothing else), but more important even than this, they were encouraged and supported in the darkest days of deprivation and destruction by the buoyant cheerfulness, understanding and good-will which characterised the editorial approach throughout.

As a result, the magazines established themselves more firmly than ever before both as all-purpose household manuals and as valued friends, ready with a listening ear and sympathetic, sound advice in the non-material as well as the material areas of everyday living. Close ties of friendship, not to say dependence, were forged during the war between the women's magazines and their readers, most of whom were discovering for the first time what it meant to be fully responsible for their families in the absence of their menfolk. These ties remained strong, and with the coming of peace and the gradual return to normal life contributed to the build-up of a mass readership in the post-war era.

It was some time after the war before the magazine industry could resume normal working conditions and meet the vastly increased demand for women's periodicals. Quota restrictions prevented the free play of market forces, and since the allocation of paper was fixed in proportion to pre-war circulation, the effect was to freeze sales in their earlier pattern, and inhibit growth. Over the economy as a whole, the years immediately following the war were occupied with an all-out export drive, with the government urging upon the nation the vital need to get industry back into full production for the sake of foreign earnings. This had first priority, and the shops remained empty of all but 'utility' * items. Rations were reduced still further, as the British people responded to a call for help from Europe where the food situation was reputed to be far worse. The only luxury goods which found their way on to the home market carried the increasingly familiar label 'export reject'.

The shortage of consumer goods severely limited the scope for advertising. Manufacturers had to be content with keeping brand names before the public in readiness for the time when their products could be released for home consumption. The amount of advertising space available to them in the women's press was in any case strictly limited. Thus the proportion of advertising carried by women's magazines remained relatively small and consisted of short messages underlining the persistence of war-time scarcity and war-time priorities. To give but three examples:†

'Among the pleasures of future peaceful days will be delicious cakes and puddings made with Turban mixed fruit . . . back in the shops as soon as conditions permit.'

'Please leave Scott's for the children and invalids—they have first claim to it.'

'Back in my own home at last. All ready for the moment when I can get an Acme.'

* Goods carrying the distinctive Government mark denoting quality control.
† *Source:* issues of *Housewife*, 1946.

Instead of stimulating consumption, manufacturers were constantly having to request their customers to 'use sparingly', or warn them that certain products were available only 'in permitted areas'. The Government was one of the biggest advertisers at this time, its communications ranging from appeals to have children immunised, through hints on how to take care of the new man-made 'wonder' fabric, Nylon, to explanations for the delays in train services.

The enforced containment of spending and the consequent limitation of the scope for advertising left magazine Editors free to concentrate on meeting the needs of their women readers unhampered by commercial considerations. Quoting James Drawbell, *Woman's Own*'s post-war Editor:

'None of the extraneous attractions which had bedevilled newspaper and magazine readers in pre-war days—the free gifts, competitions and the like—were there to get in the way of the clear message that the magazine sought to convey. This was the great time, and it would last only a few years, when magazines would sell solely on their reader value. It was a journalist's dream. We could plan our magazine as a magazine, un-baited with counter-attractions. It was the quality of the editorial, in fact, which in those early days caused the magazine revolution to happen, creating a vast new industry.'

Though their functions were in many respects the same as they are today, the magazines of 1946 differed markedly in character from contemporary women's publications. They can be divided into four groups: the story weeklies, the home-service weeklies of early vintage, their modern, mass-circulation competitors, and the higher-class ('quality') monthlies comprising fashion, home-service and 'Society' journals.

The first group, of which *The Miracle* and *My Weekly* were typical, consisted mainly of fiction, supplemented with beauty advice, occasional dress-making patterns, and a page of personal problems. The fiction was written to the usual formula: hate and revenge vied with passion and intrigue in fulfilling the expectations of sin and shame inspired in readers' minds by lurid title-pages. A new trend was evident, however. Mixed in with the rest were stories with strong human interest, often both amusing and well-written. The illustrations, too, were less crude and blatant than in the past. Both indicated the beginnings of a move away from the sensational, escapist literature of pre-war times and a new interest in real-life drama, a change which eventually drove this entire class of periodicals out of existence.

It indicated the emergence of a new group, the adolescent teenagers, whose modes of life, needs and interests were very different from those of young people of the pre-war period. Poverty and an early school-leaving age made men and women of fourteen-year-olds in the 'twenties and 'thirties. Leaping from childhood to maturity almost in the time it took them to find a job, young people were denied their period of adjustment. Not until after the war did society begin to discover that they had problems, and that adolescence could be a crucial time during which they needed the greatest possible help, tolerance and understanding from their elders.

Involved in the harsh realities of bread-winning, the pre-war genera-tion of young women needed to escape into a fantasy world which mirrored their repressed dreams of romance and riches, and fulfilled inner yearnings for thrills and adventure, the residues of childhood. But girls in the post-war era were increasingly likely to experience a measure of all of these in the normal course of everyday living. So the pulp weeklies which had catered adequately to the leisure-starved mill-girl and housemaid gradually went into decline. They survived longest in the industrial North and in Scotland, where traditions die harder and social changes are slower to penetrate. But even here, they steadily gave way to a collection of 'teenage weeklies' geared to the demands of the teenager in a more prosperous, leisured and liberal society.

Four magazines, *Home Chat*, *Woman's Friend*, *Woman's Weekly* and *Woman and Home* (which, having little in common with the 'quality' monthlies, competed rather with the weeklies), were typical of the second group of publications, the old-style 'service' periodicals, staid and faded-looking beside the slick new gravure weeklies, but still very popular. The last two mentioned were the 'giants' of the women's press before *Woman* and *Woman's Own* broke all previous circulation records. All four provided household guidance, but their coverage, though sound, was superficial and limited. Their appeal was rather to the older woman at home, with a resulting bias towards knitting and fiction, which classed them primarily as magazines of entertainment and relaxation.

This class of magazines prospered late into the 'fifties, most of them far longer than their limited scope merited, but they were kept afloat by the boom which followed the lifting of war-time restrictions, during which the reading public was far less selective than in later years. Their sustained appeal was also in large measure due to their special editorial approach. They never put pressure upon their readers, nor caused them to feel inadequate by setting clinically high standards. They were as comfortable and comforting as the woollies they encouraged their readers to knit, and exactly suited the needs of the older generation of women who rarely escaped from the confines of the home, finding their pleasures and relaxations within it—making something for the latest grandchild, or stealing the odd half-hour to put their feet up with 'a nice tale'.

At the same time such magazines served throughout to reinforce the basic philosophy which the majority of women seem to share. Whether enshrined in the 'Parson's Corner', or wafted abroad from the redolent briar of 'The Man-Who-Sees', these commonly held beliefs helped to create the intangible bond which linked them so closely with their readers. In addition to the homespun philosophising, they carried a high proportion of knitting and sentimental fiction. The importance of these last ingredients is indicated by the fact that Miss 'Biddy' Johnson, who later built *Woman's Weekly*, *Woman and Home* and *My Home* into mass-selling periodicals, once undertook to give *Woman's Weekly* (then failing) a new lease of life, provided she was given a free hand in these two areas.

In contrast to these older magazines, the new gravure weeklies were modern and dynamic in their appearance and outlook. Despite the limitations within which they had to work, they set new standards of service, laying the foundations for the comprehensive coverage they were to offer in later years. James Drawbell, recruited by Newnes to revitalise *Woman's Own*, describes his immediate post-war objectives:

'Very simply, I wanted to produce cheap magazines which would look anything but cheap, and which would provide colour, entertainment, escape (yes, escape!), understanding and reassurance to women, with contents of a higher literary and artistic quality than had been offered to them before in this medium.'[2]

Both *Woman* and *Woman's Own* placed great emphasis on 'reader-identification' as a cardinal principle in publishing for women, but both were now aiming at a far younger readership than that served by the older weeklies. At a time when rival publications were building their success on appealing to the older age-groups, they deliberately set out to woo young women. Mr Harris Kamlish, ex-Advertisement Director at Odhams, explains why:

'It was recognised that the younger women of Britain were becoming buyers over a longer period as the result of the expanding horizons of their lives. They were becoming business-women with ever-increasing buying power, and more freedom in spending what they earned on clothes, entertainment, travel and so on. But though advertisers were quick to realise the commercial significance of these new trends in terms of new markets, they were initially suspicious of the new medium being offered them.'*

While it was the job of the Advertising Departments to sell the gravure weeklies to advertisers, it was the task of their Editors to build up large and loyal readerships. The success story of *Woman* since the war, achieved through the instinctive personal flair of Mary Grieve and the co-ordinated efforts of the editorial team she trained and headed, is now almost legendary. The magazine's immediate appeal to a growing mass readership was based on her recognition of the importance of identifying with readers and establishing close ties with them. In her own words:

'This close contact with the reader has been our gold-mine since the first journals for ladies made their genteel début to the present day. This, more than anything else enabled us to forge ahead as soon as unrestricted circulations became available in the 'fifties.'[3]

This policy of 'reader-identification' translated into practical terms called for continual alertness and rigorous editorial discipline, in fact 'a deliberate daily and hourly effort to remember . . . readers' circumstances'.[4] For example, 'no advice on personal hygiene could include a casual reference to a daily bath'.[4] To forge an even closer link with readers, features such as the 'letter page' were started, which opened up a channel of communication through which women could exchange the fascinating trivia of everyday life, with the bonus of a small monetary reward. The 'letter page' has since become one of the most popular features in women's magazines; the average reader turns to it first, and then to the 'problem page'. It is also a valuable editorial guide; but the correspondence column, such a lively section of the eighteenth-century women's journals, had to wait a long time for its potentialities to be re-discovered.

Mary Grieve's achievements for *Woman* were matched by those of James Drawbell at *Woman's Own*. In little more than a decade he transformed an unexceptional 24-page weekly, selling 670,000 copies, into a competitive, 100-page 'service' magazine with a peak circulation

* Personal interview.

of over $2\frac{1}{2}$ million. His editorial approach was in many ways similar to that of Mary Grieve. As with her, 'reader-identification' was a prime consideration, and he shared her concern to meet the innermost needs of women: their desire to be wanted, understood and appreciated. But he also wanted to put them in touch with 'that exciting, outer world', to surprise them with the novel and unexpected. In his own phrase, he wanted them to 'have a ball'.

The new *Woman's Own* he envisaged would bring 'new prestige to the women's magazine world'. In the grim post-war atmosphere of devastation and shortages it would be

'. . . like a party, filled with colour, lifted from the everyday with attractive, intelligent, well-known men and women moving through its pages, and filled, not with the old-fashioned fiction suitable for the cabbie's wife, but with the popular writers of the times.'[5]

In pursuit of this ideal, he drew upon all available talent. His editorial team was carefully chosen to give fair representation to the regions, where people 'lived, thought, ate, [also dressed] and worked differently', and was deliberately composed of equal numbers of men and women. In addition, he established a close association with leading Continental and American women's magazines, frequently introducing American techniques and American material. At a time when commercial art was still widely regarded as disreputable in this country, he imported the work of American illustrators to achieve a greater degree of reader-identification with the magazine's fiction. By 1949, other magazines were following his example and were vigorously competing for American contributions.

The range of topics covered in the newer mass weeklies did not depart significantly from the traditional scope of women's magazines. The differences they showed were mainly an increase in reader-participation, greater expertise, and improvements in presentation, chiefly the introduction of colour photography, 'which began as a thin trickle in 1945'. Defending this conservatism, Mary Grieve explains:

'In holding the interest week after week of almost every second woman in the country, it was inevitable that *Woman* should concentrate on those interests which are generally held, rather than on minority interests. And sad though it is, there are fewer women strongly drawn to subjects like equal pay and racial problems than to practical skills, personal relationships, and increased self-confidence. . . . It is true, too, that the tremendous advances in colour printing inevitably fostered this policy of concentration on practical and visual appeal.'[6]

By contrast, the monthly section of the women's press was looking very different in 1946. As always, the traditional home subjects were treated at greater length and in greater depth than they were elsewhere, *Everywoman*, *Good Housekeeping*, *Housewife* and *Woman's Journal* being the leading magazines in this field. *Good Housekeeping*, long renowned for its intelligent approach to housewifery, still made the most thorough-going attempt of all to educate women in the domestic arts, centred on its Institute. *Everywoman*, too, justified its claim to be 'The Practical Home Magazine', giving advice in all departments in a manner which was helpful, friendly, and authoritative. *Housewife* covered similar ground (equally effectively, judging by its extensive and lively correspondence) though it placed more emphasis on mothercraft. *Woman's Journal*'s appeal was more decorative than practical, and fiction was still its strongest feature. But in response to post-war needs, its coverage of home subjects was gradually increasing, and it was soon devoting space to entirely new themes, such as 'How to Economise'.

Thus the monthlies at this time were still providing the best home-service coverage that the women's press could offer, and their supremacy in this area was to remain unchallenged until the mass-weeklies, freed from a restricting 48-page limit, began to swell to outsize proportions and devote more space to home topics. But, in addition to their domestic content, the monthlies carried large amounts of 'general interest' material including controversial discussions and informative articles on many subjects which Miss Grieve would have expected to interest only a minority of women. This type of content has now largely disappeared from the women's press, for reasons which will be discussed later, yet it was one of the most striking ingredients of the monthly periodicals in 1946. Miss Grieve has observed that, at this time, 'The monthly magazine *Everywoman* [was] launching on a policy of thought-provoking contents under a new editor'.[7] This was by no means an isolated occurrence, for at this stage in its evolution the frontiers of modern women's journalism were being pushed right back.

Starting with the 'quality' section of the market, a new spirit and a new approach, evoked in response to the demands of war and carried over into the peace-time emergency, began to permeate the women's press. During the war women grew in responsibility, resilience and vigour. They discovered at first hand the social condition of Britain and encountered many of her social problems, something they had not had the opportunity to do when their world was contained within the four walls of home. As in the nineteenth century, when gentlewomen, bent on dispensing charity to the poor, came face to face with the festering slums which they had scarcely known existed, so women of the middle and upper-middle classes a century later had their eyes opened to prevailing social needs, and responded similarly. In the words of a 'demobbed' ATS girl, 'Such experiences carry one forward to good citizenship, which does not allow of aimless, introvert living', and it was the widening of the concern of intelligent women to encompass issues and problems which had formerly been considered outside their sphere which was the prevailing characteristic of the monthlies in 1946.

Illustrating this widening editorial range, in *Good Housekeeping* there appeared articles on women prisoners, parents and the new Education Act, adoption, the population problem, social science, and one which revealed an awakening social conscience, 'What is bad in our social system and what can we . . . do about it?' *Everywomen* introduced a feature entitled 'This changing world—facts to set you talking', among them statistics on the extent to which the nation's health had been damaged by war. *Housewife* ran articles on new schools, women MPs, children's playgrounds, and starvation in Europe, as well as a piece on the American way of life and a critical item, 'What's wrong with the Welfare?'.

Most of these articles were carefully reasoned, buoyant, and stimulating. Many of them sparked off lively correspondence from women who showed themselves keenly interested in these extra-domiciliary questions, as interested as they were in acquainting themselves with the latest medical and dietary knowledge, and the newest theories in the psychology of child-rearing. In this they were apparently for once in advance of the rest of society. Mary Grieve recalls that 'a very forthright and explicit article on birth-control' published in *Everywoman* was condemned by the Archbishop of Canterbury, and Lord Southwood consequently issued a new policy statement:

> 'While we must be up-to-date, and if anything in advance of the times, we must not be *too* much in advance. . . . When the schools put this subject in their curriculum, it will then be time for us to deal with it in our paper.'[8]

indicating that, in his view at least, society had not progressed very far beyond the stage when women were legally classed with children and lunatics.

The contrast between these journals and the 'downmarket' weeklies, where such articles as those described above could never have appeared, where 'the whole vocabulary of dietetics . . . was unknown' and 'The world of psychology did not exist',[9] shows how marked the differences between classes still were, in terms of education at least, and how vast and how swift was the social revolution yet to come. It shows too, that the women's press was still sufficiently diversified for economic health, with the monthlies in a strong position. Equally important, editors had complete freedom to compile their magazines as they saw fit, reflecting their readers' lives fully and accurately, and balancing 'service' with 'general interest', not fearing to be controversial where they judged this to be appropriate. A good deal of their attention was claimed by the social and economic problems associated with the readjustment to normal living: assimilating the home-comers, rebuilding some relationships, breaking others, coming to terms with a contraction of role, coping with even more stringent rationing and general economic hardship, and clearing away the débris of wrecked homes and shattered lives.

Material problems were the simplest to overcome. With few goods in the shops, how could a young married couple set up house? *Housewife* threw down a challenge to their determination and ingenuity in using 'a combination of utility units, antiques and secondhand pieces', which, it claimed, could be extremely effective when properly grouped, going on to show how. Were there any substitutes for meat on the lunch-table? *Everywoman* suggested 'leek turnovers'; for soap? Again the household expert came up with some ideas. *The Lady* foresaw deeper problems, such as preventing women from buying unwisely when restrictions were finally lifted. It also feared for younger girls who had had no experience in budgeting and saving.

All the magazines continued to respond magnificently to requests for ways of making rations and coupons stretch. They advised about maintenance and repairs at home, provided instructions for making what could not be bought, and gave news of such goods as were becoming available. But material reconstruction was but a small part of the story, as *The Lady* pointed out:

> ' "Housewife, how are your cooker, your radio, your clothes, and all your other possessions? Keep them in good repair for they cannot easily be replaced." For so long now we have listened to those refrains and gratefully and conscientiously we have followed the advice of the experts who chanted them. With the end of the war, however, we seem to be concentrating much more on the condition of persons than on the condition of things . . . we have become alarmingly conscious of how worn people's nerves are, how frayed their tempers and how dim their hopes. . . .'[10]

Apart from the run-down condition of the population, which was growing daily more apparent, the correspondence to the magazine counsellors revealed grave new problems which threatened the stability of family life. The most serious of these were created by the return of the fighting forces and their preconceived notions about what they would find. This problem was encountered by women of all classes. In the cheap weeklies it was reflected in the fiction:

'I'm going back, [he said] as all men want to go back . . . simple, ordinary men to ordinary wives.'[11]

Elsewhere it was a recurrent topic in the advice columns. Just as in 1918, men were coming back home wanting to find things very much as they had left them, and expecting to take up the threads of family and business life where they had left them off. They were confused and resentful to find that women stood in their way. A fiction-writer described the reactions of one man, who was typical of thousands:

'Charles was silent. The resentment which had been smouldering within him since he returned home rose up again. The sense of inferiority which had caught him as soon as he'd seen what a fine job Janice had made of things, deepened. He was no good. He wasn't needed. A woman, his own wife, stood in his shoes and they seemed to fit her well.'[12]

A correspondent to *Everywoman* put the point of view of wives who had become accustomed to full and useful lives during the war and who found themselves largely redundant afterwards. She wrote to the magazine asking for help in developing 'outside interests':

'I am one of the many women whose husbands have returned from the forces, and who suddenly find themselves without the crowding activities forced upon them during the war. . . . Now that I am solely a housewife again, I am finding life very quiet.'[13]

This was one woman who reverted to a limited domestic role, not without difficulty, but without complaint. Others found the question of whether a wife could—or should—'become once more the "little woman"—sweetly dependent, charmingly helpless" much more difficult to resolve. As in 1918, when a similar situation faced them, women stood at the cross-roads. They could either consolidate and further their war-time gains of improved status and wider social participation, or allow themselves to be ushered back to the domestic hearth and reassume their sovereignty over the more traditional woman's kingdom.

The magazines were sympathetic but failed to sound the call to advance, at least as far as married women were concerned. They were more definite in their support of single women returning home, whose problems were no less severe, but whose needs were almost forgotten in the general concern to help in the readjustment of ex-servicemen. Loneliness, after the *camaraderie* of life in the Forces, was one problem. Also, there were the difficulties of gaining social acceptance in civilian life for modes of behaviour which had grown up out of necessity in the Services, and which were perpetuated after demobilisation. *The Lady* provided one example:

'The attitude of women of all classes to the "local" has had to be adjusted in the war years. Girls in the services, away from home, have learned to use the public houses and to go to them with men friends in a decorous way, and it is unlikely that when these girls marry or get into civilian employment again they will be willing to forego [these] cheerful meetings.'[14]

Then there were the problems of the single girls who had never been to war, but who were having to cope with the moral aftermath, working out new codes of behaviour appropriate to the changed times, very often with no one to guide them. Many of them turned to the women's periodicals for help. A century before, girls of the same age were begging editors to pass judgement on their calligraphy; in 1946, they were becoming concerned with the ramifications of 'doing wrong' before marriage, the first time the problems of courtship had been discussed so unreservedly in the women's press. They presaged the coming moral revolution and they did not pass unnoticed. One reader wrote:

'The seriousness of the problems which young people send to Mary Grant* astonishes me. They have become—sometimes through no fault of their own—involved in complicated situations which would embarrass much older and more experienced folk. Let's hope a return to peace will slacken the neck-break tempo at which we have lived during the past five years, and that growing up will once more become a delightful and less dangerous period.'[15]

The personal problems produced by the aftermath of war caught many people without their traditional sources of help, either because families and friends were scattered, or because some difficulties could

---

* *Woman's Own*'s counsellor.

only be confided to an outsider. Typical of the latter was the situation of a young girl who wrote: 'I was very foolish while my husband was away, and now am mother of a baby girl.' A clear sign of the strain on personal relationships resulting from war-time separations was the increasing coverage given by the higher-class journals to the question of divorce. Another frequent subject of discussion was the question, 'Can we afford children, and if so, how many?' On these and a variety of other problems the magazines offered sound, practical advice.

But in one important area of counselling, namely women's employment, the women's magazines acquiesced in a regressive tendency and later used their influence positively to discourage women from trying to combine work and marriage. In this they were doing no more than reinforce the traditional view of a woman's role, but as a result of the war, and women's part in it, the time was propitious for a radical redefinition of that role to encompass fuller citizenship and wider social participation. Many women were willing for their new social position to become permanent; others, with a little encouragement, might have come to share their views. But the traditionalist camp was strong, and it found a sympathetic mouthpiece in the women's press, particularly the popular weeklies. *My Weekly* reflected the conflict in its fiction, and came down firmly on the side of domesticity. In the words of one of its fictional heroines, 'I've spent a week discovering I'd rather be Mrs Peter Grant, housewife, than Rosamund Fuller, dress designer'.[16] Nevertheless, in its advice columns it did try to discourage girls from dismissing employment as a mere stopgap between school and marriage, though in advising them to put thoughts of romance to the back of their minds and concentrate on their jobs, it stressed only the value of such experience in preparing them for wife-hood, ignoring completely the benefits of some form of training as a stepping-stone to economic independence and a fuller life.

While it was now considered desirable that women should have some interests outside the home, the war having widened horizons which would never again be entirely closed, this did not extend to the cultivation and use of abilities other than those required to fit a girl to be a wife and mother, except for a minority of women. Married women were able to work as long as the emergency lasted, but when the men came home, pressures to conform to the pre-war pattern of family life were so strong that few women could resist them. In any case, their competitive position in the labour market was weak, since as far as employers were concerned, male workers had first claim upon all available posts.

By contrast, American women who had not been called upon to assume a masculine role during the war, were apparently in revolt against the erosion of the traditional privileges of the female. According to *The Lady*:

'In the American women's press, a distinct uneasiness about the present day attitude of the formerly attentive American man is to be discerned. During the war, the soldiers have been petted and the women tough and capable, but now a back-to-the-pedestal movement is called for. The campaign will be well-backed by American advertisers who cannot calmly accept an era in which American men cease saying it with flowers, diamonds, perfume, motor-cars and other merchandise. The movement need not be taken too humorously by English women. If men and women fail to take their traditional positions in the dance of life, only a greater dullness is achieved.'[17]

There was double significance in this statement. Not only was the Editor weighing in on the side of the traditionalists, but she was anticipating the intervention of commercial interests in support of them, too. The trend back to the home was already in full swing in Britain, though it was by no means universally welcomed. The question was, would we in Britain experience similar advertising pressures to those being mounted in America, to enforce it? The 'fifties provided the answer.

A final quotation from *Good Housekeeping* must be recorded. It sums up the challenge and the opportunities which confronted women in 1946, and it shows the reaction of one of the few magazines to recognise and accept that challenge on behalf of its readers. Moreover, it emphasises the kind of social influence that a women's magazine is capable of exerting (if free and willing to do so) in favour of progress and in defiance of conformity:

'... if we are to survive as a nation, Britain will have to allow our women as well as our men to use their energy and ability. Before the war, we wasted an enormous amount of the energy of women ... [in homes that were] old-fashioned, badly-planned and ill-equipped with labour-saving devices. [There was] the frustration and waste of energy when capable women could not find the right outlet for their capacity. . . . "Suburban neurosis" was the name invented by the doctors to describe the state of those women who left their jobs to marry and then found themselves lonely and cut off from their old interests, so that they passed from a state of near boredom to actual illness. There was the frustration, too, of the older married woman whose children had grown up and left home, so that she found herself in her forties with the sense that she was no longer needed and with no constructive outlet for her capabilities. Many such women . . . did find an outlet in voluntary service and local government work . . . but too many others drifted from bridge to the cinema . . . in restless dissatisfaction.

'The needs of the war changed the picture. . . . Prejudices, customs and traditions restricting women's employment were thrust aside. Women were drafted into practically every type of job and with a minimum of training, did remarkably well . . . the country could not afford to be deprived of the services of any efficient citizen for any artificial reason. Part-time schemes for the employment of married women were organised with considerable ingenuity. To many of these women it was a revitalising experience.

'Yet now that the war is over, some people seem to think that women should go back to just the kind of jobs they did before the war and accept once more the same old artificial reasons and limitations. To my mind that would be disastrous. . . . We women must assume the responsibility of making our full contribution in the field for which our personal capacity fits us. Many women will rightly choose marriage and motherhood and feel that under present conditions the making of a home and bringing up young children is a job to which they *wish* to give the whole of their time. Others, many of whom are professional women, wish to combine marriage and motherhood with at least a part-time career . . . we do need an adequate supply of women with first-class qualifications to serve on policy-forming bodies. . . . If we can carry forward into the future the spirit of individual efficiency shown by British women in the war years, then we need not fear the problems of tomorrow.'[18]

(ii) The Restrictions are Lifted: 1951–56

Five years after peace was declared Britain was still struggling to get back on economic terms with the rest of the world. The emphasis continued to be on producing goods for export, and 1951, which marked the centenary of The Great Exhibition, provided an ideal opportunity to stage a successor, The Festival of Britain, intended as a money-spinning shop-window for British goods and skills. In an all-out effort to recover our world-wide manufacturing prestige, we dressed that window with our most seductive wares, swept the hideous débris of war as far out of sight as possible, and threw open the door to customers and visitors from all over the world.

On the South Bank the Skylon symbolised the birth of a new, forward-looking Britain, and the Dome of Discovery housed more tangible signs of it. Luxury goods flooded on to the market giving the foreigner a misleading impression of affluence, for the only homes they found their way into were those of a new and rising group which *Vogue* styled 'the expense-account rich'. Behind this façade lurked the sterner realities of general scarcity and a sharp rise in the cost of living. Rationing was still in force and there was a severe housing shortage. Britain might be in the mood for celebrating, but it was a celebration on a shoestring, and for the average woman there was no remission in the struggle to make ends meet in the face of rising prices.

Nevertheless, production was fast returning to its pre-war level, even if the home market received only a limited proportion of it. This was evident from the substantial increase in the amount of advertising carried by the periodical press. A general sharpening of competition between the larger firms was indicated by their use of more subtle techniques verging on 'the psychological sell', in other words, an implied or direct appeal to the emotional drives, as in the following examples taken from various women's magazines:

> "The perfume that murmurs, "Love me!" ' ; 'It's an odd house where there's no Oxo'; 'All the best people use P & B wool'; 'You wonderful woman! That's what he'll say when you serve shepherd's pie cooked in a Pyrex casserole.'

Advertisers were now beginning to use as selling levers both the desire for security and the wish for self-advancement and personal success. Some exploited class consciousness; others, personal glamour, and many were beginning to employ what E. S. Turner has called 'word-magic',[19] a powerful mesmerising agent. In the mass weeklies, the ratio of advertising matter to editorial content averaged 50 : 50, but the range of products featured was limited mainly to foodstuffs, cleaning agents and cosmetics. All 'luxury' advertising (consumer durables, jewellery, model clothes, etc.) was carried by the 'quality' monthlies.

By 1951, the magazines themselves were beginning to take on a new look. All had increased in size following the de-restriction of newsprint in March, 1950. *Woman* and *Woman's Own* had doubled their number of pages, from 20 in 1946 to around 40 in 1951, and developments in colour photography put them still further ahead of their rivals in standards of presentation. There was a growing emphasis on visual techniques as a result of these technical advances, and photographs were gradually replacing artists' drawings as the main form of illustration. The proportion of colour work, though increasing, was still small, however. Editorially, the growth of separate departments, each responsible for a particular service area and staffed by experts, was becoming more marked, together with a greater degree of professionalism in the treatment of all topics.

The composition of the women's press showed little change. In 1949, the National Magazine Co. brought out a new fashion monthly for younger women, *Vanity Fair*, one of the first attempts to reach the expanding 'Teen-and-Twenty' market. *Vanity Fair* succeeded where an earlier teenage magazine, *Mayfair*, failed, because in the short space of three years advertisers had become much more firmly convinced of the existence of a potentially rich market amongst the younger age-groups. Also, the magazine aimed at a much wider social grouping, and was additionally fortunate in having the experience of a large and successful parent company to draw upon.

All the women's periodicals had substantially increased their sales since 1946, the weeklies showing the greatest expansion. Circulations had risen sharply with the increased capacity of the women's press to satisfy pent-up demand, but the continuing shortage of paper effectively curbed this expansion, once again freezing sales at an artificially low level. *Woman* and *Woman's Own* remained the unchallenged leaders in the weekly section of the market, while *Woman and Home* was still the largest-selling monthly. In 1951, however, almost without exception, the women's magazines began to lose circulation. For one or two, this trend became noticeable in 1950, but for the remainder, the drop in sales occurred during the second half of 1951. Because the fall was widespread, it was most probably associated with the general need to economise as a result of rising prices, aggravated by a national loss in confidence following the political upheavals of that year. The majority of magazines more than recouped their losses within a year or two, but for a few, already living on borrowed time in a sellers' market, this loss of continuity was a blow from which they never fully recovered, and they went on losing readers until they were finally driven out of print.

An important feature of the magazines of 1951 was a definite new preoccupation with the welfare of the family, and, closely allied to it, the treatment of domestic subjects in greater detail at the expense of 'general interest' and discussion features. *Good Housekeeping* was the only magazine other than *The Lady** to retain an outward-looking

---

* *The Lady*, in order to qualify for registration as a newspaper, entitling it to postal concessions, was obliged to include a fixed minimum of news and comment.

opinion feature. At the same time it considerably expanded its 'service' section by instituting a 'Family Centre', a feature which was given the widest possible terms of reference to cover all aspects of family life, including physical and mental adjustment, problems connected with marital relationships which might have a bearing upon the stability of the family, child care, and a 'good neighbour' service giving whatever practical information might be needed in the day-to-day running of a home, from shopping hints to etiquette. The Centre also ran its own showrooms where readers could come to see patterns and designs made up, receive guidance and obtain informative literature. This was an unparalleled attempt to provide a comprehensive and co-ordinated family service of a kind available through no other channel. *Everywoman* also ran a home-service centre, more limited in scope, but including an interesting new series, 'Human Problems of Today', dealing with sexual disharmony, the 'other woman', divorce, and many other problems disruptive of family life. *Woman's Journal*, too, had considerably expanded its home-making articles, giving particular emphasis to home-decorating and furnishing.

The old-style journals, *Woman's Weekly*, *Woman and Home* and *Home Chat* among others, seemed to be marking time compared with their competitors. They continued to deal sympathetically with readers' problems, but they seldom pushed out into the deeper waters of the serious difficulties encountered in courtship and marriage which other magazines were at long last beginning to tackle. Their fiction, too, continued to be purely escapist, ignoring the trend towards real-life situations evident elsewhere in the women's press. They were still basically magazines for the older woman, while the newer weeklies were slanting their content more and more towards younger readers.

Some new items indicated the progressive widening of magazine content, for instance, sports-coaching, home entertaining, careers, and 'life' articles by well-known writers, but still heading the popularity ratings were features on the Royal Family, and knitting. Medical articles, too, were compulsive reading for the majority, the introduction of the National Health Service having stimulated greater health consciousness. Dispensing medical advice was, in fact, becoming an important function of the women's magazines, the value of which can be estimated from letters such as the following, showing many a woman's need for reassurance in this area:

'I realise how difficult it is for overworked doctors to find time to explain whys and wherefores to their patients, but ignorance about our illnesses means that we are subjected to many unnecessary fears. In this respect, your "Doctor's Diary" is doing a very good job in giving us information difficult to obtain elsewhere.'[20]

In addition, many of the women's periodicals were beginning to make provision for teenagers. *Woman* included a special 'teen-page' for their benefit, and *Everywoman* carried a spread called 'Junior Fair', featuring fashion and furnishing ideas for young people. Even *Good Housekeeping* had begun to give advice to girls in bed-sitters.

In all these ways, the magazines had extended their scope by 1951. They were dealing with a wider range of subjects and treating them in greater depth, but this expansion paradoxically represented a fundamental narrowing of their viewpoint, a development closely associated with the new emphasis on home life already referred to. Woman's sphere was returning to its pre-war limits, and the social role of women was again becoming primarily domestic. The trend was confirmed, and frequently encouraged, by the women's press, partly in the general contraction of content in favour of increasing emphasis on the home, and partly through the opinions and advice given in the course of editorial comment and counselling.

A woman's proper role, and whether or not employment outside the home for married women was consistent with it, was frequently discussed. There was an interesting division of views. *Miracle*'s counsellor, advising on the difficulties encountered when a wife went out to work, had this to say:

'One thing remains, the wife's ability to do *two* jobs. Many can do them and find that the stimulation of a job outside the home makes them all the more delightful as wife and mother in it. The secret lies in a cheerful approach and the ability not to worry over non-essentials, with husband and children lending a hand.'[21]

Almost at the same time, *The Lady* reported on a meeting of the Women's Freedom League, held in conjunction with the Status of Women Committee, during which 'the critics of women who aim to combine marriage with a career were ably disposed of', an outcome which the magazine clearly approved, adding that 'It was a great loss to the nation when women with an expensive training were not allowed to use it after marriage'. These, and other comments revealed a striking measure of agreement between the top and bottom strata of magazine readership.

The mass weeklies, representing the swelling 'undistributed middle' classes of society, took the opposite line. Time and again they positively discouraged married women from trying to combine the roles of wife and worker, both directly and indirectly. A *Woman* reader wrote to the problem page to say that, having returned to the job she had before marriage and then given it up, she advised mothers not to try and take up work outside the home. Evelyn Home, *Woman's* adviser, replied:

'No two women have exactly the same capacities and I would never interfere with the right of the minority to prefer outside work. But it is safe to say that most women, once they have a family, are more contented and doing better work in the home than they could find outside it.'[22]

And elsewhere she commented:

'To almost every woman her work comes first too—the work of home-making and husband-tending.'

The same point was frequently made, indirectly, through fiction. *Woman's Weekly*, for example, ran a short story which played out the harrowing drama of a wife who went out to work (unwillingly) because her family needed money. Her children soon accused her of not being 'a proper mother', believing that her sole and selfish motive in taking a job was 'to express herself'. Feeling that her rightful place was with them, she suffered considerably, but eventually the debts were paid. The story ended happily with the mother joyfully relinquishing the work she hated, to be reunited with her 'neglected' family, free at last to devote herself to full-time motherhood—but not before every possible moral had been drawn. A forest of sub-titles reinforced them:

'Home-making is the most useful of all the talents. To make a man feel happy and comfortable and to make a child feel cherished. No Woman's Work is more important than these.'

Likewise, *Home Chat's* never-failing message was home and family first, last, and all the time. Home was the unquestioned territory of the 'little woman', and the 'perfect wife' was the one who ran that home happily and efficiently, attending to her husband's and her children's creature comforts, and dispensing never-failing love and sympathy. But she must not be too efficient, for, as another piece of situation fiction illustrated, a woman could alienate her husband by seeming too capable and fostering in him destructive feelings of inferiority; at all costs a man must be allowed his status as the head of the household. For those

readers who wished to see how far they measured up to this image of
'The Perfect Wife', *Home Chat* ran its own questionnaire, which provided a highly revealing insight into the social criteria of success in
wife-hood prevailing as late as 1951.*

In *My Weekly*, too, the value of home and family life was continually stressed, not in the form of a deliberate challenge to those still
favouring a wider role for women, but rather through a built-in bias
compounded of beliefs inextricably woven into the fabric of the lives
of the older generation of working-class women. These beliefs were
mostly taken for granted, and, as an antidote to readers' material deprivations, the Editor frequently reminded them that they possessed something precious, enduring and real in this spiritual inheritance. Each
week she contributed a short essay on how to achieve happiness and
contentment in life, pieces on accepting second best and making it the
best, living in the present, and building dreams only upon solid foundations. Sacrifices were still an inevitable part of the working-class woman's
life after marriage, and there was no attempt to hide the fact. But
sympathy and encouragement could help to soften them, and these
the magazine provided unstintingly. Even the fiction was carefully
written to show understanding and to give moral support, as in this
extract:

> 'In the old days before her marriage she had always been able to
> wear something smart when she met Howard. . . . How things had
> changed! She had been quite prosperous then, with her good
> salary and no-one but herself to spend it on . . . Mary did not
> realise that she looked utterly charming . . . but she did know that
> her clothes were far from new, and the cut was not up to date, and
> that feeling was just a little marring that evening.'[23]

Discontentment with the narrow horizons of home life was always
gently but firmly stifled. The recalcitrant were chided and reminded of
the responsibilities they had voluntarily assumed in marriage, and there
were always 'model' letters from readers who had come to years of
'discretion' to drive the point home. But the dissatisfactions persisted,
and they were significant. One reader hinted at some of them:

> 'Do other women have moments of sheer panic when they think
> of all the places they have never visited, the hundreds of books not
> yet read, the plays, films, ballets and concerts unseen and unheard

---

* See Appendix III.

while they are tied to the sink, ironing board and cooker? I do, but perhaps to be the mother of two lovely little girls like mine is more than adequate compensation for all those other things I'll never be able to do, or see, or have.'

Though she employed a stock rationalisation to tone down what would widely have been regarded as the heresy of her remarks, the writer showed herself unconvinced by it in the revealing use of the word 'perhaps'.

To balance the occasional dissenting voice there were always contributors in plenty representing the accepted point of view. A feature writer in *Woman* considered such deprivations inconsiderable when compared with all the benefits of marriage, particularly an early one: 'People who marry young gain so much that it's a pity, and dangerous, to yearn for the lost years of single blessedness.'[24]

Implied in this, and in many other comments, was a condemnation of the young wife who vaguely felt the need for 'something more' in her life besides the traditionally hallowed and all-sufficing joys of being a wife and mother. Such women were held to be unworthy of their high vocation, and the women's magazines, reflecting attitudes in society at large, generally sought to repress such feelings as being potentially destructive to the stability of the family. Later they were to recognise that, as women's education improved and their social participation widened, marriage was ceasing to be regarded as a totally fulfilling end in itself and becoming a stage in life, a state in which women could profitably develop their personal capacities and pursue new interests. But in 1951, social changes in favour of women's advancement had not begun to be felt. Society was still in the grip of retrogressive trends associated with the psychological aftermath of the war. The concept of the social role proper to women had narrowed considerably compared with 1946, and the weeklies were merely acquiescing in the trend, though their support no doubt helped to strengthen it.

The monthlies were able to take an independent line, since a proportion of their readers at least were in sympathy with a fuller life for women, and a redefinition of the roles of both sexes. *Everywoman*, for example, was an early challenger of the assumption that all domestic work is by definition 'Woman's Work'. In an article headed, 'Mother's Help is Father',[25] it speedily demolished the Victorian husband's argument, still widely used, that 'If I earn the money, it's your job to run the house'. The writer urged the 1951 husband to 'be a man, roll up his sleeves and do his fair share of running the house and family'. Many husbands were said to be sharing already in domestic chores, pointing to a new partnership in home affairs in the higher ranks of society evolving as a result of the dearth of hired help. It was a trend which took much longer to penetrate working-class households where it was still considered wrong to expect a man to help with housework. Cartoons showing a bewildered husband trying ineffectually to cope with the washing-up, and cutting a ridiculous figure in his wife's frilly apron, indicated how strongly held these attitudes still were.

Social pressures were thus responsible for an evident contraction of editorial scope in the mass circulation periodicals of 1951. As yet, commercial influences had not added their weight as architects of magazine content, but the first signs of what was to come were discernible in the women's press at this time. Advertisers were beginning to underline the current image of the ideal wife and exploit it as a selling device. To give two illustrations: the Nestlé Company published a picture of a 'dream wedding', with this supporting copy:

'Yes—but can she cook . . . will she roast bread cubes to drop in your soup?'

a question guaranteed to give food-conscious husbands food for thought, and anxious-to-please wives a clear directive as to the way to their hearts.

A second firm, Bird's Eye, recommended the same means to achieve slightly different ends. One of its advertisements portrayed a shrewd young wife slyly feeding her husband frozen strawberries, for which she was 'rewarded' with an evening at the cinema.

These were mere straws in the wind, but they heralded the onset of an intensive selling campaign directed at women in their roles as housewives and mothers which exploited and consistently reinforced traditional attitudes, and which eventually came to exercise stronger influence than social pressures in the shaping of magazine content.

These developments were only waiting upon the lifting of restrictions on consumption. Rationing ended in 1953, and by 1956 the atmosphere of the women's press had entirely changed. A whole new range of consumer goods were flooding on to the home market and instead of being taught to 'make do and mend', women now needed above all to be shown how to choose wisely amongst a bewildering assortment of unfamiliar products. It was a seller's market, and as Mary Grieve has pointed out, 'there was a real danger of women being taken for a ride by manufacturers only too keen to rush in and sell on different standards of production'. Such women not only needed advice in getting value for their money, they also needed guidance in developing personal taste and critical judgement, having previously had little scope for the exercise of either.

The women's magazines became the trusted advisers of women in this vital area of their lives. The value of the service they provided can be inferred from Mary Grieve's assessment of the challenge which shopping presents to women, and its effect upon their morale:

'A very great part of a woman's life is spent choosing, buying and preparing goods for her own and her family's consumption. . . . An immense amount of her personality is engaged in her function as the selector of goods, and in this she endures many anxieties, many fears. Success in this function is as cheering and vitalising to her as it is to a man in his chosen career, failure as humiliating.'[26]

The level of consumer guidance provided by the magazines was closely geared to the type of reader to which they catered. The monthlies tackled the subject more comprehensively and with greater sophistication than the weeklies, which were still serving the low-income groups. In the monthlies, the emphasis was consistently on the purchase of new goods, particularly consumer durables, and upon interior decoration commissioned from outside. *Housewife* carried a new feature, 'New Ideas in the Shops', a reader enquiry service, various supplements, and an entire series on home decoration designed to be 'an efficient guide' both for intending house-buyers and for those who wished to brighten up existing schemes. *Good Housekeeping* provided an ever more professional guide to all aspects of home management, now including a shopping feature, 'Market Place', and 'do-it-yourself' articles. *The Queen*, following the current trend, introduced a new series 'The Home Today', which offered advice on furnishing and interior design.

Woman's Journal was also giving much greater coverage to home service, running a 'shop-window' for gadgets, appliances and all the latest ideas, an information service, and a special new series of supplements 'designed to appeal to every woman who loves her home and must spend wisely'. In these, the reader was assured:

'you will find everything you want to know about running a house and buying sensibly for the home. Exciting colour scheming, new domestic methods, time-saving gadgets will be shown to you under the inspired and practical guidance of our Home Service Director. Our skilled and experienced team of experts will be ready . . . to answer any questions. This is a unique and invaluable home service which every home-loving woman will want to read and keep by her.'

Similarly, in *Everywoman*, home-making was given considerable prominence, and its editorial pages were filled with illustrations of the latest home equipment and ideas for building and fitting out new houses.

In the mass weeklies, the advice given was more personalised and much simplified. Here the emphasis was not solely on buying. Attention was also given to ways of renovating and refurbishing the existing contents of readers' homes. *Woman* embarked on a programme of collective tutelage intended to encourage greater reader-involvement. The 'Wooden Spoon Club', giving step-by-step cookery lessons was part of this experiment, and it proved highly successful. *Woman's Own*, too, had its school of cooking, as well as a host of other advice features. *Woman and Home* operating at a rather higher socio-economic level, offered its readers the chance to 'learn to cook beautifully with our cordon-bleu expert', but somewhat paradoxically also featured ways of 'furnishing on a shoe-string'.

Lower down the scale, *Woman's Weekly* made its attempt to meet the needs of the times with the addition of 'Cecile's Cookery Class', and 'Housekeeping hints for the young housewife who is something of a beginner', which included advice on organising the household chores, and home nursing, a new departure from the time-honoured 'knitting and fiction' formula. Only *Home Chat** seemed to have made no real attempt to respond to the challenge of prosperity by expanding its content in either range or depth.

Equal attention was being given to expanding personal services. There was a marked increase in the amount of space devoted to beauty, dress, personal hygiene and good manners. The cult of personal glamour was once more getting into full swing, and even the serious-minded *Everywoman* was obliged to bow to public demand with a series revealingly entitled 'How to dress to please men', part of which was devoted to personal grooming because 'He likes you to be soft and silky'. From now on, beauty coverage became increasingly professional, its sole aim being to improve the single girl's chances of capturing a husband. The precipitating factor was most probably the propaganda put out by the cosmetics manufacturers, who let loose upon women a formidable array of persuasive techniques meant to convince them that physical beauty was the most important of all personal assets in securing happiness for life, and one within easy reach of any woman—as near as that magic bar of complexion soap, for instance.

The beauty consultants on the magazines were encouraging but honest in the face of this commercial barrage. They duly initiated their readers into the vital mysteries of expert make-up and showed women

* Of the sample of periodicals analysed.

how to make the best of their natural endowment—even improve on it. They emphasised that most women, with a little time and trouble, could make themselves more physically attractive, and that it was rare indeed for a plain woman to find she had no redeeming feature which she could emphasise to her advantage. Even so, the beauty writers were careful to balance their instructions with a reminder that real beauty came from within and had more to do with character and natural charm than with a perfect figure and chocolate-box prettiness.

With clothing coupons, four-pleat skirts, and 'a choice of black or brown' becoming things of the past, British fashion, too, was enjoying a resurgence which gave women almost unlimited scope for the exercise of dress sense, and the magazines similar scope for helping them cultivate it. The credit for the revolution which divorced British women from the tulle and tweed uniform to which they had so long been wedded, and remarried them to twill and Terylene, belongs to an enterprising industry well supported by the women's press. The fashion monthlies, led by *Vogue*, became the guide books of well-dressed women, and of all women aspiring to the same standards who had more money than taste. There were an increasing number of the latter. The social and economic changes of the post-war years had had their effect upon the composition of the social classes, and as a result of rising incomes and widening educational and social opportunity, many women found themselves pitchforked into a style of life to which they were totally unaccustomed. They looked to the 'glossies', and these magazines grew to be indispensable both as arbiters of taste and as clearing houses for the currency of fashion, culminating in the directive: 'Buy nothing till you buy *Vogue*.'

The comprehensive and detailed service provided by *Vogue* and *Harper's Bazaar* could not be matched by the weeklies, nor was it necessary for them to attempt to do so. Their role was to help women achieve the best possible results on a limited budget: to school them in selecting flattering styles and colours, to teach them correct accessorisation, and to show them how to work out a co-ordinated wardrobe suitable for both work and leisure. This advice had necessarily to be supplemented with articles on home-dressmaking (for which both patterns and fabrics were supplied) for Editors had always to keep in mind their readers' modest circumstances. Whereas in *Vogue* the advice might be, 'Wear blue—fashion decrees it this season', the *Woman* reader would probably be told to 'wear blue—because *he* likes it'.

Side by side with these new educative functions aimed at assisting women unaccustomed to coping with the demands of prosperity, the women's magazines maintained all their usual health and welfare services which expanded commensurately with the interest of the population in these matters. Personal counselling continued to gain in importance. The problems dealt with were fundamentally the same as in previous years, but they were posed and treated with increasing frankness and in greater depth. Human weaknesses such as envy and jealousy were revealed as the underlying causes of much unhappiness in human relationships and were now discussed in separate articles. *Housewife* opted for the preventive approach and published a series on 'The Essentials of Successful Marriage', dealing with aspects as far apart as budgeting and sexual harmony. *Woman's Journal* ran a feature called 'What is the Answer?' in which questions put by readers were answered by 'eminent and distinguished experts'. The subjects ranged from what could be done with a child unhappy at boarding school, through a discussion of ways to inculcate religious beliefs in step-children, to whether or not an unmarried mother should marry the father of her child when she does not love him. Amongst the weeklies, *The Miracle* introduced a problem page for the first time in 1956, while *Woman* decided to investigate for itself one of the factors contributing to family conflict, namely nervous tension in women. The results of this research were embodied in a series which claimed to offer readers 'a wonderful new technique for happy living'.

Among the new problems which had arisen out of the social changes of the post-war years were those connected with teenage adjustment and teenage morality. Letters to magazine counsellors revealed growing tension between parents and adolescents. Parents frequently wrote asking for help in sorting out these difficulties, and there were also letters from young people themselves wanting an independent judgement on the rights and wrongs of their situation, or advice on the perennial problems of courtship, ranging from the desperate plea, 'How can I get a boy-friend?' to the even more desperate one, 'How can I tell them I'm having a baby?' Once married, getting along with in-laws was a recurrent problem. *Housewife* pointed to the causes:

'The widespread rebellion engendered against in-law interference is part of a great cultural change. . . . Probably never before in human history have so few young couples lived with their in-laws. Under the old patriarchal system, it was just taken for granted that, when a girl married, she and her husband would move into the home of his parents and bow to their authority. Today, our new democratic ideas of the family are insisting that the young couple be free and independent, living their own lives in their own way. Since in-laws are often the greatest threat to this freedom, they become the objects of popular resentment and ridicule. The core of the in-law problem is the conflict between two women of different generations brought together by their attachment to one man.'[27]

On the important question of whether or not a wife should work there was a definite hardening of attitudes despite the inescapable social fact that more and more married women were taking up part- or full-time jobs. A reader wrote to *She* asking:

'When many women have to be wage-earners as well as their husbands—has true marriage on such a basis a real chance?'[28]

She received this reply:

'It is better to live less luxuriously perhaps and have proper time to give husband and babies, and to say in truth, ours is a real home and a true marriage.'[29]

Housewife's counsellor, writing in the 'Successful Marriage' series, was against a wife working before her children were sent to school, citing Bowlby's 'maternal deprivation' theory, but felt that afterwards there were equally good arguments for and against it. *Woman's Own* carried an article condemning the working mother, taking as a test-case a letter from a 38-year-old mother of two. It was powerfully and emotively written, and is worth quoting at some length. The reader, Mrs X, was deeply troubled because a friend had cast doubts on her conviction that 'a mother's place was in the home, and that a mother's mind and physical capabilities should be concentrated on her family'. She wondered if her children would suffer 'because she had allowed her life to become so narrow', and whether she should seek other interests, in particular a job, for their sake, even though she had no inclination to do so and did not need extra money or an additional occupation. Monica Dickens had these comments to make:

'I cannot see what else can be more important than your children. To work for them, and play with them, and teach them, and always be there when they need you, is the prime duty of a mother. It does not seem like a duty because it is what a mother wants most of all to do. . . . Will her children love her more if she is an efficient career woman, who pops in and out of the house at intervals, knows a lot of stimulating people, and can talk about everything, except pleasant, trivial day-to-day matters that are the breath of family life? . . . Would you prefer your mother to be always at home looking after you and the others, or do you think you would find her more interesting if she went out and gleaned a whole lot of new ideas and connections that had nothing to do with you? . . . I hope that Mrs X does not go rushing out to look for a job. She is not cheating her children by staying at home. She is giving them the supreme gift—herself. Long after they have left home, they will be grateful to her, and perhaps model their own family life on the example she gave them.'[30]

Home Chat echoed this viewpoint:

'That the husband should be the breadwinner is not just a conventional belief that changing circumstances can set aside. It is a deep-rooted male instinct. Even a marriage partnership on an equal-shares basis goes against the grain. . . . Upsets so often happen when there is no actual need for the wife to go out to work at all. And I can't help wondering if the old-fashioned notion that a woman's place is in the home might not be right after all.

'As for career-wives, aren't they getting their sense of values mixed up? Aren't they losing something far more precious than they gain when they sacrifice their homes and their husbands for the sake of their so-called independence? I am not forgetting that, in many cases, it is sheer economic necessity that sends wives out to work. . . . But to all brides-to-be I would say this: . . . It's *your* job to keep his pride intact. This may mean giving up your own career in order to become a full-time wife, and giving up all sorts of little luxuries also. . . . The great thing for a bride-to-be to aim at is to have time enough to devote to home-making. . . .'[31]

The women's press (with perhaps the exception of *The Lady*) was thus still united in reflecting a limited 'domestic' role for women and a life-goal centred around getting married and raising a family, to the virtual exclusion of all other interests and activities, including paid work outside the home. More than this, the women's magazines continued to use their influence to discourage women from thinking in terms of a wider role. Probably only a small minority of readers were interested in wider social participation at this time. But the fact remains that an increasing number of women were taking up occupations outside the home, and their needs were altogether ignored. Since the mass weeklies in particular had to gear their appeal to the lowest common denominator amongst their readership, this policy was dictated not only by increasing pressure from commercial interests eager to create the right home-orientated selling climate for their products, but by readers themselves, the majority of whom showed by their attitudes and patterns of behaviour that they still clung tenaciously to traditional beliefs about a woman's place in society.

Magazine editors knew what they were doing when they continued to serve up, in modern dress, the 'golden formula' evolved half a century before. They were well aware that, despite the upheavals of war, the horizons of the majority of British women were still very narrow, and that their activities and interests were for the most part unchanged, being centred on the home or on the hopes of one. Intuitive editorial judgements might be considered suspect—usually they are fairly accurate—but in this case a fact-finding questionnaire, put out by *Woman's Own* in November, 1955, to construct a profile of 'the typical young British woman', tends to corroborate them. It made no claim to be a scientifically conducted piece of research—readers were simply invited, if they were aged between 15 and 25, to answer forty questions about themselves, and the experiment was apparently conducted simultaneously in sixteen other countries. The number of respondents was not given but reported as 'thousands'. The findings must therefore be treated cautiously, but the general picture they present is instructive.

The favourite pastimes of these young women were found to be dancing, knitting, reading and sewing in that order. Only one in three smoked and over half took nothing alcoholic. Almost every girl used lipstick and perfume, but 20 per cent never bought face-powder, and a further 67 per cent disdained mascara. For clothes, the order of preference was: the tailored suit, afternoon dress, skirt and sweater, evening dress. As regards the (then) vexed question of 'young men', 80 per cent of girls said they were 'allowed to go out with boys', though some of the younger ones reported that their parents wanted to choose their boyfriends for them, which they resented, while older girls faced with a similar restriction were inclined to treat this in the spirit of 'parents know best', which the magazine applauded. The questionnaire revealed a great eagerness to travel abroad as soon as the opportunity arose. On the key questions of work and marriage, the results were as follows:

'Few girls today can afford just to stay at home and not work. Very few would like such a life! . . . Nearly all want to go on working after they are married and until they are expecting their first baby. After the baby is born, more than eighty per cent want to stay at home. . . . Marriage is the most important ambition of 91 out of every hundred who are not already married. Seventy-eight in each hundred seek kindliness in their future husband more than any other quality—with intelligence a close second.'[32]

Finally, the 'life-philosophy' of these young women was summed up as follows:

'Faith will determine the future of the world, say 75 in every hundred. Only a few think that scientific progress or technical inventions will have much influence in shaping our future. International conferences do not greatly impress them. Only three in every hundred are interested in the implications of the atom bomb. Faith in themselves, faith in other people, but mostly faith in God, is what is stressed all the time. . . . This [shows] the fine inner feelings of modern young women' says the article, revealing 'Right living and right thinking . . . Love and understanding . . . and pure goodness.'[33]

Such were the ambitions, interests and values which this periodical, in common with most others, claimed for the majority of its readers in 1956, and which the women's press as a whole faithfully reflected. While the process of adjustment to the demands and opportunities of peace-time continued, the women's magazines set out to be authoritative counsellors to women in every department of their lives. But the middle 'fifties marked a turning point. To quote Mary Grieve:

'It no longer seemed appropriate that *Woman* should be speaking with quite such an authoritative, remote voice. The time of the monologue was ending; what was needed now was a place where a genuine dialogue could develop.'[34]

The reason for this modification in editorial approach was the ending of the long years of austerity and social confinement, and the growth of a new and prosperous society in which patterns of life and thought were undergoing a revolutionary change. A new challenge now faced the women's magazines, that of interpreting and satisfying the needs of educated women under conditions of affluence, and under pressure from advertisers. Their response to this challenge forms the final phase of their history up to the present.

NOTES

1 James Drawbell, *Time on My Hands*, p. 53.
2 *Ibid.*, p. 45.
3 Mary Grieve, *Millions Made My Story*, p. 96.
4 *Ibid.*, pp. 90–1.
5 James Drawbell, *Time on My Hands*, p. 50.
6 Mary Grieve, *Millions Made My Story*, p. 196.
7 *Ibid.*, p. 87.
8 *Ibid.*, p. 88.
9 *Ibid.*, p. 91.
10 *Op. cit.*, January 17th, 1946, p. 47.
11 *My Weekly*, March 23rd, 1946, p. 6.
12 *Ibid.*, May 18th, 1946, p. 10.
13 *Op. cit.*, August, 1946, p. 45.
14 *Op. cit.*, January 21st, 1946, p. 155.
15 *Woman's Own*, January 4th, 1946, p. 15.
16 *Op. cit.*, February 25th, 1946.
17 *Op. cit.*, January 28th, 1946, p. 177.
18 *Op. cit.*, May, 1946.
19 E. S. Turner, *The Shocking History of Advertising.*
20 *Woman's Own*, February 1st, 1951, p. 7.
21 *Op. cit.*, March 10th, 1951, p. 17.
22 *Op. cit.*, February 3rd, 1951, p. 37.
23 *My Weekly*, January 13th, 1951, p. 16.
24 *Op. cit.*, January 20th, 1951, p. 19.
25 *Op. cit.*, June, 1951, p. 31.
26 Mary Grieve, *Millions Made My Story*, p. 137.
27 *Op. cit.*, April 1956, p. 51.
28 *Op. cit.*, December, 1956, p. 87.
29 *Ibid.*
30 *Op. cit.*, March 8th, 1956, p. 28.
31 *Op. cit.*, December 29th, 1956, p. 17.
32 *Op. cit.*, March 1st, 1956, pp. 20–1.
33 *Ibid.*
34 Mary Grieve, *Millions Made My Story*, p. 198.

5

'Getting and Spending': 1956-1965

In the middle 'fifties, Britain entered upon a phase of accelerated economic growth which in ten years produced a socio-economic revolution founded upon affluence. Change was manifest in every area of social life as austerity gave way to prosperity, and consumption rose rapidly in both the public and private sectors of the economy consequent upon higher incomes and the downward redistribution of wealth. Between 1955 and 1965 average annual expenditure per head of the population rose by 25 per cent. The average industrial wage increased to over sixteen pounds a week, while the differential between manual and white-collar workers narrowed considerably.

Women, in particular, improved their economic position. More married women joined the labour force, and by 1962 they accounted for more than 53 per cent of all female workers, as against 41 per cent in 1950. Women's earnings in general continued to rise, though more slowly than men's, the principle of equal pay being adopted in many spheres, particularly in government employment. Teenage earnings showed the greatest proportional increases, with the result that an unprecedented amount of spending power was concentrated in the hands of young women and girls. Women now became spenders in their own right as well as being custodians of the housekeeping purse, and this new expenditure was mainly absorbed by the fashion and cosmetics industries, though a considerable amount also went on travel and entertainment.

As a result of economic expansion and higher incomes, more goods and services became available to more people. By 1965, the majority of households were equipped with television, a vacuum cleaner, a washing-machine and a lawn-mower, and a third of them also had a refrigerator. More than two out of three middle-class families owned a car, as did one in three working-class families also. The average shopping basket carried home high-grade foods such as meat, fresh fruit and dairy produce, rather than the 'cheap fillers', the bread, potatoes and cereals of less affluent years. In addition, three times as many people took holidays abroad in 1965 as in 1955, and many more were able to indulge in expensive hobbies, sports, and entertainments, such as caravanning and sailing, gardening and photography, bingo and other forms of gambling. A growing interest in 'do-it-yourself' and in furnishing and equipping the home (where, because of longer holidays with pay and shorter working hours, more time was being spent) produced a burst of spending on household goods and services.

An important effect of the general increase in purchasing power was the closing of the gap between classes in patterns of spending. The war furthered this trend by abolishing many of the social 'splinter' groups which had contributed to the highly diversified social structure of pre-war Britain. It replaced them with a class-system which was far more homogeneous in character, and predominantly middle-class. Many superficial class differences were thereby eliminated, and tastes were levelled upwards as a result of mass production which brought high quality and good design within reach of the mass of the population. These two developments, together with the growth of a state system of education, to which a cross-section of young people were exposed, helped to produce a greater similarity in the attitudes, interests and modes of life between the different social strata. The upgrading in the quality, type and variety of goods on sale in those twin capitals of mass consumption, Woolworth's and Marks and Spencer, bore mute but eloquent testimony to the scale of this socio-economic revolution.

When the first undercurrents of change began to be felt in the second half of the 1950s, they created new problems for the women's press. Editors were faced with the task of adapting to a new social climate with only intuitive knowledge to guide them. Their task was complicated by the intensification of pressure from advertisers, who, as they became aware of the vast new potential purchasing power of women of all ages, sought to exploit to the fullest extent the ideal buying climate the magazines offered by trying to secure editorial co-operation in stimulating consumption.

The trend was potentially harmful to the interests of readers in that it struck at editorial autonomy and the freedom of editorial teams to produce the kind of magazines which they felt would satisfactorily meet the needs of women in a changing society. There was a real danger, of which magazine staff were aware, that the growing power of the advertiser would so far infiltrate editorial content as to render it no more than a veiled manipulative device for influencing the spending habits of women, effectively destroying, or at best limiting, the social functions of the women's press. Thus Editors like Mary Grieve, responsible to a readership of several millions, strenuously resisted this encroachment on their territory. Others, accepting economic realities, compromised, making concessions in peripheral areas to safeguard their more central concerns. But, notwithstanding this resistance, starting in the mid-'fifties the balance of power between editorial and advertising departments began to swing in favour of the latter in response to increasing pressure from higher management.

The full significance of the growth in advertising, in terms of its effect upon the structure of the women's press and upon magazine content, could only be revealed in the long run. In the short term, the interests of readers and advertisers coincided sufficiently for its effects to be beneficial rather than otherwise. Before the war, money had been short while goods were plentiful. After it, people had money to spend but the shops were empty. Now, for the first time, production matched spending power, and manufacturers and consumers were eager to make contact through the medium of advertising. Women especially, after a long period during which they had been able to buy only essential commodities (and those in limited quantities), wanted information about the new products flooding onto the market. They were ready to be persuaded to buy, and the advertisement columns of the women's magazines were their fire-side shop-windows. Thanks to subsidisation by advertisers, they also received the less obvious benefits of larger, more colourful and informative publications for a nominal cover price.

Because women were showing a strong and growing interest in home topics, which the magazines were already catering for editorially in their service features, advertisers were in fact providing a complementary service, all the more acceptable in view of the backlog of unsatisfied demand for consumer goods. More disquieting was the nature of some advertising copy. Increasing use was being made of 'depth' techniques, particularly that which has since been christened 'the sexual sell'. The British code of advertising could protect consumers against fraudulent claims and all practices manifestly against the public interest, and magazines themselves reserved the right to refuse any advertising copy they considered undesirable, but it was more difficult to tackle advertising which exploited people's emotional responses and drives.

The following examples* are typical of the techniques then being used. The first shows an outright appeal to social snobbery:

'To people with wide social activities a car represents something more than a means of transportation. They may be attracted to its

* *Source:* Various issues of women's magazines appearing in the period 1955–56.

graceful lines. . . . But subconsciously, the possession of a Wolseley means a great deal more. Its distinguished appearance seems a natural accompaniment of their position in life, a lengthened reflection of the taste and beauty of their surroundings. When you consider [it] in that light, you may feel its ownership might be most apt in your case.'

Second, an illustration of a technique using the association of ideas· In this case, the product is beer:

'We had run down the hill into the lounge of the old Tudor pub . . . I sat toying with my new ring. It was a lovely sapphire. . . .'

Third, one of a host of advertisements exploiting the average woman's concern to do her best for her husband and family:

'A mother's love for her baby can only be measured by the care and protection she lavishes on her child . . . fourteen Royal mothers to date placed their confidence in —— .'

Fourth, two of the more obvious attempts to use sex:

'It's a wonderful way to catch a man's eye and stay on his mind.' And, 'Pagan—the perfume of sex-appeal'.

Finally, two examples of more pernicious copy, one claiming that, 'A ——'s not a luxury—it's every woman's right' (referring to expensive knitwear), and the other asserting, 'Even if we have furnished in excess of our income, we still ought to have a ——' (mentioning a hearth-rug).

Such was the type of advertising matter which women were subjected to through their magazines in the mid-'fifties. It was calculated to focus attention on their domestic role, reinforce home values, and perpetuate the belief that success as a woman, wife and mother, could be purchased for the price of a jar of cold cream, a bottle of cough syrup or a packet of instant cake-mix. At this stage, however, magazines still had it in their power to counteract, editorially, any influences which they felt were not in their readers' best interests, but that power was to be drastically reduced over the next decade.

The effects of affluence upon the editorial content of women's magazines showed themselves in a variety of ways, one of the first being a modification of the traditional editorial approach. As early as 1956, when the first stirrings of social change began to be felt, the ever-vigilant Mary Grieve, was among those who realized that a new policy was called for, to ensure that all this seething activity was captured and 'sieved back through [her] paper'. She has described what this involved:

'It meant deliberately playing-down the glamour approach—the reliance on brighter than life presentation—and there was a risk that in doing this we might drop the tempo of the paper too sharply and that women might find it drab. . . . What it amounted to . . . was that *Woman* half-turned her back on the policy of being the wonder paper which "lead" readers in the friendliest possible way, and became a partner in an exchange of ideas and experiences. . . .

'As soon as the readers' own experiences began to appear there was an immediate increase in their contacts with the paper . . . we showed women cooking in their own kitchens. . . . The health editor visited mothers in their own homes and brought their stories into the paper, instead of simply sitting in an office and writing to an unseen readership. . . .

'This emphasis on real life in the practical features had an influence all through the paper. . . . The fact that we were now going out into the country for features meant that increasingly the public would be coming to us. . . . All this activity was filtered back into the paper and greatly increased the reader's identification with what she read and saw every week.'[1]

Among the new features designed to increase the level of reader participation was 'Beauty Box', *Woman*'s own beauty salon, to which young women were invited to come for discussion sessions on all matters connected with good grooming. Another innovation was 'Expresso', a full-page feature for the teenager crammed with hints and ideas, an attempt to cater more specifically to the fast expanding youth market.

At the same time, *Woman*'s regular articles began to take on a new look as the authoritarian mode of presentation gave way to a more democratic approach. 'Social do's and don'ts' had by 1961 become 'How it's done'. The usual problem page of letters was re-styled, with the invitation to 'Talk it over' with Evelyn Home, and letters were written and answered more informally, though with a noticeable increase in astringency. The magazine gradually became younger and bolder in its outlook, with frequent opportunities for readers to take a look behind the scenes at the way various features were produced. The trend away from the traditional treatment was symbolised in its new, unconventional art-work and striking changes in format which showed a leaning toward the American pattern. By 1965, the magazine was sending its staff out to discover the latest trends and relaying these back to readers, covering fewer subjects per issue, but treating them in greater depth and with added verve.

The remainder of the women's press showed changes of a similar kind. A major effect of social change was to force the women's magazines to raise their standards of service commensurately with the changes taking place in the pattern of life of their readers. From the mid-'fifties onwards, the women's press vastly increased its coverage of domestic subjects. Even *Woman's Weekly* added articles on child care, home furnishing, gardening and health, together with a letter page through which readers could contribute their ideas and views. By 1965, an 'Over 40' club had also been introduced, giving regular fashion advice to women with figure problems. These developments were accompanied by a great improvement in the magazine's appearance. A similar transformation was evident in *My Weekly*. From a colourless, old-fashioned format, crudely illustrated on rough paper, it blossomed into colour on calendered paper, with a completely new lay-out and a liberal use of photographs. It, too, expanded its content to include domestic subjects, changing from a fiction periodical to a home-service weekly and incorporating a large selection of readers' letters.

Good Housekeeping likewise started to modernise its presentation. One reader, though delighted that the magazine was now 'easier to read' was nevertheless apprehensive lest this new bid for modernity might see the end of old favourites such as embroidery and knitting. She was assured that continued attention would be given to 'the old traditional interests of many readers'. In 1965, the magazine introduced a new home furnishing section, designed to show readers 'not only what's new and what's worth having, but also how best to use it'. Its coverage indicated the new requirements of modern living such as 'Furnishing a home office . . . a teenager's room'. In addition, the Institute was given greater prominence.

Expert help on interior decorating, cookery, dress-making and other aspects of home-making now became available to readers of *Woman and Home* also, and in 1961 this magazine, too, was given a face-lift, with a new, glossy, letterpress cover (specially designed to be eye-catching), crowning an all-round improvement in presentation. *Everywoman* also expanded its 'service' coverage, adding in particular a feature on 'Family Affairs' through which advice on child care was supplied by a member of the medical profession. By 1965 even *The Lady* was offering a regular survey of new household appliances as part of a new series, 'In the Home'. At the same time *Woman's Own* was giving advice on buying the house to put them in, while *Housewife* assisted with finance, suggesting ways of budgeting on incomes of £1,085, £1,850 and £2,800 a year, and thinking through the comparative costs of domestic help and labour-saving appliances.

Besides expanding their range of services, higher incomes and better living standards also allowed the women's magazines to show a wider selection of goods and to raise the tastes of their readers still further. The 'Great Food Revolution', as *Good Housekeeping* termed it, greatly affected the eating habits of the population. By 1961 the magazine could report:

'We are living very well, buying more solid nutrition than ever before at an average price of nearly £2 per head per week, and spending much of it on a dazzling variety of new frozen, canned, "instant" and pre-cooked offerings. The overall spectacle of the food available to us is one of exuberant, colourful and clean abundance. . . . Vastly improved packaging has multiplied the sale of cakes, biscuits, processed fish and meat products. The most recent report of the National Food Survey Committee reveals that "convenience foods" have increased the total intake of energy and nutrients from such sources by one-third and contributed to an even larger increase of vitamins C and D.'[2]

The magazines reflected all these changes in their cookery articles, in higher quality ingredients, in the variety and sophistication of recipes, and elsewhere in a new preoccupation with nutritional values and dietetics. More time was being spent in collecting food, but less actually preparing it, since manufacturers had reduced much of the drudgery of the kitchen by marketing pre-cleaned and prepared foods. Hence, cookery ceased to be an eternal battle to make cheap ingredients stretch and look appetising, and became an absorbing new hobby, for men as well as women, who were now willing to experiment with foreign recipes and new foods. The growing popularity of the *delicatessen* for all classes was evidence both of greater purchasing power and more catholic tastes.

The same trends were making themselves felt in furnishing and equipping the home. Once, an Editor could not hint at a daily bath, knowing that for most of her readers this was out of the question. Now, though a large number of British homes were still without baths, running hot water and indoor w.c.s, the majority were properly equipped, and Home Editors were suggesting bathroom suites in pastel shades and fitted carpets to make bath-time more luxurious. The dreams of yesterday were fast becoming reality. Washing-machines were standard equipment, along with spin driers, vacuum cleaners and 'pop-up' toasters. Central heating, the ultimate in home-comfort, was no longer the prerogative of the rich, and the women's magazines made it part of their job to keep readers informed about this, and all other appliances, gadgets and services contributing to the comfort of a modern home. They also paid more attention to home decoration, advising on colour schemes and furnishings and slowly educating readers in design and colour harmony.

A similar revolution was taking place in the sphere of fashion. The vast expansion in cheap, ready-to-wear clothes of good quality and design, brought the *haute couture* look within the reach of every girl and woman who had the fashion sense to make the best of her appearance. Fashion and beauty coverage in the women's press continued to expand and improve, and the high standard of the advice put out by the magazines undoubtedly contributed to the striking improvement in the way women dressed, used make-up and wore their hair. Even knitting and dress-making began to enter the realms of high fashion.

Apart from raising the standard of the services they offered, the women's magazines were, in addition, paying greater attention to leisure activities and entertainment. Articles on T.V. personalities were early innovations. The rise in car ownership brought motoring articles into the weeklies for the first time, and as more people began to take holidays abroad, help with foreign travel arrangements became an important new service. A widening range of hobbies was also reflected, including gardening, sailing, reading, and record-collecting, as well as coverage of music, theatre, and the arts. The growing popularity of 'do-it-yourself' often found a wife painting the kitchen, and the magazine experts were there to help her. If she was unsure of her rights and liabilities, particularly as a shopper, hire-purchaser or property-owner, regular legal guidance was available, and if she had money of her own (as an increasing number of working wives had) she could seek the advice of the financial experts in matters concerning investment and insurance.

Thus, in the ten years 1956-65, affluence greatly increased the buying power of women and brought a whole new range of commodities within their reach, which in turn allowed the women's press to raise its sights and to encourage women to raise theirs, at least in terms of housekeeping standards and personal taste. Affluence also helped widen women's horizons—through T.V., which became a 'window on the world' in every home, through travel, and through outside work. The need to keep pace with this unprecedented spending spree led the magazines to preoccupy themselves with the mechanics of acquisition and with materialistic goals. But the 'new society' also bred a whole new set of social problems, most of which the magazines are only now beginning to recognise, much less come to grips with, and in this area they failed to meet the needs of their readers.

Many of these problems sprang from population trends. Demographic change has contributed more than any other single factor to the changing patterns of life of women in modern Britain. For the first time, the sex-ratio has swung in their favour. This has improved the marriage prospects for younger women, and the trend since the war has been for more girls to marry, and to marry earlier, with the result that married women are forming an ever-increasing proportion of the population. There has been a sharp rise in teenage marriages, and more than half our young women marry before the age of twenty-one, while the vast majority are married by the time they are twenty-five. The earlier the marriage, the more likely it is to end in divorce, and one in five teenage marriages comes to grief in this way.

Fertility patterns, too, have altered. The large rise in births immediately after the war was anticipated, but the continuing increase, maintained until 1964, was not foreseen. Associated with it, there has been a slight increase in the average family size, and in addition, a widening differential in respect of Classes I and II, which are now producing larger families than in the recent past. Because women are having small families, averaging between two and three children, and having them early in marriage, the period of child-bearing and rearing has been greatly compressed. They now reach the late thirties and early forties with the bulk of family responsibilities behind them and with nearly half their lives left in which to enjoy the freedom they have regained.

An even greater freedom has been granted to women in recent years, one which is radical in its effects. The 1960s have brought them sexual emancipation by placing in their hands the means by which they can control their own fertility. One of the greatest of its ramifications is the possibility it opens up of an entirely new sexual role for women. Freud laid the foundations for this by making women conscious of their own sexuality. Modern science has given them the means to explore and exploit it without the risk of conception. In addition, oral contraception has brought release from the physical and psychological bondage of recurrent pregnancies, which was formerly the greatest single barrier to the full participation of women in the social and economic life of the community.

These changes, coinciding with the growth of new codes and values culminating in 'the new morality', have created special problems. So, too, has the changing geographical distribution of living accommodation and employment. Mary Grieve has drawn attention to 'the birth of the new towns, with all their problems of loneliness and psychological disturbance, as well as the practical problems of new home-making'. 'Suburban neurosis' is becoming increasingly familiar together with the dismal plight of the bed-sitter brigade and the growing army of 'business widows'. There are the difficulties facing the two-job women, trying to combine paid employment with running a home, usually with insufficient domestic help, nursery facilities, or co-operation from employers. There are the 'captive' wives,* tied to the home twenty-four hours a day, and the redundant wives, who, with their children gone and husbands fully occupied at work, feel that their usefulness is at an end, and have no training or experience to help them make a new start. Added to these are all the problems associated with adapting to life in a complex, fast-moving, technological society in which pressures on the individual are multiplied and intensified at the same time as community life and support is weakened. Families are subjected to internal tensions as the gulf between one generation and the next widens due to education and accelerated social change, and as couples try to adjust to a new concept of marriage which accords the wife higher status than that of a mere sleeping partner in the family firm.

These problems, having a social origin, were outside the ordinary run of personal difficulties the magazines normally had to cope with via their problem pages and tended to escape notice. But if social pathology was neglected in the late 'fifties and early 'sixties, personal service to the individual considerably improved. Mature counsellors, psychologists, psychiatrists and other experts collaborated to treat particular topics in some depth. For instance, in 1961, *Woman's Own* ran a series intended to help women 'Get more living out of life'. It dealt with harmony in marriage, discussed sexual adjustment, and also featured a series of real-life situations focusing on special problems, for example what it means to be 'the mother of an unmarried mother', of particular relevance in 1961 when every fourth mother conceived out of wedlock, and every twentieth child was born illegitimate.

At the other end of the scale counsellors were coping with fourteen-year-olds who felt they should be allowed boyfriends, and were inclined to agree with them—a measure of the social implications of the fall in the age of puberty which today has advisers torn between ignoring sexual promiscuity amongst the young, and dispensing contraceptive advice to forestall the consequences. In 1961, the teenage magazines were still giving an uncompromising 'no' to the question, 'should I sleep with my boyfriend to avoid losing him?' while their fiction re-

---

* The term is Hannah Gavron's. (See *The Captive Wife*, Gollancz, 1966.)

mained naïve and innocent of all signs of moral conflict. Nevertheless, there was some attempt to provide a platform for the discussion of important points in the teenager's philosophy. *Boyfriend*, for example, dealt with such subjects as 'Good looks don't matter', and 'How to be stood up and be happy'. Opposing points of view were put by teenagers wherever an issue was in doubt, as in the discussion of what factors should influence a decision to marry. One writer asserted: 'You've got to be certain', the other that 'You can't be certain', a disagreement which afforded a valuable opportunity for airing the issues involved.

Through all its counselling, the weekly section of the women's press in general preserved its traditional view of a woman's role. Despite the social changes which were beginning to modify it, particularly the increasing number of working wives and mothers, the weeklies continued to deal mainly with the problems encountered in preparing for, or experiencing, wife- and motherhood. *Woman's Realm* tended to venture a little further than the other mass weeklies. To give one illustration: in 1965 it discussed 'the Mature Marriage', *viz.* the situation a couple find themselves in when the children have left home and they are once more on their own. Taking a realistic approach, the article stressed the dangers inherent in a woman living vicariously through her grandchildren, and the importance of a healthy sex life in middle age, which it emphasised was 'neither obscene nor ludicrous'. It also recommended part- or full-time work, voluntary or paid, to fill the empty days. The magazine has since raised many other issues through its fiction, for example 'mixed' marriage (seen from the parents' point of view), the dangers to which 'latch-key' children are exposed, and the woman, 'a quietly competent housewife, devoted, compassionate—unwanted', who unaccountably turns to shop-lifting.

The monthlies were able to launch out into rather deeper waters, though they were gradually reducing features in order to expand their home service content. *Good Housekeeping*, with a tradition of adventurous feature-writing behind it, was still offering a good selection in 1961, many of which looked beyond domestic issues. Some examples indicate its range: 'First impressions of the Weights and Measures Bill', 'The p.s. baby', 'The truth about heredity'; 'The needs the welfare state doesn't meet—and willing women can'; 'Birth control'; 'Adoption'; and 'Is neighbourliness on the decline?'. *Everywoman* continued its series on 'Human Problems of Today', drawing heavily on psychological knowledge to cope with such worries as the fear of failure. Mostly, however, the new problems facing women were neglected even by the monthlies. The working mother was almost entirely ignored. In January,

1965, *Housewife* included an article on 'The New Homemakers—the "Two-Job Women" ', but made no attempt to deal with the subject in depth. However, the recognition and acceptance of the phenomenon was a significant advance in itself.

Meanwhile, as late as 1961, Monica Dickens in *Woman's Own* was still roundly condemning married women who took outside work as 'second best mothers' and inferior wives:

'Ask any man if he'd rather his wife worked or stayed at home and see what he says. If she is listening, he may echo all her excuses about her job making her a more interesting person, how proud he is of what she achieves. But if you could get him alone, I believe he would tell you he would rather she stayed at home and looked after his children, and was waiting for him with a decent meal and a sympathetic ear when he got home from work. . . . You can't have everything in life. You can't have deep and safe happiness in marriage and the exciting independence of a career as well. . . . It isn't fair on your husband. You may kid him along for a while with the idea that your job makes you more attractive and stimulating, with more to talk to him about; but men don't want to talk about a woman's work. They want to talk about their own.'[3]

Many important topics widely aired on T.V. and in the national press were still considered taboo for women's periodicals. *She* blazed a lone trail of outspokenness when it erupted onto the women's publishing scene in 1955, showing a healthy disregard for the customary 'unmentionables'. As a new and important experiment in publishing for women, it deserves special consideration. Published by the National Magazine Co., *She* owes its inimitable character to the personal aims and interests of the man who founded it, and to his highly individual attitude to the female sex. To put it in his own words:

'The women's magazines of the time just didn't reflect women as I knew them. Of course women have softness, but they are also funny, vulgar and tough. They are in touch with the harsh realities of life. No-one who undergoes child-bearing could be anything else.'*

He wanted to create a magazine especially for this type of woman, but to break away from the usual formula was not easy and required a staff that was not cliché-ridden. He recruited women who were entirely

---

* Personal interview.

outside the world of publishing, among them Miss Nancy Spain, and Miss Joan Werner-Laurie who became the magazine's Editor. Together they created a periodical which primarily interested them, and which they hoped would interest others, a magazine intended above all to be entertaining.

From the very first issue, *She* showed that it was going to be entirely different. It concerned itself with people in a way that no other magazine did. Moreover its layout was new. Discarding the cherished belief of Art-Editors that white space is important, the magazine was closely packed from cover to cover, visibly giving the fullest possible value for a shilling. It was also printed on cheap paper to keep its price low. In its catholicity of appeal, the magazine cut across age and class divisions (even to some extent those of sex), and managed to suit a broad spectrum of tastes. It was aimed at a particular interest group rather than a collection of readers sharing certain social or economic characteristics, so that it reached a wide cross-section of society. In its content there was a consistent attempt to maintain a male-female editorial balance. Women's interests were equated with those of men, and so the articles appearing in *She* were calculated to appeal to both sexes.

Then, as now, the overall character of the magazine defies analysis in conventional terms. It is broad, rather than intellectual, and appeals in a robust way to women who are down-to-earth and frank, and who disdain the niceties of the typical women's magazine. In 1963, Miss Laurie, in a reply to a critic who complained of over-refinement in women's magazines, gave her own version of what *She* was offering readers, and why:

'I plan *She* . . . on the basis that my readers are fully adult, reasonably intelligent and have a lively sense of humour. On average, not more than twelve a month cancel because of "lack of refinement".

'In November 1962, I published in *She* a major article on abortion. The same issue included an article by a mother of a thalidomide baby—a subject tackled way back in 1961. *She* has dealt in full detail with menstruation, hysterectomy, breast cancer, lung cancer, leprosy, brain tumours. The current issue has a feature on muscular dystrophy, the November issue one on infertility. We have even told our enchanted readers what a bidet is for.'[4]

She was given a mixed reception. Many hailed it enthusiastically as the kind of magazine they had been waiting for; others loathed it. After a shaky start, and a long period during which the reading public grew accustomed to its racy style and unvarnished approach to life, it has reached a circulation of more than 300,000. Styling itself as a magazine 'full of daring editorials, controversial attitudes, and gay, sophisticated features', it claims to 'set today's trends' rather than follow them, and to be 'Britain's gayest, liveliest magazine for women'. *She*'s success can be attributed to its individuality, and to the fact that it appeals to a group of women not catered for elsewhere in the women's press. The magazine commented on its own career in March, 1965:

> '*She* made her impact among people looking for a magazine which reflected the modern mood, and which was neither patronising nor smug. *She* was never aimed at little women struggling over hot stoves and kitchen sinks. . . . Over the years, *She* has been called vulgar, dirty and even pornographic—but the original policies will go on, and for the next ten years *She* will continue to be as controversial, as stimulating, and at times as naughty as she's ever been.'

The ever-increasing scope of *She*'s feature-writing (a penetrating documentary on lesbianism took this a stage further) proves editorial determination in this respect. But, though the magazine is succeeding with this approach and outpacing many other monthlies, its performance, compared with the huge sales of a more conventional monthly like *Woman and Home*, is modest. Nevertheless, though catering to an attitude group is unlikely ever to yield large circulations, as *She* has proved, it is possible to make converts over time, and if slow growth can be tolerated while the reading public catches on to a new idea, it can be a very profitable enterprise.

She entered the field at a time when conditions were changing for the orthodox monthlies. The 'quality' journals particularly were finding it increasingly difficult to attract new readers among the younger generation. Readers were becoming harder to please. A few years earlier, in the boom conditions of a seller's market, it was enough for a magazine to boast a square back and a high cover price to assure itself of a readership amongst the socially aspirant. A woman with social pretensions would take care to equip herself with a selection of 'approved' titles to display conspicuously on her coffee table. Not only did they give her the right procedural clues, but they also served as tangible 'evidence' that she had already 'arrived'. A story featured in *The Lady* described one such woman who, having suddenly 'come up in the world' was anxious to adopt the style of life appropriate to her new station. She moved to a better-class neighbourhood, where she started taking morning coffee in 'Ye Olde Coffee Shoppe'—the provincial woman's equivalent of the Athenæum:

'There was a table in the "shoppe" littered with glossy-covered magazines. Real high-class ones! Mrs Harper picked up one to read. . . . She must get into the habit of buying some of these magazines regularly.'[5]

But during the middle 'fifties, such characterless 'glossies', stiff with sepia-toned gentility, became socially obsolescent. Growing numbers of upper-middle class women, particularly in the younger age-groups, turned to the mass weeklies which were steadily outstripping the more expensive monthlies in standards of presentation and service, and even in size:

'The professional man's wife, struggling to manage her money so that her children could get a better education was just as glad of the practical recipes, the well-designed clothes, the hints on value-for-money, as was the welder's wife. . . .'[6]

The expanding middle class, recruited from above and below, created a mass readership which the cheap, but excellently-produced gravure weeklies were ready-made to absorb. By 1964, women's magazines of the 'service' weekly type were read by 60 per cent of the upper and middle classes (ABC1), 71 per cent of the lower-middle classes (C2), and 63 per cent of the working and poor classes (DE).[7] The trend spelt death to any magazine which could only offer mediocrity on shiny paper, and most of them subsequently perished.

Homogenised readerships, and the universality of appeal of the mass weeklies account for the fact that, although magazine readerships are astronomical by pre-war standards, they are distributed amongst far fewer titles. In 1934, there were upwards of twenty-five women's story papers alone in print. Today there are less than forty women's magazines all told. The contraction has come about as a result of the death of most of the old-style periodicals. In the last decade, *Home Chat*, *Home Notes*, *Weldon's*, *Wife and Home*, *Woman's Companion*, *Woman's Illustrated*, *Woman's Pictorial* and *Woman's World* have all ceased publication, many of them having lived for years on borrowed time during the period when scarcity created an artificial demand for any kind of women's periodical literature. Some firms were content to let magazines run down gradually, while they reaped the profits of advertising rates geared to much higher sales figures, but eventually audited circulations, a more demanding reading public, and heightened competition from the gravure weeklies, forced them out of print.

The 'service' weeklies have taken over as the leading publications

F*

for women of all ages and classes and their success has been due to the fact that they have managed to evolve a formula appropriate to women in all walks of life, an achievement made possible by the social and economic changes, already mentioned, which created similar modes of living, tastes and aspirations among large numbers of people. But they have owed nearly as much to the perpetuation of traditional attitudes regarding the social role and status of women, which has meant that the vast majority of women have continued to share the same domestic orientation. This situation has recently begun to change, however. Consequent upon the spread of higher education, the widening horizons of women's employment and their broadening social experience, there are signs of a new form of stratification developing within the female population based not upon socio-economic characteristics but upon common interests and attitudes, a trend which has far-reaching implications for all the mass media.

The magazines which folded in the ten years 1956–1965 have been replaced by as many new titles. One of the most successful of these newcomers has been the 'service' weekly, *Woman's Realm* (1958) which, four years after its launching, reached a peak sale of nearly one and a half million copies. It was originally started partly to use up idle print capacity at Odhams, and partly to relieve circulation pressure on *Woman* which had passed its 'economic ceiling' of three million, with the additional motive of providing a cheaper advertising vehicle for firms unable to afford space in that publication. There seemed to be little room for a new mass weekly in the intensely competitive market of the late 'fifties, and *Woman's Realm* was not expected to do particularly well. Its enthusiastic reception is once again attributable to an exceptional Editor, in this instance, Miss Joyce Ward, who created its initial formula. In a personal interview she has explained how she was intrigued by the success of small, 'dowdy' papers like *Home Chat* and *Woman's Weekly*, and decided that if they could do so well with such limited resources, a modern magazine written to a similar formula, but with all the advantages of modern production methods and expertise, plus colour, should do even better. With a queen on the throne, it was indeed a 'woman's realm', and so the title was born.

The approach decided upon is highly significant for the light it throws upon what makes for success in women's journalism in contemporary Britain. *Woman's Day*, brought out the same year, and written (apparently) to much the same formula, failed to achieve similar results, and survived for only three years on sliding sales, a curious parallel which points up the extraordinarily delicate balance between success and failure in women's publishing. Miss Ward says of *Woman's*

Realm during her tenure as Editor that it aimed above all to make women feel wanted—that it tried in every way to assist them in all their daily tasks, encouraging them to take pride in their custodianship of the home and to look upon their work as important and valuable. Thus every feature had to have a visible connection with the domestic scene, which limited the magazine's scope but at the same time allowed it to treat these subjects more fully.

The intention throughout was to heighten the enjoyment of home life for women who did not go out to work and so had few connections with the world outside. To find out how best to help these women raise their sights, the editorial staff conferred with representatives from Marks and Spencer and Butlin's, two institutions which have played an important part in improving the standards, educating the tastes and widening the experience of the mass of the population. Readers' letters, too, were collated and used to guide policy, since it was considered vital to establish a close link and a two-way flow of ideas between magazine staff and the women they were writing for. With this end in view, and because *Woman's Realm* was intended for a slightly older readership than *Woman*, only experienced staff were recruited, mainly women in their forties.

From the very first issue the magazine 'went like a bomb' and has achieved considerable popularity in the North of England, testifying to the success of Miss Ward's determination to avoid 'London conditioning', to which many a magazine has fallen victim. Judging by its correspondence, it draws the bulk of its readers from amongst home-bound housewives, as well as attracting a large number of lonely women in bedsitters. It has proved yet another triumph for Odhams, showing that, even in an apparently saturated market, there is usually room for a magazine which 'touches the right buttons'.

Flair (1960) and *Honey* (1961), two new fashion magazines, have built their success upon the growing economic independence and the wider social horizons of young women. This process gathered momentum in the middle 'fifties, when it began to force itself upon the attention of manufacturers. The fashion trade made an early bid for this new spending power, switching from the quality garments required by older women, to the mass production of fashions for the younger generation. The high-fashion demands of teenagers have, in fact, transformed the 'rag trade' and the journals associated with it. Older women today complain that their needs are largely disregarded but the economic facts are that they do not have the consumption potential of teenagers and girls in their early twenties. They have money, but they are conditioned in a way that prevents them spending it on themselves, either through guilt, or competing claims. The young female wage-earner, bearing in mind that food occupies a very small place in her budget, may have as much as £12 a week to spend on clothes, cosmetics and hair-dressing. Mary Quant and Caroline Charles owe their fashion empires as much to this new pattern of income distribution, as to their flair for fresh, stream-lined, space-age design.

Emphasising this point, *Flair* was initially geared to a more expensive range of ready-to-wear fashions than it is today. When it was launched in 1959 it was intended to appeal to the 30–40 age-group. After only one year, a change of policy brought it into the mass market of young women between the ages of 18 and 30, and it began featuring clothes in the medium price range. Belonging to the group of 'sub-glossies', which give glossy presentation at a cheaper price, *Flair*'s function is that of a wholesale catalogue, showing fashion-conscious women what is available, and how to make their selection in good taste while getting good value. One of *Flair*'s major contributions has been to ensure that the clothes it illustrates are readily available; it was one of the first magazines to print lists of stockists, thereby saving eager purchasers untold frustration. The Editor believes that it is immaterial to the reader whether an item is featured editorially or in an advertisement, but she regards it as vital that all garments shown should be readily obtainable.

Honey is likewise a display vehicle for the latest and best in the world of fashion and beauty, but it was originally more broadly based than it is today. It was brought out after surveys by Mark Abrams had demonstrated the potential spending power of a growing teenage market, and it was initially intended as a magazine of general guidance for young women, as it might be put over by a 'big sister'. This approach did not find favour with readers, and after a difficult start, *Honey* eventually achieved *rapport* by appealing to them on their own level.

In February 1965, *Honey* published this profile of its readers:

'*Honey* readers—aren't interested only in fashion, beauty and beat. You talk about holidays, careers, boyfriends, cooking, cars. About 50 per cent of you go abroad . . . and we find that contrary to the opinion of those know-all statistics men, your careers mean more to you than a stop-gap before marriage. You talk in several languages learned at night-school. You learn to cook the cordon-bleu way; you plan to revolutionise design and industry . . . [you are] everything that is young, gay, and going far.'

These were girls with several 'O' levels, and possibly some 'A' levels also, earning perhaps £10–£15 per week. Thus, while the magazine's prime function is to stimulate interest in fashion, it has also tried to include general features of interest to the educated girl, for example, 'Smoking Facts', 'Community Service Volunteers', 'Jobs Worth Having', and 'How to convert a bed-sit', to give only a sample.

Honey has sought wherever possible to break with the usual pattern of contents and to make each issue different from the last, with a minimum of regular features. The problem page was eventually discontinued and the panel of experts disbanded, to forestall boredom, though the Editor recognised that such features offered a valuable service. Instead, the magazine opted for a more adventurous brand of fiction, portraying life more realistically. For instance, it published the story of a girl who became pregnant just as she was about to enter London University. She succumbed to convention and married the father of her child, only to experience bitter resentment and frustration which culminated in a desperate bid to escape. This attempt at realism extended to the fashion features in which coloured models were used for the first time.

The magazine has also tried to reflect life in all parts of Britain. To achieve authenticity, special editions have been published from the North and South West regions, the editorial staff taking the magazine 'on location' to make contact with far-flung readers. As an additional service, to help readers get the clothes they want, *Honey* has sponsored its own boutiques in department stores all over the country, and encourages girls to badger shops for anything they cannot get so that their requirements are brought to the notice of manufacturers.

Honey was joined in 1966 by a younger sister, *Petticoat*, whose arrival testified to the new interest which advertisers were showing in the consuming potential of three million young girls aged 16–24, and particularly the youngest members of that group who were, according to the promoters, 'just about to blossom', and therefore ripe for guidance in all the arts of cultivating an attractive personal appearance.

The growth of the teenage market also produced a new group of fiction magazines. As a result of the post-war attrition in the women's press, one complete group of periodicals disappeared, the old pulp-fiction weeklies. To some extent the old approach survived (and still survives) in the North and in Scotland, where magazines like *Red Star* and *The People's Friend* continued to have a following. But in the South, readers wanted fiction based on real-life situations rather than larger-than-life romanticism. Thus, the story monthlies, *Woman's Story*, *True Story* and the rest, gained as the older fiction magazines went into decline. Alongside them, there grew up a new type of periodical for younger girls, the 'romance comic', of which *Marilyn* (1955), *Mirabelle* and

Romeo (1956), *Valentine* (1957), *Roxy* (1958) and *Boyfriend* (1959) were typical. *Mirabelle* was originally intended for girls of eighteen and upwards, but the publishers later discovered, to their astonishment, that it was most popular with the 13–16 age group. Largely due to the drop in the age of puberty, older teenagers were reading periodicals which not long since would have been considered suitable only for their mothers, with the result that the 'service' magazines were stretching further and further down the age-scale.

The 'romance comics' were written in picture-strip form. From the start they aimed at complete 'reader-identification', telling simple stories in the first person and featuring stereotyped heroes and heroines carefully created in the teenager's own image. There was one theme throughout which can broadly be described as 'the slings and arrows of outrageous fortune' which supervene to deflect Cupid's own (though Cupid could be guaranteed to reassert himself in time for the last few balloons of dialogue to explode into an ecstatic embrace). The moral code throughout was unimpeachable, and only on the problem pages was there any sign of the problems it posed for the modern teenager. Those writing for advice were dealt with sensibly and summarily, with no room for self-indulgence or self-pity. Pop-stars frequently lent their names and their personal weight to these columns, and at least one took his advisory role extremely seriously. These problem pages served to counteract the naïvety of the fiction which tended to portray a simplified world in which every dream came true if one wished hard enough, and where 'consequences' seldom entered.

Recognising that the counsellors in teenage magazines bear a particularly heavy responsibility both because of their potential influence, and because they are probably one of the few remaining independent sources of help to which a young person in trouble can or will turn, failing family and friends, one Editor, Miss Patricia Lamburn, who is responsible for a group of youth magazines, is experimenting with a new type of fiction. It is designed to reflect the everyday problems of young women (married and single) and to work towards their solution in a way never attempted by the limited 'romance comics'.

True Magazine, taken over by Pearson's and restyled, exemplifies this new approach. It is produced for young married women between the ages of 19 and 29 and aims at providing fiction different from that usually found in the women's press. It is the Editor's view* that, because *Woman* and *Woman's Own* built their success in an era when women had exhausted their capacity for feeling, they crystallised a

* Given in a personal interview.

stereotype for magazine fiction which was no more than glamorous escapism, altogether detached from real life. This formula has never been changed. Heroes and heroines have been socially upgraded in response to a changing social structure increasingly dominated by the middle classes, but they persistently inhabit an unreal world which is a pleasant focus for day-dreaming, but useless as a stage for acting out the real challenges of everyday living. *True Magazine* sets out to strip away this false glamour, and deal in a down-to-earth way with love in all its aspects—relations between mothers and their children, the colour question, the molesting of children, and other topics which deeply concern women.

These stories have to be well-written and convincing because of the importance and relevance of their subject matter; superficiality in these areas would never be tolerated. Their main purpose is to bring women vicarious satisfaction and emotional release from seeing their own problems tackled and brought to a solution, and great care is taken to ensure that readers gain something from each, whether it is a thought, a moral judgement or general guidance. The Editor feels that this is a very real way in which a magazine can instruct and educate its readers for their own good, without seeming to preach. By acting out the problems of the colour bar, for instance, Miss Lamburn believes it is possible to prepare women for coping with inter-racial living in their own neighbourhoods. Another important area which she hopes to explore through story-telling is life in the new towns. The loneliness of new urban and suburban living is a problem which has so far been disregarded by the women's magazines, and one which she thinks urgently needs attention.

True Magazine, therefore, unlike any of the fiction periodicals which preceded it, has the special *raison d'être* of guiding young women and chanelling their emotions. This underlying purpose invests it with considerable sociological significance, so that its progress will be followed with interest. At present it is fast gaining readers, and its circulation stands at 261,000.* Besides fiction, it carries a number of features (fashion, beauty, child-care, knitting and a problem page) primarily so that readers shall feel they are getting good value. Conscientious housewives might tend to regard money spent on an all-fiction magazine as unwarranted self-indulgence.

Hers, which appeared early in 1966, has been planned on similar lines, with the difference that it contains a higher proportion of 'service' features, being intended for newly-weds and those with young children,

---

* ABC figure for July–December, 1968.

women for whom romantic illusions have vanished before reality. For these two magazines to achieve their aims it is vital that editorial staff should keep in close touch with the lives and outlook of their readers. With this end in view, Miss Lamburn toured the British Isles to find out how life is lived beyond the metropolitan area, and what women in the rest of the country are doing and saying and thinking. She talked to representatives from the YHA and other organisations in touch with various sub-groups in the population, to social workers, and anyone else able to supply relevant information about women in contemporary Britain, their needs, interests and problems. Her tour emphasised the special difficulties encountered by women living in isolation on new housing estates, another area which can helpfully be explored through fiction.

It has not been easy to sell these two magazines to advertisers who find it difficult to accept that this type of market can be as valuable to them in the long run as the 'service' periodicals they normally patronise. *True* and *Hers* therefore carry little advertising. In this, too, they are breaking new ground, endeavouring to make profits on the number of copies sold rather than on the sales of advertising. This has given the editorial staff greater freedom to experiment with a new formula and other new ideas, the results of which are already highly encouraging for both magazines.

The same formula is being used in the remodelling of *Rave*, another teenage weekly taken over by Pearson's. It is being developed as a major publication reflecting a complete range of young interests and one markedly different from the usual teenage publications. Its staff are themselves young—between 19 and 21 years of age—and they interpret, and recast in their own idiom, ideas fed to them by their Editor. The magazine runs serious features side by side with the world of pop music, which receives dispassionate scrutiny, unlike the near-idolatrous approach of other magazines. Throughout, the magazine staff are trying to capture the new social codes and standards, and the marked religious feeling (quite independent of Church affiliations), which is growing up amongst young people today.

The Editor feels that the young need guidance, not in small matters, but in sorting out and facing up to the larger issues such as religion and sex. As many parents have apparently opted out of their responsibilities in this direction, she believes that perhaps magazines can exert a beneficial influence of their own. A series entitled 'This is Your Life' set out to reveal the standards by which the 'stars' lived their lives—'stars' were the pivot because of the weight they carry with teenagers. Subjects including rape and the colour bar have been featured. One story told of a young girl found raped and murdered in a park, and posed the question: 'How did the evening come to end like this?' in the hope of suggesting ways in which the girl might have been unwittingly responsible for the tragedy. This honest, authoritative approach, dramatically presented, is calculated to rivet the attention of young readers. Wherever problem pages are included, the Editor regards it as imperative that any appearance of lecturing and moralising should be carefully avoided.

While the story monthlies have generally been putting on circulation, the 'romance comics', the staple fare of the secondary-modern school-girl in the 'fifties, have lost popularity. Since 1958, *Boyfriend*, *Marilyn*, *Marty* and *Roxy* have all folded, though *Mirabelle* is managing to hold its own, and *Jackie*, a more recent (1964) entrant put out by D. C. Thomson, is doing well. The rapid turnover in titles is at least partly due to the fact that such literature is essentially transitory. It is linked to current crazes, particularly pop-music, and is therefore highly perishable. This does not mean that teenage publications are incapable of achieving lasting success, merely that any periodical leaping onto a bandwagon must expect to go out of favour when that bandwagon grinds to a halt.

Also contributing to the decline in the 'romance comic' is the fact that the whole character of the adolescent market is changing and re-forming due to the earlier physical maturation of girls. So advanced are they, that by the mid-teens the superficial picture-strip is inadequate to meet the needs created by their widening social experience, and these are better served by adult magazines. Many teenage girls now have a full social life outside school hours, as well as outside their working time, and for those with real fish to fry, a fictional date with Darlene at the discothèque is likely to be superfluous. Stories are shunned in favour of 'service', as the socially experienced girl switches to the fashion and beauty magazines which offer practical advice on how to attract a boy and hold his interest. In this chain of events, however, there would seem to be a place for story magazines which portray some of the situations in which girls may find themselves and suggest how to cope with them.

This is the place magazines like *Hers* and *Rave* are trying to fill, setting an example to the rest of the publishing trade in the art of combining good business with a conscientious attempt to exploit the potential influence of a magazine for the social good, rather than allowing such periodicals to be used merely as a selling medium. They show that, notwithstanding the fact that they exist primarily to make profits, women's magazines can be important instruments assisting in the social and personal adjustment of women of all ages, helping them towards happier and more fulfilling lives. This is not simply a matter of showing them how to cook well and dress attractively, but of helping them cope with the everyday problems of life in a complex and demanding society. Using the entertainment value of fiction to gain a platform for the staging of these real-life dramas, and a commentary upon them, is an important new trend at the younger end of the women's press where editorial freedom to exert a beneficial influence is nowhere more vital.

NOTES

1 Mary Grieve, *Millions Made My Story*, pp. 198–201.
2 *Good Housekeeping*, May, 1961.
3 *Op. cit.*, January 28th, 1961.
4 *The Listener*, October 31st, 1963.
5 *Op. cit.*, February 8th, 1951, p. 127.
6 Mary Grieve, *op. cit.*, p. 135.
7 W. D. McClelland, 'Women's Press in Britain', p. 151; a special tabulation based on the I.P.A. *National Readership Survey*, 1963.

6

The Little Woman Becomes Big Business

The tide of prosperity carried the women's magazine industry into the forefront of big business. The vast growth in circulations, together with the increasing consumption potential of the female population (their expenditure on clothes, footwear and cosmetics alone rose by 78 per cent in money terms between 1956 and 1965), finally convinced businessmen that no other medium could guarantee them access to this vast new market as effectively as the women's press, nor provide them with such a favourable selling climate. To quote Mary Grieve:

> '. . . it dawned on the businessmen of the country that the Little Woman was now Big Business. . . . American home economy had long been based on the sure knowledge that it was the women who spent the money on consumer goods, including consumer durables. The vast and profitable women's magazines in the States were founded and prospered on this fact. But Britain was a man's world, and still is in decisive matters. So it took our tycoons longer to believe that it is Mrs Jones, not Mr Jones, who chooses the goods that go into their home and down their throats.'[1]

The realisation that the women's magazines were capable of influencing the buying decisions of the bulk of British women began a new era in the history of the industry. The vast increase in advertising, beginning in the 'fifties, brought rich profits which soon attracted the attention of the giant publishing corporations. Late in 1958, with a view to expansion into the field of magazine publishing, the Mirror Group acquired the Amalgamated Press (incorporating Kelly-Iliffe). This 'Sleeping Giant', formerly owned by Lord Northcliffe, had passed to Lord Camrose in 1923, since when it had fallen into decline through lack of investment, presenting a progressively weaker challenge to its rivals. Re-named 'Fleetway Publications', and with the vast resources of the

Mirror empire backing its revival, it took only six months to bring it back into effective competition. New photographic studios and test kitchens were installed at Fleetway House to increase editorial resources, and the magazines themselves were remodelled to bring their presentation into line with the high standards set by the gravure weeklies.

To consolidate their own position in the face of this new threat, Odhams replied with a successful bid of £1·8 million for the Hulton Press. A few months later, it gained control of George Newnes with an offer of £13 million, out-bidding the *News of the World*.

The leading women's magazines were now gathered into two rival groups, a situation which, aggravated by the proliferation of titles and the insufficiency of advertising, inevitably gave rise to cut-throat competition between them. Promotion costs soared, and *Woman's Illustrated* and *Woman's Day* were together losing £700,000 a year when Cecil King (Chairman of the Mirror Group) approached Christopher Chancellor (Chairman of Odhams) with a 'rationalisation' scheme intended to be mutually beneficial. Initially, he proposed the setting up of a joint holding company for all women's magazines in which the Mirror Group would have a 51 per cent controlling interest, but would refrain from exercising its voting rights for a period of five years.

Odhams declined to take up this suggestion, and King's next proposal was for a 'negotiated merger' through an exchange of shares, at a cost to Odhams of £10 million. Unable to foresee a sufficient return on such an investment, and believing that a rejection of the Mirror offer would result in a take-over bid for the whole firm, Odhams sought an alternative agreement with the Thomson Organisation. A merger was subsequently announced, but Odhams' fragmented shareholding remained vulnerable to a better offer, and no sooner had Lord Thomson publicly discounted the possibility than Cecil King put in a counter-bid, winning control of the firm in 1961 after a bitterly-fought battle.

As a result of this change of ownership, the bulk of the women's press has been completely reorganised financially, administratively and editorially, a process which is still continuing. During the first phase, 1961–1967, it reaped the benefits of unified control and co-ordinated decision-making at management level, while retaining the stimulus of competition. A Publications Management Committee was specially formed by IPC to ensure that the three constituent firms, Fleetway, Newnes and Odhams, would still operate in effective competition, reviewing 'such items as trade terms, advertising rates and new launches'.[2] As a result, individual magazines continued to work in ignorance of what their rivals were planning, though they co-operated in implementing IPC's general policies laid down by the Managing Company. In addition, budgetary control was introduced, giving Editors clearly-defined financial limits within which to work, while a second 'Publicity and Promotions' committee was made responsible for co-ordinating 'expenditure on all publicity and promotions, including the sales of special issues, gifts and offers', which considerably reduced promotional and other costs.

Editorially, IPC's aim has been to introduce the principles of 'product differentiation' and 'specialisation of function' in an industry which has long suffered from wasteful duplication. It has been the fault of many magazines in the past that they have been characterless substitutes for one another, undifferentiated in the mind of the reader when she scans the bookstall. The new policy is to invest every magazine with its own 'brand image'—an individual character which will give it special appeal; also, to build for each title a reputation in one particular service area. In this way it is hoped to limit duplication, and to achieve a greater measure of complementarity between the family of periodicals now owned by IPC. To this end, a drastic pruning programme has been put into operation, euphemistically known as 'rationalisation', during which magazines have been killed, merged, or re-launched with new profiles.

Women's magazines are today run according to strict business methods and are answerable to cost-accountants. Their primary aim is to attract the maximum amount of advertising, which is the source of their profits. The result has been to produce a complete reorientation of policy, both in the conduct of existing publications and in the launching of new ones, based upon the 'economic' rather than the 'social' profiles of readers. Publishers are now chiefly interested in their disposable incomes and spending patterns, a knowledge of which is vital in the creation of suitable selling media for advertisers. Reader-research has therefore been concentrated in these areas to the almost total neglect of social characteristics.

An important development (for the effect it has had upon the shaping of magazine content), has been the discovery of the economic significance of the 'family cycle'. Dr Mark Abrams[3] has plotted the female spending curve against it. He has shown that three out of four girls become wage-earners at the age of sixteen, averaging £6 per week if they belong to the working class, and £8 per week if they are middle class. Half of them marry before they reach twenty-one years of age, and 80 per cent before they are twenty-five. While single, and during the first two years or so of married life when they tend to remain at work, these girls are at the peak of their spending power. Between 16 and 24, average expenditure on clothes for both classes combined is 30 per cent, and cosmetics account for a further 5 per cent. Once married, and with the birth of the first child imminent (usually after two years), which forces her to leave her job, the woman of twenty-four relinquishes her personal income and must contrive to support the family on her husband's salary alone until she is free to re-enter the labour market. Though some manage to combine family care and paid employment while their children are still young, most married women who return to work do so sometime after the age of thirty-five.

Thus, while the single woman under twenty-four years of age had a personal income which was spent mainly on herself, the married woman in the 25-35 age-group has only her husband's income, which is primarily expended on her family and her home. During this period she spends mainly on household goods and food. At this stage, too, the gap between the classes in terms of spending power begins to widen. While there is no appreciable difference between their financial status when single, after marriage the middle-class girl tends to retain more of her spending power; she also recoups it more quickly later. This is because the working-class husband does not improve his earnings a great deal after marriage, while his middle-class counterpart tends to marry with far better prospects, and can expect successive and remunerative promotions with age and experience.

These inequalities in disposable income increase with age. The working-class teenager usually takes a job and contributes to the family exchequer, while the middle-class adolescent is still at school and is a drain on it. This, however, is offset by the continued rise in the income of the middle-class breadwinner. By the age of forty, women of both classes are drifting back into employment, though the taxation system discriminates heavily against the middle-class wife by assessing incomes jointly. As a result, she probably benefits less from her extra earnings than does the working-class woman, whose contribution does not rocket the family income into the super-tax class.

Research of this kind has shown manufacturers that it is not necessarily in their best interests to aim at undifferentiated markets such as the mass weeklies offer. The cost-per-thousand (readers) is high, and the message will probably be wasted on a large proportion of them. For basic commodities, mass advertising is still the most economical, but in the specialised consumption areas, such as fashion, furnishing, and domestic appliances, concentrated selling, using media specially designed to reach the appropriate market, gives the best results. The monthlies are now making their bid for this kind of specialised advertising. Their continued existence depends upon proving to manufacturers their efficiency in reaching the particular markets they are interested in. This task is being made infinitely more difficult by competition from commercial television, and by long press-times, which are a serious draw-back. Issues carry dead-lines on advertising copy frequently three months in advance of publication, which make them unsuitable for manufacturers who require immediate communication. For them, T.V., the daily press (both of which can bring a message before the public in a day or so), and the weekly periodicals (with shorter press-times) are the preferred media.

The planners have been hard at work creating new magazines and re-styling others to meet these requirements. In March, 1966, *Everywoman* was spectacularly re-launched, promising its patrons 'A New Deal in Women's Monthly Advertising', with 'a print order boosted to 300,000 at no increase in advertisement rate'. According to the advance publicity, it had been 'Re-designed, Re-structured, Re-thought, Re-directed' throughout, 'with bold editorial outlook, new sophistication, dramatically increased fashion coverage' to offer 'the most excitingly modern medium in popular monthly journalism.'[4]

'E', as it then became, had its sights fixed on the 'top-geared younger women', a group imbued with 'the young idea'. The Editor, Miss Graeme Hall, visualized her ideal reader as being married to a rising young executive with future expectations of affluence. As she put it, 'It may be rabbit today, but there's mink around the corner'.* The average age of such women was put at 23, but it was intended that the magazine should appeal to all women between 16 and 40 who shared its outlook. It was seen as the prevailing characteristic of this group of consumers that they are chiefly interested in buying time. Because many of them work and therefore spend much more time outside the home than in it, they will save themselves time and labour in every possible way. These are the women who, before they marry, buy cheaply, and buy often. They do not bother to get shoes mended—they throw them away. To keep abreast of fashion they purchase clothes in the cheaper ranges, which they can exchange for the latest fashion idea at the drop of a wage-packet. But, once they become engaged or married, they acquire a sense of responsibility and begin to compare values. *Everywoman*'s fashion department, upgraded and expanded in the new magazine, set out to guide such women to the right shop-windows, and assist them in their choice.

This 'buying of time' extends throughout their purchasing. If necessary, these young women will pay higher prices for the convenience of buying what they need at a single store, and so avoid the time wasted in 'shopping around' for something cheaper. They want frozen food

* Personal interview.

and 'instant' meals, with a handful of 'fancy recipes' they can fall back on for entertaining, for they do not make cookery a hobby. They want time- and labour-saving gadgetry. Their homes are in fact their 'status backgrounds' and they will change their décor and furnishings frequently to keep in step with the latest trends, nearly as often, in fact, as they change their clothes. Since they earn for a while after marriage, they can afford to do this. There is a lull when the children arrive, but they are soon placed in nursery school, and the trend is for these young wives to make an early return to work. Then they are back to where they were before marriage, when, after paying for their keep, they had on average £9 or £10 a week to spend on beauty, fashion, records and travel. All of these consumption patterns conditioned *Everywoman*'s editorial approach, and were emphasised in selling the magazine to advertisers.

In accordance with IPC's policy that each one of its women's publications should acquire a reputation for excellence in a single area, *Housewife* was completely re-styled to make it 'the unquestioned leader in cookery'.[5] It also dealt 'authoritatively and informatively with all trends that . . . help to make the home gayer, happier, more efficient or more beautiful'.[5] A full-scale re-launch, planned for March, 1966, had to be cancelled at very short notice owing to the failure to win co-operation from the printers. They were unwilling to acquiesce in *Housewife* changing over from a square-backed two-and-sixpenny monthly, to a saddle-backed monthly priced at two shillings, since for them it would have meant under-used print capacity in a section of their plant. Instead, *Housewife* experimented within its existing framework, improving its presentation, and re-designing its content to appeal to the younger woman.

These changes were backed up with a powerful promotion campaign which publicised the new *Housewife* as a magazine geared to 'the young and prosperous', guaranteeing the advertiser 'maximum potential in a rich and expanding market'. Some idea of that potential can be gained from the various points in a profile drawn up by the promotion department. *Housewife* was planned to reach the 'quality' market of young, modern women, aged 25-35, who are 'successful wives and mothers in every respect', and who, socially, are 'on the way *up*':

'The *housewife* reader will demand much from life. She may already own, or be considering, the second car. She will belong to clubs, meet her friends often, dine out, travel widely abroad. And her out-going life will reflect itself in her home life. She will cook more exciting and attractive foods; shop more discriminatingly, spend more time on entertaining and leisure activities.'[5]

Housewife and *Everywoman*, both in serious difficulties, were the only two monthly periodicals to be completely remodelled in this way, but other magazines have unobtrusively been undergoing similar changes in an attempt to give them an individual character and a special focus. There have been marked changes in the content and presentation of *Good Housekeeping*, for example, all directed towards improving its attractiveness as an advertising medium. Like IPC, the National Magazine Co. has recognised the need to specialise, and has decided that in future, *Good Housekeeping* will concentrate on home service, cutting back on 'general interest' features and expanding its coverage of food and household appliances, two areas of considerable value to advertisers. At the same time it is attempting to upgrade the reputation of the Good Housekeeping Institute for probity and expertise. In addition, the magazine has been given an overall visual 'face-lift' in the hope of attracting more young women to replace and augment an ageing readership.

Another important development has been the creation of new magazines specially designed to reach particular markets of interest to advertisers, among them *Annabel* (1966), *Petticoat* (1966), and *Family Circle* (1964). *Annabel*, brought out by D. C. Thomson, is intended to appeal to 'the growing number of young marrieds'. Quoting from its pre-launch publicity, the magazine was the product of 'three years' continuous research', and designing it was clearly a systematic process. The prototype was put together on the basis of deductions made from various social statistics, for instance:

'*Annabel* knows that close on a million babies are born in Britain every year, and that young wives want to read all about parenthood. And that involves everything from prams and pedal-cars, to looking pretty while pregnant.'

While the emphasis in this last statement was commercial rather than social, the proprietors throughout their research were trying to create a magazine which was socially as well as commercially acceptable. Unlike other magazines created purely to exploit the potential of certain groups of consumers, with no prior testing to discover if the formula devised was appropriate to the social as well as the economic requirements of readers, *Annabel* did make some attempt to comply with the former.

The Editor, in a message included in the pilot issue, filled in some of the background:

'The big challenge facing us was three-fold. Could we formulate a new magazine for the young wife which was in tune with life, which was different, and which would sell? . . . Each successive stage of the magazine's development was tested on a cross section of young wives and underwent changes until we arrived at a dummy issue which we felt was near our objective. . . . We are now sure we have a magazine with an identity of its own—and it is geared to go! The title is something of a breakaway from tradition . . . "*Annabel*" is my young wife or yours. She expects a great deal more from a woman's magazine than her mother did. We mean to give her a magazine in which she will find the kind of information she seeks, and the kind of reading she really enjoys.'

Apart from this freshness of character, *Annabel*'s formula is standard, with particular emphasis on knitting for the family: '*Annabel* means to become a by-word for reliability and attractive patterns.' The assumption is that 'a young wife's heart is where her home is', and the magazine is essentially home-loving. Three years of research have not, apparently, yielded any firm evidence that women today are clamouring to have this time-honoured formula changed, but it has indicated that women's interests and their social experience have widened, and that this must be taken into account when writing for them:

'*Annabel* knows that young women paint kitchens, experiment with pastas, pay parking fines and want to know all about what other young wives are doing . . . [that] today's young wife is as much at home on the beach at Rimini as at Blackpool.'

The editorial staff aim at providing 'unrivalled coverage' of all these aspects of the young married woman's life, and as an added attraction the publishers are offering glossy magazine presentation at the low price of two shillings. No published figures are as yet available by which its initial success can be gauged, but the magazine is aiming at a target of 300,000.

Petticoat was launched by Fleetway to reach a very different, but immediately profitable market, the 14–19 year olds. The first publication to realise the value of teenage custom was *Mayfair*, a small 'quality' monthly which appeared in 1946. Though short-lived, it was a foretaste of things to come:

'At last, teens, here's your own magazine. In it, you will find features on fashion, beauty, films and careers as well as stories— all set with *Mayfair*'s seal which marks them as being of interest to you and therefore worthy of their appearance in the magazine. We will also introduce to you the names of reliable manufacturers —names which we think will be useful when you go shopping for clothes, cosmetics or just window-shopping. This way, you will get to know just where to go for that new suit or that special hair-do you've been planning for so long; we hope you'll like this idea and that it will save you many a weary shop-hunt and help you obtain the very best value for your money.'[6]

The magazine was clearly produced with the object of tapping the spending power of a new group of consumers. The offer to introduce readers to the names of 'reliable manufacturers' of clothes and cosmetics is evidence that the proprietors contemplated establishing a close link with commercial interests. The intention was further substantiated by a statement published a year later:

'Today, in spite of almost overwhelming difficulties, controls and restrictions, we are publishing our thirteenth issue, and we . . . have many thousands of readers at home and abroad. It has taken three years of uphill fight to achieve recognition for the teenager in the commercial world. But results have justified our persistence.'

By this the Editor meant that stores were beginning to cater for the teenager, and that more activities were being planned for this group. The fact that *Mayfair* lasted only a short time was probably due to the fact that it was planned as a 'junior glossy' for the daughters of the wealthy, and that this was too limited a market to tempt advertisers. Teenagers did not constitute an attractive consumer group until teenage earnings in the mass of the population had risen sufficiently to give them a surplus to spend on clothes, sweets, cosmetics and entertainment. Prior to this, the pattern was for the young wage-earner to turn over his or her entire wage-packet in return for keep, and to receive back a few shillings as pocket money. With the growth of affluence, parents, remembering their own poverty-stricken youth, began to demand less and less from their offspring, many of whom eventually made no contribution to the family exchequer at all, leaving them with large sums to spend on themselves.

Publishers first exploited the teenage passion for film-stars, pop-music, and romance in the crop of picture-strip weeklies (already described) which came out in the mid-'fifties. Earlier, *Vanity Fair* (1949), had been brought out to capitalise on the fast expanding fashion market amongst the late-teens and twenties and was joined by *Flair* in 1960. *Honey* made a big hit with this group in 1961, but the young teens were not catered for until the arrival of *Petticoat*. Created as a younger sister to *Honey*, *Petticoat* was geared to the fast growing early-teen fashion trade. The potential of this market is best summed up by quoting from a pre-launch folder, giving a preview of the magazine, which was distributed amongst prospective advertisers:

'*Petticoat* will be a brand new opportunity in a brand-free market. *Petticoat* offers you a potential two million young women in the 15–19 age group. *Petticoat* will be telling them about the clothes they ought to buy, the beauty products they ought to try, and fashion accessories, holidays, books, careers, and pastimes that are big news for Miss 1966.

'Girls in the *Petticoat* market command more than £250 million a year of uncommitted spending money. . . . Statistics show that over 70 per cent of all girls aged 15–19 have left school and are earning for themselves—the highest incidence of earners in any age group. These potential *Petticoat* readers spend far more heavily on footwear and stockings than any other age-group—an average of six pairs of shoes and forty pairs of stockings a year for each girl—and the largest amount of nail-varnish, eye-shadow, mascara, eye-liner and deodorant!'

According to the figures published in this folder, the expenditure of these two million girls was apportioned thus:

Cosmetics	£8½ million
Outerwear	£33 million
Underwear	£13 million
Stockings	£22 million
Footwear	£26 million

a total of over £174 million annually. This teenage market, conveniently for the advertiser, can be treated as a homogeneous entity. It has been established that, in this age group, patterns of expenditure are unaffected by class differences. Everywhere the demand is for up-to-date clothes which can be bought cheaply, worn hard and discarded in a few months. 'Serviceable' is a word which has entirely dropped out of the teenage vocabulary, along with 'good quality', 'practical' and 'hard-wearing'. Marks and Spencer pioneered the mass production of good design, and other firms are following their lead. The result is that women are slowly being emancipated from the doctrine that clothes should be bought to last, and are discovering that 'cheap' does not necessarily any longer mean 'nasty'. The effects are being felt all over the fashion industry, but it is the teenage passion for novelty and variety which is at present underwriting a large section of the 'rag trade' and the periodicals which are its shop-windows.

The most remarkable of the new magazines tailor-made to reach pre-researched markets is *Family Circle*. It is unusual in several respects. First, it is wholly a 'service' magazine, from which fiction has been rigorously excluded. Second, it is one of only two* women's magazines to be distributed through retail grocery outlets. Third, it is a conspicuous example of Anglo-American co-operation in the publishing world. *Family Circle* is owned jointly (and equally), by Cowles Communications Inc., publishers of American *Family Circle*, and the Thomson Organisation. The magazine's success owes much to the judgement of Cowles' experts who initially drew attention to the potential of British grocery chains and later contributed advice in all departments prior to its launching. In addition, many American firms advertising in American *Family Circle* have subsidiaries in this country, a connection which has proved valuable to the British magazine.

Family Circle was the first attempt by the Thomson Organisation to break IPC's monopoly in women's publishing, and the decision to experiment with a new sales outlet was taken in the knowledge that it offered perhaps the only possible way of entering the field. The magazine, a square-backed monthly sold at 1s. 3d., was created as a result of a merger between two supermarket publications, *Trio* and *Family*, Sainsbury's own magazine. It is not, in fact, a 'supermarket magazine', but a women's periodical specialising in home service and designed to appeal to the young housewife. It is commonly thought to be a supermarket publication because it is distributed solely through grocery chains, an assumption which materially assisted Thomson's in gaining the acquiescence of retail newsagents. The promoters regarded these stores as a promising new point of distribution, since there was a complete absence of rival publications. Also, they were convenient for the purchaser—a woman shopper could collect her copy at the same time as she selected her other merchandise, and moreover, the buying climate of the store pre-disposed her to do so. Most important of all, exposure to 'concentrated housewife traffic' was guaranteed.

* The other is *Living*, a sister publication launched by Thomson's in 1967.

To discover the sales potential of these 'solus outlets', an investigation into housewives' shopping and reading habits was commissioned from Marplan Ltd. The results, as interpreted by Thomson's own research unit, showed that such a magazine could reasonably aim at reaching 60 per cent of the women using these stores, taking into account the fact that the average housewife visits her grocer three times a week, and in fact uses more than one store. Costings based on projected sales and advertising revenue indicated the likelihood of a profitable investment, and it only remained to secure the co-operation of the grocery chains.

In return for handling *Family Circle* they were offered a profit of one-third, and 100 per cent s.o.r. (sale or return) terms. As a further selling-point, other benefits which would accrue to the stores in the long run were stressed, such as the increased trade which would result from the magazine's educational function of teaching the housewife to feed her family better (*Family Circle* was to emphasise cookery). Six out of the eight chains approached agreed to act as outlets, with Tesco holding off and Sainsbury refusing because they already possessed their own magazine. Later, a compromise was reached: Sainsbury's *Family* would merge with *Family Circle* and be replaced by special editions of *Family Circle* inset with Sainsbury's own supplement.

As the position stood in November, 1965, *Family Circle* was being sold in 10 per cent* of the main retail stores all over the country, which between them represented 30 per cent of the total annual grocery trade. The proprietors made themselves responsible for displaying their magazine in these stores, setting up specially designed dispensers for them, which were periodically serviced by a mobile marketing force. The installation and servicing of these dispensers by the publishers' own representatives was a policy proposed and fought for by the Americans.

In choosing to distribute their new magazine through supermarkets the promoters could be sure of reaching a substantial number of women, but not necessarily the right kind of women. *Family Circle* was created with the object of reaching young housewives with a full-time interest in home-making, particularly those with young families to feed and clothe, since these would constitute an attractive and well-defined market for manufacturers of domestic products, on whose backing the future of the magazine would depend. The magazine was therefore very carefully tailored to appeal to these home-centred 'primary' readers.

The concept of 'primary readership' was defined and evaluated by M. Agostini, the author of the winning paper in the Thomson Gold Medal award for media research, 1964. 'Primary readers' are those who

---

* The current (1969) figure is 14 per cent, or 18,000 of this country's 123,000 retail outlets.

buy a publication because they are personally interested in it, while 'secondary readers' constitute those members of a household who read a copy as a result of it having been introduced into the home by a primary reader. 'Tertiary readers' receive their copies from friends or relatives, living away, or see them in the course of visits to the hair-dresser, doctor and so on. Agostini pointed out significant differences in the quality of readership between the three groups, with primary readers having the highest value in terms of interest in, and attention to, what is being communicated. Thus, in order to maximise the impact of any publication, and in particular its advertising content, it is neces-sary to secure the highest possible number of primary readers.

This the publishers of *Family Circle* have sought to achieve by 'excluding from the editorial plan, items calculated to appeal to non-housewives, such as fiction and romantic features'. (This presumably has also had the effect of eliminating casual readers, as well as restricting the amount of 'passing on'.) *Family Circle* was planned to fulfil the functions of a work of reference on home subjects, thereby encouraging a high level of reader retention in the home, and special binders were made available to facilitate this.

This three-point plan, embracing a young-housewife readership, 'double selectivity' (i.e. highly concentrated exposure to housewives, and the elimination of casual appeal), and a high level of retention in the home, was offered to the advertising world together with more realistic advertising rates than *Trio* had been able to offer. These new rates were based on the decision to aim at a readership of a slightly higher class than the mass circulation weeklies, a policy which has brought *Family Circle* into direct competition with the 'service' monthlies, in particular *Woman and Home*, and has permitted the publishers to drop their rates into the monthly range. The cost-per-thousand to the advertiser is well below that of other monthlies, and special discounts are given to advertisers of products sold through supermarkets. The commercial response has been excellent, but, as part of editorial policy, the propor-tion of advertising material to editorial content is not allowed to exceed fifty pages in a hundred-page issue. For issues over this size, the propor-tion is increased *pro rata*. Food and chemists' lines predominate at present, though the research unit believes there is good potential in the markets for furniture, decor and household supplies, and it is likely that advertising in *Family Circle* will eventually expand in these directions.

Measured by the criterion of the advertising it has managed to attract, *Family Circle* is an unqualified success. But it is less easy to estimate how far it is matching up in other respects to the pattern originally planned for it. The task is complicated by the existence of characteristics which have never before been measured. Nevertheless, it was essential to have some estimate of the magazine's performance, however tentative, and the proprietors have used several research media, including the IPA surveys, specially commissioned reports from Attwood Statistics Ltd., and the N.O.P., together with surveys carried out by Thomson's own research unit. The measurement of readership for monthly magazines is generally known to be unsatisfactory, and it was no surprise to discover in the figures published by the IPA in March, 1965, a serious underestimate of 642,000 readers when the known sale of the magazine was 733,000. Even so, this latter figure involved the publishers in a rebate to advertisers. To secure commercial support and engender confidence, the American publishers insisted upon the unprecedented (in this country) step of offering advertisers a guaranteed sale. The policy was put into effect with a guaranteed minimum circulation of 750,000, a large figure which *Family Circle* only just failed to reach. The policy, though resisted at the time, is now considered to have been sound, since it gave advertisers both initial security and a subsequent bonus when sales rose. With the usual practice of relying on ABC 'estimates' during a launch period, advertisers stand to lose substantially until the market settles down.

Ever since, the magazine's sales have been rising steadily. An interim analysis has shown that it is achieving its objectives of reaching young housewives in the C_1C_2 class, and maximising its 'primary' readership: 62·8 per cent of its readers were shown to be under the age of 45, and 61·4 per cent had children under 15. The class breakdown indicated that the magazine was reaching a slightly higher class of readers than had been expected, 20·2 per cent being in the AB group, and 62·2 per cent in the C_1C_2 category. On this showing it would seem that *Family Circle* is succeeding in fulfilling its promises to its patrons.

Editorially, *Family Circle* sets out to be a down-to-earth 'service' magazine for the 'one hundred per cent housewife'. Stripped of all frivolity, sentimentality and romance, it is planned for use as a cumulative 'home manual' (one way of ensuring continuity of readership in the absence of serial fiction). It specialises in cookery and aims to give the best coverage in this area of any women's magazine. This policy is based on two assumptions, first, that the biggest task facing any woman is that of feeding her family, and second, that the younger housewives of Britain are largely ignorant in this sphere and need step-by-step guidance, their mothers in general having failed to impart to them even the most elementary knowledge of domestic skills. Although the magazine is meant chiefly for young women, it is anticipated that it will also be of use to the older generation who were similarly denied domestic training, unlike their Victorian forbears who were called upon to be versatile home administrators and comprehensively trained for that calling as women today seldom are.

The food featured in *Family Circle* is chosen for easy preparation and attractiveness. Similarly, the fashion section is tailored to the same simple formula, showing cheap, attractive, up-to-date clothes which follow prevailing trends rather than setting them. It is geared to the average woman's needs and tastes, whereas other publications tend to get rather further ahead of their readers. In the home-furnishing department, however, the policy is to keep one step in advance of present buying habits. The reader is given something to aim for, bearing in mind that financial circumstances change, and what cannot be managed today may possibly be afforded tomorrow.

Recently, *Family Circle*'s '100 per cent service' formula has been modified. Fiction is still excluded, but its range of features is being widened to include fashion, child-care, and other topics which look away from the kitchen and have a more personal interest. The magazine is still committed to devote 30 per cent of editorial matter to food, but the limits this imposes are now beginning to show. As a deliberate policy, the 'clinical' approach of earlier issues is being softened to give the magazine a warmer personality. American *Family Circle* is similarly giving a wider interpretation to the concept of 'service' to secure fuller reader-involvement.

In its concern to meet real needs *Family Circle* is bent on achieving the highest possible standards of service, backed by thorough testing in all departments, even in knitting, where an employee makes up all designs specially prepared for the magazine. Such care is regarded as essential in building up reader-confidence. In addition, periodic surveys are carried out to discover which articles are most popular and useful, and results have so far accorded well with the forecasts. Firm evidence of the magazine's wide and growing appeal is provided by its circulation figures. In the second half of 1967 it passed the million mark,* and has become Britain's largest-selling women's monthly magazine.

Family Circle's meteoric rise has variously been attributed to its high proportion of colour (a big selling point), its incomparable value, its favourable selling pitch, and its practical, professional approach. The reader is getting an obvious bargain; so is the advertiser. For the first time, he is not buying access to a heterogeneous mixed-quality readership, but a pre-selected circulation amongst 'primary' readers for whom

---

* *Family Circle*'s growth rate is controlled to match the circulation levels which are guaranteed to its advertisers six months in advance.

Family Circle is a 'trade magazine' and who give it intensive use over an extended period. Consistent editorial quality is vital, and to achieve it the publishers have appointed as Editor a fully-trained domestic economist whose qualifications fit her to set and maintain the high standards required.

In November, 1967, *Family Circle* was joined by a sister publication, *Living*. Again, American experts co-operated in creating an economically viable magazine, which was brought out to counteract the threat of a competitor to *Family Circle*. Other courses of action were considered; the choices included bringing out *Family Circle* twice a month, selling another of Thomson's magazines alongside it, improving trade terms, reducing its cover price, and adding supplements. These alternatives were discarded in favour of bringing out a new magazine. There appeared to be scope for an additional publication: *Family Circle* normally sold out in two weeks leaving the dispensers empty—also it was reaching only 1 in 12 of the housewives using these grocery stores.

To reach those readers not attracted to *Family Circle* the 'editorial mix' had to be different, in particular more broadly-based. Consequently, *Living* includes leisure interests and activities, fiction and features. This has the disadvantage of bringing it into direct competition with established 'general interest' magazines, particularly the weeklies which have a lower cover price. It therefore sets out to offer a higher standard than its rivals, giving purchasers the fullest possible value.

Living's advertising and editorial departments are independent of *Family Circle*'s, but co-ordination is ensured through their joint management. *Living* has reached its guaranteed net sale of 500,000, and advertising support is also satisfactory. However, advertisers are reluctant to patronise both magazines on the grounds that they are merely getting a duplicated readership. *Living*'s major task will be to attract an entirely different type of reader, which will extend the advertiser's 'reach'. Meanwhile, *Family Circle* is finding it difficult to attract advertising outside food and related products, but the position is likely to improve with the widening of the range of commodities available in supermarkets.

IPC claim that their relationship with newsagents precludes their entry into the supermarket field, but have replied with four other magazines, *Intro* (Odhams, 1967), *Woman Bride and Home* (Odhams, 1968), *Fashion* (Fleetway, 1968), and '*19*', (Newnes, 1968).

Intro, produced by *Woman*'s editorial team, lasted only six months. It was a magazine of bright ideas and awkward dimensions which failed to catch on. Aimed at the younger 'with it' generation, it presented a lively mixture of fashion, beauty, entertainment, fiction, letters and features, in an entirely new way. It was colourful, direct and honest, and had an individual style, but, to quote one Editor, 'It made the mistake of thinking that when you write for the young you cannot fail if you throw together a mixture of pop, fashion and sex and splash bright colours around'.* 'Gimmicks' were soon abandoned, and by the time the magazine folded it had developed a coherent and promising editorial approach, but being an expensive weekly (1s. 6d.), carrying little advertising, time was not in *Intro*'s favour.

Woman Bride and Home is the latest example of a magazine serving a specific group, one whose attention-span is estimated to be a mere two years. It is a practical magazine catering to the many engaged girls whose needs are too specialised to be covered in *Woman*. *Woman Bride and Home* was launched 'on the back' of *Woman*, and is its satellite—the editorial staffs of both liaise to prevent clashing. The magazine appears six times a year and covers every aspect of preparing for marriage.

March, 1968, saw the appearance of the first major fashion magazine for the older woman to be published for almost forty years,† namely, *Fashion*. *Fashion* is a direct challenge to *Vogue* which has been steadily losing sales, and is edited by a former Editor of *Vogue*, Miss Ailsa Garland. In choosing to direct the magazine at the over 25s, the proprietors showed that at Fleetway, as elsewhere in the IPC,‡ it was beginning to be recognised that the 'youth cult' had left too many women inadequately catered for, for too long. *Fashion* is lavishly produced, surpassing its rivals in page-size and in its (Continental) standards of colour reproduction. Besides fashion and beauty, it offers a range of supplementary features on 'the home, food, art, travel, motoring, education and all the other subjects that interest and stimulate the contemporary woman'. Wherever possible, overseas stockists are given for items featured in the magazine, a sign that the Editor sees a future for *Fashion* in the export markets.§

Priced at 4s., and aiming at a circulation of 150,000, *Fashion* must include a minimum of 70 advertising pages to achieve viability. Some critics feel that by staying close to *Vogue*'s formula it may fall foul of the tide against which most fashion 'glossies' are struggling, namely the diminishing appeal of specialist fashion literature. One Editor has predicted the emergence of a completely new set of fashion journals reflecting the changed conditions within the fashion trade and the new,

---

* Personal interview.
† The last was the English edition of *Harper's Bazaar* (1929).
‡ In 1968, Odhams were also contemplating filling the gap left by recent closures with at least one magazine intended for post-teenage consumption.
§ This point was brought out in an interview given by Miss Garland to Ernestine Carter, fashion columnist, in the *Sunday Times* (March 10th, 1968).

differentiated market, in which teenagers and twenty-year-olds have a concept of fashion all their own.

'*19*' exemplifies the coming trend. In outlook it resembles *Honey*, but is 'less virginal, and more exciting in its fashion coverage'.* It is designed as a sophisticated fashion vehicle for the 17–22 group, which the Editor sees as 'an emerging force to be wooed and won at a professional level'. In many respects it resembles its American namesake *Seventeen*, whose success in reaching the high-school girl, and in establishing merchandising links with stores has greatly impressed British women's publishers, some of whom would like to expand in this direction. Like *Seventeen*, '*19*'s interests go deeper than fashion. Editorially, it aims at reflecting contemporary attitudes honestly, and with feeling, both in its fiction and in its features. Perceiving the simmering but submerged problem of colour prejudice, '*19*' came out with a penetrating article on the subject (prepared much earlier) at the time of the public outcry caused by Mr Enoch Powell's remarks concerning integrated living.

'*19*' is selling well amongst better-educated girls, those with 'O' and 'A' levels. It has also been well received by advertisers. Its primary objective is to establish its authority, going for sales and leaving over for the time being the possibility of developing a merchandising role. *Honey* is already engaged in this, but it is a costly venture when fully extended, as the experience of American magazines such as *Mademoiselle* and *Seventeen* shows.

The re-styling of existing monthlies, and the appearance of new, custom-built magazines, slanting their content towards the areas most profitable to advertisers, testifies to the change in the balance of power from the editorial to the business side in publishing for women. Leading periodicals are intensifying their advertising campaigns and supplying increasingly sophisticated data concerning the consumer coverage they are able to offer. *Woman* achieved spectacular success in 1965 with a nation-wide campaign to establish its importance as an advertising medium, which, almost as a by-product, gained it an extra hundred thousand readers. The campaign took the form of a series of four '*Woman* Shopping Weeks' (for Food, Fashion, Furnishing and Beauty) designed to 'link magazine readers and shoppers, advertisers and retailers, in a fully co-ordinated promotion of specific markets over a seven day period'.[7] More than 60,000 supermarkets and shops participated in the Food Week alone, and 'more than £200,000 was invested in this issue, the highest investment ever made in any single issue of

---

* Personal interview.

Woman'.* A special *Times Supplement*,[8] in which reporters investigated every aspect of the magazine's production, was arranged beforehand to give 'a complete picture of *Woman*'s giant marketing power'. *The Times* was chosen to undertake this important survey because of its reputation for independent criticism.

Campaigns of this kind emphasise the stark economic reality that even the giants of women's publishing stand or fall by the amount of advertising they can attract. With the intensification of competition between periodicals for advertising custom it has become vital for them to demonstrate both their efficiency as advertising media and their superiority over other methods of mass communication. Advertisers need to know the number of readers they are getting for every pound they spend on advertising space, which means they require to be supplied with accurate circulation figures.

Before the war, when the 'balance of power' was in the publishers' favour, advertisers experienced considerable difficulty in obtaining correct sales figures for the publications they sought to patronise. The position was slightly improved with the setting up of the Audit Bureau of Circulations in 1934, but still only a few women's publications subscribed to it. Membership increased after the war, but the women's press was still conspicuous by its under-representation until 1961, when IPC decided on membership for its latest acquisitions. Even today, audited figures are not available for all women's magazines, notable exceptions being *Queen*, *Vogue*, and the D. C. Thomson group. The National Magazine Co.'s periodicals joined the ABC as late as 1967, but the trend is for new publications to register immediately with the Bureau, and to pursue a policy of frankness with regard to their sales.

Publishers normally make available all necessary information regarding the circulation of at least the leading women's journals. But these figures alone give an incomplete picture of the actual number of readers reached. Total consumer coverage, which is what advertisers are interested in, can only be ascertained by supplementing audited sales figures with readership surveys. The first attempt to measure readership regularly was made by the *Hulton Readership Surveys* begun in 1946. These were designed to yield information on the readership of leading newspapers and periodicals classified according to age, sex, marital status, class and region, together with additional tables showing the reading habits of special groups of consumers. They ceased publication in 1956 and were replaced by the *National Readership Surveys* sponsored by the Institute of Practitioners in Advertising. To supplement these,

* Personal interview.

publishers have commissioned other readership studies from agencies such as Marplan, or from internal research departments where firms can afford to maintain them.

A mass of data has been produced in recent years, all of it designed to help the advertiser select 'that combination of women's magazines that will most effectively communicate his message to the correct section of the population at the correct time and at the correct time intervals'.[9] Much of this research is in depth, employing highly sophisticated techniques. One of the more important surveys was that commissioned by *Woman* from the Odhams Research Division, published in 1964 under the title *A New Measurement Study of Women's Weekly Magazines*. It broke entirely new ground in media research attempting to improve on the IPA Surveys which were generally accepted to be unsatisfactory because of their failure to allow for parallel and replicated readership, a serious source of inaccuracy.*

The study had four main objectives. The first was 'to estimate "Issue-Readership" in such a way that distortion due to replicated and parallel readership was eliminated [showing] how costs per page per thousand are modified when [these] are excluded'. Second, it attempted to enumerate 'Reading Days', 'the total number of days on which a reader is exposed to an issue of a publication', an entirely new quantification, which again affects the true costs of advertising. Third, it tried to measure 'Page Exposure', i.e. 'the average number of pages or "spreads" to which an average reader is exposed on an average day', the first time that statistics of this kind had been made available in Britain. Finally, a pioneer attempt was made to investigate the 'audience attitude' dimension, and to measure some of the qualitative aspects of the leading weeklies, using a structured questionnaire.

It is an impressive study, showing 'scrupulous attention to detail and a rigorous application of the best possible research methods' but according to one review, 'the results are complex and often confusing and do not present to a media planner a clear pointer as to how to select the best magazine'.[10] The confusion arises partly from too much sophistication—interpreting this kind of data would present problems even to a qualified statistician—but more especially out of the basic fact that 'the pattern of readership for magazines bears very little rela-

* Changes in the NRS have now been made which took effect in the period January–June 1968. They are designed to clarify the concept of 'readership' for advertisers. 45 more publications are now covered, and information on 'intensity' of readership is provided for 85 periodicals. Sample size has been increased from 16,000 to 30,000 and the number of sampling points increased to 1,200.

tion to the pattern of circulation'. In the monthly section of the market, the first four magazines in order of circulation in the first half of 1966 were *Family Circle, Woman and Home, She* and *My Home*, but the first four magazines in terms of IPA readership for the same period were: *Vogue, Woman and Home, Good Housekeeping* and *Family Circle*. There was less discrepancy in the placing of the mass weeklies, but although they appear to show a higher correlation between readership and circulation size, 'it is by no means a correlation of one.... Some magazines do gain more readers per copy than others.'[11]

This paradox accounts for the apparently conflicting claims made by the various magazines in their promotion campaigns. Blinded by technique and bewildered by a mass of statistics that seem to indicate that every magazine is the 'best buy', how does the advertiser make his choice? The following suggests the most likely approach:

'Research once again can provide only guide lines for media selection and cannot be expected to provide the complete answer to the media planner. . . . Until somebody traces through the life of a magazine and shows the way magazines are dealt with, how they are read and what people do with these magazines in real life, no amount of mathematical models and logical hypotheses will convince a media planner of their relative values. . . . The sensible media planner will look at the figures and try and understand them, but will still base his media planning on the facts that he knows are true. These are the circulation and the rate charged for space.'[12]

Thus, whatever refinements are introduced into the measurement of readership, the fact remains that the hard currency of mass media advertising is the number of copies sold, so that the prime concern of the publisher is to safeguard his circulation. This does not necessarily mean boosting sales as far as they will go. In view of the run-on-loss situation facing most publishers, he will rather aim at reaching an optimum circulation figure at which costs are minimised and the advertising rate is maximised. This optimum figure varies from magazine to magazine, and can be arrived at only after several important variables have been taken into account.

The most crucial is the printing process, as each method has its own cost curve, with widely differing break-even points. For instance, photogravure, which is costly to prepare, becomes an economic proposition at between 500,000 and a million copies. Theoretically, there is no limit to the savings reaped thereafter, but an effective 'ceiling' of three million is placed on it. After that point the marginal revenue from advertising falls below the marginal costs of production simply because the advertising rate cannot be further raised with increasing circulation, and the proprietors lose on every copy sold. Thus it can be a positive embarrassment to a magazine to acquire more than its optimum number of readers. This happened to *Woman* when its circulation approached three and a half million in 1957, and *Woman's Realm* was launched the following year to absorb the excess.

For magazines on very tight cost schedules, an appreciable increase in sales which is not large enough to carry them on to a new advertising rate, can mean a substantial loss. If the reverse occurs, it is the advertiser who suffers, since publishers are notoriously slow to adjust their rates downwards. Occasionally, the disparity between a magazine's value in terms of circulation and its advertising rate becomes too great, and advertisers withdraw their support, with the result that the magazine has to cease publication. This was the case with *Woman and Beauty*.

The weeklies charge high rates for their mass coverage, but it is felt that, '. . . on the whole, the market is still willing to bear [them]; . . . it is extremely unlikely that any new competitor could enter the field at a rate competitive with the established magazines. They are in an entrenched position and represent a major advertising monopoly force'[13] as 'one of the most economic and effective ways of reaching the mass housewife and woman audience'. They have managed to retain their position in the face of competition from other media such as television and the national press and represent 'a unique selling force in the British advertising scene . . .'

Their success in achieving this position is the more remarkable because they are a more costly proposition to the advertiser than either the daily press or T.V., both of which have the added advantage of immediacy. In 1963 it was estimated that to advertise in the daily press cost 0·07d. per thousand readers per message, on television, 0·15d. and in the women's press, 0·28d. for a four-colour page in a weekly selling between one and three million copies, and 0·35d. for a black-and-white page in a monthly with an average circulation of 250,000. Advertising rates for all magazines have in fact been rising faster than those for any other medium.

Table 1: Changing cost of potential audience of 1,000
1964 = 100

Medium	1961	1965	Unit
National newspapers	95·3	100·9	column inch
Magazines	87·2	106·4	b. and w. page
T.V.	101·5	95·5	second

Source: IPA, *Trends in Audiences and Advertising Costs*, 1966.

Nevertheless, the women's magazines have continued to attract a large share of national advertising because they reach more women consumers more effectively than any rival medium. The boom in women's periodicals has in fact parallelled the boom in domestic consumption and the vast expansion in advertising which has accompanied it.

Until 1961, the growth in advertising expenditure averaged 10 per cent a year, a rate of increase of only one-tenth of one per cent over twenty-five years when measured against the rise in national income. In absolute terms, the amount spent in 1963 totalled £501 million compared with only £98 million in 1938. The Press's share in 1963 was £161 million (32 per cent), the bulk of which was divided between the national dailies and London evening papers (£68 million), and the periodical press (£40 million).[14]

Since 1961, the battle of the periodical press to maintain its required proportion of advertising has intensified in the face of growing competition from commercial television, the T.V. magazines and the colour supplements. The rising importance of T.V. as an advertising medium can be gauged from the fact that it increased its share from a negligible 3·4 per cent of total advertising revenue in 1953 to a substantial 21·4 per cent (£85 million), ten years later. By 1965 it was attracting £106 million a year. Between 1963 and 1968, advertising revenue for the three leading magazine companies has shown considerable fluctuations, making assessment difficult. Certainly, over the industry as a whole magazines have not done as well as other sections of the press, but IPC magazines, particularly the weeklies, have a poorer record than most.

Table 2: Advertising Revenue for Fleetway, Newnes and Odhams, 1963–68

	Advertising Revenue £000		
Year	FLEETWAY	NEWNES	ODHAMS
1963	3,023	7,483	9,301
1964	3,121	7,722	9,828
1965	3,439	8,305	9,996
1966	3,270	8,611	10,113
1967	3,172	8,581	10,340
1968	2,623	8,519	9,380

Source: Extracted from Buckmaster and Moore, Report on IPC, 1969.

However there are signs that here, as in the U.S.A., advertisers may be losing faith in commercial T.V. as a reliable advertising medium. The first half of 1968 brought an encouraging 33·9 per cent increase in magazine revenue, contributing to an 18·8 per cent rise for the whole year, but it is too early to say whether the trend is significant.

In the United States, competition from commercial television has forced magazine publishers to provide 'split-run' facilities and regional editions for the benefit of advertisers. *McCall's* alone publishes twenty-six regional editions and in addition offers 20 'spot' markets covering particular metropolitan areas. These allow advertisers to concentrate their selling campaigns in areas most profitable to them, and also enable them to patronise advertising media which would otherwise be too costly. As yet, British magazines have not ventured into these areas, but there is growing conviction within IPC that 'regionalisation' will have to come, although initially it may create production problems and inflate costs. The new, intensely competitive situation will demand greater flexibility on all fronts. It has been suggested* that there may have to be a change of policy regarding periodicity. For the convenience of advertisers, *Vogue* now comes out twice a month in Spring and Autumn which are periods of concentrated demand for advertising space, and other magazines may find it necessary to follow suit.

The vast expansion in advertising, and the ability of women's magazines to attract a considerable portion of it, has made them the big business which they are today and has brought about what amounts to a revolution in the approach to publishing for women. But the golden

Table 3: Profit Margins 1963–68

Year†	FLEETWAY Per cent	NEWNES Per cent	ODHAMS Per cent
1963	2·5	13·5	8·6
1964	4·1	14·5	13·0
1965	4·7	15·4	12·9
1966	6·9	13·3	13·1
1967	6·5	11·8	10·2
1968	7·8	11·5	6·1

† Ending February.
Source: Extracted from Buckmaster and Moore, Report on IPC, 1969.

years of huge profits and seemingly unlimited growth are over. Fluctuating, but generally declining profit margins reflect both the volatility of advertisers and the vulnerability of those publishers who are largely dependent upon an advertising subsidy. It is significant that Fleetway, with a comparatively low yield from advertising (one-fifth of its total

* Theodore Peterson, 'Magazines: Today and Tomorrow', in *Gazette*, Vol. 9–10 (1963), p. 228.

revenue), had a more satisfactory trading record than either Newnes or Odhams, which drew approximately half their revenue from this source.

With the women's press having to fight harder each year for its share of a limited amount of advertising, commercial interests are now being 'accommodated' to a greater extent than ever before, and there is evidence that the actual content of magazines is being affected. One Director, referring to women's magazines in general, described them as 'commerce-ridden'. The most important effect of advertising pressure has been to induce the monthlies to 'retreat even further into the kitchen and the boudoir'.* Features which cannot be used to sell goods are wasted space as far as advertisers are concerned, and Editors are forced to keep them to a minimum. Whereas the monthlies could once be relied upon to recognise the fact that for many thinking women there is more to life than chores and children, in recent years they have been obliged to abandon this policy of broadmindedness. There has been a steady contraction in 'general interest' features and discussion of affairs in the world outside the home, and a substantial balancing increase in 'home service'. Before the war, magazines like *Good Housekeeping* and *Everywoman* carried serious, thought-provoking articles on subjects of interest to women as citizens.† Since the war, the proportion of mentally stimulating content has dwindled almost to nothing, pushed out by the rise of 'consumerism' and the demands of advertisers who want every available space devoted to persuasive selling—editorial or otherwise. So complete has been the muffling of intelligent writing for women that *Nova*, appearing in 1965, crammed with outspoken features specially written to appeal to the educated and lively-minded, believed itself to be making a break-through in publishing for women.

The effect of advertising pressure on the weeklies has been somewhat different. Their vast sale, built upon the trust and confidence of millions of readers, lessens their vulnerability to pressure from outside. But advertisement rates are tied to circulation figures, and since it is the weeklies' huge share of the mass market which attracts advertisers, it is vital that sales should be maintained at the required levels. This has promoted an extremely conservative attitude to progress. Editors have not dared to experiment with variations on a tried and trusted formula for fear a sudden drop in sales figures might scare the business fraternity. They have therefore been pursuing a policy of gradual evolution, endeavouring to keep pace with social change without getting too far beyond their readers. Like the monthlies, they have tended to concen-

* The phrase is Katharine Whitehorn's.   † See Chapter 3.

trate their research in areas more profitable to advertisers than to Editors, which has further hampered their progress, if indirectly.

Thus, during the past ten or twelve years, the influence of advertising has been responsible both for curbing the general expansion of the women's press, and for narrowing the scope of at least one section of it, so that the function of the majority of women's magazines has remained, or has become, that of servicing the domestic industry and its unpaid personnel, providing at the same time a glamorous shop window for a huge assortment of manufactured goods. This is clearly the most potentially restrictive of all the pressures exerted by advertisers, and that which has affected the character of the women's press the most.

The growing 'accommodation' of retail traders is showing itself in a variety of other ways. Editorial backing for products is frequent, either in the form of deliberate editorial mentions, or through the 'advertising magazine' features included in most periodicals, which are given special introductions by editorial staff; for example, 'Ideas for better living' (*Housewife*)—a collection of small-ads with covering editorial copy; *Woman's Realm*'s 'Bywells'; the '*She* Shop' and *Woman*'s 'Advertisement Shop'. Special positions are more frequently conceded and advertising features barely distinguishable from editorial content are creeping in.

There are more 'special offers' run in conjunction with manufacturers to launch or publicise products, and supplements featuring special areas of consumption (home-heating, carpeting etc.) are regularly included. *Woman* has recently introduced its own mail-order catalogue called 'Shopping Post' which is given away with the magazine. Proprietary foods are mentioned in some cookery recipes, and from time to time fashion features have been used to push branded fibres.* Wherever a proprietary item is included in any photograph, the manufacturer is credited. Stockists' lists of all advertised products are also made available.

The more serious the economic position of a magazine, the more uncompromising are its attempts to win the support of manufacturers. One monthly switched to Duplex binding to facilitate the insertion of colour advertising, despite the fact that it reduced the number of 'double spreads' available for editorial matter. It also guaranteed next-matter positions to all its advertisers, a promise which proved technically impossible to fulfil.

---

* The fashion journals lost considerable custom when the big fibre manufacturers changed their policy and begain advertising on T.V. Smaller clothing firms, which depended upon their support, were forced to withdraw their advertising.

Not all pressure from advertisers is direct. It is not uncommon for food manufacturers to woo cookery editors and their staffs with sight-seeing tours of their factories at home and abroad and with gifts, hoping to elicit an editorial mention. They are well aware that advertisements incorporated in the editorial text have considerable influence, and can result in a greatly increased demand for a product. Magazines can actually create a demand for a commodity which is not marketed, and have occasionally used this power to encourage manufacturers to fill a 'long felt want'. Alternatively, a large manufacturer may indicate to an advertising manager that if a magazine were to expand its content in a certain direction which would give scope to his products, then he would be prepared to patronise it. Where the economic viability of publications is at stake, it may be very difficult, if not impossible, for editors to refuse to comply, even when they know encroachment of this kind will inevitably limit their freedom to print what they believe is in the best interests of the reader.

On the other hand, several Editors of mass-selling publications have personally testified that the policies of their respective firms have allowed them to resist strenuously any pressure to slant content in favour of advertisers. It is well known that behind-the-scenes agreements can place a magazine in danger of selling its birthright (i.e. the reader's faith in editorial integrity) literally for a 'mess' of copy, and when a periodical is thriving it can argue strongly that such concessions would endanger the very circulations that advertisers are anxious to reach. The Editorial Director of Odhams Publications, Mr Archie Kay, explains:

'. . . Far from conflicting with commercial interests, it is good business to be honest and impartial. Editorial staff have fought and won the battle to exclude advertising which is undesirable, and any that is indistinguishable from editorial content. They see this as an essential part of retaining the reader's trust, for women are quick to detect dishonesty and insincerity of any kind. It is an axiom that no good magazine will ever take advantage of its readers. Magazines with established circulations have no need to resort to "sharp practices".'*

In general, it is admitted that, in the case of the mass weeklies, a measure of 'co-operation' with advertisers is unavoidable, but only in lesser areas to permit a firm stand where ground cannot be yielded without seriously undermining a magazine's integrity. Minor conces-

* Personal interview (1965).

sions in advertisement placing continually have to be made. Guaranteed positions cannot normally be sold in advance for technical reasons, but still, co-operation over placing occurs to a far greater extent than would have been possible ten years ago. When a manufacturer is taking thousands of pounds' worth of space, six-column advertisements extending onto an editorial page have to go through. Again, for a huge sum, the 'centre spread' is occasionally turned over to an advertiser. Regular patrons are informed in advance of the contents of future issues so that they may not miss a particularly advantageous selling opportunity.

With all advertising ventures, it is the Editor's job to ensure that nothing conflicts with the policy of the magazine. It is part of the policy of the mass weeklies that nothing may be artificially grafted on in order to attract advertising, but must spring naturally from the services normally provided, for to brook interference with the editorial content of a trusted weekly is to court disaster. As more than one Editor has pointed out, it is as important to the advertiser as it is to the Editor to produce a good magazine that people will have faith in and want to buy. By sacrificing its integrity, a magazine stands to sacrifice its readership.

This policy does not always hold good for the monthlies, which necessity has made far less resistant to commercial blackmail. One staff member provided this insight into their situation:*

'Magazines have been forced to beg for advertising and to make concessions in return that would have been unheard of fifteen years ago. There has been a continual battle between management (run largely by accountants) and Editors, who have the interests of their readers at heart and wish to retain their autonomy. The fight is a losing one. Content is planned with an eye on what will best serve the interests of the advertiser. It will soon be impossible, if it is not so already, to include a feature on the Portobello Road, because there would be howls of protest from furniture manufacturers who do not want to see readers encouraged to buy secondhand. Even now, an Editor can only slip in the occasional article on 'make do and mend'. Instead, she has to feature new and expensive furniture which she knows most of her readers cannot afford. The whole policy of a magazine is nowadays dictated from above where only the advertiser counts. Because of the limitations on space, and the necessity of filling it to the advertiser's advantage, the order has gone out to dispense with 'general interest' features in favour of 'home service', because manufacturers do not like content

* Personal interview (1965).

which cannot be used to sell goods. An editor has to comply, despite the knowledge that readers' interests are much wider.'

A perennial problem for all women's magazines is the ratio of editorial to advertising matter. Editors know that readers will not tolerate more than a certain percentage of advertising without complaint, and appreciate neither issues distended with advertisements, nor those which are disturbingly thin, which can happen when the skeleton of editorial content is insufficiently padded. Both smack of a raw deal. Too much advertising also interferes with editorial continuity. The difficulties arise because advertisers tend to concentrate their space-buying in two peak periods, Spring and Autumn. If firms could be prevailed upon to spread their demands for space more evenly, the overall proportion of advertising could be kept lower and more constant all the year round.

On the basis of this evidence, it would seem that the attempt on the part of editorial staffs to balance the needs of readers and advertisers without loss to either has proved impossible. As long as publishers opt for a system under which magazines are sold at an uneconomic price, and the difference is made up by an advertising subsidy, Editors are vulnerable to an intensification of pressure from advertising departments with every increase in costs. The extent of the dependence on advertising can be gauged by the fact that in 1963, the weeklies offset 67 per cent and the monthlies 82 per cent of their costs from this source. It has been estimated that *Woman*, when it sold for eightpence, cost the publishers roughly two shillings per copy. *Harper's Bazaar*, when it sold for half-a-crown, was making only enough to cover the paper it was printed on. Until recently, publishers maintained that it was impossible to charge a more economic price for magazines, despite the fact that Continental firms were managing to do so. They claimed that the British public was conditioned to paying an unrealistic price for its reading matter and that to make increases of the order necessary to dispense with the advertising subsidy would result in the collapse of the industry. They shrank from raising cover prices by as little as a penny, and felt bound to sugar the pill with bumper issues, free gifts and supplements.

Now, there are signs that IPC for one may be considering changing its former policy. Due to the general economic situation, the reading public is growing accustomed to rising prices over a wide range of consumer goods, including newspapers and periodicals. Magazine representatives are beginning to predict a future in which cover prices will bear an economic relation to production costs, and there will be no further

Table 4: Cover Price Changes (Women's Weeklies)

	1962	1964	1967	1968
Woman's Own	6d.–7d.	8d.	—	10d.
Woman	6d.–7d.	8d.	—	10d.
Woman's Realm	4½d.–5d.*	6d.	7d.	8d.
Woman's Weekly	4½d.–5d.	6d.	7d.	8d.

* March, 1961.

Source: Buckmaster and Moore, Report on IPC, 1969.

reliance on an advertising subsidy. The stimulus to this new thinking has undoubtedly been the increasing difficulty of attracting sufficient advertising to sustain the magazine industry as a whole.

Meanwhile, production costs have been soaring throughout the industry and are weighing particularly heavily on 'prestige' periodicals with circulations of under half-a-million which are costly to produce because their appeal depends on a glossy appearance and a high standard of colour reproduction. For this, an expensive grade of coated paper is necessary, combined with the slower, and so less economic, letterpress or litho printing methods. A 'new' method, web-offset, has been hailed as the salvation of these journals, and is confidently expected eventually to oust letterpress as the chief method of printing medium-circulation publications. In fact, web-offset is not new, merely redis-covered. Sheet-fed litho was known in this country at the beginning of the century and a web-fed version has been experimented with in America for the past eighteen years. However, it is only during the past eight that it has proved itself in Britain as a viable alternative to existing methods for executing medium size print orders, and for some years yet there will be insufficient capacity available to allow many firms to take advantage of it. The process has several advantages. It is faster than sheet-fed offset, and units can be used for both colour and black-and-white work. It is a less expensive method for making printing sur-faces than photogravure, and it gives better value for the same outlay in reproductive quality, though to achieve it, it must be used with a coated paper.

Web-offset has received considerable publicity since Lord Thomson pioneered its use, along with the latest computerised techniques, in the printing of a provincial newspaper, the *Reading Post*. *Hers* is printed by it (as was *Intro*) and some sections of *Nova*. It is still the centre of controversy, and there are those who feel its choice over other processes is a matter of taste only. Offset imparts a soft, feminine quality in reproduction. Those who prefer a sharp image are inclined to choose an alternative method. Where half-tone reproduction is used, sheet-feeding is necessary to ensure a high standard, and so letterpress continues to hold its own for contracts of this kind.

Nevertheless, web-offset is beginning to prove its worth for periodicals whose circulation falls in the region of 200,000–350,000. Its economic 'floor' is debatable, but it probably becomes profitable at runs of over 30,000 copies (b. and w. and 2 cols.) and 50,000 (4 cols.). Depending on the type of work, it is said to be able to compete favourably with photogravure on runs of between 500,000 and a million, and sometimes beyond it. Around the million mark, and for the cheaper journals, photogravure is unsurpassed. Once the cylinders are prepared, it can print in four colours on cheap, mechanical-groundwood paper, giving an excellent result and reaping unlimited economies of scale. But for the middle-range publications it would seem that web-offset has good prospects of becoming more widely used. Already it has achieved enough success to vindicate the faith of Gilbert Smith of Hazell Sun, who prevailed upon the firm's management to install a single experimental plant on the basis of what he had seen in the United States.

The more widespread use of web-offset is one possible way of reducing the costs of printing and the bill to the publisher. Another is the application of electronics to various stages in the printing and preparation processes to allow the industry to become as fully automated as possible. During the past twenty years, an electronic revolution has been in progress, the greatest impact of which has been in the composing room. Teletype-setters have been developed which can set lines of type from tapes punched by an operator sitting at an ordinary type-writer keyboard. These can be prepared anywhere, at any time, and telegraphed to central offices. Another advance is photo-typesetting, which dispenses altogether with hot-metal type, and substitutes 'cold-type', namely photographic proofs which can be used to make plates for offset and gravure printing. These photo-setters now operate in conjunction with coded tapes. The most recent development is computerised teletype-setting, by which justification is carried out automatically. The compositor sits at an ordinary electric type-writer and as he types the copy, the characters are translated into symbols on a tape. This tape is fed into a computer which justifies the copy and makes such editorial changes as may be necessary. The corrected tape then passes through the 'print-out' unit, where photographic proofs are made from it.

Electronics are also being used increasingly in colour preparation work. Electronic colour-scanning is reducing the time taken for colour re-touching by automatically calculating the corrections required for each colour separation negative in order to achieve accurate reproduction of the original. Electronic engravers are now available which can reproduce an original illustration in black and white half-tones, in relief, directly onto a plastic plate, and in about one-seventh of the time taken by the conventional method. Full-colour half-tones can also be produced electronically. Finally, electronic devices are also being used on printing presses to control register, and these have substantially cut the proportion of waste.

Backing colour with colour has recently become possible and further refinements to increase colour-printing capacity are urgently being sought. A new system of reproducing original colour photographs onto printing surfaces is at present being experimented with by Cosmocord, the firm which developed it. A prototype, claimed to be more efficient and considerably cheaper than conventional methods of colour reproduction, has already allowed the new entertainment magazine *Zeta* to operate on a greatly reduced advertising rate, having cut printing costs by 50 per cent. This breakthrough has been pursued by Cosmocord's Managing Director, Mr Gordon Allen, formerly a Director of International Printers, IPC's Printing Division.

All these advances are helping to cut costs. There would be scope for considerably greater reduction if co-operation between printing firms and the printing unions could be improved. It should be emphasised here that newspaper and magazine production are entirely different branches of printing, each with its own techniques and special difficulties, but some problems, connected with the general state of the printing industry, are common to both. The chief area of conflict is that surrounding the introduction of automated techniques in the preparation, printing, and assembly of magazines. Theoretically, costs could be slashed by the introduction of an electronic, computerised production-line, but only at the price of heavy redundancy. Both sides accept that automation must come: the argument is over the speed and method of its introduction.

The machinery for joint consultation is widely regarded as unsatisfactory, in addition to which, old prejudices concerning the supposedly conflicting interests of capitalists and workers still operate, producing deep-rooted antagonism and suspicion. These attitudes exist side by side with a desire on the part of more enlightened union executives to co-operate with management to achieve an economically efficient industry which will benefit workers, management and public. Union representatives now attend courses and discussion groups on economics. They enlist professional help in evaluating managerial policies and interpreting cost-schedules, when the latter are used by management to justify actions not considered to be in the interests of employees. The unions have accepted the introduction of many automated processes, and have on occasion themselves requested the introduction of labour-saving equipment. The optimum number of men required to operate certain printing presses is settled by joint consultation, according to technical requirements.

Nevertheless, managements claim costs are artificially high as a result of restrictive practices sanctioned by the printing unions, namely, over-manning, resistance to the introduction of automated techniques, the demand for 'incentives' where presses are run beyond a certain speed, and the maintenance of an artificial shortage in skilled trades such as colour re-touching. To give some examples: the paper wastage allowance is an expensive item in the publisher's budget; on a printing run of $2\frac{1}{2}$ million copies, the allowance is $12\frac{1}{2}$ per cent, representing a loss of approximately £7 10s. 0d.* on every ton of paper consumed by the mass weeklies. Electronic devices are now available, capable of reducing this percentage, but their introduction has been resisted by the unions. Again, where high-speed presses capable of a greater output are introduced, the unions demand higher pay for performing the same press-minding functions, which offsets any saving. Union representatives claim that to mind a machine delivering twice the normal number of copies per hour, although it involves no more physical exercise, requires greater mental concentration, which should be compensated for.

Also, it is frequently claimed by managements that printing shops are over-manned by as much as a third, due to the enforced retention of workers after they have been supplanted by labour-saving equipment. A tour of any printing works reveals large numbers of men apparently standing idle except for the occasional straightening of a pile of printed copies. The unions refute the charge of over-manning on the grounds that the size of machine crews is determined at executive level according to technical requirements, and that any apparent slack is a necessary provision against those emergencies when more men are suddenly needed. If men are withdrawn from a machine, the unions argue that their wages should be distributed amongst those who remain, since their work load must be heavier. And if output is increased, it is further argued that the men responsible are entitled to a share of the higher profits which ensue.

On the crucial question of automation and redundancy, union policy is to safeguard all existing jobs, while agreeing to a slow run-down as men leave and are not replaced. They claim that their concern is not to ensure that a firm is employing the same number of men in ten years'

* 1965 prices.

time, but that all those men already fully employed should be assured of their jobs as long as they want them.

Clearly, there is a need for a far greater measure of co-operation between management and the unions in achieving more efficient production, and there is room for a reappraisal of policy on both sides along the lines suggested by the Cameron Report. The frequent disputes and stoppages are in fact strangling the industry and placing an unnecessary strain on publishers as costs climb higher and higher. The printing industry as a whole is suffering from the loss of prestige caused by publishers being forced to take their contracts abroad. *Family Circle* is printed in Turin,* and the new glossy, *Fashion*, in Darmstadt. In the case of the latter periodical, the publishers took their contract to Germany because it was impossible to obtain the high quality reproduction required in fashion journalism, in this country. To prove this, and gain the acquiescence of the printing unions, two identical dummy issues were run off in both countries. These revealed notable differences in photographic detail and texture, attributable to inferior workmanship in the preparation and re-touching processes. The point was conceded, but even so, union trouble delayed *Fashion*'s launching by six months.

The high level of overheads makes publishers particularly sensitive to increases, which they are unwilling to incur for purely aesthetic

Table 5: Breakdown of Publishing Costs, IPC, 1967–68

	Women's Weeklies %	Other Publishing Interests %
Paper and ink	30·3	16·7
Printing	40·0	31·3
Editorial	7·5	12·5
Distribution	2·3	1·5
Other	19·9	37·0
TOTAL	100·0	100·0

Source: Extracted from Buckmaster and Moore, Report on IPC, 1969.

improvements to their publications. A glance at any bookstall reveals the inferiority of British periodicals beside their Continental and American rivals (who, incidentally, charge an economic price for their journals). The chief reason is the cheap grade of paper on which many of

---

* For 'political reasons', *Living* is unable to reap the economies of using the same plant.

them are printed, which gives poor quality reproduction. Foreign journals favour more expensive, coated papers, but while British paper manufacturers can offer a wide range of these, specially formulated for use in conjunction with different printing processes, the mass-selling publications cannot afford them. Even chemical additives, such as those used by the French, are out of the question. Amongst women's periodicals, the *Queen* stands out as an example of what can be achieved using the best quality paper by a magazine which has the financial independence to be a law unto itself.

For the IPC, printing costs are mainly an internal matter. The Corporation's subsidiary, International Printers Ltd. (IPL), prints around 75 per cent of the publications put out by the Magazine Division, a percentage which will eventually be increased. At present, and for a further seven years, *Woman's Own* is under contract to Sun Printers, Watford, and is therefore vulnerable to the cost increases which an independent printer must periodically pass on to his customers, at least in part. Mr Arnold Quick, before he accepted the Chairmanship of the Magazine Division, was responsible for rationalising IPC's printing interests, during which process the number of its printing plants was reduced from 24 to 12 in only five years.

Inflated costs are not the only problem facing the women's magazine industry. There is also the growing difficulty of marketing a highly perishable commodity in a fiercely competitive situation. Efficient distribution is the Achilles heel of periodical publishing. Its organisation has changed little since the war, and this inflexibility in the face of vastly different economic conditions is forcing many publishers to seek new outlets and to devise sophisticated and ingenious ways of advertising their magazines. The bulk of periodicals still reach the reader through a network of retail newsagents, numbering around 50,000, who draw their supplies from wholesalers, of which there are approximately 450. This system remained satisfactory while newsprint was rationed, but when the publishing trade entered upon a new era of expansion, it soon proved inadequate. Every year, larger, glossier and more ambitious publications flooded the market, and the problems were no longer those of simple allocation, but of providing the conditions under which a proliferation of almost identical magazines in direct competition with each other, could bid fairly for the customer's attention.

The problems of retail distribution stem from the failure to bring this section of the trade into line with the modern requirements of efficient marketing. Newsagents are a heterogeneous collection ranging from the general store which also sells newspapers and periodicals, to the modern news agency which sells nothing else, of which there are only a handful in existence, all experimental. Standards of display in these outlets vary greatly, but they are all congested. Much space is wasted or badly used; titles are obscured, and new publications rarely get a fair showing except during their launch period. The attitudes of newsagents do not help. There is general apathy and a lack of interest in making improvements amongst the majority, who are evidently content with things as they are. They do fairly well out of existing sales, and tend to regard new titles as being more trouble than they are worth to handle. Creative selling is not encouraged by the fact that newsagents know they are endangering a large percentage of their profits by having just a few copies of an expensive 'glossy' left over at the end of the week. Hence they tend to 'play safe', carrying only a limited number of titles, and those in moderate quantities. The larger newsagents can be obstructive in other ways. One chain of retailers refuses to accept publishers' advertisements for subscriptions, and through this and other practices is said to have a 'paralytic hold' over distribution.

A drastic reorganisation of retail outlets based upon research is badly needed. In the meantime sales promotion rests heavily on the shoulders of the publisher. In recent years one after another has been driven to experiment with new outlets and costly promotion campaigns, the latter designed to create interest and stimulate 'demand' sales, rather than relying on chance transactions-on-sight. Launching a new magazine can cost publishers several hundred thousand pounds.

Tackling the problem from the other end, attempts have also been made to improve the terms offered to distributors. The average discount currently allowed is 40 per cent of the cover price. The wholesaler receives about 15 per cent of this (plus or minus 5 per cent, taking into account the differential transport costs incurred by his location in London or the provinces), while the retailer can expect 25 per cent.* More complicated issues are involved as regards conditions covering the return of unsold copies. The Periodical Proprietors' Association, a committee of publishing houses formed to discuss problems within the trade and to enforce internal regulations, has a fixed policy barring sale-or-return (s.o.r.), except during an initial launch period. This is contrary to current practice in the United States, where s.o.r. is the universal rule.

At present, members of the P.P.A. are bound to their agreed policy, but in practice, unofficial 'see-safe' agreements with wholesalers and retailers are an effective substitute. In time it is likely that British

---

* IPC's average allowance is within the range 35–40 per cent, 10–15 per cent of which is retained by the wholesaler, the remainder going to the retailer.

publishers will be forced to acquiesce in s.o.r., since it is already being practised by non-members. But one hundred per cent s.o.r. leaves the publisher vulnerable to heavy losses. A 25 per cent return is thought to be the highest figure that he can economically accept. Thus accuracy in forecasting sales will become increasingly vital.

The requirements of maintaining advertising revenue have, for the weeklies, involved maintaining circulations at an optimum level, and for the monthlies, reaching out to scoop up new groups of potential readers, particularly the young. Editorial staffs have frequently been directed to produce a formula tailored to fit the reader-profiles the research teams have constructed, within the specifications laid down by the advertising departments. All of them work closely together; the days are past when the circulation manager and his staff were the 'poor relations' and the Editor's word was law. Today, magazine policy emerges out of top level decision-making and co-operation in all the different branches of magazine production. But however successful these policies are in producing the kind of publication which attracts advertisers and which women want to buy, in the last resort profits depend upon an efficient method of getting it to them, a problem to which magazine publishers are now giving their urgent attention.

NOTES

1   Mary Grieve, *Millions Made My Story*, p. 136.
2   Buckmaster and Moore, *International Publishing Corporation*, p. 76.
3   In a Public Lecture, 'Women as Consumers', delivered at Bedford College (University of London), March 4th, 1969.
4   Circular to advertisers.
5   Pre-launch circular to advertisers.
6   *Op. cit.*, preface to launch issue, September, 1946.
7   Promotion material.
8   *Op. cit.*, October 16th, 1966.
9   'Mediascope' by Marplan, in *World's Press News*, October 4th, 1964.
10 *World's Press News*, September 4th, 1964, p. 31.
11 *Ibid.*, p. 30.
12 *Ibid.*, p. 31.
13 *Ibid.*, p. 30.
14 All figures in this section are taken from *Facts about Advertising*.

7

New Magazines for the 'New' Woman

A comparison of a sample of pre-war magazines with a set of those currently on sale shows the magnitude of the industry's achievements during the past twenty-five years. The look of pallid undernourishment which characterised the periodicals of the 'thirties has disappeared, and the magazines of the 'sixties are glossy and robust, bright with colour and ideas. The improvement testifies to the change in their fortunes and their growth from a relatively insignificant branch of the publishing trade into a vast empire. They have also grown fatter: their issues distended by advertising which now makes up, on average, at least 50 per cent of their content, the proportion varying according to the total amount of advertising available, the season, and their success in securing special contracts.

The scale of their growth in terms of circulation is difficult to estimate accurately, since audited figures for women's magazines were not available before the war. However, W. D. McClelland, IPC's Research Director, puts the 1934 total for women's weeklies at between 3 and 3·5 million copies sold per week.[1] By 1964, this figure had risen to 12·1 million (16·3 million, if sales of monthlies are included) which represented a ratio of 0·8 of a copy per person per week. It was then estimated that five out of six women saw at least one women's magazine every week, readership being well maintained at all ages. Though the highest percentage of readers fell within the 16–24 age-group, readership between the ages of 25 and 44 was almost as high. Girls of 11 and over formed a substantial section of the market, and even amongst the elderly, the figure did not fall below 50 per cent. Current readership figures show a similar pattern.*

The greatest expansion since the war has been in the 'service' weekly group. Six magazines, *Woman*, *Woman's Own*, *Woman's Weekly*,

* See Table 6.

216

Table 6: Readership of Women's Weekly Magazines—All Women, 1967

Age	Woman %	Woman's Own %	Woman's Realm %	Woman's Weekly %	Popula-tion %
16–24	22	22	22	15	17
25–34	16	17	16	14	15
35–44	17	16	18	17	16
45–54	17	17	16	17	17
55–64	14	14	15	17	16
65 and over	14	14	13	19	14
Social Grouping					
AB	11	11	10	9	12
C1	20	18	18	18	18
C2	39	39	40	36	35
DE	31	32	33	37	35
Area					
London and S.E.	35	33	33	29	34
S.W. and Wales	11	11	12	13	13
Midlands	18	19	22	20	16
N. West	14	13	13	14	12
N.E. and North	16	15	15	15	15
Scotland	8	9	6	9	9

Notes: AB = upper and professional classes; C1 = middle class, clerical; C2 = skilled workers; D = unskilled; E = old age pensioners, etc.

Source: Buckmaster and Moore, Report on IPC, 1969.

Woman's Realm, *Woman's Mirror* and *Woman's Day* have at various times topped the million mark, with *Woman's Own* reaching a peak circulation of $2\frac{1}{2}$ million weekly, and *Woman* nearly $3\frac{1}{2}$ million. In 1964, the first five of these titles made up three-quarters of the total weekly sale of British women's magazines and were 'read in the average week by two-thirds of all women in the country aged 16 and over'.[2] *Woman's Own* at its zenith (1957) had increased its sales by seven times since 1938; *Woman* at its peak (also 1957) by nearly five times, and *Woman's Weekly*, which is currently reaching an all-time record of 2 million, is selling four times as many copies as in 1938. *Woman's Realm*, launched in 1958, achieved its peak circulation of almost $1\frac{1}{2}$ million four years later.

For most magazines, however, this 'golden age' in women's publishing came to an end in the early 'sixties, since when the industry has not only failed to increase its growth rate but has begun to decline. The trend dates from the beginning of 1958 when a number of magazines suffered a sharp drop in circulation. Within ten years, some had lost a third or as much as half their readers, and several were driven out of print, among them the monthlies *Woman and Beauty*, *Modern Woman*, *Everywoman* and *Housewife*, and the mass weeklies *Woman's Day*, *Woman's Illustrated* and *Woman's Mirror*.

The pattern has been remarkably similar for all magazines. Since 1962, *Woman* and *Woman's Own* have been losing readers at an average annual rate of 3·6 per cent and 3·1 per cent respectively, and despite fluctuations in their recent performance, it seems clear that the drain is continuing. *Woman's Realm* and *Woman's Weekly* have also been losing readers, but to a lesser extent and more slowly, averaging 2·3 per cent and 1·9 per cent a year, but the latter magazine began to pick up in 1967 and is now forging ahead, largely due to the introduction of colour. *Woman's Mirror* had the sorriest record of all, its sales having dropped to more than 600,000 below its record figure at an average annual rate of 7·7 per cent for the period 1962–66, before it ceased publication early in 1967. Altogether, in the first half of 1958 there were seven 'service' weeklies selling more than half a million copies per issue, with a combined weekly sale of over 12 million; in the second half of 1968, there were four such weeklies, with a total circulation of under 7½ million.

The extent of the decline was at first masked by a number of mergers which temporarily boosted the sales of the 'host' periodicals, but it later became clear that the readerships of defunct magazines were not being wholly reabsorbed, representing a net loss to the trade. The trend was also partially camouflaged by inaccurate sales figures, and in some cases by no figures at all where publishers, worried about their effect upon advertisers, chose to suppress them. The true picture emerged only when IPC, having won control of the bulk of the women's magazine industry in 1961, insisted on ABC membership for all its publications, and other publishers followed suit.

Though the plight of the industry was now fully recognised, there was confusion and uncertainty as to the corrective measures it should adopt. Speculation about the causes of the decline was widespread, but there was a dearth of concrete information. Research departments within the larger publishing houses had in the past paid little regard to the women's magazines. They had consistently reaped satisfactory profits without costly excursions into the sophisticated realms of attitude measurement, and managements had not considered it necessary to authorise research into them at a deep level. Such surveys as had been commissioned were limited to establishing reader profiles in demographic and economic terms. These were sufficient to fulfil the requirements of advertisers, though the research experts were well aware that they were inadequate and that some attempt should be made to try and measure the satisfactions which readers were, or were not, getting from their magazines; also their attitudes to certain aspects of magazine content, to mention just two possible approaches.

The amount of qualitative research available for editorial and managerial guidance was thus extremely small. The National Magazine Co. had, in 1961, commissioned a survey from Marplan Ltd., which was designed as:

> 'A continuing, comparative study of [women's] magazines as products, combined with a thorough analysis of reader and purchaser characteristics . . . not only of who buys what, and where and how magazines are used, but also of the attitudes held towards them, and the reasons, both conscious and preconscious, for their purchase and readership.'[3]

The 'New Measurement Study' produced by Odhams' Research Division in 1964[4] also included a specially compiled 'Satisfaction Index' to show which magazines were regarded by readers as being more, or less 'good' and 'interesting', and *Family Circle's* publishers made similar, though small-scale attempts to discover which aspects of its content, and which of its covers, were most acceptable to readers. But Editors who wished for a fuller assessment of how their publications were being received had to rely on their own observation and the inbuilt 'barometer' of readers' correspondence.

In the absence of any major research capable of casting light on the reasons for the decline in the popularity of women's magazines, IPC commissioned an important study from the psychologist Dr Ernest Dichter, President of the Institute of Motivational Research, New York. Dichter, whose work was well known to advertisers, had at various times been called upon to advise American publishers* and had assisted in the re-styling of the Canadian women's magazine, *Chatelaine*. In 1964 he was asked to prepare a report on *Woman's Own*, and to assess

---

* It was on the basis of a study by Dr Dichter that American *Family Circle* decided to take the unprecedented step of omitting fiction to become a 100 per cent 'service' magazine.

its performance both in relation to the needs of the present and the possible requirements of the future, and in relation to the other 'service' magazines, particularly *Woman*.

The study took the form of a sample survey during which 180 'depth' interviews and 455 'projective tests' were carried out among readers and non-readers of the magazine. Dichter interpreted the findings against his own socio-psychological knowledge of trends in the female population. He pointed to the changes occurring in the 'needs, problems, goals, tastes and self-images'[5] of English women, due to wider and better education, exposure to mass media such as T.V., affluence, and the growth of women's employment, particularly after marriage. There was, he said, 'an inexorable movement towards greater independence, responsibility and social mobility for women',[6] bringing with it new interests and activities for them, wider social experience, and a greater cultural awareness.

He claimed that, as a result of these trends, a new type of woman was emerging, the 'balanced' woman:

> '. . . the kind of woman who can combine, adjust and compromise femininity with independence, personal fulfilment with family responsibilities, and modesty with basic human values as she perceives them.'[7]

He contended that to classify such women by age had ceased to be meaningful (since age no longer presupposed a particular stage in the 'family cycle'), and that instead they should be grouped according to their outlook, experience and activities. This was the more necessary because differences between age-groups were also lessening due to the fact that 'young girls mature and become independent earlier and the older women stay young and active longer'.[8]

Dichter saw in these changes far-reaching implications for a mass weekly like *Woman's Own*, among them the need for a more realistic approach, especially in fiction, a wider range of features related to the broadening horizons of women's lives, improvements in format, type, and art-work to bring them into line with modern tastes, and the acquisition of a special character and a stated purpose with which groups of readers could identify. He emphasised the need to start thinking in terms of 'market segmentation' by 'interest or orientation',[9] rather than by class or age, and to start catering to those women who were more advanced, 'professionally, culturally, decoration-wise and food-wise',[10] fostering 'reader-involvement' and a 'dialogue' between magazine staff and their readers. He warned:

'. . . these, and similar changes . . . are your guide lines as to the direction in which your readership is now, and will be moving. Understanding and utilising these trends will permit you to match, or perhaps to gently lead such trends. Failing to understand, or ignoring them, can create a situation in which continuing to do what has been successful in the past will eventually prove disastrous as your audience moves off in another direction.'[11]

He concluded his report with a 51-point plan intended for editorial and promotional guidance in bringing *Woman's Own*'s format, formula and publicity into line with the changing requirements of contemporary women.

Though it was carried out specifically for *Woman's Own*, the general findings of the Dichter study were seized upon by IPC's management as supplying both the diagnosis and the cure for the malady from which the women's press as a whole was suffering, while editorial offices seethed with conflicting opinions as to the validity of its claims.

A small group of *avant garde* editors were solidly in favour of a 'revolution' in women's publishing. One of them commented:

'Once the necessary research is carried out, it will show, contrary to the beliefs of many people responsible for the mass weeklies, that women's lives have undergone extensive changes, and that women's magazines have failed to keep up. The old formulas are no longer good enough, and the danger in such ostrich-like attitudes is that the realisation may come when it is too late to do anything about it.'*

But others were more sceptical:

'It is true that better education has increased most people's social awareness, but it has not necessarily made women more intelligent. The goals of the average girl are still to find a man to love, to set up house, and to lead a happy married life. Women's lives may have been changed by affluence, but women are still women underneath, and the things they care about have not changed.'*

Nevertheless, Dichter's report was accepted, and its recommendations formed the blue-print for new developments throughout IPC's group of women's magazines. A new generation of younger Editors was

* Personal interviews.

given the task of re-defining the whole concept of publishing for women. Recruited from the *Sunday Times*, where his methods had been spectacularly successful, Mr Clive Irving was installed as Editorial Director and began the task of translating Dichter's suggestions into clear-cut editorial policies.

For Mr Irving, and his fellow-thinkers within IPC, accurately reflecting the needs of women in contemporary Britain meant producing publications which dealt with everyday living intelligently and realistically. It meant 'being prepared to tackle issues like the morality of living on the H.P., explaining how supermarkets work, taking a deep look at the birth pill and all its implications',[12] and involved 'breaking a lot of taboos about what can be discussed, and the manner in which things can be discussed in women's magazines . . . the strain of living with a successful husband . . . sexual impotence . . . the Other Woman—the kind of things which until now have been only dealt with as brief footnotes to readers' letters in the old-style agony columns'.[12] As he said:

'The idea that a woman's magazine has to place a genteel filter between a subject and its reader must be hopelessly out of date at a time when any other medium . . . can open up any issue for adult discussion. Women's magazines have been wearing their skirts too long.'[13]

The results of this new thinking soon became apparent. Mass weeklies and monthlies alike were given a new, modern look to strengthen their visual appeal and improve their image. The weeklies, with large, conservative readerships to consider, were cautious in making changes, avoiding sudden and dramatic alterations in their format, while the monthlies, having smaller circulations, could afford to be more adventurous. Though differently paced, both sections of the industry embarked upon a thoroughgoing programme of modernisation, introducing new type-faces and illustrative techniques, and building up to a bolder style of presentation more in keeping with the artistic ideas of the 'sixties.

More important were the effects of the new theories upon the traditional formula and editorial approach. Two experiments along the lines indicated by Dichter were particularly significant. In March, 1965, a new publication was launched by Newnes, proclaiming itself to be 'The New Magazine for the New Kind of Woman'. If anyone was puzzled (and many people were) as to the identity of this 'new' female, a glance at the supplementary copy revealed that her distinguishing characteristics were a lively intelligence and a keen interest in what went on around her. Society was apparently witnessing the arrival of the 'thinking female', together with a magazine created especially for her. That magazine was *Nova*.

Nova is the embodiment of the 'intelligent' approach to women's publishing, and its launching was a direct outcome of Dichter's findings. Despite sensational and ill-considered publicity during its launch period—the result of handing over the magazine's promotion to an outside agency—which, in stressing the novelty of intelligence in women, offended many potential purchasers, *Nova* is slowly digging itself in, and sending out its antennae in search of an 'attitude group' of which the following woman is typical:

'She could be 28 or 38, single with a job, or married with children (and perhaps a job too), a girl with a university degree, or a girl who never took school seriously. The social permutations are endless. What remains constant is that our new kind of woman has a wide range of interests, an inquiring mind and an independent outlook—not to mention that her numbers are multiplying.'[14]

It is now accepted that such women are not new, only newly-discovered. Nevertheless, the publishers claim that they are exploring an entirely new market, the size of which is still an unknown quantity, and are filling a yawning gap in the range of women's periodicals. At the time of its launching, *Nova*'s Editor commented:

'What is there for women like this to read? No end of house-keeping and fashion items, escapism unlimited, and reliably happy endings. The standard explanation is that an intelligent woman can always read whatever an intelligent man reads—but does she really have to digest the *New Statesman*, skim through the *British Medical Journal*, fillet *New Society* and wade through *The Times* just because her horizons don't stop at furnishing hints or royal gossip? . . . At Newnes we believe she is hungry for a magazine of her own, one that looks at life from her own attitude, and ranges over her many interests . . . [*Nova*] is not an implied criticism of existing women's magazines, but an assertion of the emergence of readers with new requirements.'[14]

Finding the appropriate formula has been a matter of trial and error. In its early issues *Nova* took the radical step of throwing over-board all the traditional ingredients of a women's magazine, replacing them with a slick brand of 'intellectualism' calculated 'to make reality entertaining', coupled with highly sophisticated art work and striking *sans serif* text. This approach is now believed to have been invalid, and *Nova's* current policy is not to eschew the traditional subjects, but to treat them in a new way. Mr Denis Hackett (one of *Queen's* ex-consorts, who was *Nova's* second Editor and later its Editorial Director) did not see *Nova* purely as a women's journal, but as a serious magazine aiming at a high literary standard which would be acceptable to both sexes. He contended that, at this level, there can be no distinction between editing for male and female readers.

Under his direction, *Nova* acquired a strong, bi-sexual personality, and in its pursuit of frankness and realism crashed through many of the old barriers in women's journalism. For example, in October, 1965, it published a fully illustrated article on the use of psycho-prophylaxis in child-birth, which incorporated close-ups of an actual confinement. Similarly, in its articles on sex, innuendo and vague generalisations have given way to concrete facts and expert opinions supplied by prominent medical representatives. Nor is Royalty any longer sacrosanct. *Nova* has published a critical analysis of 'Two experiments in Royal marriage' (those of Princess Margaret and Princess Alexandra), a move away from the customary approach, cosy and complacent, which has been described as 'knitting your own Royal Family'.

Converting women, who are notoriously resistant to change, to a new idea in women's publishing has been slow and difficult. *She*, which blazed a similar trail in 1955, took some years to establish itself, and *Nova*, in many ways an 'upmarket' version of *She*, is evidently needing a similar period of grace in which to gain acceptance. Its performance has so far been unstable, with sales figures varying according to the strengths and weaknesses of individual issues. Technically, the magazine is a brilliant production—artistically equally so. But it is as an editorial prototype that its progress is being most closely watched by the other women's monthlies, whose future pattern of development may well be influenced by its performance.

The weeklies had a similar experiment to observe in their own camp, notably the 'Dichterian' transformation of *Woman's Mirror*. The magazine was in rapid decline when it was selected as a testing-ground for new ideas and approaches which it was hoped ultimately to introduce into the weekly section of the women's press. To quote Clive Irving at the time of its re-launching, 'What is happening to *Woman's Mirror* is a good indication of how we see the future women's market'.[15] Starting in September, 1965, the magazine began to break out of the customary confines of women's journalism and to experiment with a more realistic, intelligent view of modern living. The new era was marked by an issue whose cover bore a full-page colour photograph of a foetus, part of a series showing stages in the development of a human embryo within the womb. On the strength of this feature alone the magazine was a sell-out within three days.

The series was a foretaste of the powerful new brand of feature writing which was to be an important aspect of the remodelled formula. Service features underwent a similar transformation in which they were no longer treated as 'an abstract exercise in curtain patterns, furnishing design and cutlery, but in a way which [related] these things to the people who have to live with them and to their sociological setting'.[15] These new approaches were likewise reflected in the magazine's distinctive art work, particularly in its new logo contracted to the initials 'WM', which suggested modernity and vigour and was, in addition, a useful distinguishing mark on bookstalls. Dichter stressed the importance of relating covers to inside content, a policy which has since been implemented in all IPC's women's magazines.

The new *Woman's Mirror* was homed onto what the proprietors labelled 'the mortgage generation', a group who:

'As well as being more demanding about the kind of house they live in . . . want all the things that go with it, even if it is all bought on the Never-Never . . . [and who] apart from these materialistic things . . . have a much wider curiosity about the world around them.'[15]

The magazine had a larger percentage of its readers in the under-35 group than the other weeklies, and it was hoped that in breaking away from the traditional formula *Woman's Mirror* would increase its appeal to young housewives.

From the first, the weekly section of the trade was sceptical about its chosen methods. The majority view was that the magazine was trying to do too much, too soon, and would only succeed in shocking its readers rather than stimulating them. Several observers believed that the magazine was pursuing a dangerously radical policy for a weekly. Advocating more caution in the application of the new prescription of realism, one Editor commented:

'Women are certainly more knowledgeable than they were—but this does not mean they want to see pictures of dead babies on the covers of their magazines.'*

* Referring to *WM*'s 'foetus' cover.

These opinions were given within a few weeks of *Woman's Mirror'* re-launching, before the female reading public had had time to pass its verdict. A year later they had done so conclusively enough for IPC to announce its decision to merge the magazine with *Woman*, which took place in February, 1967, bringing the experiment to an end.

Dichter's theories concerning the effects of social change upon the lives and interests of women were thus instrumental in giving birth to *Nova*, designed solely as a features magazine to explore the 'educated' women's market—one is tempted to christen it the 'intelligentshea'—and in bringing about the re-launch of *Woman's Mirror*. They were also used in the attempted resuscitation of the two moribund monthlies, *Everywoman* and *Housewife* (previously described), both of which were slowly perishing on account of dwindling circulations and the inability to attract sufficient advertising to keep them financially buoyant.

Over the years, *Everywoman* had become dull and characterless, 'impregnated with the spirit of the Women's Institute, devoted to good works, and implicitly subscribing to the view that a woman's life is over at thirty-five', as one critic described it. When, in 1966, it was completely reoriented to appeal to the 'emerging' group of grammar-school educated women, its new formula was directly related to Dichter's findings regarding the widening social interests and experience of women, particularly their increasing tendency to combine marriage with employment and the general upgrading in their tastes and cultural level.

The new *Everywoman* was founded on the assumption that home and family are not enough for the coming generation of women; that young women of today crave the mental stimulus and sociability of work outside the home, believing they are better wives and mothers for it, and have a completely different set of aspirations and a totally different outlook from their predecessors. *Everywoman*'s Editor described these young women as 'individualistic, optimistic, willing to experiment, and highly critical' as well as being fun-loving and interested in everything going on around them.

As mentioned earlier, the basic editorial approach was to help the 'two-job' women by saving them time, not only in housekeeping and entertaining through quick, stand-by recipes and hints on labour-saving, but also in cultural areas, by providing general features giving 'potted' information for the benefit of those who have no time to glean it elsewhere. Romantic fiction was also given its place on the strength of the Editor's belief that 'no woman ever outgrows her liking for romance

. . . and at heart every woman wants to fall in love'.* However, following Dichter's recommendations, it was treated in a more sophisticated way with greater emphasis on real-life situations.

The magazine was one of the first to attempt to implement Dichter's prescription for 'market segmentation by interest or orientation'. *Everywoman*'s fashion articles were designed to appeal to all age-groups. The Editor explained that female dress was becoming less related to age and more to personal outlook:

> 'It is becoming the rule that all women are, or can be, young, so that a woman no longer asks, "Is it too young for me?" but "Do I like it?" Everything depends on her attitude of mind and it is as common today to find older women in pale pinks and blues as it is to encounter toddlers dressed in aubergine and violet.'*

Everywoman (or '*E*' as it was subsequently known) was re-styled in all these ways to achieve a formula which dealt 'in a forward-looking, knowledgeable way [with] the arts, social trends, every thought-provoking contemporary subject',[16] placing special emphasis on fashion and beauty. Throughout, particular attention was paid to presentation which was claimed to be 'as good as modern art can make it'.

Housewife was given a similar, but more limited editorial 'boost'. The publishers announced to the advertising world that they had 'planned a new *Housewife* to reflect every aspect of successful living for the young wife and mother', and Dichter's theory that affluence and education have generated a new attitude to home-making was clearly responsible for its new editorial approach. Having dropped its age profile, it now focused on 'lively women between 25 and 35', women for whom 'the house is still a vital part of life . . . a creative workshop . . . a place to experiment . . . a base for full and happy living'. Here, too, the intention was to reach an 'attitude group' rather than an age- or income-group. The new *Housewife* was created for the woman who was gay, fashion-conscious, and 'interested in new opinions, new ideas, new patterns of behaviour', able 'to think for herself' and 'set her own trends', an outlook which the magazine was committed to share. Confining itself to home subjects, it concentrated on guiding young housewives through their first attempts at home-making, showing them in particular how to get value for money, bearing in mind the needs of those young couples who had reached that point in the 'family cycle' at which resources are lowest and pressure on them greatest.

* Personal interview.

The minimum initial print orders for these two re-styled 'quality' monthlies were advertised as 275,000 for *Housewife* and 300,000 for *Everywoman*. Neither magazine reached its target. After an initial rise of 23,000, *Housewife* again went into decline. It survived until early in 1968, when it was merged with *Ideal Home*. The merger was carefully phased, with *Ideal Home* gradually broadening its editorial range and becoming more 'human' in its approach in the hope of retaining as many *Housewife* readers as possible. *Everywoman* did considerably better in terms of the new readers it managed to attract, but it failed to gain sufficient advertising support and perished a year earlier, being merged with *Woman and Home*. The merger involved careful study of *Everywoman*'s copy to determine which of its best features could be readily absorbed into the larger monthly. It was decided to expand the scope of *Woman and Home* to take in *Everywoman*'s ready-to-wear-fashion and beauty features which are now run in the 'host' magazine by *Everywoman*'s Editors. The changeover was so skilfully made that some readers still write to *Everywoman* at *Woman and Home*'s address.

Everywoman, *Housewife* and *Woman's Mirror* were obvious candidates for kill-or-cure experimentation along Dichterian lines since all of them had been losing sales heavily. Such drastic measures were neither necessary nor appropriate for other, more successful, titles. Nevertheless, it was felt that all magazines would benefit from at least a moderate 'face-lift', and Dichter's assessment of the needs of contemporary women as well as his suggestions for more effective communication, were helpful to many Editors in rejuvenating their periodicals.

Dichter's ideas penetrated even the mass weeklies, where traditionalist views are nowhere more tenaciously held, but it soon became clear that the scope for their implementation was limited. When *Woman's Mirror* merged with *Woman*, an attempt was made to impart some of the former magazine's progressiveness to its host. The change was too drastic and too abrupt, and had an adverse effect on sales. Similarly, *Woman's Own* was forced to back-pedal when it found it was getting too far ahead of its readers, and both magazines have reverted to a policy of 'quiet evolution'. Nevertheless, they have achieved considerable improvements in presentation which now has stronger impact, clarity and crispness, partly due to a more dramatic use of colour photography. Both are also continuing to widen their scope, and subjects are treated in a more intelligent, searching manner. Though cleverness and 'gimmicks' are taboo for *Woman*, the Editor has been experimenting with new articles: clean food, alcoholism, thalidomide children, the 'Pill', sex from a man's point of view, Sally Trench's experiences amongst the 'meths' drinkers, and a campaign to get nationwide facilities for cervical cancer smears. She is also prepared to introduce articles on abortion and mixed marriages as soon as readers appear to be ready for them. Only a short time ago it would have been impossible even to mention these topics, a measure of the broadening in the average woman's outlook in recent years.

Another problem receiving attention is the pressing one of how women can occupy their time once their children have left home. Ten years ago this would not have been recognised as a problem—the 'twilight years' being accepted as the natural and inevitable price to pay for the privilege of motherhood. Today, life really does begin again at forty or earlier, and the women's magazines are beginning to realise that a surfeit of knitting is not the answer to the vacuity many women experience. Barbara Buss gives her views:

'Affluence is giving women the freedom to be persons in their own right through increased leisure. Some women are still only interested in their homes and families, but today this role is dynamic. A woman has to grow with her children and keep in step with her husband too.'*

She sees it as *Woman*'s task to keep pace with this development, even to keep a little ahead of it. But the criterion of what the magazine can include is still whether or not it is accepted in the population at large. *Woman* can talk about abortion when it is a common topic of conversation and not before.

As this Editor further pointed out, it is difficult to know how far, if at all, women's attitudes and habits of life have altered to match their broader horizons. In the realm of merchandise the changes are easier to see, and it is in this area of *Woman*'s content that progress is most evident. For example, such 'exotic' ingredients as wine, peppers and avocado pears can today be introduced into recipes where once this was impossible because such things were neither widely available nor widely desired (or if they were, could rarely be afforded).

This change in consumption patterns has in fact created new problems for the magazines. It was an easy matter for them to raise levels of taste when people had very little. They could keep one step ahead of their readers merely by featuring washing-machines or refrigerators which were but dreams on the horizon for most women in the early 'fifties. Today, these dreams (and many more) are a reality, and Editors must seek new goals to present to their readers, which are

* Personal interview.

becoming more and more difficult to find. Meanwhile, the mass weeklies are trying to involve themselves more fully in the lives of their readers, entering homes all over the country to produce features which more accurately reflect their ideas and activities.

Woman's Own, the launching-pad of this major revolution in women's publishing, has likewise been facing up to the effects of social and economic change and the need to broaden its scope. Under its present Editor, George Rogers, the magazine has begun to take into account the fact that a large number of its readers are working wives. In the past it had often carried articles condemning women who sought employment outside the home except in dire necessity, but this attitude is now being eradicated. In addition, the breaking of the 'conspiracy of silence', which for so long made many subjects taboo in the mass weeklies, has given the magazine more freedom in its treatment of sexual matters. It recently ran a feature 'What to tell your children about sex', which covered lesbianism and transvestism. It evoked a heavy, critical response from readers, some of whom were subsequently invited to come to London and participate in a further discussion, after which a number changed their views.

Its fiction, too, has become tougher, frequently departing from the ritualised 'happy ending' and, following the new trend towards realism, relating more closely to life as it is lived today. In cookery, foreign recipes have been cautiously introduced and have proved extremely popular, being welcomed especially by those readers for whom cookery has lately become a creative, artistic and interesting hobby.

Changes in *Woman's Own*'s editorial approach have also taken place following the recognition of altered relationships within marriage which are tending to produce a greater degree of partnership in home affairs. Dichter drew attention to the fact that there are now many more joint undertakings between couples than there were a few years back, whether it is painting the kitchen, choosing new curtains or perambulating the baby. This trend is reflected in the magazine in articles specially written to appeal to both husband and wife, and in illustrations showing couples co-operating on various projects. In America, *McCall's* heralded 'togetherness' 12 years ago.

Woman's Own, which has always taken a more astringent editorial line than *Woman*—there is currently a circulation gap between them of more than half a million—has dared to be more progressive than its rival, particularly in the expansion of its 'general interest' features, but for the moment is not pressing further ahead. *Woman's Realm*, because of its smaller circulation, has been ready to take similar chances in keeping up to date and its topical articles bring an enthusiastic mail. Its fiction, too, is changing in accordance with the modern taste for realism and the magazine is also getting younger. Initially, it was created for the older, full-time housewife, but recently it has been slanting its content to appeal more to younger women in an attempt to broaden the base of its readership.

Woman's Realm's Editor, Josie Argy, is emphatic that older women must still be catered for, particularly as they will be forming an increasingly large section of the population owing to demographic trends. She feels they have special needs which must not be neglected in the rush to woo the young housewife, but she admits that keeping a balance between the two age-groups is not easy. Now that men are taking a greater interest in domestic affairs, articles are occasionally included for their benefit and the magazine has a large male following. Its continued success is attributable to the Editor's determination never to underestimate the capacity of women to appreciate articles and illustrations of exceptional quality. There tends to be less glamour and escapism in *Woman's Realm* than in some other magazines and an avoidance of excessive romanticism and sentimentality in its features, but many readers have expressed their approval of this approach. As one correspondent wrote: 'How nice it is to be treated like an intelligent human being.'

Of all the 'service' weeklies, *Woman's Weekly* has changed the most, at least as far as presentation is concerned. In October, 1966, it 'went gravure', introducing full colour for the first time. In order not to damage the magazine's image, the transition into colour was made gradually. The traditional pink-and-blue emphasis was retained on the cover, and early colour features were carefully chosen to incorporate these colour tones. The Editor also strictly limited the proportion of 'bled off' illustrations, which she felt would change the look of the magazine. A slight technical modification allowed the page-size to be fractionally increased, yielding 2,400 extra words per issue, and the magazine also changed to a whiter paper.

Woman's Weekly's 'new look' has brought it nearly 200,000 new readers and increased revenue from the higher advertising rate for colour. Its rapid growth has confounded those critics who had written it off as a social anachronism, doomed to perish in the face of the new trends sweeping through the industry. Its Editor, Jean Twiddy, sees its future as one of gradual development rather than radical change. The direction of that development can already be detected in the magazine's features which are more sophisticated than those of five years ago. It has already dealt with drug addiction, and the Editor believes it will be possible gradually to expand the range following the

Table 7: Male Readership of Women's Magazines—1967

Magazine	Percentage of all readers who are male
Weeklies:	
Jackie	23·8
Valentine	23·3
Woman's Own	20·4
People's Friend	19·3
Woman	19·0
Woman's Weekly	17·4
Woman's Realm	17·3
My Weekly	17·1
Petticoat	10·5
Monthlies:	
Rave	35·8
Nova	28·5
She	21·6
Good Housekeeping	19·6
True Story	18·4
Family Circle	18·1
Woman's Home Journal	14·3
Woman and Home	14·1
Vogue	13·7
Annabel	13·7
True Romances	13·0
Mother	11·9
My Home and Family	9·4
Flair	9·1
Honey	8·5
Vanity Fair	8·3

Source: National Readership Survey, 1967.

pattern set by T.V., giving the magazine wider appeal for the increasing numbers of grammar-school educated women who are not being adequately catered for at present.

Though *Woman's Weekly* and its two sister papers *Woman and Home* and *My Home* (which are written to much the same formula), have progressed beyond the 'lavender and roses' image, their big pull still lies in their sincerity and the friendship they offer to lonely, unsure women, elements which their Editor believes must be preserved despite and throughout all the other changes which are steadily overtaking them. *Woman's Weekly* will therefore continue with its policy of combining warmth with practicality, emphasising knitting and fiction but providing a more balanced 'service' formula than in the past.

The monthlies have also benefited from the infusion of Dichter's ideas. Typical of them is *Woman's Home Journal* (formerly *Woman's Journal*). The problem facing this magazine is shared by most pre-war journals which are encumbered with dying readerships and a staid, middle-aged image which is failing to attract the new, younger readers they need to insure future circulation. Starting in 1964, *Woman's Home Journal* embarked on a programme of rejuvenation through which it has gradually been acquiring greater youthfulness and vitality, dropping its age profile to focus on women between 25 and 45. Its Editor during this period, Ailsa Garland, widely experienced in publishing—she was appointed the *Daily Mirror's* first woman Editor by Cecil King and was also Editor of *Vogue*—was aware of the pressing need to catch up with the vast changes which have been overtaking women in the 1960s, and to educate readers away from the old formula which was 'nice, genteel, and pretty'. However, she felt strongly that realism carried to the point of crudity had no place in women's magazines.

Today *Woman's Home Journal* is trying to effect a compromise between these two extremes. It is gradually developing along new lines, attempting to build for itself a reputation for high quality fashion, excellent fiction (for which it has always been well-known), and home service. Special discussion features on social problems such as delinquency are also being quietly introduced to test readers' reactions to topical subjects, changes which are part of an all-round upgrading of the magazine's editorial content and presentation designed to check the slow drain of readers and encourage new recruits from the younger generation without more drastic changes in its hitherto very successful formula. In the period since this policy was put into effect, readership amongst the under forty-fives has increased far more than was anticipated, an indication that it is proceeding along the right lines.

Like the IPC, The National Magazine Co. has found it necessary to mount a rescue operation for its 'prestige' service periodicals *Good Housekeeping, Harper's Bazaar* and *Vanity Fair*, but without comparable research to guide it. For many years *Good Housekeeping* led the 'home service' field, strengthened by its renowned Institute and GHI Seal of Guarantee. It began losing circulation in 1957 and by July, 1965, its sales had dropped by 25 per cent. The publishers had to decide between two alternatives: widening the magazine's appeal to include more general (and perhaps controversial) features, following in the steps of its own early trend-setter *She* and, more recently, of *Nova*, or contracting its content right down to a core of household service. The management opted for the latter policy as being the most effective way of competing with the other 'glossies' in attracting the advertising revenue it needed for survival. This decision was determined as much by the recognition that 'specialisation is the only way of meeting cut-throat competition in the publishing world today', as by the fact that 'past surveys have shown that *Good Housekeeping* has been purchased for its "service" features rather than its fiction or articles', to quote Mr Marcus Morris, the firm's Managing Director.*

Assuming that the magazine would be able to hold and increase its sales on a more authoritative 'service' formula backed by a much improved and expanded Institute, resources allotted to the latter department were increased, with the intention that the Good Housekeeping Institute should ultimately provide the most comprehensive and professional guide to housewifery available anywhere in the women's press. The functions of the GHI Seal of Guarantee having been largely superseded by the growth of nation-wide consumer protection organisations, it was discontinued. Advice in this area is still available to any manufacturer or reader requiring it, but it was hoped this would be rendered increasingly unnecessary by the higher standard of regular editorial coverage.

This expansion in 'service' was balanced by a contraction in fiction and features, but a correspondence column has since been introduced as a means of forging closer links with readers, reflecting their views and achieving the identification which is felt to be crucial to the magazine's future success. Special attention was also given to improving its general lay-out and art work. *Good Housekeeping*'s Editor, Laurie Purden, stressing the importance of this aspect, commented:

'In Britain, publishers have always tended to lag behind in this area, and it is only during the last five years or so that there has been any noticeable attempt at improvement. Now, visual excitement is being demanded more and more by readers who have been made more visually conscious by television, and standards of presentation are soaring. But there are dangers in trying out too many new techniques before readers are ready for them, as *McCall's* found when they allowed the visual to take over completely in the period after the war when the American periodical press was setting new

* Personal interview.

trends in presentation. Today, we tend to accept good photography, colour, space and clarity as the norm, but we owe them to such pioneers as Jimmy Drawbell who was one of the first to realize the potentialities of the new American techniques and campaigned for the introduction of more colour into women's periodicals. *Queen* was another pace-maker whose example sparked off new ideas which have since filtered right through to the weeklies.'*

Implicit in all these measures was the recognition that, in order to survive, *Good Housekeeping* had both to bring itself up to date and embark upon a policy of specialisation. In choosing to concentrate on providing a comprehensive home-making service, an important consideration was the fact that approximately 400,000 new houses are built in Britain every year, half of which are privately owned. When the actual number of new households formed *per annum* is also taken into account, there is obviously great scope for a publication offering expert guidance and information on all aspects of equipping and running these new homes. *Good Housekeeping* has transformed itself with this potential readership in mind; like *Woman's Home Journal*, it badly needs the infusion of new, younger patrons to replace those who have grown old and fallen away. Since the new policies were put into effect it has shown a consistent increase in sales, but, in common with other monthlies, its chief problem is still to attract enough advertising.

Change has also overtaken *Harper's Bazaar* and *Vanity Fair*, both of which have been in decline for some years. The former was completely re-styled in February, 1968, to give it a broader appeal. Renamed *Bazaar*, the new magazine set out to attract the affluent older woman, covering a much wider range of topics, including 'rich living, gourmet eating, pasha weekends, couture cars, art as an investment'—to quote the first of the re-styled issues. The publishers hoped the new formula would reduce competition from the other 'quality' fashion magazines but the change did nothing to halt its declining circulation. The magazine has since undergone a second re-styling, reverting to its original title under the banner 'The return of the Beautiful Magazine', and featuring 'a new type-face, and a whole clutch of new columnists covering everything from cars and clematis to cognac and the latest gossip in the opera world'. Enlarged to a hundred pages, and equipped with three new Editors (for Fashion, Beauty and Features) and a new Art Director who has 'completely re-conceived the whole *Harper's Bazaar* look', the first of the new issues appeared in March, 1969,

* Personal interview (1965).

proclaiming the 'old fashioned virtues' of 'beautiful pictures, desirable clothes, and intelligent writing'.

Vanity Fair has been similarly re-formulated. When the present Editor, Hazel Meyrick-Evans, joined the magazine, she set out to reproduce the formula which *Elle* exploits so successfully, interspersing fashion with written articles and solid information. Then the decision was made to cut back on extraneous features and concentrate on fashion, following the trend towards specialisation. Circulation continued to drop and current managerial policy is once more releasing the magazine from its narrow confines with the aim of giving it a 'total personality'.

While the declining magazines search for ways to regain their popularity with readers and advertisers, the few journals which have defied the general recession, increasing or at least maintaining their sales, stand out as the 'object lessons' of women's publishing. *She*'s achievements have already been described.* Among the periodicals of pre-war vintage, *Mother* is doing particularly well, having increased its circulation by 75 per cent since 1959. *Mother*'s readership is concentrated in the 25–35 age-group, 86 per cent of whom had an income of under £1,000 a year in 1965, which implies a circulation mainly amongst women of the skilled working classes. In view of the fact that more than a million babies are born in Britain every year, the Editor, Mrs Veronica Snobel, feels there is considerable room for expansion with the help of better promotion and improved presentation. The American magazine, *Parents*, with a million sale, shows what can be done in this field, but unlike *Mother* it does not have to rely on book-stall sales. Because it is highly specialised, *Mother* cannot hope to retain its readers as long as an ordinary 'general interest' women's monthly, and therefore expects a high turnover in its readership. Its success depends on its ability to attract a constant supply of new readers, which means keeping abreast of the latest developments and trends. There are fashions in child-care and *Mother* has to follow the lead of the medical profession in this and all other aspects of motherhood, treating the same subjects in progressively different ways according to current medical opinion.

The magazine is performing an important, professional service in instructing the young mother. While it has no direct liaison with the Ministry of Health, it nevertheless upholds government policy on all medical matters. Its articles are vetted, and readers' enquiries dealt with, by a panel of medical men which comprises a leading paediatrician, an obstetrician, a G.P., and a psychiatrist. These experts set extremely

* See Chapter 5.

high standards, and the Editor is aware that their advice may not be an unmitigated blessing to women with no training or experience, no home help, inadequate equipment and a limited income. Failure to measure up to the magazine's expectations regarding cleanliness, patience or tolerance, can undermine a young mother's self-confidence, which is the reverse of what the editorial staff are trying to do. The 'commercial mum' as she is presented through television and press advertising reinforces the happy, well-run family ideal which is totally divorced from reality.

In view of this, the Editor considers it important that the magazine should strip off this façade occasionally and show that the staff understand the difficulties women have to contend with in the far-from-ideal world of everyday. This new policy of realism is evidently appreciated. The Editor claims that on the occasions when more perceptive, intelligent articles have been included, the response has been very encouraging. Far from causing horror at the near-blasphemous contradiction of the 'joys of motherhood' gospel, one item, 'Family Holidays are Hell', elicited an enthusiastic correspondence—an outpouring of sheer relief at having secret experiences and beliefs confirmed. The Editor feels that more of this should be attempted. She would like to reach the group of mothers who are seriously in need of the help and confidence the magazine is able to give. At present, it is mainly read by those who are already conscientious in their approach to motherhood, and she regards preaching to the converted as something of a sterile enterprise.

The proprietors are unwilling to tamper with so successful a formula, and the exploration of controversial areas such as abortion and combining motherhood with an outside job can only take place gradually, but it is the Editor's intention to press ahead in this direction. The case of a small boy molested by a man in a children's playground has already formed the subject of a short story, a notable advance. The magazine underwent radical re-shaping in 1964, when its size was increased, more experts were recruited to its staff (replacing the professional journalists who had previously produced it) and its services were generally upgraded. The proportion of fiction was also reduced to allow it to concentrate on mothercraft in accordance with the new policy of specialisation. In February, 1968, the magazine was completely re-styled and given 'square-back' presentation to project a more modern image.

Another successful periodical is *The Lady*. It is the only remaining privately owned publication for women in Britain and is run by a small staff of eight, most of whom have been with the magazine for many years. The Editor, Miss Margaret Whitford, herself joined it in 1932, and is largely responsible for rescuing it from the doldrums of the 'thirties and restoring it to economic health; also for maintaining the magazine's unbroken record of appearances all through the Second World War. In 1935, *The Lady* was selling a mere 12,000 copies. Today, that figure has been increased to 77,000, which, though small fry compared with the mass weeklies, is nevertheless a remarkable achievement for a black and white magazine of Victorian vintage written off by many as the social anachronism its title implies. Formerly, *The Lady* catered mainly to the 'polite' section of Society, but during the war when publications of all kinds were in short supply, the magazine attracted readers from all walks of life. Today, its readership is believed to be predominantly middle-class and rural, but the fact that it has a considerable male following says much for the universality of its appeal. It has a large 'pass-along' readership which the proprietors hope to see converted into new sales.

The primary attraction of *The Lady* is probably its large 'classified advertisement' section, a service unusual in the women's press. But there is a solid core of readers for whom the editorial content has a strong appeal. *The Lady* is a magazine intended to provide solid reading matter. Indeed, its continued registration as a newspaper depends upon the inclusion of a certain percentage of hard news. It concentrates on topics of general interest on the assumption that there are many women whose concerns are not bounded by the four walls of their homes. 'We regard our readers as human beings, not merely housewives' commented the Editor,* hence the magazine ranges over some novel territory.

Its fiction is a strong feature and has a characteristic stamp. Sketches of domestic life, written in satirical vein, are particularly popular. The fashion articles, instead of parading a selection of the latest clothes to emerge from the large fashion houses, concentrate on providing a comprehensive guide to fashion trends, which the provincial reader can refer to when she shops in town. *The Lady*'s travel guide is another popular service feature, as are its correspondence columns which attract some 4,000 letters a year. Travel, dress, and careers in that order elicit the greatest response. In the past, all controversial topics have been rigorously excluded as a cardinal principle of editorial policy, but the Editor hopes to introduce articles in which experts will discuss current social problems, reviving an era when the magazine possessed a sensitive social conscience, particularly with regard to the Women's Movement.

One characteristic differentiates this magazine from most other women's periodicals. It is entirely impersonal in its approach and

---

* Personal interview.

factual in its treatment of events. There is no attempt whatsoever to establish a close relationship with readers and they seldom comment on what the magazine has to offer. The Editor believes that this policy generates reader-loyalty, rather than reader-dependence. The result is an expertly tailored production, entertaining as well as utilitarian and full of interest, which discharges its obligations to readers competently and unemotionally but in no way unfeelingly. No longer 'The Magazine for Gentlewomen', it has widened its appeal and adapted itself to a changed class structure. But the aura of quiet refinement and gentility is still there, and it has not forgotten 'the importance of being earnest', attributes which commend it to well over 300,000 readers every month, an achievement which many of the monthlies would be happy to equal.

Homes and Gardens is another example of a pre-war magazine which has not been seriously affected by the present trend of falling sales, and its ability to gain readers and hold them in a field where other publications have lost ground or folded completely is significant. Part of this success is no doubt due to the tremendous resurgence of interest in all aspects of home-making in recent years, particularly cookery, which has now become almost a cult amongst the young. Following the American pattern, the material evidences of 'house-proudness' have taken over as the chief status symbols in Britain also. But *H&G*'s popularity is mainly attributable to good value: for three shillings the reader gets a large, immensely varied magazine, flexible in its approach, and of high editorial quality. The necessity of working within a budget which does not run to 'big-name' fees, taxes editorial ingenuity and produces some original feature ideas.

The magazine's strongest feature is its home-decorating service through which it undertakes to advise readers on colour-schemes, and sends out colour-matched folders which include wall-paper, paint, curtain material and carpet samples. This service is entirely free, and no other periodical offers a comparable scheme, a fact which, together with its furnishing section, gives it a big pull with the trade. Its cookery is traditional, to suit older palates, and its fashions are intended primarily for the older woman also. Its service for the antique collector, though a minority interest, is again appreciated by older readers. However, the magazine's reputation in other fields evidently encourages younger women to seek the advice of its experts, for *H&G* receives a larger mailbag from them on the subjects of beauty and fashion than does its specialist rival, *Flair*, notwithstanding the fact that it carries no beauty articles.

The Editor sees the function of the magazine as being primarily one of service backed up with entertainment. It has evolved a special character and remains true to it by scrupulous attention to detail which ensures that editorial continuity is preserved. However, its core of loyal patrons represents a dying readership which needs to be replenished from the younger generation. Hence its policy in recent years has been to 'hedge' against the future by injecting sufficient new life to attract new readers, but nothing so radical that existing readers will be disturbed. Its editorial team, under Lady Georgina Coleridge, is cautiously bringing the magazine into line with the broader interests and horizons of women, recognising the need for an adventurous element but refusing to subscribe to the shock tactics and sensationalism that some other journals have resorted to for the sake of impact. To quote Lady Georgina:

> 'Women's lives and interests have widened enormously in recent years. T.V. is partly responsible, but so are the greater opportunities for foreign travel. Today women are selective in their tastes and harder to please. They have become more houseproud, and they are more mobile too, so that they know Britain better than their mothers did. *H&G* aims at being a friend to these readers, and a useful one. There will always be room in it for controversial subjects discussed in a matter-of-fact way. But dabbling in dope, adultery or violence is not its function. Such territory is already adequately covered by the daily newspapers.'*

Thus *Homes and Gardens* will continue with its carefully-balanced blend of culture, entertainment and home service, spiced with humour, aiming as in the past at variety, value, and the highest literary and 'service' standards. But its policy will no longer be to exclude the outside world for the sake of preserving an 'in-group' appeal. To quote a former Editor, Mr. John Mendes:

> 'The time has come for greater realism both in fiction and in features, and for the modernisation of its design and presentation. This will be kept within reasonable limits. The fate of *Home Magazine* which underwent radical changes to bring itself up to date and folded soon afterwards, is a lesson which no publisher can afford to ignore. There is a real danger in trying to do too much, too soon. The present preoccupation with introducing more intelligent subjects into women's magazines is probably more relevant for publications catering to women in the lower ranks of society. A

---

* Personal interview.

woman who only sees *The Daily Mirror* is probably in greater need of intellectual stimulation than one who has access to the "quality" opinion papers and other media dealing with current affairs in a responsible way. For this reason, it is probably better that the "quality" women's magazines should confine themselves to home topics which their readers are not getting elsewhere.'*

Clearly, there are lessons to be learned from those magazines which are continuing to find favour with the reading public without sweeping editorial revisions, and the fate of *Woman's Mirror*, *Everywoman* and *Housewife* would seem to add weight to the views of the Editor who said:

> 'There is a danger in any policy which tends to elevate women's magazines onto too high a plane. Magazines like *Nova* are appealing only to a fringe group of women who are more sophisticated than they are educated, and with everyone's eyes turned on the glossies, managements and Editors alike are tending to forget that a large proportion of female readership is made up of very ordinary women, who above all need emotional release which they can never find in magazines devoted to "witty literacy".'*

This opinion is further strengthened by the recent success of *Woman's Weekly*, which gained almost one hundred and fifty thousand extra readers in a single year merely by offering its traditional formula in bright new packaging.

The Editors who paid lip service to the root-and-branch reforms considered necessary by the Management to stop the rot in the core of women's publishing were never happy with either the diagnosis or the remedy. Only the passage of time and the reactions of the female reading public could show that the Dichter study was a somewhat misleading piece of psycho-social research, which was further distorted at the stage of implementation by those who seized on the concept of the 'emerging woman' and created the fully-fledged 'New Woman' as the pivot of the industry's future development, brushing aside Dichter's reservations and qualifications. Dichter, in fact, never stated that the universal decline in the popularity of women's magazines was due to editorial tardiness in catching up with social trends. He merely indicated that *Woman's Own* could improve its appeal by modernising its image and expanding and improving its content in certain areas, at the same

* Personal interviews.

time stressing the many aspects which were already well-received. His findings were nevertheless regarded as conclusive evidence that the industry's troubles stemmed from editorial inadequacies, and they were further distorted by Dichter's own failure to make clear the fact that social trends do not affect a population uniformly, or at an equal rate. Publishers have realised their error, and Dichter's, and are beginning to take into account the complexities of social stratification along several dimensions in planning for the 'seventies.

NOTES

1 W. D. McClelland, *Women's Weeklies*, p. 10.
2 W. D. McClelland, *Women's Press in Britain*, p. 152.
3 Marplan Ltd., *Markets and Media*, 1963.
4 *A New Measurement Study of Women's Weekly Magazines.*
5 *A Motivational Research Study on the British Woman in Today's Culture*, Vol. 1, p. 19.
6 *Ibid.*, p. 29.
7 *Ibid.*, p. 33.
8 *Ibid.*, p. 21.
9 *Ibid.*, Vol. 2, p. 221.
10 *Ibid.*, Vol. 2, p. 231.
11 *Ibid.*, Vol. 2, p. 168.
12 *World's Press News*, September 17th, 1965, pp. 10–12.
13 *Ibid.*, p. 12.
14 *World's Press News*, March 12th, 1965, p. 44.
15 See note 12.
16 Promotion material.

8

The Women's Press in America

In the mid-'fifties, the American women's magazine industry entered a period of recession. It was due to a combination of rising costs, diminishing advertising support and a sudden drop in news-stand sales, and it claimed such well-known titles as *Collier's*, *Coronet*, *Everywoman's* and *Woman's Home Companion*. *Collier's* and *Woman's Home Companion* were two of America's longest-running periodicals, founded in 1888 and 1873 respectively, and at the time they ceased publication were each selling over four million copies a month. Crowell-Collier withdrew them because they were involving the firm in heavy losses (estimated at $7·5 million annually), converting a profit on its other publishing enterprises into an overall deficit of $2·5 million.

Those magazines which survived underwent a gradual editorial transformation which brought readers flocking back. In marked contrast to contemporaneous trends in the British women's press, the American industry embarked upon a new phase of expansion with circulation soaring in all but the fiction sector, a trend which was maintained until the late 'sixties. Since 1967, however, the picture has begun to change. The problems of the wider magazine industry have intensified and spread to the mass-selling women's magazines. Owing to the scarcity of advertising,* a number of women's journals are known to be in difficulties, the extent of which is masked by contracts secured at large discounts. There has also been a deterioration in sales; 14 out of the 21 leading women's magazines had either lost readers or failed to improve their circulation in the six months ended June, 1968, and for eight of them the decline dates from the second half of 1967.

It is too early to judge whether this represents a new period of

* The early 1969 issues of a number of titles showed a substantial fall in advertising. In common with *Life*, *Look* and *Reader's Digest*, whose advertising sales had dropped by 27 per cent, 16 per cent and 18 per cent, advertising in *McCall's* was down by 12 per cent over 1968.

decline or is merely another temporary recession. Advertising appears to move in cycles as firms shift their patronage from one advertising medium to another following the latest market research findings. The decline in circulation may equally prove to be a passing phenomenon. However, there is at least the possibility that the American women's press, like the British, has passed its peak and will have to come to terms with a new market situation. By its previous recovery from the recession of the 1950s, the industry has shown that it is flexible enough to adapt to changing conditions, and there are aspects of this recovery, in particular the evolution of new editorial approaches to match changes taking place within the female population, which justify closer examination for the relevance they may have to the future of our own.

(i) American Women's Magazines: a Profile

Due to the attrition experienced in the previous decade, the American women's press comprises fewer titles than our own, and total circulation in proportion to a national female population of over 100 million is considerably lower. There are (1968) 21 women's periodicals with sales in excess of half a million per issue, and these can roughly be grouped into four categories: 'shelter', 'fiction', 'fashion' and 'service'. Although the majority of these publications are aimed at the middle classes, adherence to the principles of individuality and specialisation has helped to minimise duplication, and there is clear differentiation between them.

The 'shelter' magazines are wholly practical, dealing with the more technical aspects of housing (building, landscaping, decoration, etc.) rather than the subtle arts of home-making. Because they are highly specialised and are not intended to appeal solely to women, despite their strong feminine interest, they are excluded from this survey.

'Fiction' periodicals fall into two groups: the cheap 'pulp' magazines, such as those put out by the firm of Martin Goodman, and higher grade publications of the type published by MacFadden Bartell. In common with other, similar groups, Martin Goodman publications appear bi-monthly and are sold to advertisers as a complete 'package' consisting of *My Confessions, My Romance, Romantic Confessions, Secret Story* and *True Secrets*. These titles speak for themselves as to the type of fiction they offer, but though they provide as much sex interest as they dare without offending the delicate sensibilities of advertisers, an inbuilt moral code imposes strict editorial limits, and readers who buy on the strength of titillating covers and captions are usually disappointed. However, this does not seem to prevent them coming back for more. As with British magazines of a similar type, there is a small amount of non-fiction content, and the intention is to expand this gradually, introducing columns dealing with, for example, medical queries and personal problems.

Though their titles are indistinguishable, the MacFadden group, comprising *True Confessions, True Experience, True Love, True Romance* and *True Story*, differs substantially from its competitors both in appearance and editorial approach. They appear monthly, are higher priced and project a more polished image. Only their titles are temperature-raising. The entire group sold 6 million copies a month in 1967, and claimed a readership of 15 million among home-oriented women in the middle-income ranges. As with most other fiction magazines, the proportion of news-stand sales is high (two-thirds) and the amount of advertising carried correspondingly low (approximately 38 per cent).

True Story, with a circulation of almost $2\frac{1}{4}$ million, is the unchallenged leader in the field, possibly due to the fact that it is basically a 'service' magazine covering the usual range of domestic subjects, but featuring a very high proportion of fiction. The magazine has had some difficulty imprinting this image upon the minds of advertisers with whom memories persist of a very different *True Story*, banned two decades back on account of its torrid fiction, and it has taken an intensive promotion campaign to convince them of its respectability. Its fiction today deals with happenings within the home and is intended to provide both wish-fulfilment and an emotional outlet for mothers with problems, supplemented by recipes and advice on baby-care. It is, to quote MacFadden's President, Frederick Klein, 'Peyton Place in print', but backed by a strong 'service' element which elicits a large reader-mail. *True Story*'s editorial staff take this 'service' function seriously. Testing is carried out in the magazine's own kitchens and laundry, and the Household Editor regularly visits readers in their own homes to promote a closer relationship with them. A measure of their success is given by the fact that an increase in its cover price to fifty cents resulted in no loss of sales.

On this dual basis *True Story* has managed to hold its position while other fiction magazines have lost considerable ground since the 'fifties, some having suffered cuts in their circulations of up to 50 per cent. Compared with other sections of the periodical publishing industry, they are clearly in decline. Mr George Delacorte, Chairman of the Dell Publishing Co., another big publisher of fiction and 'movie' magazines, attributes this decline to the rise in the educational level of

Table 8: Breakdown of Editorial Content in a Selected Group of

Magazine	National Affairs %	Foreign Affairs %	Amusements %	Beauty and Grooming %	Building %	Business and Industry %	Children %	Farming and Gardening %
Good Housekeeping	2·8	1·6	3·1	3·3	1·6	—	3.2	0·5
Ladies' Home Journal	2·9	2·0	6·1	2·9	0·8	0·1	5·5	0·0
McCall's	4·2	0·9	4·3	3·3	0·1	1·6	5·3	0·2
Redbook	1·3	1·0	0·5	4·7	1·0	—	7·9	0·1
Family Circle	—	—	0·2	6·0	1·8	0·5	4·7	1·7
Woman's Day	0·1	—	1·4	6·2	1·8	2·2	8·4	1·7
Ingenue	0·5	—	5·6	10·5	—	1·5	—	—
Seventeen	—	1·2	5·1	8·3	—	1·9	—	—
Modern Romances	—	—	—	3·1	0·2	—	6·7	0·1
True Confessions	—	—	2·4	3·0	—	—	2·2	0·1
True Story	—	—	—	3·7	—	—	3·0	—
American Home	—	—	—	1·2	21·9	—	0·4	9·8
Better Homes and Gardens	—	—	—	0·2	18·0	—	0·1	0·2
Glamour	0·1	—	2·5	24·9	—	1·7	—	—
Harper's	0·0	0·4	3·2	10·7	0·0	0·2	0·0	0·1
Mademoiselle	—	0·4	1·4	12·8	—	3·5	0·2	—
Vogue	0·8	0·9	3·4	9·4	0·2	—	—	1·3

Source: Magazine Editorial Reports, Lloyd H. Hall Co. Inc., New York, August, 1967

American Women's Magazines for the Period Jan.–Aug., 1967

Food	Health	Home Furnishing	Sports, Hobbies, Recreation	Travel and Transport	Wearing Apparel	Cultural Interests	General Interest	Miscellaneous	Fiction	Total Editorial
%	%	%	%	%	%	%	%	%	%	%
17·8	5·5	10·8	0·3	1·2	11·1	7·3	8·6	3·3	17·8	54·8
18·1	5·2	9·8	0·1	0·2	11·2	10·3	8·5	3·0	13·4	48·1
17·0	3·8	9·2	1·5	2·3	9·9	16·1	5·5	2·2	12·7	54·7
11·3	3·0	3·2	0·8	2·5	8·5	8·6	2·5	2·9	40·1	61·3
30·2	8·1	18·5	1·3	3·5	9·6	5·5	4·6	3·5	—	55·6
24·5	1·1	20·3	1·4	6·7	12·0	1·8	3·5	3·1	3·7	63·2
4·9	0·6	1·4	0·5	1·7	29·5	15·7	—	7·2	16·3	56·0
4·8	1·5	5·1	1·6	2·7	39·1	12·1	2·2	4·3	10·2	34·1
3·4	1·9	0·8	—	—	0·5	5·8	1·1	2·9	73·6	66·2
2·7	0·2	1·0	—	—	—	3·6	1·5	2·6	80·7	72·7
9·5	1·8	2·7	—	—	1·4	2·6	4·8	2·8	67·8	62·5
16·1	0·9	37·7	0·8	1·7	0·6	1·8	3·2	3·8	—	43·0
22·4	2·9	25·7	1·0	9·4	0·9	0·1	5·4	3·8	—	48·5
1·2	0·8	2·8	0·6	5·1	41·0	9·1	4·1	5·3	0·8	45·1
0·1	—	1·2	0·4	3·1	63·0	8·1	4·1	2·6	2·5	50·6
0·1	0·2	2·2	0·6	6·3	44·4	12·5	3·3	3·2	7·5	47·4
0·3	0·7	3·3	0·2	3·0	59·0	6·4	8·0	2·2	0·5	54·6

the population, as a result of which the reading public is no longer satisfied with simple stories and is turning instead to paperbacks, which are booming. Dell have responded with a new range of 'purse books', wallet-size for carrying in the handbag, dealing in depth with single subjects such as hair-styling, numerology, or choosing Christmas gifts for men. These are proving a popular innovation, and the range is continually being extended.

MacFadden's are likewise recognising the implications of the trend in education. *True Story*'s editorial content has already been upgraded, and its level will be raised still further as soon as the effects of a new generation of college-educated women are felt. An even more significant development is that the firm is diversifying its holdings, entering in particular the fields of book publishing and broadcasting.

The 'fashion' magazines, dominated by *Seventeen* (which is also published in Braille), are a small but select group operating in close association with the rag-trade. Sleek and sophisticated, they are content with moderate sales in the interests of retaining the appeal of exclusiveness. *Vogue* and *Harper's Bazaar* vie with one another in clothing the older woman; *Mademoiselle* serves the collegiates and young careerists, while *Seventeen* has become the 'bible' of the high-school student. *Glamour* has cornered the beauty market and is leader in its field.

While their *raison d'être* is to keep their readers abreast of the coming fashions in dress and beauty, the fashion journals nevertheless take a broad view of their function. *Mademoiselle*, under the direction of the renowned Mrs Betsy Talbot Blackwell, sets out to serve 'the whole young woman', stimulating her mind as well as clothing her body, advising and informing her, particularly with regard to college entrance and careers, and entertaining her with good fiction. The focus of the magazine is the college campus, and each year it draws twenty 'Guest Editors' from colleges all over America to assist in the preparation of the summer 'College Issue'. These young women provide a 'hot line' of communication between the magazine and its collegiate readership, ensuring authentic and up-to-the-minute representation of the society of the 18-25s. Often these temporary Editors join the magazine's permanent staff.

Launched in 1935, *Mademoiselle* was the first periodical to provide fashion coverage for the younger woman. At this time women needed to take employment outside the home and it was socially acceptable for a women's magazine to focus on careers. *Seventeen*, brought out in 1944, started life in a very different era when society was once more orientated toward the traditional domestic role for women. Today, the social pendulum appears to be swinging back, and like *Mademoiselle, Seventeen* now shows a sustained concern for teenage girls in every department of their lives. Counselling is one of its most important functions and a variety of problems, 'from sex to crooked teeth', are dealt with in a straightforward, sisterly way. The magazine's aim is to inspire confidence and to suggest guide lines for behaviour as well as taste.

Though the median age of readers is 17·1 years, *Seventeen* spans the 13–19 age-group, which for most American girls means the high-school years, and for the fortunate the early period in college. It is an entrenched favourite with teenagers and according to 1967 estimates reaches every one of them in three issues. The editorial staff believe it has achieved success both because it shows a sincere desire to help teenagers, which has won their confidence, and because it never 'talks down' to them. Also important is its determination to avoid the East Coast orientation shown by some other periodicals. *Seventeen*'s Editors 'range far afield to keep attuned to the interests and attitudes of readers'.

The magazine tries to represent all modes of thought, to project a social conscience, and to reflect teenage involvement in family life (e.g. by including recipes for girls who must cope with the cooking when mom is at work), but it does not escort a girl beyond her engagement. This policy is strictly adhered to in the interests of readers, despite the fact that advertising could be considerably increased by departing from it. *Seventeen*'s August, 1967, issue, which ran to 452 pages, breaking all previous advertising records, shows that it has no need to do so.

Vogue, too, explores fields other than fashion, finding that the days have gone when it sufficed to provide shiny, showy literature, suitable for display on the coffee-tables of affluent homes. Readers are no longer satisfied with mere visual excellence, and under the Editorship of Mrs Diana Vreeland, *Vogue* has acquired not only a more youthful character but a greater liveliness and licence of subject and language. Non-fashion material occupies 16–24 pages per issue, and includes reviews, one important article, a portrait of a house or garden, and a feature, 'People are talking about . . .', which keeps readers *au fait* with the latest ideas and events. *Vogue*'s art coverage is famous, and in support of these various extensions of the magazine's editorial range its publishers argue that the economic viability of a fashion magazine now depends upon backing its ephemeral fashion coverage with more enduring content. Similarly, *Harper's Bazaar* was devoting almost 40 per cent of its editorial content to non-fashion subjects in the period January–August, 1967.

The 'service' periodicals constitute the largest section of the American women's press and that which has seen the greatest changes as a result of falling sales and heightened competition for advertising. After a rough passage in the 'fifties, seven leading titles emerged, streamlined and modernised, to face the challenge of the 'sixties. The large magazines have grown bigger and the smaller ones more specialised: all have grown younger, and all have, until recently, been gaining circulation, *McCall's* leading its rivals with a current monthly sale of over $8\frac{1}{2}$ million.

At *McCall's*, Robert Stein, a publisher and Editor with wide experience and deep insight in writing for women, believes that, aside from the basic responsibilties of informing and guiding women in the fundamentals of caring for a home and raising a family, it should be part of the magazine's monthly task 'to amuse, delight, stimulate and surprise'[2] them with 'literary and provocative' journalism far removed from the 'aimless chatter and cozy nonsense' of former years. Starting some years back, when Herbert Mayes began experimenting with new visual techniques to achieve greater impact, the editorial team at *McCall's* has been striving to create 'a world to delight the eye, challenge the senses and awaken the imagaination',[2] while at the same time encouraging 'new involvement and understanding'. Their aim is to reflect 'all the richness of [American] society and [to give] the reader confidence in choosing among those riches, both material and spiritual',[2] but equally to underline the areas of social poverty and suggest what women can do about them.

Translated into more specific terms, this editorial approach has produced a whole new range of articles and features in the realm of science, the arts, and world affairs. The magazine has carried interviews with outstanding men and women of our time, ranging from the Protestant theologian Dr Reinhold Niebuhr to Madame Indira Gandhi, and has begun to explore many areas once regarded as strictly male preserves. Fuller coverage has been given to finance and investment, motoring and travel, as well as to the more intimate territory of personal feelings and relationships. The qualities of grace and perception, considered by Mr Stein to be highly important in writing for women, have been imparted through the contributions of 'the finest novelists, playwrights and critics'. As a result of these new policies, *McCall's* now carries a higher proportion of cultural and current affairs features than any other 'service' magazine, and has become America's largest-selling women's periodical.

In contrast, *Ladies' Home Journal* is concerned less with visual impact and dramatic *reportage* and more with building a reputation for substance, depth and reliability in its coverage of home management, striving for a relationship with readers that is warm, intimate and personal. It claims to be 'The magazine women believe in'. Like *McCall's*, however, it manifests considerable literary freedom and balances the 'service' emphasis with a strong debating role, creating controversy and inviting criticism. It deals constructively with topical issues such as race conflict, the effects of the Pill, and parent-child relationships, and tries to cater to the new generation of working mothers with special articles. *The Ladies' Home Journal's* Editor, John Mack Carter, recognises that there are a whole new set of competing claims on women's time, and stresses the importance of matching the pattern of editing to changing patterns of work and leisure. He feels that, as they become more discriminating, readers will not tolerate magazines which waste their time, and that it is an Editor's principal task to gain their attention (and hold it) with top quality writing. Far more than in the past, the magazine now sees itself as catering to an attitude-group, and has widened its scope accordingly. This policy was begun early in the 1960s, when Curtiss Anderson (then Editor) described the thinking behind it:

> '. . . an integral part of our editorial concept is to achieve a still higher level of editing that will attract those alert young women who do not now have strong allegiance to any women's magazine.... Through selective editing beyond the traditional confines of our field, and in combination with discerning selectivity in our circulation policies, the *Journal* plans to cultivate this audience.... As a magazine whose purpose is to lead—rather than reflect—[the reader's] tastes, the *Journal* will not be limited to any single editorial style.... Our editors will strive to open her eyes and mind ... awaken her to new responsibilities ... challenge her greater intellect ... speak without condescension about her way of life.'[3]

This statement, and subsequent editorial trends, are in line with the decision made by the Curtis Publishing Co. in 1958 not to enter a 'circulation race', but to opt for selectivity and the kind of 'service' magazines which would establish close *rapport* with readers and demonstrate to advertisers their ability to motivate as well as reach. *American Home*, committed to a similar policy, claimed an encouraging response from both advertisers and readers.*

The lush presentation of *The Ladies' Home Journal* and *McCall's* is lacking in the supermarket magazines *Family Circle* and *Woman's Day* (sold at 20 cents), but they have nevertheless built circulations in the region of 7 million respectively. The fact that they are cheap and favourably positioned is offset by the freedom of the grocery chains to

---

* The policies described above relate to the period prior to the acquisition of *The Ladies' Home Journal* and *American House* by Downe Communications.

sell a full range of women's magazines, unlike Britain, where *Family Circle* and its sister publication *Living* have no such competition. Since all other 'service' magazines rely on at least a proportion of subscription sales, the achievements of American *Family Circle* and *Woman's Day* in maintaining a high level of on-the-spot sales have been considerable.

The two magazines are very similar in content and approach, with the exception that *Woman's Day* carries fiction and *Family Circle* does not. Both aim at helping the housewife cope with the demands of home and family, but both interpret this 'service' function broadly. For Geraldine Rhoads, Editor of *Woman's Day*, it means being the 'all-inclusive vehicle of a quality of life', and 'reassuring women that the job they are doing is worthwhile'. She stresses the need for practicality and reliability in all departments, and behind-the-scenes testing is comprehensive and thorough. For Arthur Hettich, in charge of *Family Circle*, 'service' covers 'all that pertains to a woman in her home environment, not least personal relationships'. Under his direction, the magazine is moving towards a warmer, more personal approach, one that is hoped will encourage greater reader-involvement through features presented 'in terms of people'. Both magazines show a trend towards greater realism, and an attempt to relate editorial matter more closely to their readers' way of life. Their articles reflect the widening scope for creativity within the home, the vastly increased range of choices in everything from goods and services to family planning, and the tendency amongst women toward greater social involvement.

Good Housekeeping is unique among the 'service' magazines in possessing a nationally known Institute and associated Seal of Guaranty. It is also one of the most profitable of the women's periodicals, choosing to keep promotion costs low and circulation at an optimum level. In 1966, it was the fourth most profitable magazine in the U.S.A. and only *Seventeen* carried a higher number of advertising pages. Its readers, to quote its Editor, Wade Nichols, 'are generally women of the three levels of the middle class; generally a little better educated than the average without being sophisticated or "in" members of any intellectual élite; a bit sharper than most without being rashly experimental in anything'. To these women, in the 20–40 age-group, *Good Housekeeping* is an all-round 'business adviser', the business being the serious one of functioning effectively as a woman in a complex and demanding environment. Its Editor has a down-to-earth conception of what it means to be a housewife and mother:

'... everything from shopping and household maintenance and decorating and darning some guy's dirty socks to raising children, steering a husband economically and sexually and probably spiritually, taking the lead in establishing social contacts and community status, and possibly even managing a supplementary career.'

Instead of 'glamour and magic', he offers 'the stern and sure and proven path of the ancient maxims and eternal truths',[4] a traditionally high level of credibility, and consumer guidance and protection based on guaranteed advertising.

Since Wade Nichols joined *Good Housekeeping* in 1959, the magazine has been committed even more firmly to a policy of 'reader-identification', but it has been gradually and cautiously modernised to give it new youthfulness and vitality. Its presentation has been improved, its fiction used to explore the real and personal situations of modern living, and its articles given strong, urgent, controversial appeal. It tackles questions such as civil rights and hospital administration and is no longer reticent about giving its own viewpoint, though it does not seek to impose this on the reader. Contributions from the Institute continue to bulk large in every issue, and the knowledge that they are backed by advanced testing in the magazine's laboratories is an important source of reader-confidence.

A more recent competitor for the younger end of the 'service' market is *Redbook*. It is directed at the 18–34 age-group and edited for young married women aged 20–26. Formerly a short-story magazine, *Redbook* was completely remodelled under Wade Nichols and Robert Stein, and is now divided equally between service, 'general interest' and fiction. Currently edited by Sey Chassler, it sets out to give serious, usable information and guidance to those young women who are just entering parental and community life, in a way that respects their intelligence.

Aware that these young women are faced with a host of new domestic and social responsibilities, *Redbook* endeavours to give constructive help by providing them with the raw materials for decision-making, clarifying situations and choices, contributing expert opinion (from such authorities as Dr Spock and Margaret Mead), and inspiring confidence. It also brings a new perspective to bear on family and social life, dealing with the problems which are an intrinsic part of the young married woman's world: education, equality, the economy, the law. But even here it is careful to heed Anne Morrow Lindbergh's warning that 'modern communication loads us with more problems than the human frame can carry',[5] and assigns priorities. Under Robert Stein's Editorship, the magazine chose to emphasise race conflict and the nuclear threat, and this policy remains unchanged. Edited with sincerity and dedication, *Redbook* holds to 'its mission, its thesis and its purpose' which is 'to respond colourfully, creatively, imaginatively and energetically to [all the] requirements of the entering, participating woman', assuring advertisers that 'these things . . . are in the truest sense "editorial support" in every classification'.[6]

Also aimed at the 18–34 group, but at its unattached members, is the much-publicised *Cosmopolitan*. In 1951, the magazine was moribund and making an annual loss of $1·5 million. Two years later its budget was cut to $30,000 per issue, and had it not been for an outstanding $2·5 million debt to subscribers, it would have been completely withdrawn. The early 'sixties brought a further setback following a new drop in news-stand sales resulting from a wave of cut-price subscription offers and the growing preference of advertisers for more lavish journals. The publishers were unwilling to invest in an expensive 'face-lift', and by 1964 the magazine's advertising had dropped by 20 per cent while its circulation was down almost to guarantee level.

Then Helen Gurley Brown assumed the Editorship, and during her tenure sales have climbed towards the million mark and advertising revenue has risen by 200 per cent, added to which *Cosmopolitan* has acquired considerable notoriety as the feminine answer to *Playboy*. *Life* has described it as 'a monthly amplification of Mrs Brown's bestseller *Sex and the Single Girl*', the embodiment of the thesis that 'with a little help any girl can catch a man'. But despite the ballyhoo which surrounds her—Hearst did no promotion on its revolutionary Editor—Mrs Brown has a serious mission: to tap a hitherto ignored audience and to cater to its special needs. The fact that these needs are connected with the intimate craft of being a woman rather than the skilled trade of being a housewife is the reason for the welter of publicity *Cosmopolitan* has attracted.

Identifying with the 'swinging' single girl has given *Cosmopolitan* a new market, and Mrs Brown's individual editorial style has given it a distinctive personality expressed through frank, constructive articles, for example, '54 tips for the divorcée who loves her children *and* a man'. Home-making and general domestic subjects are entirely excluded. The editorial philosophy is founded upon the belief that women need two things: someone to love and some useful work to do. *Cosmopolitan* tries to assist in the satisfaction of both these needs, focusing on the single, widowed or divorced and tackling the special problems which arise in their working lives and in their personal relationships. It pays particular attention to careers, for the benefit of those women who are seeking new ways to fill their days, their children having left home. *Cosmopolitan* is in fact a specialised 'service' magazine of an unorthodox type, packaged to emphasise its sex-appeal, but its success has left advertisers in no doubt as to its commercial potential.

Two newcomers to the 'service' field are *'Teen* (1960) and *Ingenue* (1959), both catering to the youth market. *'Teen* is a fairly conventional, but slick production encompassing the usual teenage interests, with a mind of its own in discussing topics such as drugs and smoking. Besides a high proportion of fashion and beauty, and lively coverage of the film and 'pop' worlds, the magazine finds space for some strong and courageous features—in August, 1967, it even dared to be 'Sick of Twiggy'.

At *Ingenue*, Mrs Silvy Reice (a former Editor) was responsible for initiating an even more independent line with teenagers, 'helping them to deal with the inward problems of adolescence, urging them to take an interest in the world around them, encouraging them to develop their own creative potential'. Deeply involved in achieving meaningful and productive communication with them, she wrote:

'Our aim is to speak to the real teen, the alert, aware, increasingly sophisticated and well-educated offspring of an affluent society . . . to report and reflect current teenage moods and mores rather than to create and "sell" teens a dream image. . . . We do seriously accept the responsibility of our influence on young people and we never hesitate to take positions on issues that are not popular with all of our readers.'[7]

Produced for 13–19-year-olds from well-to-do backgrounds, *Ingenue*, under Mrs Reice's guiding hand endeavoured to strike a balance between 'service' and entertainment. Fashion, beauty and 'fun' features were blended with food and decorating articles carefully related to the teenager's environment. There was full coverage of teenage problems—'how a girl co-exists with her parents, finds a boyfriend, loses weight, gets into college'—and space was found for readers' own literary contributions. The latter were regarded as important for editorial guidance since they reflect the emotional climate of teenage culture and herald changes occurring deep within it. Poetry sent in by readers revealed a growing anti-war philosophy and mounting rebellion against social conformity long before this was detectable elsewhere.

An important aspect of the editorial intention was the channelling of the growing social awareness and involvement of teenagers into practical action. Teens were encouraged to study closely their responsibilities as citizens. One article asked: 'Can teens make our highways safer for humanity?' Another described a scheme for visiting American soldiers wounded in Vietnam begun by a group of teenagers in a New York hospital. A third announced: 'Our hospitals are in trouble and teens can help.' Yet another urged readers to help tackle the problem of poverty. A special *Ingenue* 'Care Corps' was formed by Mrs Reice through which teens could act in concert.

In its attempt to inculcate social consciousness in the younger generation, *Ingenue* has pointed the way towards a new role for the youth media and a constructive use for their considerable influence. The fact that it has found favour with an estimated three million readers demonstrates that there is a definite place for a magazine which credits young American women with interests wider than fashion and the cosmetic arts.

(ii) Shaping Magazine Content

The foregoing profile of American women's magazines shows them to be predominantly youthful, aiming at intelligent and broad-based coverage of all subjects relevant to the lives and interests of the different groups of women to which they cater. Rising demand has been a measure of their success with the female reading public. Though the most visionary of Editors have their sights set higher still, they have already managed to create a brand of journalism far removed from the gossipy, inconsequential productions of earlier years, and one that is gradually moving towards new importance and integrity.

It is a self-criticism that American women's periodicals have in the past been 'too much concerned with the trivial details of housekeeping and personal attractiveness ... too reticent about pursuing the serious social and political issues',[8] and too often inclined 'to foster a cheerful unreality about the deep internal questions of faith, understanding and personal fulfilment'.[8] To some extent these weaknesses still persist, but they are steadily being eradicated and are giving place to serious, responsible coverage, in depth, of topics which assume both a wider social concern amongst women and a deeper interest in achieving meaningful personal relationships. Three interacting sets of factors have contributed to this evolution: social change, editorial freedom within a commercial framework, and research.

(a) Social Change
The growing youthfulness of American women's magazines is part of a deliberate policy to capture young readers, and is a reflection of the interest of advertisers in the rapidly expanding youth market. As a

result of demographic trends, young women are forming an increasingly large proportion of the total female population, in addition to which their personal wealth, and the influence they exert over the spending patterns of the households to which they belong, make them a prime commercial target. Significantly, the only new women's magazines to appear in recent years have been those directed at the very young, namely *Teen*, *Ingenue* and the short-lived Hearst publication, *Eye* (1968), which catered for both sexes.

The youth market falls into four groups: children, teens, collegiates, and young adults, of whom the 18–25s are the fastest-growing section, followed closely by the 13–17s. The following table shows the trend:

Table 9:
Size and Expected Growth of the Young Female Population 1960–80

Age-group	1960 (million)	1965 (million)	% Change over 1960	1970 (million)	% Change over 1960	1975 (million)	% Change over 1960
13–17	7·3	8·7	+19	9·7	+33	10·3	+40
18–25	8·2	10·0	+22	12·1	+47	13·5	+64
25–29	5·6	5·7	+ 3	7·0	+25	8·6	+56

Source: U.S. Census.

Projected to 1980, these figures show further increases over 1960 of 41 per cent, 75 per cent and 74 per cent for the three groups. The under 21s now constitute 40 per cent of the female population, and it is estimated that this figure will have risen to 50 per cent by 1971. The age of marriage continues to fall. Over 40 per cent of brides are teenagers, and more young women marry at eighteen than at any other age, having their first child at nineteen. Unlike their parents, today's young couples expect to equip their homes immediately, using the instalment plan, which means that, both before and after marriage, they are among the nation's best customers.

Seventeen and *Mademoiselle* exploit this buying potential in the specialised fields of fashion and beauty, while *Redbook* focuses on the newlyweds and their multiple household needs. The rest of the youth magazines provide a more general shop-window for advertisers interested in reaching young women, and throughout the remainder of the women's press magazines have been dropping their age-profiles, hoping to scoop up enough young readers to allow them to compete. *Good*

Housekeeping is one periodical which has been particularly successful in changing its image.

This new emphasis on youth has left the older woman inadequately catered for, as many Editors realise without being able to do more than cast a glance in her direction. In 1966, *McCall's* Editor protested that, despite the prevailing cult of youth, his magazine did not consider middle age (and beyond) to be 'some form of incurable disease'. Betsy Talbot Blackwell is another sympathetic Editor who cherishes the hope that some time in the future it will be possible to give older women a magazine of their own, but until advertisers can be convinced that there is sufficient potential in this sector of the women's market, it is unlikely to be realised.

The higher intellectual level now displayed by American women's magazines is attributable to social change of a different kind, namely the 'educational explosion'. Figures published by the U.S. Department of Commerce show that, in the period 1940–65, the number of high-school and college graduates increased three times as fast as the total population. An even more pronounced rate of growth is predicted in the decade 1965–75. In 1940, the median number of school years completed was 8·4; by 1975, it is expected that this figure will have risen to 12·1 years, giving the average American an education which extends beyond high-school. It has already increased to more than 11 years.

This expansion in education has helped to create a new reading public, literate and intellectually curious, whose level of receptivity is continually rising. No longer obliged to screen readers from the real world, the magazines have been able to move away from bland, safe, 'formula' editing into hitherto unexplored territory. Quoting Robert Stein:

> 'Now we can take conventional areas of interest which are un-changing—interest in food, fashions, their appearances and the appearances of the home, child-rearing and harmony with husbands—and go on from there in a remarkable fashion. We can be a lot more sophisticated in the basic areas.... But we can discuss serious subjects that have to do with our society and culture and the world in general—how things run, what the problems are, how we're going to survive. The possibilities are much broader and deeper now than they have ever been. What is exciting about the mass magazine for women ... and this has become apparent only in the past few years—is how far we can go, how wide we can range, how seriously we can approach our subject matter.'[9]

Today, more than 50 per cent of American women over 20 are high-school graduates, an increase of 87 per cent in fifteen years. In 1950, 25 per cent of such graduates went on to higher education. Since then the numbers have increased by 200 per cent, and the proportion of women in the 18–34 age-group who have had a college education is three times that for women aged 35 and over.[10] In ten years, this proportion, too, will have doubled, and Editors forecast steadily increasing scope for intelligent journalism in the women's press.

Associated with this growing intellectual sophistication is the broadening of the base of women's magazines in America. This is not entirely due to trends in education. An influential factor has been the increasing employment of married women outside the home. As they participate in wider social and commercial life, they are gaining new knowledge and experience which renders unacceptable to them any periodical which minces words or distorts the truth. Editors have been quick to sense this, and a greater frankness and realism is apparent in all women's magazines. This extends to the fiction, which now mirrors real-life situations and problems with the aim of encouraging therapeutic 'reader-identification'. It is now possible to extend the range of such identification due to the many new interests married women are beginning to acquire, and their consequent exposure to a wider variety of social situations.

Taking up paid employment is only one of a number of new freedoms which have opened up for American women in recent years, with far-reaching implications for magazine content. Women are, to quote a member of the McCall Corporation's Research Department, 'in a different frame of mind today, and ready for different magazines'. In 1962, Curtiss Anderson drew attention to the change:

'Woman has always been a mutable creature. But never, as in the last decade, have so many women changed so much in elevating their standards of taste and broadening their fields of interest. . . . There is evolving an important new group of women endowed with an intellectual curiosity that takes them beyond the traditional feminine role of homemaker. They want to do more and know more.'[3]

He also voiced the belief that Editors of women's magazines were aiming too low; too often settling for a formula which, whilst it might increase total circulation, left the needs of more intelligent and discerning women unsatisfied. Subsequent developments have supported this view, and it is generally agreed today that stereotyped editing is inappropriate for women who are buying books, attending lectures, filling concert halls and museums, and 'searching for meaning in their lives on a wider scale and in a deeper sense than ever before'.[2]

The changing attitudes of women are manifest in all classes and age-groups, with teenagers everywhere taking the lead. Young women have for some years been regarded as an economic entity; very recently they have become a social group also, affluent, vocal and aware. In the 'fifties, teenagers were silent and passive: in the 'sixties they have found their voice and raised it in support of a new social order, many of them carrying their words into action. Those who write for them claim that in ten years teenagers have matured an extra five in outlook, and that the creative impulses generated within their ranks are spreading upwards and outwards to affect the whole of society, not *vice versa* as in the past.

These developments have presented Editors with a new and difficult challenge. Led by *Ingenue*, whose framework is well suited to the task, magazines are beginning to recognise the teenage desire for social involvement and to cater for it. The field is wide open for periodicals which will effectively meet their wider needs. 1968 saw the appearance of *Eye*, a magazine which responded to the challenge of a young, avid readership with intelligent, realistic journalism. Steeped in youth culture, *Eye* reflected the predominating interests of the young—records, the pop world, films, fashion, etc.—but treated them critically and constructively. It also devoted considerable space to wider topics: serious, provocative articles (e.g. 'Your Professors Wage War') encouraged readers to form opinions on social issues, while editorial features prodded them into action, stressing the personal gains to be derived from voluntary social service and involvement with other people's problems:

> 'Helping others is one of the easiest, most satisfying ways to find identity and self respect. . . . Have you ever thought of asking in your town if there are people who need people? . . . If you give a damn, some of the poverty and misery might vanish.'[11]

The editorial approach throughout was incisive, mature and realistic, often serious but nowhere lacking in humour. The reviews were full and frank: columnists appraised their subjects honestly and responsibly, and chastised producers and consumers alike where an important principle was at stake, as in the following film review:

> '. . . what concerns me is this: I know that most of you are going to dig *Head*. . . . The fact is, the movie's a computer's dream. . . .

'But ... let's talk about motives ... what happens when there isn't an underlying philosophy? What happens when a film gets made because a couple of guys want to make movies when they grow up and want to make a lot of money on the way? You get a film like *Head*, for one thing. It has absolutely no reason for being. ... In its awful attempt to entertain, it insults. In short, its greatest appeal will be to ... swinging mums and dads with the love beads and the whips. This film is precisely their image of where we're all at, and it is clearly insulting. ...

'I urge you to use your power and not see *Head*. ... If you see it and love it a lot, think about what's going on in the world now and ask yourself if this film really has a right to take up your time and your own beautiful head. ...

'Also, think about motives a lot when you look at a film. If a film's sole reason for being is nothing more than somebody's wanting to make a movie, it's a betrayal. ... Film producers are bendable and beatable. It is NOT necessary to see every film that hits town ... that defeats the power we have as product buyers. When you get stuck with a drag like *Head*, write a bitchy letter to its producer at Columbia. Tell him you won't see his next one to get even for his last. And tell him why. Make it simple and unemotional. You'll get results.'[11]

Eye's 'problem page' was run by the 'House Shrink', a qualified psychologist and former student counsellor whose aim was to give correspondents enough information to allow them to find their 'own best solution'. One girl, struggling with an instinctive rejection of traditional goals and priorities, received in reply a 480-word survey of the potential life-chances of a female 'drop-out', ending with this verdict:

'If the woman's psychological condition and her financial resources do not permit her to invest in schooling and competence, she is left with either dreams, or the long-shot chance of a constructive marriage.'

For another, describing at length her bewilderment over her boyfriend's erratic behaviour, the diagnosis was short and to the point: 'Your friend has found another friend and doesn't know how to tell you'.[11]

From its letter page, which teemed with readers' comments on past features, it would seem that *Eye* was a magazine the young identified with, and took seriously. Its early withdrawal, in May, 1969, owing to lack of patronage, deprived the teenage press of a team of writers clearly committed to helping the younger generation interpret their environment, evaluate it, and make some contribution to it.

The extremes of change evident in the teenage section of the women's press are part of a current which is affecting all women to a greater or lesser degree, with important implications for all women's publishing. In the words of Robert Stein:

'This generation of women will not settle for easy, pat answers about themselves or the world they live in. . . . They are freer to make their own choices than any women who have ever lived and they have more to choose from—more ideas, more attitudes, more styles of living. In our lifetime, they have moved from the problems of having to make do with too little to the problems of having to cope with too much.

'To serve women today, a magazine must do more than simply reflect these changes. In every way possible, it must help open the way for them.'[12]

(b) Editorial freedom

The freedom of American women's magazines to develop along lines which match the changes taking place within the female population has been crucial to their success, and should be axiomatic for all women's publications. However, the fact that Editors operate within a commercial framework means that editorial scope is co-extensive with the enlightenment of advertisers regarding the type of 'editorial support' which is most effective in selling their products. This situation has frequently hindered the progress of women's magazines in the past.

For many years, American Editors, in common with their British counterparts, served under the double burden of boosting sales and maintaining advertising ratios. The cut-throat competition which was a feature of the 'circulation race' in the 1950s bred methods which are still shuddered at in American publishing circles. But this battle has now ceased. Rising publishing costs, which have brought diminishing returns on multi-million sales, have forced the publishing firms to review their circulation policies, with the result that many magazines now work to an optimum sales level, allowing circulations to expand slowly but doing nothing to stimulate them once they have passed the 'break-even' point. Only the cheaper periodicals which rely on single-copy sales, stand to increase their profits by free expansion. The 'quality' journals, which depend on subscriptions peddled at rates cut by anything up to 50 per cent, draw their profits from sales of advertising.

Hence they devote at least 50 per cent of their content to it,* compared with the cheaper fiction monthlies, in which the proportion of advertising carried may be as low as 25 per cent.

Far from competing for readers, the women's magazines of America now co-operate, through the medium of the Magazine Publishers' Association, in furthering the interests of the industry as a whole. In the face of a common threat—commercial T.V.—conferences discuss common problems, for magazine proprietors have found that there is much to be gained from pooling their ideas. In consequence, Editors have had more scope for experimentation, and the quality of women's journalism has noticeably risen. In one remarkable instance of magazine co-operation, a group of leading Editors interviewed the late President Kennedy on the subject of the nuclear threat, putting questions to him on behalf of all American women. Afterwards, individual versions of the transcript were published simultaneously in all the participating magazines.

Though the 'circulation race' has been called off, the intensive battle for advertising has continued unabated. The market research agencies of Starch, Nielsen, Simmons and Politz, among others, supply the ammunition in the form of a mass of statistical data which is syndicated to all magazines, since advertisers are suspicious of results originating in publishers' own research departments. Advertisers take a good deal of persuading that the women's press is a worthwhile investment when measured against the mass exposure and immediacy guaranteed by radio and T.V. Hence publishers pour millions of dollars annually into promotion and research, blinding the advertiser with claim and counter-claim, all of which are the result of sophisticated manipulation of the same sets of statistics. Every magazine purports to lead the field in some area, whether it be gross readership, net sales, consumption potential, page exposure, reader-loyalty, editorial coverage of particular consumption areas, advertising pages, or cost-per-thousand. In assessing these figures, businessmen must further take into account methodological differences in producing them, balancing, for example, Politz' small but carefully proportioned sample against Simmons' disproportionate one which is two and a half times larger.

Computers aid the advertiser in determining the type of 'media mix' best suited to his needs, but in the final analysis, the decision about which magazines (if any) to invest in is an emotional one, and an

---

* Editorial: advertising ratios for the leading magazines in May, 1969 were: *Woman's Day*, 59: 41 (due to 'heavy editorial investment'); *Good Housekeeping*, 56: 44; *Family Circle*, 51: 49; *LHJ*, 48.5: 51·5; *McCall's* 41: 59.

important element in that decision is his evaluation of the subtly different buying climates which the magazines offer. In broad terms, the advertiser is looking for periodicals which women have confidence in, as indicated by high and maintained circulations and evidence of *rapport*. Falling sales suggest that readers' requirements are not being met, and advertisers quickly withdraw if a decline sets in. Hence it is seen as the prime responsibility of Editors to ensure that readers are given what they want in a palatable form and to foster a close relationship of trust.

It was a serious falling off in circulations, and the subsequent loss of advertising support, which finally convinced the publishers of American women's magazines that they could no longer attract readers (or advertising custom) using the traditional approaches. As a result, the leading magazines have been modernised, a process which has included increasing the range, and sometimes the proportion, of 'non-service' content to reflect the greater social involvement of women described earlier. Such a trend might be expected to have been strenuously resisted by advertisers, who are normally sensitive to any changes which might divert attention away from their messages. Yet Editors have evidently enjoyed a large measure of freedom in pursuing the new policies. The reason would seem to be that they have substantially succeeded in convincing advertisers that it is the character of the magazine *as a whole* that determines its effectiveness as a selling medium.

Mr Sey Chassler, Editor of *Redbook*, defending this thesis at a *Redbook* Sales Meeting in 1967, said:

'There is hardly one of you who isn't constantly after me in one subtle way or another for something called 'editorial support' for particular categories . . . but [it] is the last of the reasons I take into consideration. First of all, I must put out a magazine dedicated to a specific purpose. And I must produce a serious, responsible magazine. I must have a thesis, and I must, every month, prove that thesis. I must make sure that whatever I put into the magazine, or allow to be put into it, supports the purpose to which the magazine is dedicated. And a magazine must be dedicated. . . .

'There are dozens of magazines which feature women's breasts. But only one . . . is internationally famous and financially successful. Only one . . . has convinced advertisers of its viability. Why are naked women classifiable as editorial support in one magazine and not in others? Because Hugh Hefner . . . has a purpose and a dedication . . . a point of view beyond the keyhole.

In short, because *Playboy* believes in what it is doing, its advertisers believe in it. And advertisers believe in its audience.'[6]

The Editors of the leading American women's journals echo this philosophy. They claim that they would never prostitute their magazines for the sake of advertising revenue. Robert Stein underlines the point:

'No good editor . . . takes things he disbelieves or things which go against his basic convictions, and tries to exploit them because they might be commercially viable. Eventually, those editors who try lose the confidence of their readers.'[13]

Editors (and advertisers) have learned that women want 'non-service' content and are ready to supply it. But the larger the audience, the more conservative the Editor still has to be; 'way out' material offends advertisers and readers alike. However, editorial scope is yearly increasing with the growing receptivity of the population, and having discovered that limited magazines mean a limited audience, advertisers are beginning to acquiesce in the trend.

American Editors appear to have won overall freedom to produce the kind of magazines they believe in, but pressures in specific areas persist. During the most intensive period of competition, 'accommodation' of advertisers to secure contracts was blatant and widespread. Today, there is little evidence to suggest that Editors are being forced to concede more than they can personally justify, but magazines specialising in important consumption areas (e.g. food or furnishing) are undoubtedly subjected to considerable pressure, particularly when the insertion of a special feature would clinch a large advertising contract. At the least, Editors are bound to delete anything manifestly deleterious to the interests of advertisers. One Editor admitted having to censor a cookery article which advised against 'spoiling' a good casserole with soup-mix. There are also things they clearly cannot do, such as comparing values. *Good Housekeeping* obviates part of the need for this by featuring only those products which have been tested by its Institute and awarded the Seal of Guaranty. As well as being beneficial to the consumer, this is good advertising technique, for although it means closing the magazine's columns to a number of firms —$3·5 million worth of goods were rejected in 1966—the remainder enjoy an enhanced reputation for quality and reliability.

In addition, there are the accepted 'benefits' which advertisers expect, and pay for. Favourable positioning is one important concession; editorial mentions, too, are bargained for, but few magazines allow them except in the form of *bona fide* 'credits' which are considered a necessary part of the service and are often linked with schemes to help readers find the nearest stockist of the goods they are interested in. The fashion journals work particularly closely with the stores, planning joint promotions, giving extensive guidance on running fashion shows and setting up special displays, as well as putting out advance information to the retail trade on the latest trends in colour, fabric and design, often supplemented with elaborately presented samples.

In deciding how much to concede to advertisers, most Editors adhere to the criterion of what they judge to be the 'best interests' of readers. In 1963, Betty Friedan charged the American women's press with being in league with businessmen, brainwashing readers with the 'feminine mystique' to persuade them to stay at home, and encouraging them to discharge their pent-up frustrations in the creation of a beautiful, fully-equipped habitat. She claimed that the process began in teenage magazines which were 'deliberately designed to turn teenage girls into housewife buyers of things'.[14]

These accusations are emphatically denied by Editors today. They maintain that, far from exerting a powerful influence over the formulation of magazine content, advertising pressures are 'less than they used to be, and far less than is commonly supposed'. It is further argued that power struggles in the higher echelons of management have at times proved a great deal more inhibiting to editorial freedom than any commercial considerations, especially in cases where magazines are economically unsound.

In reconciling these opposing viewpoints, it must be remembered that Mrs Friedan's assertions relate to an era when the social and economic climate of women's publishing was very different and characterised by cut-throat competition. Editors had barely begun to realise that social change had seriously undermined the appeal of the traditional home-centred formula, and with economic viability uppermost in publishers' minds, they also lacked freedom of manœuvre. Mrs Friedan, however, claims active editorial collusion in restricting magazine content to the domestic area. This charge is difficult to substantiate, the more so because it is based upon a highly selective and unrepresentative sampling of women's periodicals which ignores a considerable amount of non-domestic, outward-looking content. Trends since 1963, particularly the widening of editorial scope in these 'non-service' areas, have cast further doubts upon the validity of her assertions, at least in so far as they relate to the women's press in contemporary America.

(c) Research

Much of the success of American women's periodicals in remodelling themselves to suit the changing needs and interests of women in the 1960s is due to the instinctive flair of Editors in assessing the type of content most acceptable to their readers. There is no substitute for that 'sharp sense of reality' which helps an Editor stay tuned to their varying wavelength. Nevertheless, there is at least limited recognition within the American women's press that research is of value in reinforcing editorial judgement. Quoting Robert Stein:

> 'In some cases we're working with research organisations and foundations to do basic research which goes far beyond reporting, simply to find out what the reality of the situation is before we can begin to figure out what we're going to say about it, how we're going to treat it in a magazine... on some of the most serious subjects we find that we are investing as much as two years' time....'[15]

Provided that it is used in the right way, many Editors feel that research into the attitudes of readers towards certain aspect of editorial content can also be helpful. *Good Housekeeping* runs monthly investigations into the reception of the two most experimental items in each issue, trying to find out at what point the reader stopped reading, and why. A sample of 350 readers is used and the reports are not seen by the management, being confined to the editorial departments concerned. Although there was initial resistance to the practice on the grounds that it might be used to 'rate' editorial staff, it is now fully accepted as a valuable means of identifying readers' requirements and ascertaining what they can comprehend and enjoy. *Ladies' Home Journal* also carries out a monthly survey, and *Family Circle, Glamour* and *Ingenue* are among other magazines which find reader research useful. It is not available to all Editors, however. Publishers are either unwilling to incur the expense, or they are dissuaded by editorial opposition.

Using reader research in the initial formulation of magazine content is a different matter and is generally considered to be unwise, if not fatal, since it can result in the compilation of a predictable editorial 'formula'. It is held that the successful magazines are those which stretch their readers, deliberately going beyond their known interests and tastes. *McCall's*, for example, operates at a level which is estimated to be five years ahead of its readers' present ideas. Kate Lloyd, Features Editor at *Vogue*, sums up the feeling: 'If we find out what people want, it's already too late.'

Though reader research is not widely employed to reveal opinion, another possible use for it is at present being studied, namely, to differentiate readers according to psychological variables. Susceptibility to persuasion has been found to be related to age and self-images, and it is hoped to be able to discover more about the psychological mechanisms causing readers to respond to one magazine rather than another. If these factors can be related to personality characteristics, the results could be highly significant for advertisers interested in the more subtle 'typing' of audiences. It would give them some idea of the kind of reader they could expect to reach through (say) *McCall's* and the differences between these women and those who subscribe to (say) *The Ladies' Home Journal*. They would then be able to refine their advertising techniques accordingly.

Most research into women's magazines and their audiences is not for editorial guidance but for the benefit of advertisers, to assist them in achieving the most concentrated coverage possible of the consumer groups they are interested in. In addition, the women's magazines have, in the last six to eight years, introduced regional editions and 'spot markets' to define these groups still more closely. They are now contemplating refining the service still further by attempting to break down readership according to demographic and other characteristics so that special editions can be matched with them. To give two examples: high-grade advertising would, under this system, be inserted only in issues destined for high-income neighbourhoods, and copy relevant to a particular profession would reach only known members of that profession. Selectivity of this kind could be achieved by computers using specially programmed subscription data.

In all these ways research is being used to convince a growing number of advertisers, disenchanted with commercial television as an advertising medium, that the women's magazines can offer them an attractive alternative giving a high degree of 'market selectivity', maximum impact, and effective 'editorial support'. The great achievement of magazine Editors has been the complete re-definition of this latter concept to encompass intelligent, progressive journalism which fully involves women (and sells goods) because it deals with the totality of their concerns—non-domestic as well as domestic. In so far as they have succeeded in selling this concept to their commercial patrons, they have won for the American women's press the freedom it now enjoys to experiment with new ideas and techniques, and to develop, within the framework dictated by social, cultural and economic change, according to the insights of those with long experience in writing for women—those who understand what women's publishing is really about.

NOTES

1 'The World of *Seventeen*' in *Madison Avenue Magazine*, December, 1964.
2 Robert Stein, *The Third Force: A Presentation.*
3 Article on *The Ladies' Home Journal* in *Madison Avenue Magazine*, April, 1962.
4 Wade H. Nichols, Editor of *Good Housekeeping*, in a Luncheon Address, April 14th, 1964.
5 Anne Morrow Lindbergh, *Gift From the Sea*, p. 124.
6 Sey Chassler, Editor of *Redbook*, at a Sales Meeting, 1967.
7 *Ingenue* publicity handout, September, 1967.
8 Robert Stein (when Editor of *Redbook*) at a Luncheon Meeting, May 29th, 1963.
9 Roy Newquist, *Conversations*, pp. 386–7. (Interview with Robert Stein.)
10 All figures quoted are taken from *The Educational Explosion and the Magazine Influence.*
11 *Eye*, February, 1969.
12 See note 9, p. 390.
13 See note 9, p. 393.
14 Betty Friedan, *The Feminine Mystique*, p. 231.
15 See note 9, p. 393.

N.B. All other quotations in this chapter are taken from personal interviews with representatives of the American women's magazine industry.

9
Conclusions

Towards the 'Seventies

This study of the women's press in Britain has two aims: first, to trace the history of publishing for women, and to show how this huge industry, which now serves a readership of millions, grew up out of a mere handful of journalistic novelties introduced in the eighteenth century; and second, by examining a representative sample of the periodicals which have appeared during the past century and a half, to clarify what is being communicated to women, and why. We come now to a summary of these findings and an evaluation of a mass medium of communication which we must now regard as one of our more important social institutions since it is capable of exerting considerable influence over the bulk of women in this country.

The women's press is frequently described as a post-war phenomenon, with total disregard of its earlier history. However, though it is only in the last twenty-five years that women's publishing has become big business, that expansion has been built upon foundations laid as far back as the mid-nineteenth century, and its spectacular success in appealing to a mass female readership derives from a formula developed more than fifty years ago.

As we have seen, the origins of the women's press are discernible at the end of the seventeenth century, and magazines intended primarily for women (but often addressed to men also) proliferated throughout the 1700s, long before a recognisable magazine industry came into being. These early periodicals were heterogeneous and transitory, put out by enterprising authors, both male and female, whose variable literary talents and uncompromising views guaranteed them a short life, if a merry one. But they pointed the way for more serious and enduring attempts to capture the attention of the female reader. By 1800, at least two journals of a stable character and considerable standing had emerged, *The Lady's Magazine* and *The Lady's Monthly Museum*, and these became the patterns upon which the early Victorian women's periodicals were modelled.

By the third quarter of the nineteenth century, there was a growing demand in 'polite society' for periodicals fit to be the leisure companions of the Fair Sex—very little other reading matter was considered suitable by those rigorously guarding the pure character and morals of women—but the Upper Ten Thousand did not constitute a large enough group to support more than a handful of such magazines. The birth of a full-scale industry waited upon a complex of social and economic factors which included the spread of literacy, higher wages, technological advances in rotary-printing and paper-making, and upon general industrial expansion and the growth of the middle classes. All these conditions were fulfilled during the last fifteen years of Victoria's reign when a 'publishing explosion' occurred. Women's periodicals of all types, and intended for consumption far lower down the social hierarchy than the customary 'sixpennies', flooded onto the market, headed by Harmsworth's prototype for future mass-selling, middle-class weeklies, *Home Chat*.

This period of expansion marked the beginnings of a clearly definable 'women's press'. Publishers were waking up to the fact that publishing for women, if approached in the right way, could be a profitable enterprise. But what was the right way? After a series of experimental soundings which had a high mortality rate, the successful 'formula' emerged. It was based upon the pre-eminent domestic role of women and their home-centred interests and attitudes. Publishers proved that, as long as they concentrated on the domestic sphere and tried to promote a warm, friendly relationship with readers, they were sure to succeed. This, together with the speedy demise of any magazine which displayed a wider social awareness, encouraged them to stay close to the fireside, and thus the *Kinder*, *Küche*, *Kleider* formula crystallised.

The First World War pruned away all superfluous titles, but its effect in broadening the lives of women stimulated new growth as soon as peace came. The years between the wars saw a gradual increase in the size and efficiency of publishing firms like Odhams, who began to see in the women's sector a market worthy of investment. Odhams brought out *Woman*, which blossomed into the first mass-circulation women's weekly of the 1940's, closely rivalled by Newnes' *Woman's Own* which had appeared in 1932 with far less promotion. Crucial to their expansion was the introduction of colour-gravure, which had been first applied in Britain to the production of *Woman* in 1937.

The process opened up a host of new possibilities, chief among them being the capacity to print cheap, colourful magazines by the million, and the chance to open up a huge market for women's journalism. But the economic viability of the rotary-gravure method—which only begins to reap economies of scale on printing runs in the region of a million—depends upon the existence of large, fairly homogeneous readerships capable of sustaining large print orders, and Britain in the 1930s had too rigid a class structure to give the necessary degree of market uniformity. *Woman* failed to reach its guaranteed sale of 500,000 on a print order of one million, and only two other magazines, *Woman's Own* and *Woman's Weekly*, had circulations of more than 300,000.

Britain returned to peace and in the course of social reconstruction, some of these pre-war inequalities were eradicated. During the 'forties, consumption increased among the lower-income groups, social services were improved and extended, and tastes, attitudes and patterns of life among certain sections of the working class began to converge upon those of their financial betters. Such changes gave the women's magazines the mass market they had previously lacked and also offered them new scope to educate and guide large numbers of women who were floundering in a bewildering sea of new responsibilities, new choices, and new opportunities. Advertisers, recognising the potential of that expanding market, saw their opportunity too, and joined forces with the women's press, subsidising its expansion in return for the use of its selling power. Circulations soared in every sector of the industry and transformed women's publishing into a giant economic enterprise, the glittering profits of which attracted a series of take-over bids culminating in the monopolistic ownership of the industry by the International Publishing Corporation (IPC).

Towards the end of the 'fifties, the boom broke. Sales dropped sharply over the whole market and many titles perished, the old-style weeklies being the first to succumb. The decline has continued steadily during the 'sixties, with but a few exceptions, and has produced an estimated drop in total circulation of over 3 million.

An important result of the decline has been to stimulate a thoroughgoing reappraisal of women's journalism, a questioning of the traditional formula, and experiments with new editorial approaches. Confronted with the problem of why women's magazines were losing popularity, IPC's analysts, following Dichter's lead, concluded that magazine content was not in step with readers' requirements. It was their verdict that the women's press was in decline because it had failed to keep pace with the accelerated social change of post-war years, and that in closely adhering to the traditional approach which softened reality into cosy complacency, it was failing more and more to attract the new generation of young women who are more socially experienced, affluent, educated and culturally aware than were their predecessors. They prescribed an all-round upgrading in the intellectual level of magazine content, a more professional and creative treatment for home-service articles, greater realism in fiction and features, and a general modernisation of presentation.

In the four years since they were first tried, these new policies have had disappointing results. They have not succeeded in reclaiming the millions of 'lost' readers, and occasionally they have proved disastrous in newly alienating others. In some cases they have given a temporary boost to sales, but mostly the slow drain of readers has continued, masked by a series of mergers. Only among the fiction monthlies is there any sign of continuing expansion, an interesting reversal of trends in the American women's magazine industry. Nor has the associated policy of specialisation produced a sustained increase in commercial support. Over the whole industry securing sufficient advertising remains a paramount problem.

The policies inspired by Dichter have not, apparently, succeeded, but it would be a mistake wholly to condemn Dichter's theories in consequence. His study is open to criticism on a number of counts, among them the small size of the sample, bias in selecting only those of respondents' remarks which confirmed his view of the 'emerging "balanced" woman', and the tendency to generalise from American social trends and the policies followed by American women's publishers.

Nevertheless, Dichter's assessment of the social changes affecting British women was broadly correct. His error lay in assuming, without fuller investigation, that these trends were more advanced in the population than they actually were, and that the English woman reader was ready for the type of magazine which was proving successful in America. He allowed that many women were resisting emancipation, that it was not 'a smooth-flowing and universally popular trend', but having stated this qualification, he proceeded to base all his recommendations on the needs of those who had accepted an expanded social role because, 'The signs . . . point to emancipation, reluctant or not, sooner or later'.[1]

The 'new generation' of Editors ignored the *caveat*, and all other reservations (stated or implied) in the study. They accepted Dichter's conclusions and set about a drastic and uncompromising reformulation of traditional editorial policies, magnifying the fundamental flaw in Dichter's work.

If British publishers had researched into the lives and character of these 'new' women as carefully as they investigated their buying potential, the pitfalls inherent in taking over unmodified American policies would have been apparent. Educational progress in this country as far as women are concerned has been far more limited than in the United States. British girls, on average, leave school over a year earlier, and only a very small percentage of them go on to higher education.* The pressures to do so are far less intense than in America, and there are fewer opportunities. Moreover, the typical American female's involvement in community affairs is greater, not only through her work, but through the multitude of societies and clubs to which she belongs and through the many responsibilities which devolve upon her as chief guardian of the family in her husband's frequent absence. The American woman's attitude to 'culture', too, is different. She regards it as something to be acquired by hard work rather than absorbed by natural osmosis and she is indefatigable in pursuit.

Further, the social position of women in both countries is markedly different, as are their patterns of life, values, and to some extent their ideology (or lack of it). It is a paradox that, whilst the social emancipation of women is considerably more advanced in America than in Britain, the pressures toward conservatism and social conformity are so strong that it would be impossible to publish magazines of the British type for young American girls. *Petticoat* has been quoted as being 'much too way out' for American audiences. At the teenage level, if nowhere else, social changes have pushed British publishers ahead of their American colleagues.

The above are generalisations. The fact remains that far too little is known about the effects upon women of the social developments of recent years, the changes in their life patterns, or the growth of their attitudes, interests, and aspirations. Much more research is needed to clothe the stark statistical profiles. But there is enough evidence in the educational statistics alone to show that the 'intellectual revolution' is proceeding more slowly here than in the United States. Their response shows that the majority of British women have not yet changed sufficiently to make them ready for ultra-progressive journalism, even though they may have moved beyond the confines of the traditional formula.

But, whatever the speed of social change, the problem for Editors on both sides of the Atlantic remains that of 'pacing' the evolution of their magazines to match it. As one American Editor remarked, 'We can't go back to the comfortable and shallow world of Andy Hardy, but not all of us are ready for Andy Warhol . . .'[2] This echoes the sentiments of an

---

* In the academic year 1965–66, only 3·4 per cent of girls leaving school and 7·4 per cent of boys were destined for the universities; 80·9 per cent of girls and 83·5 per cent of boys were preparing to enter employment. (*Statistics of Education*, 1966, Vol. 2.)

English Editor who declared that not all women 'wanted Picasso with their peas'. Mr Alex McKay of IPC sums up the perplexity of many magazine publishers:

'Women's magazines like *Woman's Weekly* are still inhabiting a world in which everyone lives happily ever after. This outlook belongs to grandma's day—and grandma, incidentally, was a lousy cook! We have got to bring people closer to life, give them reality as well as the fiction. But how quickly should we move into this area, and can we afford to risk our older readers dropping off?

The new *Woman's Mirror* showed how quickly *not* to move into it. Its failure to win acceptance with the majority of readers emphasised that, while a new generation of women is growing up who want more from their magazines than in the past, there remains a large mass of readers for whom the sophisticated techniques of minority publishing are inappropriate. To their cost publishers have discovered that 'there are thousands of little women whose lives have not changed all that much and whose education has not significantly improved'* and that 'even for women who are affluent, highly educated and socially experienced there are needs connected with the fundamental character of the sex which "with it" magazines fail to satisfy'.* Such women still constitute the bulk of magazine readership, and though their numbers may be dwindling, they are the mainstay of women's publishing and are likely to remain so for some time.

The fact that millions of women favour the traditional formula does not mean that it cannot be improved, in their interests, and in ways they would appreciate, to make it more relevant to life in the 1960s. There are many gaps which need to be filled. Throughout the history of the women's press women's magazines have been tackling serious subjects with an encouraging response. Their reputation for pap and frivolous nonsense has come from critics who have never analysed magazine content systematically, but have dipped into issues at random, failing to appreciate that, due to the special cumulative and cyclical nature of women's publishing, single issues can never be representative of what is published over a whole year.

When magazines were produced primarily for entertainment, as in the eighteenth century, they were provocative and stimulating. As the position of women changed and their domestic role came uppermost, magazine content, too, changed its emphasis and concentrated more on

* Personal interviews.

fitting women to be home-makers. Now, in the second half of the twentieth century, women's magazines provide 'service' first, entertainment
second, and mental stimulus hardly at all. This is a major criticism and
the chief complaint of literary critics and others outside women's
publishing. The following comments are typical:

'While they [give] women plenty of—mainly sound—advice on
how to dress, eat, housekeep, have their babies, and even make
love, they have never attempted to tell them what to do with
their minds'[3] . . . 'one would have thought that in time a little social
conscience might have been introduced into them, or at least an
awareness of new things . . . for instance the new voices and new
attitudes that have invaded the theatre'[4] . . . 'It seems to be assumed
that the woman reader is not interested in savings, insurance,
investments, stocks and shares. There is nothing about finance in
her papers. There is nothing, either, about mortgages or leases, or
the law of landlord and tenant. . . . There is nothing about jobs,
careers or equal pay. Nor do the controversies about education
penetrate her papers, so far as I can see. I can find no reference to
day nurseries, comprehensives, or university places.'[5]

This latter examination of women's magazines was evidently cursory,
for many of these topics have begun to figure increasingly in the women's
press in the 'sixties, though they are under-represented. But there is still
a marked absence of informative features and opportunities for the
discussion of a whole new range of topics which are now of interest to
women, particularly the need to redefine morality in the context of their
recent sexual emancipation.

Many Editors do not regard social comment as one of the functions
of the women's press. Mary Grieve, after a long career in publishing,
remarked that it would seem to her to be 'as inappropriate to find in
Woman a serious political article as to find a guide to weaning in the
Economist'.[6] A writer in the *Daily Herald* shared her view:

'[To] criticise them [women's magazines] for their unconcern
with more public events . . . is a misunderstanding of their purpose
and capacity for influence. The women's magazines are extremely
specialised. In psychological terms they enable the harassed
mother, the overburdened housewife, to make contact with her
ideal self: that self which aspires to be a good wife, a good mother
and an efficient home-maker.'[7]

Editors are justified in maintaining that national issues and political and religious controversies are outside their territory. Magazines have limited space which must be allocated according to priorities, and in Britain these subjects (and a wider range of cultural topics) are covered by the daily and Sunday press, the weekly supplements, radio and television. Television coverage particularly has expanded and improved in recent years, considerably reducing the scope of competing media. The American public is less well served by T.V., and the greater concern to provide information about, and discussion of, social and political issues in American women's magazines is partly attributable to the fact that readers expect them to fill these gaps.

Nevertheless, there are many other stimulating subjects which could be given space to balance the intellectual limitations of an unrelieved diet of domestic features. As one Editor commented:

'Women are not dispassionate observers of the social scene. They will always prefer people to things and so the personalised approach succeeds every time in the treatment of home topics. But it must also be remembered that women no longer live in a "home ghetto", and that while sex-for-effect and gimmicks generally are not welcomed, they do want lively articles which reflect the wider horizons of their lives. Today more women go out to work, and T.V. has brought the world into the living-rooms of those who do not. This gives magazines the scope to stimulate rather than confining themselves to service, though the fact remains that some of them are better fitted to provide general features than others.'*

Without shifting their ground more than a fraction, the magazines could extend their coverage in a way that would be acceptable to readers. What is required is not the 'intellectualisation' of magazine content—which is in any case a false concept because better education has nothing whatever to do with basic intelligence, which is randomly distributed throughout the female population regardless of educational opportunities—but the widening of the base of magazine content in recognition of the fact that women have, and always have had, fertile minds, though they have not always had the leisure in which to give them free rein. Now they have more leisure than ever before, and need more to get their teeth into than gossip and guinea-winning letters.

Mr W. D. McClelland, IPC's Research Director comments:

* Personal interview.

'The housewife who started *Forum* showed that a market for a publication providing intelligent, wide-ranging articles for women does exist. . . . What is certain up to the present time is that women's magazines have done nothing to stimulate interest in this kind of material. Undoubtedly they have been guilty of seriously under-estimating the capacity and quality of their readership.'*

It is socially desirable that the women's press should make good these deficiencies, for, as *The Economist* pointed out, 'Furnishing the mind (and not necessarily with politics) is at least as important as furnishing the kitchen'.[8] But the fact that it is desirable does not auto-matically guarantee its implementation. The fundamental dichotomy in women's publishing remains: that women's magazines, though they are designed to render an important social service, are produced pri-marily for profit.

This raises the whole question of what factors are dominant in deciding the content and role of women's magazines in modern Britain. Two broad sets of determinants can be distinguished, social and economic, though they are frequently interdependent. The social factors operate in several different ways. First, there is the effect upon magazines of the social climate in which they have to operate. This establishes the basic framework of a periodical, and conditions its tone, viewpoint, and approach. Magazines are inevitably imbued with the spirit of the age in which they appear, and each period has a character of its own. Contrast, for example, the gloomy piety of the mid-Victorian era with the gaiety and precociousness of upper-class Edwardian society, a difference which is immediately apparent upon opening a magazine of either period.

Second, there are the more specific social influences which directly affect the role which women's magazines are called upon to play. An important example is the servant shortage which, from the late-nine-teenth century onwards, forced women of the upper and middle classes to assume an ever-increasing share of the domestic burden, until, by the late 1930s, the majority of them were entirely responsible for running their homes, a task for which they were largely untrained. Magazine editors had long realised the significance of the trend, and by the end of the nineteenth century had begun schooling their readers in the essen-tial skills of housewifery, not as before, so that they might supervise their servants more efficiently, but to equip them for whatever duties they might personally be called upon to perform in an understaffed

* Personal interview.

household. This service has since developed into one of the most important and valuable of all the functions of the women's press.

Third, there are the various demographic trends which have focused attention upon new social groups, inspiring both the creation of special magazines to cater to them, and the reformulation of existing periodicals to slant them in the required direction. The growth of a 'teenage culture' and the trend towards earlier marriage are two such developments, which have exerted considerable influence over the present structure and content of the women's press .They have been responsible, respectively, for the appearance of two new types of publication, the 'strip-romance' weeklies and teenage fashion magazines, and for the general lowering of age-profiles.

The latter trend has resulted in the serious neglect of the older reader, once the mainstay of women's publishing, in favour of an overwhelming preoccupation with the young, particularly the 'young-marrieds', so that the women's press is now predominantly 'teen and twenty' in its orientation. It is also showing an increasing tendency to reach down into the 'pre-teens', another rapidly emerging group, who are fast becoming spenders in their own right and accordingly are attracting the attention of advertisers.

Finally, the most important of the social determinants of magazine content is the social condition and role of women. It is this factor which, more than any other, has influenced the character and functioning of the women's press throughout its history, so much so that women's magazines could be regarded (certainly up to 1950), as particularly reliable indicators of prevailing attitudes to women and accurate reflectors of the way of life of the feminine groups to which they catered: their beliefs, their interests, their hopes and their problems. These attitudes and patterns of life have always circumscribed the scope of those writing for women.

The vast majority of women's periodicals are by tradition trend-followers rather than trend-setters. The *status quo* is their frame of reference and the image of women they portray is a conventional one· Thus the range of subjects covered has always been closely geared to the social role considered proper for women, and the scale of values and priorities projected has reflected those held by women themselves. This has meant that no significant modifications in the formula for women's periodicals could take place without having been preceded by corresponding changes in the social condition of women.

We have seen this circumstance operating with regard to the predominantly domestic orientation of the women's press. The degree of home-centredness of women's periodicals has varied inversely with the extent to which women have been involved in wider social concerns. For example, the Victorian magazines which catered to a female sex virtually in domestic bondage rarely betrayed the existence of a world outside the home, keeping their readers amused with endless exercises in fancy-work, light fiction, fashion drawings and a few home hints. But as soon as war drew women into the forefront of social action, the women's press quickly developed a commensurate degree of social awareness. However, this lasted only as long as women's freedom to participate in non-domestic activities outside the home, a freedom which narrowed considerably with the return to peace.

In all of these ways social factors can determine the range and type of women's magazines and their editorial content. They may operate directly—by influencing demand, as when a new need encourages the introduction of a new content category, or when a new social group such as the teenagers emerges, which requires special provision—or they may function indirectly, by conditioning the attitudes of readers and Editors regarding a woman's 'natural' role and interests, which leads to a mutually accepted definition of what is appropriate in a women's magazine.

By contrast, technological and economic factors affect content from the supply side. The history of publishing for women is inseparable from the history of paper and ink manufacture, printing, and retail distribution. Technological progress in all three areas is responsible for both quantity and quality in contemporary women's magazines. New, automated methods of reproducing colour illustrations have transformed the appearance of the women's press and made possible the exploitation of visual techniques in the presentation of editorial matter; refinements in paper-making have banished rough-textured newsprint, the hall-mark of the cheap periodicals of the past. Rotary-gravure has, in addition, helped to bring down production costs for the mass-circulation periodicals, and web-offset promises to do the same for the medium-sized journals, though the benefits of these processes together with automation and the use of computers are being cancelled out to a considerable extent both by workers' restrictive practices in their application and by inefficiency in management.

Costs, however, form only part of the equation which determines the price to the consumer and the profit margin to the producer. Under the existing financial structure of the industry, the crucial factor is the advertising subsidy. Women's magazines are normally sold at a fraction of what they cost to produce. The deficit and the profits come from advertising revenue, and on the principle that 'he who pays the piper calls the tune', the implications as regards the determination of magazine content are obvious and disturbing.

The post-war history of the women's press is bound up with the growth of this new economic influence upon the formulation of magazine content. Before the war, any modification in magazine content was directly related to social developments, for instance the introduction of employment bureaux and advice on home occupations when the problem of penniless 'surplus women' became acute, and the new emphasis on motherhood and child care following the trend towards smaller families. Though advertising had long been a valued source of income eagerly solicited by publishers, at that time it appears to have been merely an adjunct to the women's press with little influence upon it. Also, the magazine industry of the 1930s was relatively small and fragmented, and of minimal economic significance.

Since the war, the situation has radically changed. The enormous expansion in women's publishing, coinciding with the concentration of unprecedented spending power in the hands of women (particularly young women), has given the magazines potential influence over the buying decisions of the majority of women consumers and made them a magnet for advertisers. For the first time Editors have been subjected to commercial as well as social pressures. They can no longer plan issues solely on the basis of what they feel their readers want; they must also consider what it is in the best interests of advertisers for them to publish, and it is fast becoming the rule that 'anything goes'—in or out—on the strength of these latter considerations.

The balance of power has evidently swung in favour of the economic determinants of magazine content, and while it is impossible to estimate accurately their weight relative to social factors, it is clear that their influence is decisive in top-level policy-making, often overriding readers' known interests and preferences. This is not to say that these are disregarded: women's magazines make profits only as long as they continue to please the female reading public. But it does mean that certain types of content, i.e. those with a selling potential, are favoured at the expense of 'think pieces' and general features; that the feminine image portrayed is predominantly of women in their domestic role because this is the only kind of selling climate advertisers are interested in, and that editorial criticism in the area of consumption is almost entirely stifled.

The latter is a serious inadequacy. Women may have greater scope than ever before to indulge their acquisitive instincts, but as the U.S. Secretary of Commerce pointed out in 1965, '. . . the increasing specialisation of manufacture and labor means that today's family is far removed from the source of new products and services'.* Therefore, women rely to a considerable extent upon the mass media for information and expert guidance in making choices:

'Magazines particularly play a dominant role in bridging the gap between buyer and seller, between producer and consumer, between those who have needs and those who have something to offer to meet those needs. By creating a exciting awareness of what is new and useful in the home, in the school, and in the world of leisure, American magazines have evolved into a vital force for progress.'†

This is equally true of British women's magazines, but the new role imposes additional responsibilities. In the women's press, as nowhere else, editorial judgements and recommendations are taken on trust by readers and integrity is vital. Editors recognise and respect this. Nevertheless, commercial pressures seriously limit the type and extent of consumer advice the experts can offer, particularly restricting their freedom to compare products and values. Reference has already been made to one British Editor who complained that it was impossible to give full coverage to 'making and mending' and buying secondhand. The emphasis has to be on buying *new* and buying *now*, whether or not the advice is appropriate to readers' known circumstances.

The encroachment of advertising into editorial territory has been strenuously resisted by editorial staff, but it is a losing battle. Wherever possible, editorial content is now used to sell. Fashions, food, furnishings, cosmetics, household equipment—all are legitimate and traditional subjects covered by the women's press. But magazines now feature branded products, even in recipes; they run special advertising supplements, permit the most advantageous next-matter positioning of advertisements, even where this involves splitting up editorial content to the frustration of readers and editorial staff alike; they give editorial support to advertising features, and arrange sales-promoting campaigns such as the *Woman* 'Shopping Weeks'. And there are indications that behind-the-scenes agreements are made to expand content in particular areas in return for more advertising custom.

There is evidence, too, that advertising agents have in the past submitted stories or horoscopes for inclusion in women's magazines specially written to reinforce the advertiser's message. Some years ago,

---

* In a letter to the President of the M.P.A., September 21st, 1965.
† *Ibid.*

when the medical profession condemned a certain detergent for its harmful effect on the skin, the firm's advertising agency wrote beauty articles for women's magazines on the care of the hands after wash-day, a positive approach intended to counteract the negative line taken by the national press. Similarly, horoscopes can be used to suggest that *now* is the ideal time to arrange a summer holiday, buy a new dress or invest in a hair-do.

Advertising agencies have at times been able to have their copy inserted under a Section Editor's 'by-line' without the Editor's knowledge. These Editors and their staffs are also liable to be 'wooed' by firms wishing to push new products. An 'innocent' invitation to a cocktail party may acquire unexpected significance for a magazine representative when a new product becomes the topic of conversation. More seriously, content such as 'general interest' material, which has no direct selling value to the advertiser may be deliberately cut back in favour of 'service'. *Family Circle* is an example of a magazine which has opted for a total 'service' formula omitting fiction and general features entirely, while *Good Housekeeping* deliberately reduced its 'non-service' content in 1965 in the hope that stronger emphasis on 'service' would have greater appeal for advertisers.

With every rise in production costs, the need to safeguard and increase advertising revenue has intensified, and it has now reached the point where women's publishing is dominated by wider financial considerations. Within the IPC, decisions affecting women's magazines are made at the top in the context of overall planning. The decision to launch a new magazine tends to be taken only when it has been shown by intensive research that there is a particular market, useful to advertisers, waiting to be exploited. Readership profiles are drawn up to establish the basic characteristics of that market in consumption terms, and the editorial department is required to produce a magazine to fit these specifications. Similarly, a complete re-styling may be decided upon to maximise the selling power of a magazine in a particular area of consumption, the blue-print for which is again provided by the management. Finally, a magazine may be killed because it is failing to attract sufficient advertising revenue to keep it economically buoyant, even though it may still be popular with readers.

The social responsibility the women's magazines carry is so overwhelming that the only considerations which should be allowed to shape their content are the best interests of their readers. Given the present financial organisation of the industry in which subsidisation by advertisers plays a crucial part, it is clear that this requirement cannot easily be met except under conditions of severe pressure from falling sales. As a result, this huge and highly influential medium of communication is at the mercy of commercial interests which encourage extreme conservatism with regard to progress, over-concentration on the home environment, and the reinforcement of a limited domestic role for women. The consequences for society are potentially serious, for women's magazines are far from being the innocuous purveyors of light entertainment that they are often made out to be: they are the nation's most powerful sales force to women, not merely of consumer goods but of a feminine image and desirable standards of female achievement. This is where their main sociological significance lies.

Whether the provision of so influential a medium of communication should remain in the hands of private enterprise would seem to depend on the extent to which social and commercial interests can be reconciled. American experience in women's publishing offers some hope that an acceptable compromise can be reached. As the foregoing profile has shown, American women's magazines are dedicated to the task of helping women to function effectively in a complex and demanding social environment. Their strong, controversial, and wide-ranging articles emphasise the need for enrichment in personal relationships but also point in the direction of social consciousness, social involvement and social service. Some magazines may still err on the side of artificiality and a materialistic outlook, but they show clear signs that they are gradually assuming a fuller and more important role and one which, judging by their sales record, is approved by their readers.

American Editors have formulated and pursued policies which have led them into areas traditionally regarded as unprofitable to advertisers; yet they have emerged with greater autonomy and enhanced status. Women have the magazines they prefer (or are in process of getting them), and a growing number of advertisers are giving preference to women's magazines over television for their 'recall value'.

There are lessons here for British publishers. The American magazine industry has prospered because editors have substantially succeeded in convincing advertisers that the character of a magazine *as a whole* determines the response to advertising messages, and that editorial autonomy and integrity are their ultimate guarantee. American advertisers are beginning to accept that their interests can best be served by magazines which take the broadest possible view of their role and aim at expanding the horizons of the woman reader rather than acquiescing in her domestic confinement. The logic is reinforced by recent research which indicates that 'there is a definite association between advancing education and increasing product usage in the case of a large number of consumer products'.[9]

These arguments notwithstanding, a measure of co-operation with advertisers is generally regarded as being in the interests of readers and is encouraged. Joint meetings, held to discuss the mutual needs of publishers and advertisers, often result in the satisfaction of many of the demands women express, through the medium of their magazines, for new products or refinements to existing ones. The fashion journals particularly regard 'creative merchandising' as an important part of their work; *Mademoiselle*, for example, sponsored the revival of 'Paisley', while *Seventeen* claims to have the strongest merchandising arrangements with stores of any magazine, and continually inspires new designs for teenagers. American *Good Housekeeping*'s Sales Promotion Manager contends: 'You can't lock the door between editorial and advertising; exactly the same procedures are followed for testing [both]', and this view is shared by all who produce American women's magazines. It is the basis of their continued viability.

To create magazines in tune with today's needs, American publishers have called in Editors with insight, spirit, and dedication, and have given them the freedom to express themselves limited only by the consideration that women's magazines exist to make profits. Further, they accord Editors the highest status, commensurate with their acknowledged pre-eminence in the publishing hierarchy. As one Editor put it: 'It's more difficult to get to see me than the Managing Director!'

In contrast, British Editors have received far less recognition, and their relationship with management has too often been that of a subordinate to a superior, though their status tends to vary from firm to firm. Occasionally they have won seats on the Managerial Board, but more frequently, because their presence conflicts with the dominant interests of financiers and accountants, they have not been welcome in the Boardroom. Far from being free to produce the kind of magazines they know women want, they have been subjected to arbitrary (and often ill-informed) interference from above, and committed to a progressively greater degree of 'editorial support' in the high consumption areas following increasing pressure from their advertising departments.

Although commercial influence on Editors is considerable, it must not, however, be held entirely responsible for the limitations of contemporary women's magazines. On the basis of available evidence it seems unlikely that the relaxing of economic pressures would immediately result in less home-centred, socially conscious publications, at least as far as the mass weeklies are concerned. The formula for them, laid down more than half a century ago when a 'woman's sphere' was far narrower than it is today, has endured despite Dichterian attempts to modify it. The fact that it has withstood the emancipation of women, two world wars and the social upheavals following them, the growth of affluence and multilateral social change indicates that the majority of women find in it certain ingredients which satisfy their deepest needs.

The *New Statesman* has argued that women's magazines 'present a cosy picture of the world because that is what sells' and Mr Charles Curran, quoting Sir Robert Ensor, has suggested why it sells:

> 'Journalists, he said, were obliged to be realists about women. Thus certain propositions had been adopted as working certainties by the newspaper trade. One was that women in the mass have very little interest in doctrines, or arguments, or serious speculations of any kind. Their concern was not with ideas or principles, but with persons and things. Their main interest was in their feminine roles.'[10]

It must be accepted that certain aspects of women's publishing are so basic as to be strongly resistant to social change—viz. anything connected with the female psyche and its ultimate fulfilment in the role of wife and mother—and that these aspects will inevitably be represented in any magazine designed to appeal to a mass female audience. They represent the demarcation line between the sexes and are the sole justification for the existence of a separate press for women.

The emancipationists fought for the abolition of all discrimination based on sex. Today, the pendulum is swinging away from a preoccupation with the similarities between the sexes and towards a recognition and acceptance of sexual differences, with the corollary that society is concerned less with equality and more with equivalence. But, although the position of women has steadily improved, with a wide range of opportunities opening up for them in public life, the chief aim of all but a tiny minority of women is still to marry and have a family. They seldom set their sights beyond this; indeed society makes it very difficult for them to do so. Most girls receive an education which is not calculated to fire any ambition in them beyond proficiency in domestic science, and the numbers who progress into the higher reaches of learning where a social consciousness might be awakened, or acquire any training which might later fit them for some interesting occupation in addition to housewifery, are still relatively small.

Thus, whilst they may continue to be unmoved by social questions, women will always be interested in topics fundamental to the craft of being a woman, as the majority still define it. As one Editor remarked:

> 'Women will always want to know how to make themselves more attractive, their homes prettier, and their children better cared for.

... The real success of the weeklies is grounded in their fulfilment of the basic needs of women which have nothing to do with social revolutions.'*

Any magazine which might contemplate changing this emphasis has the following experience of *Woman* to deter it:

'*Woman* had a social conscience once, when it was first launched —the social conscience of the late John Dunbar, then Editorial Director of Odhams and once a member of the I.L.P. Dunbar thought it should deal with social problems as well as flower arrangements and fancy menus to tempt young husbands. Its sale dropped to a third. Not until Dunbar accepted the facts of life as they appertain to women's weeklies and freed it of its social conscience did its circulation begin to rise. It is a lesson no one running women's magazines forgets.'[11]

This truth is as much responsible for the domestic focus in women's publishing as pressure from manufacturers interested in selling food and equipment to housewives. In the past publishers fastened upon this 'lowest common denominator' in writing for women as the surest way of building and maintaining multi-million readerships. In the 'forties and 'fifties it was possible to be 'all things to all women'—the deprivations of war and the restrictions of peace were great levellers.

But the era is passing when women's magazines can prosper by appealing at a low level to an undifferentiated mass of women. Social changes are at work, leavening the 'lump' and breaking it down into sub-groups, some of them newly-created, others newly-revealed. *She* proved some years ago that these groups are there, and that catering for them can be a profitable enterprise; *Nova* has confirmed it. What remains in doubt is the size and special characteristics of these sub-groups, and it is in this area that research needs to be concentrated.

Publishers are now becoming aware of these trends. In planning for the future they are taking into account both the widering interests and experience of women and a new form of stratification within the female reading public, based not so much upon age and class as upon shared ideas and experiences, which may unite along a single attitude dimension women of all ages and backgrounds who can be reached by a single magazine which reflects those attitudes. *Fashion*, the latest magazine to enter the field, claimed in its pilot issue that it would 'appeal to

* Personal interview.

the woman with a certain attitude of mind—the woman who really cares how she looks—rather than a specific age or income group'.

American experience confirms that, as women become more discriminating, 'formula' editing must be discarded in favour of individuality and inventiveness. While mass circulation periodicals will continue to 'reflect' rather than 'lead', there are signs that in the future they will have scope for greater originality consequent upon the formation of attitude groups. Those who fear 'market saturation' has been reached can find reassurance in the fact that:

'. . . if you have something to say in a magazine addressed to women, it doesn't matter that there are now more than a dozen large magazines of different kinds for women. You can still find an audience for whom your magazine can be valuable. In a way you invent your readership by having an idea and a conviction, then having the skill and the imagination . . . to make it materialise. Then you can find the people for whom your magazine will be valuable, interesting, exciting. You do this without regard for what anyone else is doing.'[12]

Two British magazines have already built their success on this principle, *She* and *Nova*. It is not a new approach. The history of magazine publishing demonstrates that periodicals which show initiative and high editorial quality can succeed even where a market is reputedly saturated. *Woman's Realm*, launched in the teeth of competition in 1958, is one example.

An analysis of those publications which have managed to increase or at least maintain their circulations in the face of decline over the entire industry suggests that the reason for their success lies in their ability to offer the reader special value. *Family Circle*, *Hers*, *Homes and Gardens*, *Honey*, *The Lady*, *Mother*, *She* and *Woman's Weekly* have this in common: that they offer a service, or an approach, or some new idea in publishing which gives each of them a distinct character and an individual appeal and commends them to a particular group of readers. Their success indicates that there is still scope in women's publishing for expansion, if that expansion is carefully directed on the basis of systematic research.

It can be argued that in planning for the future publishers should look more closely at the economic factors contributing to the decline in the popularity of women's magazines. Up to now, it has been widely accepted that Editors were at fault in not keeping up with the social changes overtaking their readers, but there are other possible explanations for at least a part of the overall drop in sales. The striking fact about the circulations of the leading women's magazines over the past twenty-five years, when represented graphically,* is that the pattern is very similar for all of them. This suggests that the causes for these simultaneous fluctuations are more likely to be found in the state of the market itself than in particular editorial deficiencies, which would tend to affect the circulations of individual magazines differently and at different times. It must be remembered, too, that where there is a structured market, its constituents may be affected in various ways to produce the same overall result.

The monthlies have suffered through competition from the fast-growing gravure weeklies which, in size and presentation, now offer equivalent value at a quarter of the price. This situation is aggravated by the problem of 'dying readerships' with which most monthly magazines of the older type are burdened. Editors cannot afford to lose these loyal, ageing readers, but catering for them requires an approach which is anachronistic in present day social terms, and unappealing to the younger women whom these magazines must attract to insure their future.

The weeklies have problems of a different kind connected with the limited field in which they now have to work. Women today want less authoritarian guidance and more 'ideas', and Editors are finding it increasingly hard to supply new angles without straying outside the consumer sphere, which company policy discourages. Whereas, twenty years ago, the deprivations of post-war life gave them plenty of scope for originality with little fear of duplication, today it is almost impossible for the women's magazines to avoid overlap. The result (for the reader) is diminishing returns on multiple purchases. A woman can no longer expect to get three times the value by buying three magazines as she would by buying one, and this applies as much to three different issues of the same magazine as to three separate publications. It is possible, therefore, that women are not only cutting down on the number of different titles they buy, but are also buying less regularly than in the past, being drawn only to those issues which have special interest for them. The marked fluctuations in magazine sales during a single year seem to support this.

Thus, the decline in circulations may represent a complete re-drawing of the 'demand curve' for women's magazines. The vast expansion of magazine readerships in the ten years after the war was to some extent artificially induced by war-time shortages. Demand for reading-matter

* Appendices VII and VIII.

built up and created an insatiable appetite which gorged itself as soon as restrictions were lifted. The boom kept many old-style publications afloat long after they would normally have folded under the pressure of mounting competition and rising standards, and inflated the sales of others to a level which soon came to be accepted as normal but probably was not. Since then, the magazines have had to compete with television, the colour supplements, paper backs and the growing popularity of lending libraries. It may well be that publishers will have to accept that the market is suffering an inevitable contraction which has less to do with the failure of Editors to provide what is needed than with a slackening demand for this type of literature.

Patterns of circulation in the American women's magazine industry are interesting by comparison since they show an opposite trend, settling on a 'plateau' in the first half of the 'fifties and expanding rapidly thereafter. The 'plateau' represented a drop in news-stand sales (which has been attributed *inter alia* to increasing geographic mobility after the war*), but apparently did not signify a permanent disenchantment with women's magazines since they were later more than replaced by subscriptions. For publishers, the growing competition from commercial T.V. was 'the essential difficulty'† which the large magazines responded to with a 'circulation race', while the smaller journals opted for specialisation.

The sustained expansion in the American women's magazine industry up until 1967, contrasted with the recession in our own, may be partly attributable to the different functions of the two groups of magazines relative to other mass communications media in the respective countries. It has already been noted that American magazines are important purveyors of information over a broad range of subjects, supplementing regional broadcasting services which are generally inadequate. Commercial T.V. has not killed off news magazines such as *Time* and *Life*, *Look* and *Newsweek*, but in this country it has long since driven *Picture Post*, *Illustrated* and *Everybody's* out of print.

American women habitually resort to magazines, a practice which increases with education; 59 per cent of all women college graduates in 1966 were 'heavy magazine readers', compared with 40 per cent of high school graduates. (Educational level and exposure to T.V. were negatively correlated.)[13] Thus, with the rapid expansion occurring in higher education for American women, it is to be expected that magazine consumption should also rise. Similar figures are not available for British women's magazines, but it is likely that they would show a

* By Theodore Peterson.
† A statement by Robert Stein in a letter to the writer, March 12th, 1968.

negative correlation between magazine readership and educational level, and perhaps a higher correlation between education and the use of public libraries.

However, the past success of American women's magazines in increasing their sales is relative and gives a misleading impression of the current state of the industry. In America it is now generally accepted that the heyday of magazine publishing is past. Expansion has not been keeping pace with the growth in population and the mass magazines have now begun to lose ground. The recent decline is seen as the inevitable sequel to a period in which mass circulations have been artificially maintained by 'high pressure direct mail' and reduced subscription rates, while the reading public has been growing less dependent upon periodical literature for information and entertainment.

At the same time, high publishing costs and diminishing advertising revenue have not only cut back profits, but are now resulting in losses for magazines such as *McCall's*, which is estimated to have lost $3·5 million in 1968. Abnormally attractive issues can make matters worse. The William Manchester Story won *Look* magazine an extra million readers but lost its publishers $500,000 because the advertising rate could not be raised in time. All over the industry publishing firms are diversifying—going into real estate, broadcasting, paperbacks, hardcovers and other profitable fields outside magazine publishing.

It is currently being argued that magazines cannot continue to survive as advertising media and that their future viability depends upon restoring 'the primacy of editorial'. It is felt that creating regional and demographic editions offers only a temporary solution and one which benefits the advertiser while ignoring the reader. Specialisation of function in line with contemporary social needs is seen as a possible alternative, and proposals are being considered for magazines dealing with urban problems, locality-oriented periodicals, and a newly-formulated publication for parents.

Although the women's publishing industry on both sides of the Atlantic can no longer hope for the huge profits of the past, it still has an encouraging future in prospect. The women's magazines may have lost a major part of their entertainment function to television, but this releases them to concentrate on, and develop, their role as purveyors of information over a wide range of specialised 'service' areas. This is a function which no other medium is so well fitted to perform. Magazines are relatively inexpensive, provide a continuing flow of topical information during the course of a year, can be used as cumulative works of reference and allow the reader to choose her own pace, with unlimited opportunities to refer back.

More than this, the women's magazines are in a unique position to assume a positive role of leadership in helping women to adjust to their new position in a changing world. As Dr Dichter pointed out:

'The ambivalent attitudes towards modernity and emancipation have created a new need for models and influentials. As women try to feel their way in a world which they may, at the same time, want and fear, the practical and emotional value of "models" increases. Trend-setters, thought-leaders and the like can help to turn cultural concepts into humanised forms which assist the individual to imitate, to evaluate, to reject or to implement her own attitudes towards modernity, independence and the like.'[14]

There is no lack of scope in this area, once Editors feel they can move into it without undermining the confidence of advertisers.

American Editors claim to have few connections with the women's press in Britain, and therefore little knowledge of recent trends here. They rarely buy British material; sales are more frequent in the opposite direction. The one magazine representative who did comment on women's publishing in this country had this to say:

'British women's publications look dead. They lack enthusiasm and the go-ahead spirit, and they are suffering from underinvestment. The difference between the two industries is that, while the British businessman accepts limitations to his activity, it is not in the nature of his American opposite number to do so. For him, the sky's the limit.'*

This outlook is responsible for the dynamic approach found everywhere in American publishing. If Britain is a nation of cautious shopkeepers, America is a land of travelling super-salesmen financed by investors who are ready to back them heavily with capital in the expectation of a worthwhile return. Such businessmen, with much to gain and a great deal to lose, make things happen. They will simply refuse to take 'no' for an answer. A striking example of this drive, combined with opportunism, was a publication called *Twiggy*, put out by Martin Goodman in 1967 to capitalise on the sudden craze for this lean young British fashion model. Only one issue was published, put together in just two nights by the regular editorial team, and it sold a quarter of a million copies. Highly priced at fifty cents for only 68 pages, most of which were filled with material from photo-agencies, the magazine made a handsome profit.

* Personal interview (1967).

While Britain has its share of businessmen with enterprise and initiative, their freedom to operate is habitually restricted by a variable economic climate. The small percentage of subscription sales allows circulations to fluctuate freely in sympathy with seasonal economic trends (and advertising custom with them). Magazines are marginal purchases, the first items to suffer when women have to economise, and custom has therefore to be battled for not only month by month but, in the case of the mass circulation periodicals, week by week. The result is that much investment capital which might be used to improve the magazines is spent instead on their promotion, to the advertiser and to the reader.

Marketing is a crucial area and is currently the focus of attention. The experts are now less concerned with possible editorial deficiencies than with probable managerial inefficiency, and following the failure of the motivational researchers to stimulate sales, it is now the turn of the management consultants to get to grips with the industry's problems. IPC have called in McKinsey and Co., the American firm which is also advising the B.B.C. and the Bank of England.

McKinsey's interim findings have produced a fundamental change in the traditional philosophy of magazine publishing and have set on foot a complete re-structuring of magazine management within the IPC. Announcing details of the coming changes in August, 1968, Mr Arnold Quick, Chairman of IPC's Magazine Division, advanced the latest theory regarding the industry's recession. Describing the thinking that led to the consultations with McKinsey, he said:

'We tried to find out what was wrong. Are we in a socio-economic squeeze, as Cecil King and Lord Thomson reiterate? Or are we bad marketeers? I believe we are bad marketeers. We have been publisher-oriented, dedicated to producing a product and not doing enough about selling it and extending its availability to likely buyers ... the deficiencies have been in management....'[15]

To remedy these 'deficiencies', IPC have evolved a new concept in managerial control. The formation of the Magazine Division under the Chairmanship of Mr Arnold Quick, announced in May, 1968, did not alter the internal management structure of the constituent publishing firms, but, as a result of McKinsey's recommendations, this is now undergoing radical change. The customary Board of Directors has been abolished, and each individual magazine now has its own 'Publisher', an executive responsible for profit and loss and internal co-ordination, and with the authority to make running decisions. These junior executives are in turn responsible to a Chief Executive, the head of the Magazine Group to which they belong.

The separate publishing houses of Fleetway, Newnes and Odhams are being phased out, and their publications distributed between five newly-created Magazine Groups, each of which covers a specific section of the market. The first of these, 'Women's Weekly Magazines', came into being in November, 1968, and the remaining four, 'Women's Monthly Magazines', 'Young Magazines', 'Practical and Juvenile Magazines' and 'Special Interest and Miscellaneous Magazines', are (at the time of going to press) in process of being established. There is accompanying geographic rationalisation designed to centralise and unify magazine administration which has in the past been carried out from thirty-seven different buildings.

The chief object of this reorganisation is to facilitate collective marketing and the rationalisation of advertising rates. The Magazine Division has already announced a number of new services to advertisers, including 'a collective rate card structure for the four women's weeklies ... offering volume and series discounts and special positions' (September, 1968), and similar discount arrangements for the monthlies (January, 1969), together with 'test marketing facilities in the regions, merchandising help at the retailer level and market research'.*

It is also hoped to achieve quicker and more flexible decision-making within individual magazines by delegating a measure of responsibility to internal executives with an all-round knowledge of their problems, and to promote co-ordinated research and development, including diversification into allied fields. The most important change of policy, however, is that the tough, internal competition, strongly encouraged in the past when Fleetway, Newnes and Odhams operated separately under the co-ordinating hand of IPC's Managing Company, is to be abolished in the interests of managerial efficiency and profitability. This is a step which, according to Mr Quick, should have been taken many years ago, and is expected to yield dividends in the current financial year (1968–69). Buckmaster and Moore forecast that it will enable the Division to maintain an annual profit of around £4 million, despite the continuing fall in the circulations of the mass weeklies.†

---

* It is claimed (Buckmaster and Moore) that these schemes have already given 'considerable impetus to the forward bookings of the major IPC consumer magazines for 1969'.

† In the year ended February 23rd, 1968, IPC Magazines showed a profit of £3·2 million on a turnover of £46·9 million. The women's weekly magazines contributed most of the Division's profits (63·9 per cent) and accounted for just under half its total sales. The women's monthlies contributed only 6 per cent (sales 10·6 per cent). Profits for the Group were £7·2 million on a turnover of £152·9 million.

A Chart Prepared by IPC Magazines Showing its New Management Structure

ORGANISATIONAL STRUCTURE OF IPC MAGAZINES LTD.

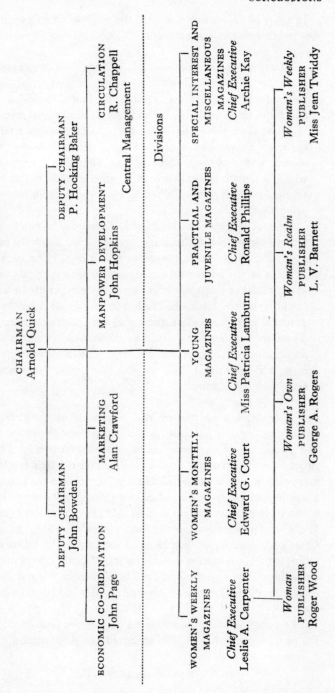

CHAIRMAN
Arnold Quick

DEPUTY CHAIRMAN
John Bowden

DEPUTY CHAIRMAN
P. Hocking Baker

ECONOMIC CO-ORDINATION
John Page

MARKETING
Alan Crawford

MANPOWER DEVELOPMENT
John Hopkins

CIRCULATION
R. Chappell

Central Management

Divisions

WOMEN'S WEEKLY
MAGAZINES

Chief Executive
Leslie A. Carpenter

WOMEN'S MONTHLY
MAGAZINES

Chief Executive
Edward G. Court

YOUNG
MAGAZINES

Chief Executive
Miss Patricia Lamburn

PRACTICAL AND
JUVENILE MAGAZINES

Chief Executive
Ronald Phillips

SPECIAL INTEREST AND
MISCELLANEOUS
MAGAZINES

Chief Executive
Archie Kay

Woman
PUBLISHER
Roger Wood

Woman's Own
PUBLISHER
George A. Rogers

Woman's Realm
PUBLISHER
L. V. Barnett

Woman's Weekly
PUBLISHER
Miss Jean Twiddy

In 1961, *The Economist* discussed the possible choices open to magazine publishers. In view of current developments they are worth quoting:

'A really cold-blooded "multiple publisher" of magazines within particular fields of advertising, might be concerned with his combined advertising revenue rather than that of individual papers, and could think of the whole lot in terms of marginal revenue and marginal cost. Where he is generally under pressure from rising costs, as all publishers are today, he might consider whether closing one magazine, some of the advertising revenue from which, if not all, he could capture in others, would reduce his total revenue as much as it would reduce his costs (including competitive promotion).

'But . . . this may not hold good. There may be an incentive to keep two journals if advertisement rates for one cannot be raised by killing the other. Again, the strong reader loyalty that each of two journals in the same field can command may prompt caution in killing either goose: advertisers may feel it is imperative to advertise in both; and two established papers in a field may deter the always potential newcomer more than one, even a thicker one, would. There are innumerable variants on the economic circumstances of a magazine: there is much room for cross-subsidisation in a combine; and magazine publishers, like other entrepreneurs, are not simply economic men.'

The arguments concerning the 'wastes of competition' are well known: so, too, are the stultifying effects when competition is absent, and the social dangers inherent in monopolistic ownership. The Second Royal Commission on the Press underlined the deleterious effects of the narrowing of consumer choice following attrition in the national press. Co-ordinated policy-making, if carried through at editorial level, could conceivably produce the same result. Mr Quick has already announced IPC's intention to develop the four women's weeklies 'as a totality'. Cross-subsidisation, too, can be disadvantageous. The Editor of a mass-selling women's magazine recently asserted* that if it were not under an obligation to 'make profits for the combine', it could, without damaging its economic position, reduce its advertising ratio and improve its editorial coverage.

The extent to which the saving on competitive promotion, the benefits of unified control, and co-ordinated planning, marketing and re-

---

* In a personal interview.

search will outweigh the stimulus of real competition in the British women's press will only emerge over time, and the effect on magazine content and the consumer will be watched as closely as the effect on profits. Administrative improvements and the more effective deployment of resources could well work to the consumer's advantage if they permit the expansion of reader-research, greater editorial flexibility and better methods of distribution. It is an encouraging development that, as part of a new promotions policy designed to advertise magazines as 'consumer products' stressing the total editorial concept rather than specific, periodic attractions such as 'special offers', IPC are now beginning to conduct research into readers' preferences concerning editorial content. They are also currently sponsoring experimental improvements in distribution and display which will expose magazines to potential purchasers over a longer period. In some regions these have increased sales of weeklies by as much as a fifth, and monthlies by two-fifths, and it is estimated that, given the co-operation of the retail trade, national increases of 'between 2 and 10 per cent' are possible. If, however, the new emphasis on collective marketing* does no more than increase the efficiency with which magazines are sold to advertisers, then the reader is more likely to suffer than benefit, and the magazines will clearly be developing in a manner contrary to the social interest. It is also likely to be to their own ultimate disadvantage, as recent American experience testifies.

The fact remains that neither the re-shaping of their management structure to promote efficiency, nor improving their position *vis à vis* the advertiser can insure the future of the women's magazines in the face of a diminishing audience. Nor will better marketing to the consumer help matters (except in the short run) if the product is commercially biassed and socially retarded. Whilst gains will no doubt accrue from these measures, it should be recognised that the industry's problems do not stem from a single area, but from a complex, interacting set of factors, economic, social and cultural, which cannot be dealt with in isolation.

Moreover, large-scale reforms inspired wholly by American theories of business management, and based on American experience, need to be carefully examined before being implemented within our own magazine industry, where different considerations apply. IPC have already had one lesson bearing upon the wisdom of introducing unmodified American theories, *viz.* in the field of motivational research.

---

* IPC's marketing budget has risen by £0·5 million since the reorganisation and the 'total promotion budget for its magazines is now over £3 millions'.[17]

Nor has the latest report from McKinsey gone unchallenged. The resignation of a number of top IPC executives in other Divisions indicates that there is at least an element of doubt as to the suitability of some of these latest proposals, though they have been unanimously supported by the main Board. But the full import of McKinsey's investigations for the future of IPC will not be known until their reports are complete, and it will be some time before it will be possible to fully evaluate the new administrative structure and the new policies.

Finally, we come to an evaluation of women's magazines in modern Britain. The majority of them are 'trade papers', domestic manuals for the woman who is already a housewife, or expects to become one. Between them, these periodicals in a single year cover most aspects of running a home and caring for a family, together with extensive advice to help women improve their personal appearance and overcome their problems. Those subjects which cannot be adequately dealt with in weekly or monthly articles are more fully covered in supplementary leaflets and guides which are usually free. The women's press has acquired extensive testing facilities, professional help, and commercial contacts to ensure that the highest standards are maintained, and in the information and guidance which it makes available to women for a few pence, it is providing a secondary network of social welfare services, the value of which in promoting higher standards of nutrition, child-care and general home comfort, as well as personal adjustment, it is impossible to calculate. Successful home-making requires skills which few women now have the opportunity to acquire before they marry, and no other single agency combines guidance in so many departments of married life as does the women's press, or presents that help so attractively and encouragingly.

Women's magazines also have entertainment value—their fiction, features, gossip, correspondence and competitions being ideal 'fillers' of those odd moments in every woman's day when she takes a few minutes' break and wants to relax with something that is bright, interesting, and not too demanding either of time or concentration. They may bring her emotional release, or help re-charge the batteries of her own inventiveness by providing useful ideas, whether it be for a new hair-style or for 'making potatoes a party dish'.

To give magazines their due, it must be placed on record that they are edited 'not only with professional acumen but also with sincerity, responsibility and a deep regard for individual problems and social values'. Their Editors know that women are sentimental creatures and cater for them accordingly, recognising the therapeutic value of day-dreaming and wish-fulfilment (which they regard as harmless anodynes), and the importance of achieving identification with their readers. Magazines have a valuable role to play in ministering to the submerged needs of all sorts and conditions of women, particularly those who, due to the break-up of kin and community groups in modern society, are lonely and isolated, and want encouragement, approval, understanding and friendship.

This function is pre-eminent, and will always be one of the strongest claims of women's magazines upon the loyalty of readers. In times of distress, magazine counsellors are trusted to be wise and impartial, and they are assisted in this by the fact that they never meet those they are trying to help and can therefore be objective in their judgements. It can be argued that, for the same reason, they can only give general advice and run great risks through ignorance of the character and situation of their correspondents. However, experience has made these advisers extraordinarily perspicacious, and they can at least point readers in the right direction, if only by indicating appropriate professional sources of help.

The women's magazines also act as unofficial C.A.B.s, supplying information on procedures, rights and obligations at law, as well as replying to a multitude of miscellaneous queries. Their overall role is comparable to that of a nationwide 'Women's Institute', providing an arena in which women can meet, exchange ideas, views and experiences, and derive from it mutual help and support. Under our existing social system, housewives and mothers inhabit a closely-confined world. Many are lonely, insecure and over-taxed by the day's demands, which they must frequently cope with unaided. The trip to the supermarket is often the high-point of their day, for it is the place where a woman makes most of her social contacts. Here she meets other women who share her viewpoint, understand her worries and sympathise with her difficulties.

Women's magazines offer a similar experience. Turning the first page of a mass weekly is like entering a women's club—a woman knows she is on 'home ground' in more senses than one. This is her territory, her profession; she knows the rules and she shares the implicit goals and values. Here she finds warmth, friendship and identification, as well as a little harmless escapism. There is colour, humour and vitality to raise her spirits, and often a money-saving offer to give a fillip to her wardrobe. Over the years a special relationship can grow up between readers and their magazines, a strong bond compounded of trust, loyalty—and habit.

The critics who denigrate these periodicals are usually those who bring only objective judgement to bear upon them. A writer in a literary journal once poured scorn upon the pages of guinea-winning letters from readers, calling them 'a revelation of artless naïveté'. Yet Mary Grieve, an Editor of long experience, regarded them as one of the most important ingredients of a women's magazine. These two views contain the essence of the debate which periodically rages over the evaluation of women's magazines, and they illustrate the relevance of the subjective element in that evaluation. The critic gave as an example the following letter:

'Last Christmas, my husband gave me a gorgeous crimson under-set trimmed with black lace, which he had bought himself. It did not fit me, but I wouldn't part with it for anyone. I am nearly sixty-one.'

Writing for a small and intellectual readership, the critic could see no value in this letter, measured by all the usual objective, literary criteria. Yet some Editor, writing for a female readership of millions, decided it was worth a guinea to the magazine that printed it (and to get into print that letter had to be selected from a postbag of thousands). Why? Because, in its amusing simplicity, it embodied a handful of values of the utmost importance and relevance to many women, values which it is fashionable to ridicule on the part of those whose lives and interests are not so closely circumscribed, and to whom sophistication is all-important. Since the mass-selling magazines have these values woven into their very fabric, a short analysis of the letter in question may help to clarify the reasons for its appeal—and theirs.

First, the age of the writer: most women's magazines focus on young women, yet older women are forming an increasingly large proportion of the population, and they bulk large in magazine readership. Editors are well aware of their needs, even though, as a result of pressure upon them to concentrate on age-groups with a reputedly higher consumption potential, they tend to be squeezed out editorially. Ageing and its attendant difficulties, many of them psychological, is something which deeply concerns women, and for them, more so perhaps than for men, staying young and preserving an attractive appearance is intricately bound up with community status and personal morale. Modern society glorifies youth and youthfulness, and is losing its respect for age and experience. To show signs of age is to forfeit one's place in a top-geared world. Even the women's magazines are abetting this trend by pretending that 'women don't grow old nowadays'. But they do, and however good the camouflage, they are still sensitive underneath to the passing years, and are apprehensive in case they may lose the interest of their menfolk as their physical charms wane. The 'crimson underset' is a symbol whose significance most women would understand. To this sixty-one-year-old, the fact that her husband presented her with a gift so obviously suited to a much younger woman, meant that in his eyes she was still young, and that he still saw in her the girl he married. It was too small—he had not even noticed her thickening figure! Women reading about this experience would be able to share in it to the full and perhaps find in it some hope for themselves.

Then there is the fact that this was a gift the husband 'had bought himself'. Women often have little by which to reassure themselves of their husbands' continued appreciation and affection other than these material tokens, and those which come spontaneously, and have clearly involved special thoughtfulness and effort, as in this case, are priceless. They restore the self-confidence which women, with no one to guide them, can quickly lose in the welter of responsibilities marriage brings. Indoctrinated with the notion that to get and keep her man a woman must retain her physical attractiveness, and knowing that, confined to the home, she cannot keep pace with his interests and activities outside, a wife as she grows older may feel threatened by the fear of failure. A forgotten Christmas present can seem a petty cause of depression to a husband unless he appreciates that to his wife it may signify that she is no longer wanted. This particular act of thoughtfulness must have warmed the hearts of the millions of women with whom it was shared, each of whom would undoubtedly have indulged in the same sentimental gesture of refusing to part with so special a gift.

The value of all such contributions from readers is acknowledged even by the more sophisticated monthlies. In the opinion of the Editor of *Good Housekeeping*:

'Honest views from readers on any subject should always have a place in a magazine. In some measure they can provide a kind of antidote to the serious side of life. Occasional "relaxed" articles can do the same. As one reader wrote in response to a serious piece which admitted that real children were a very different proposition from model "magazine" babies, "You made us laugh about something we would normally worry over". This reaction reveals the very real risk that impossibly high standards projected in a magazine can undermine confidence and create problems rather than dispel them. Basically, those who write for women must understand them and be knowledgeable about the lives they live, if they are to avoid frightening them to death.'*

* Personal interview.

The foregoing study of the character and functions of British women's magazines shows above all the value and social significance of what they are communicating to the women of Britain, a value which can never be measured statistically, or expressed in the profit and loss account on a firm's balance sheet. Like all mass media of communication, they wield tremendous influence, both economic and social, and this places a heavy burden of responsibility upon those who produce them. In the past, it has mainly been the Editor who has shouldered this burden, interpreting, for the most part by instinct and intuition, the needs of readers, and satisfying them according to personal judgement exercised within the limits imposed by managerial policy. As has frequently been stressed in this study, there is no substitute for a good Editor, and the empathy he or she brings to the job. The most successful periods in the histories of our longest-running magazines are co-extensive with the tenure of particular Editors, and continuity in this respect is crucial.

However, at a time when social change is affecting every aspect of women's lives, there is urgent need for research to provide Editors with a more accurate picture of those they are writing for than can be gained from readers' letters or their own intuitive judgements, valuable though these are. The Editor who exclaimed: 'What *do* women want from their magazines?—I don't know!' is typical of many who are feeling their way in a fluid, transitional, social situation. It is an encouraging development that, as part of a new policy to promote each magazine as a total editorial concept, IPC are now beginning to conduct research into readers' preferences concerning editorial content.

Attention has been drawn in an earlier chapter to the lack of research into the psychology and the sociology of magazine readership, and publishers badly need concrete facts in these two areas to guide them in planning ahead. Such research is vital if the argument about the future of women's magazines is not to be conducted wholly in commercia terms.

Society's interests can never be served by influential periodicals which are so closely circumscribed by financial considerations that they cannot readily respond to changing social requirements. As Mr Gardner Cowles (Chairman of Cowles Communications Inc.) once remarked:

'Communications is more than a business. It involves intimate sensitivity about the wants and needs and tastes of people.'[18]
'In the last resort it is profits, not sociological truths which guide the publisher and influence his decisions.'

If commercial pressures are permitted to distort and retard the natural evolution of the women's press, publishers may discover—too late—that sociological truths are the very stuff of which profits are made.

NOTES

1 *A Motivational Research Study on the British Woman in Today's Culture*, Vol. II, p. 172.
2 Roy Newquist, *Conversations*, pp. 383–97. (Interview with Robert Stein.)
3 *The Economist*, June 27th, 1964.
4 *New Statesman*, August 24th, 1962.
5 Mr Charles Curran in *The Spectator*, November 19th, 1965.
6 *Millions Made My Story*, Mary Grieve, p. 178.
7 *Daily Herald*, February 5th, 1961.
8 See Note 3.
9 *The Educational Explosion and the Magazine Influence.*
10 See Note 5.
11 See Note 4.
12 See Note 2.
13 See Note 9.
14 See Note 1. Vol. I, p. 31.
15 *The Financial Times*, August 12th, 1968.
16 *World's Press News*, August 16th, 1968, p. 2.
17 Peter Hillmore, 'Hard sell for magazines' in *The Guardian*, May 16th, 1969.
18 *Inside Cowles' Communications Inc.*

Appendix I

Periodicals intended primarily for the woman reader 1693–1968

The following list contains all those publications for women encountered during the course of this research. It includes only those periodicals providing home service, general information, fashion or fiction. 'Family' journals and specialised magazines such as those dealing with maternity and child welfare, women's rights, and the organs of the various women's associations are excluded, as are those early 'pocket-books', diaries, and annuals intended for use as engagement diaries. This is not by any means a comprehensive list of all women's magazines ever published: it would be impossible, given the existing system of cataloguing, to compile such a list without inspecting every undescribed periodical at present held by the British Museum—in addition, many women's papers are known to have been misplaced or destroyed, or else never received. But the following bibliography represents the only collected list of women's publications in existence, and has been compiled over many months from records and holdings at the British Museum and other libraries. An attempt has been made to sort out the discrepancies which frequently occur between different catalogues in respect of dating, press-marks, titles, etc., and to establish which of those periodicals, still listed, have in fact been destroyed. Where possible, press marks have been given to facilitate future use of this material. (Under the current system, monthly magazines are quoted as being held at the B.M., while 'weeklies' are available at Colindale. However, this does not always apply, as this list shows, and in addition, publications which change from being monthlies to weeklies are frequently split between both libraries.) Also included are a few titles claimed to have been 'destroyed', but which are still in existence.

Unfortunately it has been impossible to investigate many nonspecific titles, which may also be women's publications, but it is hoped that, through continual cross-reference, searching of catalogues, and personal inspection of obscure titles, this list represents at least the leading periodicals for women, published between 1963 and 1968. Approximately 170 of these titles have been individually examined and classified; the remainder are known to be women's publications, but have not been personally inspected by the writer. They have been included in order to present a more complete picture of the composition of the women's press over the past 250 years.

The publications are arranged alphabetically, in periods which correspond to those used for analysis in the main survey.

N.B.: W = Weekly; F = Fortnightly; M = Monthly; A = Annual

Eighteenth-century women's periodicals (seen)

Title	Dates	Press-mark
Female Spectator by Eliza Haywood	1744–1746	B.M. (1st) 629e 3 (last) pp. 5251 g
Ladies' Complete Pocket Book	1769	B.M., pp. 2469 cl(i)
The Ladies' Diary (or Woman's Almanack) by John Tipper, Coventry then: merged with The Gentleman's Diary to form The Ladies' and Gentlemen's Diary	1704–1840 (A) 1841–1871	B.M., pp. 2465
The Ladies' Magazine by Jasper Goodwill	1749–1753 (F)	B.M., pp. 5124
The Ladies' Mercury	1693 (W)	B.M., 816m 19 7)
The Lady's Magazine inc. with The Lady's Museum in 1832 and contd. as	1770–1832 (M)	B.M., pp. 5141
The Lady's Magazine and Museum of the Belle Lettres later:	1832–1837	
The Court Magazine and Museum	1838–1847	
The Lady's Monthly Museum then: The Ladies' Museum (united with The Lady's Magazine)	1798–1828 (M) 1829–1832	B.M., pp. 5153 (i)
Le Journal des Dames then: Month's Fashions contd. as	1797–1837 (M)	Colindale
Le Journal des Modes	1868–1913	

Additional titles (recorded but not seen) 18th Century

Female Guardian	1787	Oxford
The Female Tatler	1709–1710	B.M. pp. 5348 ca (Destroyed)
The Freethinker by Ambrose Phillips	1718	

Additional titles (recorded but not seen) 18th Century—continued

Title	Dates	Press-mark
Ladies' Journal (Dublin)	1727	
Lady's Curiosity (Weekly Apollo) by Nestor Druid	1752	Oxford
Lady's Magazine (or Universal Repository)	1731	
The Lady's Museum by Charlotte Lennox	1760–1761 (M)	B.M., pp. 5139 (Destroyed)
Lady's Pocket Magazine	1766	Birmingham P.L.
Lady's Weekly Magazine by 'Mrs. Penelope Pry'	1747	
The Old Maid by Mary Singleton (spinster)	1755–1756	
The Parrot by 'Mrs. Penelope Prattle'	1728	
The Visiter	1723–1724 (W then bi-W)	
The Young Lady	(W)	

Also: Various publications by Richard Steele written to appeal as much to women as to men, *The Lover* (1714), *Town Talk* (1715), *Tea-Table* (1716), *Chit-Chat* (1716), *Theatre* (1720).

Nineteenth-century women's periodicals (seen)
(i) 1800–1825

La Belle Assemblée then:	1806–1832	B.M., pp. 5142
The Court Magazine and Belle Assemblée (united with The Lady's Magazine)	1832–1848	
The Female Preceptor	1813– ?	Fawcett Library
Ladies' Fashionable Repository	1809–1895	B.M., pp. 5114 ba
The Ladies' Pocket Magazine	1824–1840	B.M., pp. 5154
World of Fashion then:	1824–1851	B.M., pp. 5115
Ladies' Monthly Magazine	1852–1879	
then: Le Monde Elègant	1880–1891	

Nineteenth-century women's periodicals
(ii) 1826–1850

Title	Dates	Press-mark
Englishwoman's Magazine (and Christian Mother's Miscellany)	1846–1854	B.M.
The Female's Friend	1846	B.M., pp. 11256
The Keepsake	1828–1857 (A)	B.M., pp. 24746 cl
Heath's Book of Beauty	1833	
The Ladies' Cabinet from 1852 the vols. are identical with those of the	1832–1870	B.M., pp. 5170
New Monthly Belle Assemblée		B.M., pp. 5143
The Ladies' Companion and Monthly Magazine (same as the L.M.C. at Home and Abroad)	?1850–1870 (M)	B.M.

After 1852, issued as:
The Ladies' Cabinet and
N.M. Belle Assemblée

Title	Dates	Press-mark
The Ladies' Gazette of Fashion	1834–1894 (M later W)	B.M., pp. 5230
The Ladies' Journal	1847 (W)	B.M., pp. 5244 d
The Ladies' Penny Gazette	1832–1833	B.M., pp. 5149 ca
Ladies' Polite Remembrancer	1843–1845 (A)	B.M., pp. 2474 e
Ladies' Mirror and Mental Companion	1815 (A)	B.M.
Ladies' Annual Journal	1815 (A)	B.M.
Lady's Newspaper and Pictorial Times (united with The Queen)	1847–1863 (W)	Colindale

Additional titles (recorded but not seen)
(ii) 1826–1850

The Christian Lady's Magazine	1854–1857	
Household Friend	1850–1852	B.M. (Destroyed)
Ladies' Own Magazine (and Mirror of the Months)	1843	B.M. (Destroyed)
Le Follet	1846–1900 (M)	Colindale
London and Paris Magazine	1842–1891 (M)	B.M., pp. 5231

Additional titles (recorded but not seen)
(ii) 1826-1850—continued

Title	Dates	Press-mark
Mother's Friend	1848–1895 (M)	B.M., 352 n
Young Ladies' Magazine	1838	

Nineteenth-century women's periodicals (seen)
(iii) 1851–1875

The Englishwoman's Domestic Magazine* by Samuel Beeton, contd. as	1852–1879 (M)	B.M., pp. 5114 k
The Illustrated Household Journal and E.D.M. (inc. with The Milliner)	1880–1881	
Englishwoman's Review	1857–1859 (W)	Colindale
Girl of the Period Miscellany	1869– ? (M)	Fawcett Library
The Ladies	1872–1873	Colindale
Lady's Own Paper	1866–1872 (W)	Colindale
Lady's Review	1860 (W)	Colindale
The Ladies Treasury	1858–1895	B.M., pp. 6004 o
Myra's Journal of Dress and Fashion	1875–1912 (M)	Colindale
The Queen	1861– (W then M)	Colindale
Woman's Gazette	1875–1879	B.M., pp. 1103 6a
then: Work and Leisure	1880–1893	
Woman's World then:	?1866–1868 (M)	B.M., pp. 6004 p
The Kettledrum	1869	
The Young Englishwoman	1864–1877 (M)	B.M., pp. 5149 m
contd. as Sylvia's Home Journal	1878–1891	
then: Sylvia's Journal	1892–1894	
Young Ladies' Weekly Journal (then: inc. with Cartwright's Lady's Companion)	1864–1920 (W)	Colindale

Additional Titles (recorded but not seen)
(iii) 1851–1875

Blackwood's Ladies' Magazine	(M)	

---

* Certain volumes on restricted loan—classified as 'pornography'.

Additional titles (recorded but not seen)
(iii) 1851–1875—continued

Title	Dates	Press-mark
Beeton's Book of Household Management	(M)	
Journal des Modes	1868–1913 (M)	
Mother's Treasury	1864– ? (M)	B.M., pp. 357 aa
Victoria Magazine by Emily Faithfull	1863–1880 (M)	

Nineteenth-century women's periodicals (seen)
(iv) 1876–1900

Title	Dates	Press-mark
Cartwright's Lady's Companion later:	1892–1915 (W)	Colindale
Leach's Lady's Companion then:	1915–1921	
Lady's Companion (merged in Woman's Friend)	1921–1940	
The Gentlewoman (merged in Eve)	1890–1926 (W)	Colindale
Girl's Own Paper, then:	1880–1927	B.M., pp. 5993 w
Woman's Magazine and G.O.P.	1928–1930	
contd. as:		
Woman's Magazine, G.O.P. and Heiress	1931–1950 Weekly parts making up a Monthly	B.M., pp. 5993 w and Colindale
then: The Heiress	1950–	B.M., pp. 5993 w(2)
Hearth and Home (merged with Vanity Fair)	1891–1914 (W)	Colindale
Home Chat	1895–1958 (W)	Colindale
Home Companion	1897–1956 (W)	Colindale
then: Home Comp. and Good Luck		
Homely Friend for Young Women and Girls then:	1877–1879	B.M., pp. 358 ea
Home Friend (contd. as Scottish Girls Friendly Society Magazine)	1880–1925	

Nineteenth-century women's periodicals (seen)
(iv) 1876–1900—continued

Title	Dates	Press-mark
Home Notes	1894–1957 (W)	Colindale
(merged in *Woman's Own*)		
Household Hints and Mothers' Handbook	1899–1901 (W)	Colindale
The Housewife	1886–1900 (M)	B.M., pp. 6004 dab
Ladies' Bits	1892	Colindale
The Ladies' Field	1898–1928 (W)	Colindale
(merged in *Home Magazine*)		
Ladies' Gazette of Fashion	1895–1899 (W)	B.M.
Ladies' Home	1898–1899 (W)	Colindale
Ladies' Home Journal	1890–1923	
(*Enquire within*) then:		
Home Life	1923–1924 (M)	
The Ladies' Review	1892–1908 (W)	Colindale
The Lady	1885– (W)	Colindale
Ladyland by Smedley Norton	1898–1899 (M)	B.M., pp. 6004 ol
Lady's Own Magazine	1898– ?	B.M., pp. 6004 cak
Lady's Own Novelette and Weekly Supplement	1889 (W)	B.M., pp. 6004 cak
The Lady's Pictorial	1881–1921 (W)	Colindale
(merged with *Eve*)		
The Lady's Realm	1896–1915	B.M., pp. 6004 og
The Lady's World	1886–1890	B.M., pp. 6004 ob
ed. Oscar Wilde		
(contd. as *Woman's World* after 1887)		
The Lady's World (II)	1898–1926 (W)	B.M., pp. 6004 oi
Le Moniteur de la Mode	1882–1896 (M)	Colindale
Mothers' Companion	1887–1896	B.M., pp. 5992 gd 6
(merged in *Family Friend*)		
My Lady's Novelette	1890 (W)	B.M., pp. 6004 cal
Myra's Threepenny Journal	1882–1893 (M)	Colindale
The People's Friend	1869– (W)	Colindale
Red Letter	1899– (W)	Colindale
Weldon's Ladies' Journal	1879–1954 (W)	Colindale
then: *Home Magazine*	1954–1963	
(merged in *Homes and Gardens*)		

Nineteenth-century women's periodicals (seen)
(iv) 1876–1900—continued

Title	Dates	Press-mark
Woman	1890–1912 (W)	Colindale
Woman at Home, then:	1893–1920	B.M.
The Home Magazine	1920–1921	
Womanhood	1898–1907	B.M., pp. 6004 ok
Woman's Herald	1891–1893 (W)	Colindale
(Formerly Women's Penny Paper 1888–1890)		
Woman's Life	1895–1934 (W)	Colindale
(merged in Woman's Own)		
Woman's Weekly	1898–1900 (W)	Colindale
World of Dress then:	1898–1908 (M)	Colindale
Eve's Mirror	–1909	
The Young Gentlewoman	1892–1921 (M)	Colindale
The Young Woman	1892–1915	B.M., pp. 6004 oda
(merged with The Young Man)		

Additional titles (recorded but not seen)
(iv) 1876–1900

Beauty and Fashion	1889	
Dorothy Novelette	1889	
Girl's Best Friend	1898–1931	
(merged with Poppy's Paper)		
Girls' Realm	1898–1915 (M)	B.M., pp. 5993 ya
(merged with Woman at Home)		
Home Cheer	1892	
Home Chimes	1884–1885	
Home Circle	1894–1897	
(The Ladies' Paper)		
Home, Sweet Home	1893–1901	Colindale
Isobel's Home Cookery	1896–1904 (M)	Colindale
then: Home Cookery and Comforts	–1921	
Ladies' Monthly Review	1889–1896	Colindale
(contd. as The Glass of Fashion)		

Additional titles (recorded but not seen)
(iv) 1876–1900—continued

Title	Dates	Press-mark
La Mode Illustrée	1896–1899 (M)	
Latest Paris Fashions	1898–1902	
London Journal Fashions	1886–1899 (M)	Colindale
Madame	1895–1913 (W)	Colindale
My Magazine	1899	
My Paper	1895	
Schild's Ladies' Magazine of Fashion	1882–1905	
Woman's Gazette and Weekly News	1888–1891 (W)	Col. Manchester (Destroyed)
Woman's World	1898– ?	B.M., pp. 6004 odc (Destroyed)

Twentieth-century periodicals for women (seen)
(i) 1901–1919

Eve then:	1919–1929	Colindale
Britannia and Eve	1929–1957	
Everywoman	1911–1914 (W)	Colindale
Everywoman's Weekly	1915 (W)	Colindale
Contd. as Everywoman's (merged in Romance)	1916–1923	
Family (Woman's) Pictorial (merged in Home Chat)	1920–1956 (W)	Colindale
Homes and Gardens	1919– (M)	
Ladies' Home Paper	1909– ? (W)	B.M., pp. 6004 sae
The Ladies' Kingdom	1909 (M)	Colindale
Lady's Gazette	1901–1904 (W)	Colindale
Lady's Gazette (II)	1909–1910 (M)	
The Matron	1906–1916 (M)	Colindale
Mayfair	1910–1922 (W)	Colindale
Mother and Home	1909–1918 (M; W after 1915)	B.M., pp. 6003 fa and Colindale
My Paper then: The Family Favourite	1913–1915 (W) –1916	Colindale
My Weekly	1910– (W)	Colindale
Peg's Paper	1919–1940 (W)	B.M., pp. 6004 sal

Twentieth-century women's periodicals (seen)
(i) *1901–1919—continued*

Title	Dates	Press-mark
Polly's Paper	–1924 (W)	B.M., pp. 6004 sao
(merged in *Girl's Mirror*)		
Vogue	1916– (F)	Colindale
Woman Citizen	1908–1913 (W)	Colindale
Woman's Health and Beauty	1902–1920 (M)	B.M., pp. 1832 gca
Woman's Home Magazine	1914– ? (M)	B.M., pp. 6004 op
Woman's Magazine	1907 (M)	Colindale
Woman's Own	1913–1917 (W)	Colindale
(merged in *Horner's Penny Stories*)		

Additional titles (recorded but not seen)
(i) *1901–1919*

Woman's Weekly (II)	1911– (W)	Colindale
Woman's World	1903–1958 (W)	Colindale
Betty's Weekly	1916 (W)	B.M., pp. 6004 seg
(inc. with *Woman's Weekly*)		
Cartwright's Home Life	1904–1914	Colindale
Housewife's Magazine	1902	B.M., pp. 6223 d
Ladies' Daily News	1901	Colindale
Ladies' Fortnightly Leaflet	1908	
Ladies' Mirror	1903–1954	
Lady's Illustrated Weekly	1905–1906	Colindale
Lady's Magazine (II)	1901–1905	B.M., pp. 6004 om
(then: *Home Magazine of Fiction*)		(Destroyed)
Mrs Bull	1910–1913 (M)	
(then: *Everywoman's Weekly*)		
My Favourite Home Journal	?1909–1914	
My Queen Magazine	1914	B.M., pp. 6004 tb
		(Destroyed)
Paris Fashions	1901–1914	
Queen of Fashion	1911–1912	B.M.
Vanity	1915	
Women Folk	1909–1910	
Woman's Realm (I)	1908–1909	B.M., pp. 6004 oo
		(Destroyed)
Girl's Mirror	1915–1933 (W)	Colindale

Twentieth-century women's periodicals (*seen*)
(*ii*) *1920–1945*

Title	Dates		Press-mark
Everywoman	1924	(W)	Colindale
Everywoman's	1934–1940	(M)	Colindale
contd. as *Everywoman*	1940–1967		
(merged in *Woman and Home*)			
Femina	1920–1922		Colindale
Glamour and Peg's Own	1938–1956	(W)	B.M., pp. 5993 wbi
then: *The New Glamour*	1956– ?		
(merged in *Mirabelle*)			
Good Housekeeping	1922–	(M)	B.M., pp. 1524 dac
Harper's Bazaar	1929–	(M)	Colindale
Housewife	1939–1968	(M)	B.M., pp. 1524 dfc
(merged in *Idéal Home*)			
Ladies' Home World	1926–1927	(M)	Colindale
Ladies' Only	1933–1935	(W)	Colindale
The Lady's Paper (*Chic*)	1929–1930	(W)	Colindale
Lucky Star contd. as	1935–1957	(W)	Colindale
Lucky Star and Peg's Paper,			
then: *Lucky Star*	1957—		
Miracle	1935–1958	(W)	Colindale
Miss Modern	1930–1940	(M)	Colindale
Modern Home	1928–1951	(M)	Colindale
(merged with *Modern Woman*)			
Modern Marriage, then:	1931–1932	(M)	Colindale
Home-Making Magazine	–1933		
(merged in *My Home*)			
Modern Woman	1925–1965	(M)	Colindale
Mother	1936–	(M)	Colindale
My Home	1928–	(M)	Colindale
(later *My Home and Family*)			
My Lady Fayre	1926–1927		Col. Bournemouth
Oracle	1933–	(W)	B.M., pp. 5993 wbe
Red Star	1929–	(W)	Colindale
Secrets contd. as	1932–1940	(W)	B.M., pp. 5993 wbm
Secrets and Flame	1940–		
True	1944–	(M)	
True Romances	1934–	(M)	
True Story (*English ed.*)	1922–	(M)	

Twentieth-century women's periodicals (seen)
(ii) 1920–1945—continued

Title	Dates	Press-mark
Violet Magazine	1922–1939 (M)	B.M., pp. 6018 tat
Wife and Home	1929– ? (M)	B.M., pp. 6004 obc
Woman (II)	1937– (W)	Colindale
Woman and Beauty	1930–1963 (M)	Colindale
Woman and Home	1926– (M)	Colindale
Woman's Companion (merged with *Woman's Weekly*)	1927–1961 (W)	Colindale
Woman's Fair (formerly *Woman's Filmfair*)	1935–1941 (W)	Colindale
Woman's Friend (merged in *Glamour*)	1924–1950 (W)	Colindale
Woman's Hour	1935	B.M., pp. 6004 s66
Woman's Illustrated (merged in *Woman*)	1936–1961 (W)	Colindale
Woman's Journal (later *Woman's Home Journal*)	1927– (M)	Colindale
Woman's Mirror (merged in *Woman's World*)	1934–1935 (W)	Colindale
Woman's National Newspaper	1938	Colindale
Woman's Newspaper	1939 (W)	Colindale
Woman's Own (II)	1932– (W)	Colindale
Woman's Pictorial	1919– ? (W)	Colindale
Woman's Story	? (M)	

Additional titles (recorded but not seen)
(ii) 1920–1945

Home Journal	1921	B.M., pp. 6004 or (Destroyed)
Home Journal (II) (inc. with *Woman's Pictorial*)	1934–1939	Colindale (Destroyed)
Home Mail and Woman's Guide	1933 (W)	Colindale
Home Mirror (inc. with *Home Companion*)	1926–1927 (W)	
Home Romance Illustrated	1937	

Additional titles (recorded but not seen)
(ii) 1920–1945—continued

Title	Dates	Press-mark
Household and Garden Hints	1933–1934	
Ladies' Times	1920–1922	Colindale
Leisure	1936– ?	(Destroyed)
Modern Girl	1936	B.M., pp. 6004 odh
		(Destroyed)
My Favourite	1928–1934	
My House	1934	
Woman of the Day	1921	
Woman's Kingdom	1926–1930	Colindale
Woman's Supplement	1920–1921 (F)	
(to The Times)		
merged in Eve		
Woman Today	1936–1939	

Twentieth-century women's periodicals (seen)
(iii) 1946–1968

Annabel	1966–	(M)
Boyfriend	1959–1966 (W)	Colindale
(merged in Trend)		
Woman Bride and Home	1968–	
	(6 a year)	
Family Circle	1964–	(M)
Fashion	1968–	(M)
Flair	1960–	(M) B.M., pp. 7613 gc
Hers	1966–	(M)
Honey	1959–	(M) B.M., pp. 6014 bd
Intro (merged in Petticoat)	1967	(W)
Jackie	1964–	(W) Colindale
Living	1967–	(M)
Mayfair	1946–1950	(M) B.M., pp. 6004 ot
Marilyn	1955–	(W) B.M., pp. 5993 wbq
Mirabelle	1956–	(W) Colindale
Marty		
'19'	1968–	(M)
Nova	1965–	(M)
Petticoat	1966–	(W)

Twentieth-century women's periodicals (seen)
(iii) 1946–1968—continued

Title	Dates		Press-mark
Romeo	1957–	(W)	
Roxy	1958– ?	(W)	
She	1955–	(M)	B.M., pp. 6004 obu
Trend	1966–1967	(W)	
(merged in *Petticoat*)			
Valentine	1957–	(W)	Colindale
Woman Herself Digest	1949– ?	(M)	B.M., pp. 6004 odo
Woman's Day	1958–1961	(W)	Colindale
(merged in *Woman's Own*)			
Woman's Mirror	1958–1967	(W)	Colindale
formerly *Woman's Sunday*			
Mirror, National Newspaper			
for Woman 1955			
(merged in *Woman*)			
Woman's Realm (II)	1958–	(W)	Colindale
Vanity Fair	1949–	(M)	B.M.

Appendix II

How You Can Help Your Editress

In her letter overleaf the Editress tells you why she wants this information and her reason for inserting this form. It is that she may *know you*, and so be better able to gauge your outlook, your needs, and your likes and dislikes in your *own* little HOME CHAT.

And the questions have been framed accordingly. They can be answered very simply, in many cases just by a tick in the spaces provided—and elsewhere please understand that your really frank opinions and suggestions are invited.

The questions should be read carefully, answers marked clearly *in ink*, and the whole four-page section pulled out and posted in a 1½d. stamped envelope addressed to:

> The Editress, HOME CHAT, Room 167,
> > The Fleetway House, Farringdon Street, London, E.C.4.

Please send your completed form just as soon as you can. No letter is necessary with it, and should you trust us with your name and address your gift blotter will be sent to you as quickly as possible. Should you require further space for your comments or suggestions, a sheet of plain paper may be used as well.

These are important pages to every reader of HOME CHAT, *so* R.S.V.P. *All the answers given in this questionnaire will be treated as strictly* CONFIDENTIAL

1 *Where do you live?* PLACE   COUNTY

2 *Are you Married?*   YES............ NO ....
Do you do all your own Housework?   YES............... NO ....
Do you have any Assistance?   DAILY HELP ....
                                                MAID OR MAIDS ....

Do you make your own Clothes?   ALL .... SOME ....
                                                NONE.................................

3 *If you are married, have you any Children?* YES............... NO ....
If so, How Many?   ....
And How Old are they?   1ST............... 2ND ....
                                                3RD .... 4TH ....

318

Do you make your Children's Clothes?   ALL .... SOME ....
                                           NONE..............

4   *Will you please give an indication as to Your*   21 OR   **22–30**
    Age by putting a tick in the appropriate age   UNDER
    group?
                                                      ....
                                                      31–45   OVER 45

                                                      ....

5   *If you are single, what is your Profession or*   ⎫
    Occupation?   │
    ....   │ PLEASE ANSWER ONLY
                                                      ⎬ ONE OF THESE
    If you are married, what is your husband's   │ QUESTIONS
    Profession or Occupation?   │
    ....   ⎭

6   *About how much do you spend on House-*   £   **s.**   **d.**
    keeping (including servants' wages, if any)
    each **week***?*
                                                      ....
    About how much do you spend a **year** *on*
    Clothes? (including underwear, shoes, stock-
    ings, etc.)
                                                      ....
    About how much do you spend a **year** *on*
    Beauty? (i.e., expenses on face, hands, hair,
    etc.)
                                                      ....

7   *Do you own your house?*   YES.............. NO ....
    Or, if you are buying your home, what is
    the **monthly** *payment?*   £ .... s.............. d............
    Or, if you pay rent, what is the **weekly**
    amount?   £ .... s.............. d............

8   *How long have you been a reader of* HOME
    CHAT?   ....
    Do you read it—Regularly?   ....
                    Occasionally?   ....

9   *Which Regular Features (in order, please) do you like Best in* HOME
    CHAT?
        1 ....
        2 ....
        3 ....

10 *Which Regular Features do you like Least in* HOME CHAT?

....

....

....

11 *Are there any Features which do not at present appear in* HOME CHAT *and which you would like to see every week?*

1 ....

2 ....

3 ....

12 *If you read any Other Magazines regularly in addition to* HOME CHAT, *will you please say which they are?*

Weekly Magazines:

....

....

Monthly Magazines:

....

....

....

Source: Home Chat, October 8th, 1938.

Appendix III

Are You The Perfect Wife?

Quizzes are fun, and they tell us a lot about ourselves that we might not otherwise own up to. This one sets out to show you how you line up as a marriage partner.

Lock yourself away quietly somewhere, and answer each question honestly, putting the answers down on paper.

When you score—and we tell you how to do that at the end of the quiz—you'll know just how successful you are as your husband's 'better half'.

Easy to discover . . . here's our fact-finding quiz. Do it honestly, and truth will out. If your score is over twelve, your husband can count himself as fortunate. If it's sixteen, he's married an angel!

1. Which of these age groups do you consider the ideal time for a woman to get married? . . .
   (*a*) . . . below twenty-two.
   (*b*) . . . between twenty-two and twenty-seven.
   (*c*) . . . over twenty-seven.

2 When there's an outing in view, are you of the opinion that a wife should . . .
   (*a*) . . . choose the play, film, or whatever it is?
   (*b*) . . . be asked her opinion before the outing is planned?
   (*c*) . . . be ready to like whatever her husband chooses?

3 Sleep is a time when the sub-conscious runs free, and behaviour at that time tells many a story of the emotions.
   (*a*) . . . do you dream a lot?
   (*b*) . . . do you consistently over-sleep, though you're aware that it's time to get up?
   (*c*) . . . do you wake up and lie for a while, planning the day?

4 On the subject of marriage, do you consider that . . .
   (*a*) . . . the advantages are mutual?
   (*b*) . . . the primary purpose of marriage is the legal protection of women?
   (*c*) . . . marriage is a social and religious necessity?

5 'There is a woman behind every successful man.' Assuming this to be true, would you say that the ideal wife should . . .

 (*a*) . . . concentrate on looking after the creature comforts of her husband?

 (*b*) . . . assist him in his work by learning all she can about it?

 (*c*) . . . remain in the background because of the danger of nagging at the one extreme, and rivalry of talent at the other?

6 Like most men, your husband had a number of girl-friends before he met you; some were serious affairs; others mere flirtations. If you both met one of these old flames, still unmarried, would you . . .

 (*a*) . . . demand to know how serious the affair was?

 (*b*) . . . laugh at the possibility of such a woman ever being a rival to you?

 (*c*) . . . arrange things so that you never met again?

7 At the annual dance of your husband's firm, with whom do you consider your husband should dance first? . . .

 (*a*) . . . the boss's wife—because it would probably enhance his position in the firm?

 (*b*) . . . his secretary, as the girl obviously hopes he will?

 (*c*) . . . you?

8 If you ever sit back and compare your husband with other men you know (especially your brother or father), do you tell yourself that . . .

 (*a*) . . . he's got one or two faults like every man, but they really don't matter?

 (*b*) . . . he would be just perfect if only he would stop that little mannerism?

 (*c*) . . . he's just perfect?

9 Do you believe that the greatest **power** of love which human beings can show (excluding the unassailable love of a mother for her child) are between . . .

 (*a*) . . . man and woman before marriage?

 (*b*) . . . man and man, like David and Jonathan?

 (*c*) . . . members of the same family?

10 When your husband comes home with stories of troubles at work, do you . . .

(*a*) . . . listen quietly?
(*b*) . . . offer advice?
(*c*) . . . tell him about your own problems of the day?

11 A divorced man is unlikely to make a good husband. Do you consider this to be generally true?

12 Your husband manages to get a few days extra holiday, quite apart from the family fortnight by the sea. He suggests that the children be packed off to a relative while you both go away. Would your reaction be . . .
(*a*) . . . this was a thoughtful, romantic scheme?
(*b*) . . . he was being selfish?
(*c*) . . . it would be a perfectly miserable time for you?

13 Maybe your husband's tastes in clothes are a little out-of-date, but they are certainly definite. When he gives you some money to buy a new dress, do you . . .
(*a*) . . . buy something fashionable because you know that eventually he will grow to like it?
(*b*) . . . make certain to get his favourite colour?
(*c*) . . . take the advice of a woman-friend or the saleswoman?

14 Who gets the early morning tea in your house . . .
(*a*) . . . your husband?
(*b*) . . . you?
(*c*) . . . sometimes one, sometimes the other?

15 Most of us have to face the fact that bereavement is a possible future tragedy. In your thoughts about it, is your first reaction . . .
(*a*) . . . how you will manage financially?
(*b*) . . . how you will manage to go on living?
(*c*) . . . you hope you will die before your husband?

16 If your husband fell seriously ill, would you prefer to . . .
(*a*) . . . have a skilled nurse to help you?
(*b*) . . . get him into a good hospital right away?
(*c*) . . . nurse him yourself?

17 Do you consider that perfect love could only be perfect if it consisted solely of the marriage of two minds, and the physical side did not enter into it?

18   Have you ever gone to the doctor about a pain which you are assured has no physical basis?

19   Do you think that in a well-run home housework should be paid for like any other job by a stated proportion of the gross income?

20   Would you like to be back in your childhood days again?

HOW TO MARK YOUR ANSWERS

SCORE one mark for each 'yes' answer according to the following key:

THE KEY: 1 (b). 2 (b). 3 (c). 4 (a). 5 (a). 6 (a). 7 (b). 8 (a). 9 (a). 10 (b). 11. 12 (a). 13 (a). 14 (c). 15 (b). 16 (a).

Now deduct one mark for each 'yes' answer to Questions 17, 18, 19 and 20.

In this 'examination paper' sixteen marks is the best possible score you can obtain. Any woman who can boast such a score has proved, as so many wives always have, that the strange mixture of idealistic woman, helpmate, lover, and foster-mother, which all men hope to find combined in one woman, can be obtained!

If your score is between 12 and 15, your husband can count himself as fortunate among men, and far luckier than most, as he probably realises.

Between 8 and 11 is fairly good, though an examination of the questions where you made no score will show where you are failing in this difficult job of being a wife. Maybe you lost some marks on those 'minus' questions; they are the psychological ones which are really danger-signals of hidden faults. Recognise their existence and you can put them right, adding marks to put yourself in a happier grouping.

Less than 8 would indicate that you have answered the questions without sufficient thought, for very few wives who are happy in their marriage will get such a low score!

Source: Home Chat, December 30th, 1950.

	VOGUE
	—
	—
	135·0
	150·0
	150·0
	150·0
	145·0
	147·0
	145·0
	145·0
	148·0
	142·5
	142·5
	135·0
	130·0
	130·0
	125·0
	120·0
	123·0
	160·0
	170·0
	165·0
	165·0
	152·0
	142·0
	143·5
	140·0
	140·0
	133·0
	137·0
	140·0
	137·0
	130·0
	126·0
	121·0
	118·0
	118·0
	117·8

Classified list of British women's periodicals, 1968

Title	Periodicity	Price	Publisher	Circulation ooos*
'SERVICE'				
Woman (1937)	Weekly	10d.	Odhams	2,523
Woman's Own (1932)	,,	10d.	Newnes	1,977
Woman's Weekly (1911)	,,	8d.	Fleetway	1,675
Woman's Realm (1958)	,,	8d.	Odhams	1,173
Family Circle (1964)	Monthly	1/3	Standbrook	1,153
Woman and Home (1928)	,,	2/6	Fleetway	666
My Weekly (1910)	Weekly	6d.	D. C. Thomson	630†
Living (1967)	Monthly	1/3	Standbrook	510
Ideal Home (1919)	,,	3/–	Odhams	199
Good Housekeeping (1922)	,,	3/–	Nat. Mag. Co.	188
My Home (1928)	,,	2/6	Fleetway	188
Annabel (1966)	,,	2/–	D. C. Thomson	176.6†
Mother (1936)	,,	2/6	Odhams	115
Woman Bride and Home (1968)	6 per year	2/6	Odhams	173‡
'FASHION'				
19' (1968)	Monthly	2/6	Newnes	196
Honey (1961)	,,	2/6	Fleetway	190
Petticoat (1966)	Weekly	1/–	Fleetway	182
Vogue (1916)	Monthly	4/–	Condé Nast	118§
Vanity Fair (1949)	,,	2/6	Nat. Mag. Co.	114
Flair (1960)	,,	2/6	Newnes	108
Fashion (1968)	,,	4/–	Fleetway	63
'QUALITY'				
Homes and Gardens (1919)	,,	3/–	Newnes	205
Woman's Home Journal (1927)	,,	3/6	Fleetway	189
Queen (1861)	,,	4/–	Stevens	40 E.
Harper's Bazaar (1929)	,,	5/–	Nat. Mag. Co.	32

ABC figure July–Dec., 1968, except where otherwise stated.
Audited figure.   E. Estimated figure.
Average for the magazine's first six months in print (publisher's estimate).
Not an audited figure.

Title	Periodicity	Price	Publisher	Circulation 000s*
'FEATURES'				
She (1955)	Monthly	2/6	Nat. Mag. Co.	275
Nova (1965)	,,	3/6	Newnes	132
'FICTION'				
Jackie (1964)	Weekly	6d.	D. C. Thomson	451†
True Story (1922)	Monthly	2/–	Illustrated Pubs.	268
True (1944)	,,	2/–	Pearson's	261
True Romances (1934)	Weekly	2/–	Illustrated Pubs.	229
Valentine (1957)	,,	7d.	Fleetway	181
Hers (1966)	Monthly	2/–	Pearson's	180
Mirabelle (1956)	Weekly	8d.	Pearson's	175
Romeo (1957)	,,	6d.	D. C. Thomson	154†
Woman's Story (19 ?)	Monthly	2/–	Illustrated Pubs.	121
NEWSPAPER				
The Lady (1885)	Weekly	1/3	The Lady Pub. Co.	72

N.B. The fiction periodicals *Family Star, People's Friend, Red Letter, Red Star* and *Secrets*, fc which circulation figures are not available, circulate mainly in the North of England and i Scotland.

* ABC figure July–Dec., 1968, except where otherwise stated.
† Audited figure.

I. The Woman Reader (continued):

(ii) Nineteenth century (continued):

ROYAL COMMISSION ON LABOUR, *Report of Miss Collet on Statistics of Employment (Women and Girls)*, 1893, Cmnd. 7695.

WELLS, H. G., *Ann Veronica*, T. Fisher Unwin, 1909.

(iii) Twentieth century:

BEAUVOIR, Simone de, *Nature of the Second Sex*, Four Square, 1963.

BERGER, Nan, and MAIZELS, Joan, *Woman—Fancy or Free?* Mills and Boon, 1962.

BROWN, Helen Gurley, *Sex and the Single Girl*, Four Square, 1964.

CADBURY, . . . MATHESON, . . . and SHANN, . . . *Women's Work and Wages*, Unwin, 1906.

CARR-SAUNDERS, A., JONES, D., and MOSER, C., *Social Conditions in England and Wales*, O.U.P., 1958.

D.S.I.R., *Woman, Wife and Worker*, Problems of Progress in Industry, No. 10, 1960.

DOUIE, Vera, *Daughters of Britain*, Privately published, Oxford, 1949.

ELLIS, Havelock, *The Task of Social Hygiene*, 1912. (Chs. I–IV and Ch. VIII.)

FLETCHER, Ronald, *The Family*, Penguin, 1962.

FRIEDAN, Betty, *The Feminine Mystique*, Gollancz, 1963.

GAVRON, Hannah, *The Captive Wife*, Routledge & Kegan Paul, 1966.

GOVERNMENT PUBLICATIONS:

Central Advisory Council for Education, '*15–18*' (Crowther Report), H.M.S.O., 1960.

Central Office of Information, *Women in Britain*, Pamphlet No. 67, H.M.S.O., 1964.

Committee on Higher Education, *Report* (Robbins), H.M.S.O., 1963.

Department of Employment and Productivity, *Gazette*.

HUNT, Audrey, *Women's Work and Wages*, Vol. I (Report), Government Social Survey, March, 1968, SS 379.

Ministry of Education, *Statistics*.

Registrar General's *Census of Population*, 1801–1961.

Registrar General's *Sample Census*, 1966.

Registrar General's *Statistical Review of England and Wales* (Annual).

Report of the War Cabinet Committee on Women in Industry, 1919. Cmnd. 135.

Appendices and Evidence, Cmnd. 167.

I. The Woman Reader (continued):

(iii) *Twentieth century (continued):*

GOVERNMENT PUBLICATIONS (continued)

Royal Commission on Population, 1949, *Report and Papers*, Cmnd. 7695.

HUBBACK, Judith, *Wives Who Went to College*, Heinemann, 1957.

HUNT, Morton, *The Natural History of Love*, Hutchinson, 1960.

HUTCHINS, Barbara, *Woman's Industrial Career*.
Reprinted from *The Sociological Review*, October, 1909.
Women in Modern Industry, Bell & Sons, 1915.

JEPHCOTT, Pearl, *Rising Twenty*, Gollancz, 1948.

LIFTON, Robert Jay (Ed.), *The Woman in America*, Daedalus Library, Vol. 3, American Academy of Arts and Sciences, 1964.

MCGREGOR, O. R., and ROWNTREE, G., *Society: Problems and Methods of Study*, ed. A. T. WELFORD, Routledge & Kegan Paul, 1962 (Ch. 3).

MCGREGOR, O. R., 'Family, Home and Environment', in *Frontiers of Sociology*, ed. T. R. FYVEL, Cohen & West, 1964.

'Take This Woman', a series of ten articles in the *Evening Standard*, March 18th–March 29th, 1968.

MARSH, David, *The Changing Social Structure of England and Wales, 1871–1961*, Routledge and Kegan Paul, 1965.

MYRDAL, A., and KLEIN, V., *Women's Two Roles*, Routledge and Kegan Paul, 2nd ed., 1968.

PRESIDENT'S COMMISSION ON THE STATUS OF WOMEN, *Report*, ('American Women'), 1963.

PRIESTLEY, J. B., *Angel Pavement*, J. M. Dent & Sons, 1937.

ROWNTREE, B. Seebohm, and STUART, F. D., *Responsibility of Women Workers for Dependants*, Clarendon Press, 1921.

TITMUSS, R. M., *Essays on the Welfare State*, Allen & Unwin, 1958. (Ch. 5.)

UNITED NATIONS, *The United Nations and the Status of Women*, U.N., 1964. (H.M.S.O.).

WILLIAMS, Gertrude, *Women and Work*, Nicholson and Watson, 1945.

WOOLF, Virginia, *A Room of One's Own*, Hogarth Press, 1929.

II. Technological change:

History of the printing and paper trades.

The British Printer.

II. Technological change (continued):

Cameron Report, Cmnd. 3184, 1967.

COLEMAN, *The British Paper Industry 1495–1860*, Clarendon Press, 1958.

Encyclopædia Britannica. (Section on 'Printing'.)

LEECH, Miriam, and COOK, Charles, *David Greenhill—Master Printer*, privately published, Sun Engraving Co.

NUTTALL, Gwen, 'How *Zeta* slims her costs', in *The Sunday Times*, April 7th, 1968.

Oxford History of Technology. (Selected chs.)

YOUNG, Ernest W., *Printing Our Magazines*, Condé Nast, 1956.

III. The British Press:

DILNOT, George, *The Romance of the Amalgamated Press*, Amalgamated Press, 1925.

Gazette (The International Journal of the Science of the Press), 1955–
The Economist, 'Economics of the Press', September 9th, 1961.

'The Press Ahead', November 19th, 1965.

THE ECONOMIST INTELLIGENCE UNIT, *The National Newspaper Industry*, 1966.

HAMMERTON, J. A., *With Northcliffe in Fleet Street*, Hutchinson & Co.

HERD, Harold, *The March of Journalism*, Allen & Unwin, 1952.

MARTIN, B. Kingsley, *The Press the Public Wants*, Hogarth Press, 1947.

MINNEY, R. J., *Viscount Southwood*, Odhams, 1964.

MOONMAN, E. (Ed.), *The Press: A Case for Commitment*, Fabian Tract No. 391, Fabian Society, 1969.

NAYLOR, Leonard E., *The Irrepressible Victorian: The Story of Thomas Gibson Bowles*, Macdonald & Co., 1965.

Newspaper Press Directory, 1846 et seq.

POUND, R., and HARMSWORTH, G., *Northcliffe*, Cassell, 1959.

ROYAL COMMISSION ON THE PRESS, 1947–49, *Report*.

1961–62 *Report*, Cmnd. 3121.

STEED, Wickham, *The Press*, Penguin, 1938

Willing's Press Guide. .

World's Press News.

IV. Literary Background:

BOORSTIN, Daniel J., *The Image*, Pelican, 1963.

HOGGART, Richard, *The Uses of Literacy*, Pelican, 1963.

IV. Literary Background (continued):

PLANT, Marjorie, *The English Book Trade*, Allen & Unwin, 1939.

STEPHEN, Leslie, *English Literature and Society in the Eighteenth Century*, (Ford Lectures, 1903), University Paperbacks, 1963.

WILLIAMS, Raymond, *Communications*, Penguin, 1962.
Culture and Society, 1780–1950, Penguin, 1963.

V. Origins of the Women's Press in Britain:

Christian Science Monitor, 'The First "Female" Periodical', August 28th, 1939.

HARGREAVE, Mary, 'Women's Newspapers in the Past', in *The Englishwoman*, Vol. XXI, January–March, 1914, pp. 292–301.

HYDE, Montgomery, *Mr and Mrs Beeton*, George Harrap, 1951.

RICHARDSON, Mrs Herbert, 'Pioneer Journal', in the *Daily Telegraph*, January 15th, 1927.

SPAIN, Nancy, *Mrs Beeton and her Husband*, Collins, 1948.

STEARNS, Bertha Monica, 'Early English Periodicals for Ladies' in *PMLA*, Vol. XLVIII (1933), pp. 38–60.

VI. General Articles, etc., on the Modern Women's Press:

B.B.C. T.V. (Channel 1), 'Women's Own Weeklies', 6.25 p.m.–7 p.m., January 7th, 1969.

British Printer, 'Magazines for the Millions', October, 1961, pp. 105–20.

CURRAN, Charles, 'Journalism for Squaws' in *The Spectator*, November 19th, 1965.

Daily Herald, Editorial on women's magazines, February 5th, 1961.

The Economist, 'Modes and Morals', November 28th, 1953.

FAY, Gerald, 'The Women's Magazine Front' in *The Manchester Guardian*, March 2nd, 1959.

The Guardian, 'The ABC and LSD of writing for the women's weeklies', April 10th, 1963.

'The Family Magazine' in *The Guardian*, March 8th, 1965.

MCCLELLAND, W. D., 'The Women's Press in Britain', in *Gazette*, Vol. XI, 1965, No. 2/3, pp. 148–65.

'Women's Weeklies' in *New Society*, December, 1964.

New Statesman, article on women's magazines, August 24th, 1962.

Sunday Times, 'Petticoat Jungle', March 19th, 1964.

The Times, 'What Women Read and Why', July 12th, 1958.

VII. Aspects of Editorial Content:

(i) Fiction

CAMPBELL, Flann and Mary, 'Comic Love' in *New Society*, January 3rd, 1963.

COHEN, Gerda L., 'The Pelvic Four' in *Twentieth Century*, November, 1958.

The Guardian, 'Fiction in Women's Weeklies', April 10th, 1963.

HESHEL, Thena, 'Woman, Fiction and Reality', in *New Society*, January 3rd, 1963.

OWEN, Carol, 'Feminine Roles and Social Mobility in Women's Weekly Magazines', *Sociological Review*, 1962, Vol. 10, No. 3, pp. 293–6.

(ii) Problem Pages

ELLIOTT, Janice, 'The everlasting question, "Should I sleep with him?" ' *Sunday Times* colour supplement, September 12th, 1965.

LACEY, Robert, 'Dear Marje, My boy friend and I . . .', *Sunday Times* colour supplement, March 30th, 1969.

RATCLIFF, Rosemary (Ed.), *Dear Worried Brown Eyes*, Robert Maxwell, 1969.

VIII. Information on Individual Women's Periodicals:

CARTER, Ernestine, 'A New Fashion', in *The Sunday Times*, March 10th, 1968.

CHASE, Edna Woolman, and Ilka, *Always in Vogue*, Gollancz, 1954.

DRAWBELL, James, *Time on My Hands*, MacDonald, 1968.

GRIEVE, Mary, *Millions Made My Story*, Gollancz, 1964.

JEGER, Lena, *Nova*, in *The Guardian*, March 2nd, 1965.

The Lady, 'Reviewing Three Quarters of a Century's Publications', February 18th, 1960.

NUTTALL, Gwen, 'Petticoat Government for a Trendy Failure', in *The Sunday Times*, February, 1968.

THOMAS, Doina, 'Joining the Family Circle' in *Management Today*, November, 1967.

The Times, 'Woman Magazine' (Supplement), September 16th, 1965.

WHITEHORN, Katharine, 'The Reading Age of Women', in *The Observer*, March 7th, 1965.

World's Press News, 'The Thinking Behind the Novelty', March 12th, 1965.

IX. Circulation and Readership:

AUDIT BUREAU OF CIRCULATIONS, *Circulation Review.*

HULTON PRESS, *Hulton Readership Survey,* 1947 *et seq.*

I.I.P.A. Survey, 1934.

INSTITUTE OF PRACTITIONERS IN ADVERTISING, *National Readership Survey,* 1956 *et seq.*

LONDON RESEARCH AND INFORMATION BUREAU, *Press Circulations Analysed,* 1928.

X. Reader Research:

INSTITUTE FOR MOTIVATIONAL RESEARCH INC., N.Y. *A Motivational Research Study on the British Woman in Today's Culture for 'Woman's Own',* presented to George Newnes Ltd., 1964 (unpublished).

MARPLAN LTD., *Markets and Media,* a survey for the National Magazine Co., 1960–61 (unpublished).

Study of *Family Circle,* 1964 (unpublished).

'Mediascope: in Focus, Women's Magazines', in *World's Press News,* September 4th, 1964.

MCCLELLAND, W. D., *Readership Profiles in Mass Media,* IPA series on aspects of the *National Readership Survey.*

ODHAMS RESEARCH DIVISION, *A New Measurement Study of Women's Weekly Magazines,* 1964.

STANDBROOK PUBLICATIONS, *Progress Report on 'Family Circle',* January, 1965.

World's Press News, 'What Odhams' Study Found Out About Women Readers', July 10th, 1964.

XI. Advertising:

ABRAMS, Mark, *Education, Social Class and Reading of Newspapers and Magazines,* I.P.A., 1966.

ADVERTISING ASSOCIATION, *Facts About Advertising.*

How Advertising Disciplines Itself, 1964.

Advertisers' Weekly.

B.R.A.D. (British Rate and Data).

HOBSON, J., *The Influence and Technique of Modern Advertising,* IPA Occasional Paper, No. 15 (Reprinted from the *Journal* of the Royal Society of Arts, July, 1964).

IPA, *Trends in Audiences and Advertising Costs in Nine Media,* 9th Ed., 1966.

LASKI, Marghanita, 'The Image on the Penny', in *Twentieth Century,* August, 1958, pp. 151–8.

XI. Advertising (continued):

PACKARD, Vance, *The Hidden Persuaders*, Longman's, 1957.
TURNER, E. S., *The Shocking History of Advertising*, Penguin, 1952.

XII. Reorganisation of the Women's Magazine Industry:

BLACK, Sheila, 'IPC Magazines Reorganisation', in the *Financial Times*, August 12th, 1968.
BUCKMASTER AND MOORE (Stockbrokers), *International Publishing Corporation*, 1969.
CUDLIPP, Hugh, *At Your Peril*, Weidenfeld and Nicolson, 1962.
DAVIS, David, 'IPC Magazines to Split . . .', in *The Times Business News*, August 12th, 1968.
The Economist, 'Petticoat Battleground', November 21st, 1959.
'Logic of a Merger', February 4th, 1961.
'Don't Shoot the Editor', December 11th, 1965.
HILLMORE, Peter, 'Hard sell for magazines', in *The Guardian*, May 16th, 1969.
JONES, Robert, 'Rows at IPC over McKinsey Plans', in *The Times Business News*, March 3rd, 1969.
KING, Cecil, *Strictly Personal*, Weidenfeld & Nicolson, 1969.
The Sunday Times, 'Quick on the Draw', by 'Prufrock', April 7th, 1968.
The Times Business Diary, August 12th, 1968, p. 19.
The Times, 'New titles for old faces', August 12th, 1968.
World's Press News, 'Quick picks mag masterminds', August 16th, 1968, pp. 1–2.
'Women's Magazines: the Thinking that is Opening up Their New Frontiers', September 17th, 1965.
YOXHALL, H. W., 'Recent Developments in British Magazine Publishing', in *Gazette*, Vol. 7/8 (1961–62), pp. 277–85.

XIII. Consumption Patterns:

ABRAMS, Dr Mark, 'The Home-Centred Society', in *The Listener*, November 26th, 1959.
'Women as Consumers', Fawcett Lecture delivered at Bedford College, March 4th, 1965.
'What's Changed in 10 Years?' in the *Observer* colour supplement, New Year issue, 1966.
HENRY, H., 'But some consumers are more equal than others', reprinted from a Marketing Seminar, Thomson Organisation, February, 1962.

XIV. The Women's Press in America:

ANDERSON, Curtiss, Profile of *Ladies' Home Journal* in *Madison Avenue*, April, 1962.

AUDIT BUREAU OF CIRCULATIONS (U.S.A.) *Reports*.

Business Week, Article on *Good Housekeeping*, March 19th, 1966, pp. 191–8.

COWLES INC., *Inside Cowles Commnications Inc.*, Publicity brochure, 1967.

GOULDEN, Joseph C., *The Curtis Caper*, Putnam, 1965.

DAVENPORT and DERIEUX, *Ladies, Gentlemen and Editors*, Doubleday and Co. Inc., N.Y., 1960.

FULLER, Walter D., *The Life and Times of Cyrus H. K. Curtis, 1850–1933*.

GALLAGHER REPORTS

Life Magazine, 'Soaring Success of the Iron Butterfly', November 19th, 1965. (Profile of Helen Gurley Brown).

L.I. Newsday, 'Single Along with Helen', February 18th, 1967.

LLOYD H. HALL CO. INC. *Magazine Editorial Reports*.

LUCE, Henry R., *Magazines and the Great Society*, Address to the 9th Annual Conference of the M.P.A., September, 1965.

MCCOOEY, Meriel, 'Why don't you knit yourself a little skull-cap?' (Profile of Diana Vreeland) in *The Sunday Times* colour supplement, March 17th, 1968.

Madison Avenue, advertising profile of *American Home*, January, 1962. Advertising profile of *Seventeen*, December, 1964.

MAGAZINE ADVERTISING BUREAU, *A Study of the Magazine Market—Part II*.

Magazine Industry Newsletter.

MAGAZINE PUBLISHERS ASSOCIATION:
  Bibliography of Consumer Magazine Research, 1967.
  The Educational Explosion and the Magazine Influence, 1966.
  Magazine Split Run and Regional Advertising, 1967.
  Sources of Consumer Magazine Information, 1965.

MARKET RESEARCH AGENCIES (NIELSEN, POLITZ, SIMMONS, STARCH & CO.) *Reports*.

MOTT, Frank L., *American Journalism*, 1690–1950, MacMillan, N.Y., 1950.

NEWQUIST, Roy, *Conversations*, Rand McNally, 1967.

Newsweek, 'Down with Pippypoo' (article on *Cosmopolitan*), July 18th, 1966.

XIV. The Women's Press in America (continued):

PETERSON, Theodore, 'Magazine Publishing in the U.S., 1960', in *Gazette*, Vol. VI (1960), No. 1, pp. 105–18.

Magazines in the 20th Century, University of Illinois Press, 1956.

'Magazines: Today and Tomorrow', in *Gazette*, Vol. IX–X (December, 1963), pp. 215–29.

PRESIDENT'S COMMISSION ON THE STATUS OF WOMEN: 'Portrayal of Women by the Mass Media', one of *Four Consultations* presented as supplementary evidence, 1963.

Printer's Ink, 'Woman, U.S.A.', April, 1966.

PUBLISHERS' INFORMATION BUREAU, *Reports*.

REYNOLDS, Quentin, *The Fiction Factory*, Random House, 1955.

The Sunday Times, 'Taste makers, U.S.A.', November 15th, 1964.

SWAN, Carroll, *Magazines in the U.S.A.*, Standard Rate and Data Service, in co-operation with the M.P.A., 1965. *N.B.* This brochure contains a useful bibliography.

TEBBEL, John, *The American Magazine: A Compact History*, Hawthorn, 1969.

VITT, Sam B., 'Media and the Youth Market', in *Madison Avenue*, June, 1967.

WOLFF, Janet, *What Makes Women Buy*, McGraw-Hill Paperbacks, 1958.

WOODWARD, Helen, *The Lady Persuaders*, Obolensky, 1960.

WRITERS' INSTITUTE, N.Y.C., *Publication Portraits* (*Good Housekeeping, Harper's Bazaar, Mademoiselle, Redbook, True Confessions, Vogue, et al.*).

Index